Songs from the film

A HARD DAY'S NIGHT

PMC
1230

THE BEATLES

SIDE ONE

1. A HARD DAY'S NIGHT
2. I SHOULD HAVE KNOWN BETTER
3. IF I FELL
4. I'M HAPPY JUST TO DANCE WITH YOU
5. AND I LOVE HER
6. TELL ME WHY
7. CAN'T BUY ME LOVE

From the soundtrack of the United Artists film 'A HARD DAY'S NIGHT'

Words and Music:
JOHN LENNON AND PAUL McCARTNEY

Alun Owen began work on the original screenplay late last autumn. Producer Walter Shenson and director Richard Lester watched their newest screen stars at work over Christmas and the New Year on the stage of the Finsbury Park 'Astoria' in London. John and Paul began to compile a collection of new compositions for the soundtrack while The Beatles were appearing at the Paris 'Olympia' last January. One morning early in March a specially chartered train moved out of Paddington station and the first day's shooting of The Beatles' first feature film got under way.

Reel upon reel of precious film had filled the camera crew's metal cans before a title had been selected for the United Artists picture. Then Ringo casually came up with the name at the end of a particularly strenuous session on the film set. 'It's been a hard day's night that was!' he declared, squatting for a moment on the arm of his canvas chair behind the line of cameras and technicians. The film, which also stars Wilfred Brambell in the role of Paul's (mythical) Irish grandfather, was promptly named 'A HARD DAY'S NIGHT'.

The story depicts something like 48 consecutive hours of activity in the bustling lives of four beat group boys. Named John, Paul, George and Ringo. *A Hard Day's Night* is heard at the very beginning of the film as the boys sing and play over the opening titles. The number features John's double-tracked voice, producing a duet effect. Its brisk, compelling theme crops up in orchestral form elsewhere during the film as part of recording manager George Martin's instrumental soundtrack score.

John's *I Should Have Known Better* makes an early appearance in the film during a railway sequence when the four boys are seen playing cards in the guard's van of the train.

John and Paul share the vocal action on *If I Fell*, the first of four songs featured in extensive theatre/studio sequences which show the group rehearsing and finally performing in a television spectacular. *I'm Happy Just To Dance With You* gives George a chance to handle the lead vocal, *And I Love Her* hands the solo spotlight to Paul who is joined by John for *Tell Me Why*.

The last of the soundtrack's magnificent seven, *Can't Buy Me Love*, has already been a worldwide disc hit for The Beatles. In 'A HARD DAY'S NIGHT' it forms the musical backdrop to several different scenes—when the boys are seen chasing across a field after a quick-fire getaway from the television studio and when the incredible race between Beatles, fans and police takes place with the boys tearing along streets and down alleyways in double-quick time!

SIDE TWO

1. ANY TIME AT ALL
2. I'LL CRY INSTEAD
3. THINGS WE SAID TODAY
4. WHEN I GET HOME
5. YOU CAN'T DO THAT
6. I'LL BE BACK

Words and Music:
JOHN LENNON AND PAUL McCARTNEY

Creating and perfecting completely new compositions for the soundtrack of 'A HARD DAY'S NIGHT' presented John and Paul with one of the greatest challenges of their pop-penning career. In the past their song-writing had been done at a more leisurely pace. Now they had a shooting schedule deadline to meet and the entire collection of fresh numbers had to be compiled during a season of concerts in Paris and a now legendary visit to America. To assist their work the two boys had a grand-piano moved into their hotel suite at the George V in Paris.

By the beginning of March the task was complete and The Beatles had a total of almost a dozen new songs ready for final rehearsal. At every stage of its conception and production care was taken to see that 'A HARD DAY'S NIGHT' would not turn into a continuous parade of Beatle performances. After all The Beatles themselves had agreed that the film should portray as many different facets of the four boys' individual personalities as possible. Indeed the comedy content was, and is, of paramount importance, and John, Paul, George and Ringo are afforded maximum opportunity to display their on-the-spot sense of humour.

It became apparent that no more than six new songs should be introduced via the soundtrack of the film. To increase this number would have left insufficient screen-time for the action of the plot. On the other hand it seemed most unfair to hold back the remainder of the boys' new songs when each one was of such excellent quality. Eventually the decision was made to record all the material which John and Paul had written and include the extra titles on the second side of this album.

Although the voice of George Harrison is much in evidence throughout this album the solo vocal activity on the second side is shared between the songs' composers, John and Paul. Paul handles the lyrics of *Things We Said Today* and he's heard in duet with John on *I'll Cry Instead*. For the main part John's is the dominant voice featured on *Any Time At All*, *When I Get Home*, *You Can't Do That* and *I'll Be Back* although George and Paul back up his efforts strongly on all titles.

When you listen to the second side of this record you will agree that it would have been a pity to cast aside such a fabulous set of songs solely because they couldn't be fitted into the structure of 'A HARD DAY'S NIGHT'. Now, with this album in your library, you have a collection of Beatle recordings which is comprehensive and up to date. At the same time it is interesting to remember that the LP housed within this sleeve is the first-ever album release to be made up entirely of self-composed and self-performed Beatle compositions.

Produced for records by GEORGE MARTIN
Cover Notes by TONY BARROW

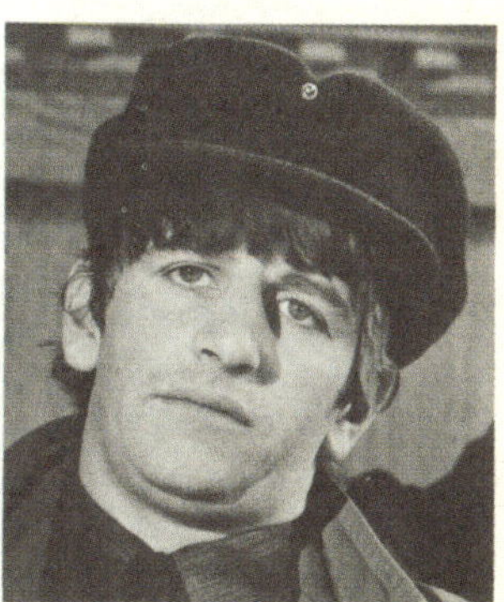

TRADE MARK OF
THE PARLOPHONE Co., Ltd.

LONG PLAY $33\frac{1}{3}$ R.P.M •

E.M.I. RECORDS LIMITED
(Controlled by Electric & Musical Industries Ltd.)
HAYES · MIDDLESEX · ENGLAND
Made and Printed in Great Britain

USE
EMITEX
CLEANING MATERIAL
The use of "EMITEX" cleaning material (available from Record Dealers) will preserve this record and keep it free from dust.

Printed and made by Garrod & Lofthouse Ltd. Patents pending PMC 1230 PCS 3058

The BEATLES
A Hard Day's Night & More

Compiled by Bruce Spizer

With additional contributions by

Bill King,
Al Sussman,
Frank Daniels,
Piers Hemmingsen
and other Beatles fans

Copyright ©2024 by 498 Productions, L.L.C.

498 Productions, L.L.C.
935 Gravier Street, Suite 707
New Orleans, Louisiana 70112
Phone: 504-299-1964
email: 498@beatle.net

All rights reserved. No part of this book may be used or reproduced in any form or by any means, or stored in a database or retrieval system without written permission of the copyright owner, except in the case of brief quotations embodied in critical articles and reviews. Making copies of any part of this book for any purpose other than your own personal use is a violation of United States copyright laws.

This book is sold as is, without warranty of any kind, either express or implied. While every effort has been made in the preparation of this book to ensure the accuracy of the information contained herein, the author and 498 Productions, L.L.C. assume no responsibility for errors or omissions. Neither is any liability assumed for damages resulting from the use of the information contained herein.

The Billboard, Cash Box and Music Vendor/Record World chart data used in this book was taken from books published by Record Research, including Billboard Pop Album Charts 1965- 1969,Billboard Pop Album Charts 1970 and The Comparison Book 1954-1982. Photo credits: Zack Smith Photography (page vi); Amity Photos/Alamy Stock Photo (page 33); www.popsiephotos.com (page 43); CBS Photo Archive/Getty Images (page 45); Dom Slike/Alamy Stock Photo (page 95); British Library, London, on exhibition (page 234 top); Cinematic/Alamy Stock Photo (page 234 bottom); Beatles Book Photo Library (page 237); David Hum/Magnum Photos (page 239); Allstar Picture Library Ltd./ Alamy Stock Photo (page 241); and PictureLux/The Hollywood Archive/Alamy Stock Photo (page 245). The Canadian images (pages 121-139) were provided by Piers Hemmingsen, Doug Thompson, Chuck Gunderson (page 138 ticket) and Bruce Spizer, with digital enhancements on some images by Ethan Alexanian. Most of the other collectibles shown in the book are from the collections of Bruce Spizer, Jeff Augsburger, Frank Daniels, Gary Hein and Perry Cox.

This book is published by 498 Productions, L.L.C. It is not an official product of Universal Music Group, Inc., Capitol Records, Inc. or Apple Corps Ltd.

Print edition ISBN 979-8-9863190-8-7

Printed in U.S.A.
1 2 3 4 5 6 7 8 9 0

I Should Have Known Better

After watching the Beatles for the third time on The Ed Sullivan Show on Sunday, February 23, 1964, I thought there would be a bit of a lull as to the Beatles. After all, the group had three hit singles at the top of the charts with "I Want To Hold Your Hand," "She Loves You" and "Please Please Me." They also had two top-selling albums in *Meet The Beatles!* and *Introducing The Beatles*. The group was back in England for what I thought would be a well-deserved rest. So I wasn't expecting there to be any new Beatles singles or albums for quite a while. I should have known better.

In late February, I began hearing "Twist And Shout" on WTIX in New Orleans. I was familiar with the song as it was on *Introducing The Beatles*, which my cousin Barry owned. (I only had *Meet The Beatles!* at the time.) And then, in mid-March, there was an entirely new song on the radio, "Can't Buy Me Love." That seemed like a pretty astute message. And the flip side, "You Can't Do That," was a really cool-sounding tune with some great guitar work. I later got to see film of the Beatles performing the song on The Ed Sullivan Show. Those new songs were soon followed by two more tunes I knew from *Introducing The Beatles*, "Do You Want To Know A Secret" and "Love Me Do."

There was also a great new album curiously called *The Beatles' Second Album*. It had the single "She Loves You" and its terrific flip side, "I'll Get You," plus great versions of songs by other artists that I was already familiar with: the Marvelettes' "Please Mr. Postman," Barrett Strong's "Money," the Miracles' "You Really Got A Hold On Me," Little Richard's "Long Tall Sally" and Chuck Berry's "Roll Over Beethoven." As great as those original recordings were, they were even better by the Beatles! I also really liked Ringo's pounding drums on "Thank You Girl." Thank you Beatles!

Early that summer, I was at the Beacon Theater on Harrison Avenue in New Orleans when I saw the preview for the Beatles film *A Hard Day's Night*. Although I don't recall which movie I saw that afternoon, I remember laughing hard at the scene in the preview where Ringo places his coat over a puddle for a young woman to walk over, only to see her fall into a man hole.

Shortly after my ninth birthday on July 2, I began hearing songs recorded for the Beatles film on WTIX, starting with "A Hard Day's Night" and "I Should Have Known Better." Both exploded out of my bedroom clock radio. I also heard "I'll Cry Instead," "I'm Happy Just To Dance With You" and "If I fell." The song I remember hearing most at night was Paul's beautiful ballad, "And I Love Her." It remains one of my favorite Beatles songs.

In August, after picking up my two older sisters at Camp Sequoia in Tennessee, my family took a car trip to New York. We stayed at a hotel that was less than a block away from the Delmonico, where the Beatles were staying. I remember having a 24-hour bug and being unable to take an afternoon nap due to the sound of girls screaming "We want the Beatles!" over and over again! My parents had no interest in seeing the Beatles in concert at Forest Hills, but we did go to see the Broadway musical *Funny Girl* with Barbra Streisand. Vice-President Hubert Humphrey, along with his Secret Service contingent, were sitting a few rows in front of us. They were very tall, forcing me and my sisters to move our heads to see around them.

We also saw *Hello Dolly* and spent a day at the New York World's Fair. It was a great trip, but because we were out of town during the second half of August, I missed *A Hard Day's Night* when it first came out.

In September, I heard the Beatles were coming to New Orleans. But being nine years old, the only way I would get to go was with my older sisters. But my sister Jan's birthday was on the day of concert, and she did not want to go. Her musical hero was Barbra Streisand. Once again, Babs foiled my chance to see the Beatles!

Although I never got to see the Beatles in concert, I finally saw *A Hard Day's Night* on October 24, 1967, when the film preempted one of my favorite shows, I Dream Of Jeanie, on NBC. By this time, many of the network's evening programs were in color, preceded by a colorful bumper with music and the announcer proudly saying: "The following program is brought to you in living color on NBC." It would end with an image of a peacock. Prior to the start of the Beatles film, the opening had the same music as the standard one, but featured a black and white cartoon penguin and custom voiceover: "The following very, very special program is brought to you in lively black and white on NBC."

By seeing the film on television, I actually got to hear the dialog that I would have missed in a theater full of screaming girls. Perhaps it was worth the wait.

The long-lasting power and attraction of *A Hard Day's Night* became apparent to me in 2002 as I was hiking and climbing the Inca Trail to Machu Picchu in Peru. There were two female college students on the trip who knew I had written a few books on the Beatles. During our first morning on the trail, as the three of us talked about the group, one of the girls asked, "Do you want to do 'A Hard Day's Night'?" I thought maybe we would sing the song, or perhaps some of the songs from the movie. But I soon realized they were doing the entire dialog from the film! They loved the movie and had watched it dozens of times on DVD. I was able to keep up with them some of the time, but they knew every line! I guess I should have known better.

A year or so later I was at a Beatlefest where four female Beatles fans dressed up as the school girls on the train in *A Hard Day's Night*. They had me sit in a chair while they recreated the hair-grooming publicity photo that I remembered from the film's bubblegum cards. Once again, I should have known better.

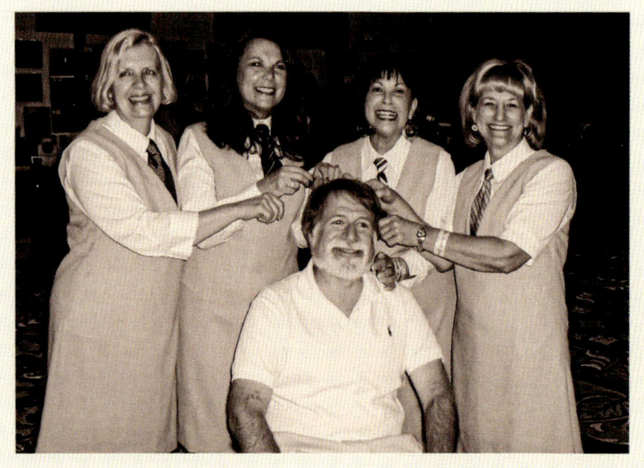

I've Been Working Like A Dog

Welcome to the second and eighth installment in my Beatles Album Series. *The Beatles A Hard Day's Night & More* is the second book chronologically but the eighth published since the series began in 2017 with *The Beatles And Sgt. Pepper: A Fans' Perspective*. That book was then intended as a one-shot issued for the 50th anniversary of the 1967 release of *Sgt. Pepper's Lonely Hearts Club Band*. From small things big things happen. It was followed by books on *The White Album*, *Abbey Road* and *Let It Be*, before I magically went backwards through the Sea of Time for a tome combining *Magical Mystery Tour* and *Yellow Submarine*. This was followed by another double feature, this time starring *Rubber Soul* and *Revolver*, with a guest appearance by *Yesterday And Today* and its infamous Butcher Cover.

Next came the first chronologically in the series, *The Beatles Please Please Me to With The Beatles*, which covers the records that fueled Beatlemania in Britain, the United States and Canada. If you don't already own that book, you need to get it for the background story leading up the group's records released from mid-February 1964 through mid-November 1964 covered in this book, *The Beatles A Hard Day's Night & More*. With the exception of the records containing songs from the British LP *A Hard Day's Night*, the albums and singles released in America during that time frame featured songs previously issued in the U.K. in 1963. They are the "& More" of this book, which does not repeat the information on the recording of those songs contained in my previous book.

Put simply, the two books described above will give you the full story on how the Beatles brilliant first three albums and associated singles were marketed and received not only in the group's native land, but also in America and Canada.

Once again, I assembled the same team utilized in the previous installments in the Beatles Album Series. Piers Hemmingsen provided the Canadian perspective. Beatlefan editor Al Sussman wrote about what was happening in 1964 in the news and in music to place the Beatles records and first film in historical context. Frank Daniels contributed a chapter on rock 'n' roll movies before and after *A Hard Day's Night*. Beatlefan publisher Bill King returned with more fan notes and an interview with film producer Walter Shenson.

As always, we were treated to dozens of wonderful Fan Recollections, including Pattie Boyd's memories of first meeting the boys on the set of *A Hard Day's Night*. This led to her first date with George Harrison and then their marriage.

On the technical side, Diana Thornton worked her magic to make the book look terrific as always and Kaye Alexander coordinated the interactions with our printer. Proof readers included Diana, Frank, Al, Beatle Tom Frangione and Tom Brennan. In the tradition, my thanks to my family, Sarah, Eloise, Barbara, Trish, Big Puppy and others too numerous and crazy to name.

Finally, as this book goes to press, I am already writing and putting together my next book, *Beatles For Sale to Help!* which will bring the Beatles Album Series to an end. It will cover those British albums, the Beatles second film and the American Capitol albums *Beatles '65*, *Beatles VI* and the *Help!* soundtrack. As you can see, I've been working like a dog.

About Author

Bruce Spizer is a native and lifelong resident of New Orleans, Louisiana, who was eight years old when the Beatles invaded America. He began listening to the radio at age two and was a die-hard fan of WTIX, a top forty AM station that played a blend of New Orleans R&B music and top pop and rock hits. His first two albums were *The Coasters' Greatest Hits*, which he permanently "borrowed" from his older sisters, and *Meet The Beatles!*, which he still occasionally plays on his vintage 1964 Beatles record player.

During his high school and college days, Bruce played guitar in various bands that primarily covered hits of the sixties, including several Beatles songs. He wrote numerous album and concert reviews for his high school and college newspapers, including a review of *Abbey Road* that didn't claim Paul was dead. He received his B.A., M.B.A. and law degrees from Tulane University. His legal and accounting background have proved valuable in researching and writing his books.

Bruce is considered one of the world's leading experts on the Beatles. A "taxman" by day, Bruce is a Board Certified Tax Attorney with his own practice. A "paperback writer" by night, Bruce is the author of 16 critically acclaimed books on the Beatles, including *The Beatles Are Coming! The Birth of Beatlemania in America*, a series of six books on the group's American record releases, *Beatles For Sale on Parlophone Records*, which covers all of the Beatles records issued in the U.K. from 1962- 1970, and his new series of books on the Beatles albums. His articles have appeared in Beatlefan, Goldmine and American History magazines.

He was selected to write the questions for the special Beatles edition of Trivial Pursuit. He maintains the popular website **www.beatle.net**.

Bruce has been a speaker at numerous Beatles conventions and at the Grammy Museum, the Rock 'N' Roll Hall of Fame & Museum and the American Film Institute. He has been on ABC's Good Morning America and Nightline, CBS's The Early Show, CNN, Fox and morning shows in New York, Chicago, Los Angeles, New Orleans and other cities, and is a frequent guest on radio shows, including NPR, BBC and the Beatles Channel.

Bruce serves as a consultant to Universal Music Group, Capitol Records and Apple Corps Ltd. on Beatles projects. He has an extensive Beatles collection, concentrating on American, Canadian and British first issue records, promotional items and concert posters.

contents

BEATLES' Early Days
by TONY SHERIDAN

ELVIS ★ BILLY J. ★ CILLA
FAITH ★ POOLE ★ PITNEY

Plus top pop news service

Registered at the G.P.O. as a Newspaper

No. 897 EVERY FRIDAY PRICE 6d. March 20, 1964

No. 6
DIANE
BY THE BACHELORS
on DECCA F.11799
A GREAT FAVOURITE
eight-by-ten
KEN DODD on Columbia CB 7191
K.P.M., 21 DENMARK STREET, W.C.2 TEM 3856

new MUSICAL EXPRESS

WORLD'S LARGEST CIRCULATION OF ANY MUSIC PAPER
—WEEKLY SALES EXCEED 275,000 (MEMBERS OF ABC)

ELVIS
VIVA
LAS VEGAS
(from his latest film Love in Las Vegas)
RCA 1390 45 rpm
RCA VICTOR

THE BEATLES ARE BACK!

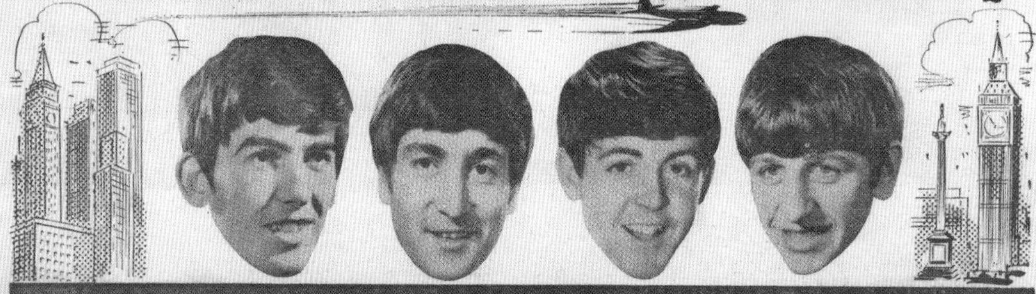

THE BEATLES
Can't buy me love

PARLOPHONE R 5114

A TERRIFIC NEW TITLE WRITTEN BY JOHN LENNON/PAUL McCARTNEY
PETER AND GORDON
A world without love

COLUMBIA DB7225

NOW...TO FOLLOW HIS
RECENT HIT "MISS YOU!"..COMES A FANTASTIC NEW RELEASE OF
ONE OF THE GREATEST SONGS EVER RECORDED!
JIMMY YOUNG
Unchained melody

COLUMBIA DB7234

EMI RECORDS LTD., EMI HOUSE, 20 MANCHESTER SQUARE, LONDON, W.1

The Beatles are Back for *A Hard Day's Night*

The front page of the March 20, 1964 issue of New Musical Express ("NME") let readers know: "The Beatles Are Back!" The EMI/Parlophone ad showed that the Beatles were back from America, with a jet flying over the heads of George, John, Paul and Ringo from New York's skyscraper-dominated skyline to London featuring Nelson's Column at Trafalgar Square and Big Ben. But the Beatles weren't just back from America, they were back with a new single, "Can't Buy Me Love." The song would later be featured twice in the Beatles first feature film, *A Hard Day's Night*.

The Beatles first American visit from February 7 through 21, 1964, had exceeded everyone's expectations. After the previous failures of popular British recording artists such as Cliff Richard and Adam Faith to achieve success in the States, music fans in the United Kingdom had reason to wonder if things would be any different for the Beatles. In the letters page of the December 28, 1963 Record Mirror, Colin Vingo of Manselton, Swansea, Wales expressed his skepticism: "So the Beatles are going to try and conquer America. Well, they might as well stay home. You have only to look at the disasters of so many British stars these last few years to realise that it's hopeless as British tastes are at the moment. The British scene is way behind the times. The Americans had groups like the Beatles years ago, when the Crickets were popular. And there is such a Negro population in the States–and I'm sure they'd never buy records they could do much better themselves." Even the Beatles had concerns, with George Harrison telling Disc in its November 30 issue: "We are not kidding ourselves about America–it's going to be hard. Look at the way Cliff Richard has tried to promote his career over there without a great deal of success."

But the Beatles proved the skeptics wrong. Their first of three appearances on The Ed Sullivan Show was seen by a record-breaking television audience of over 73 million people. They played before 8,000 screaming fans at a sold-out show in the nation's capital, and twice sold out the country's most prestigious music venue, New York's Carnegie Hall. The American singles charts and radio airwaves were dominated by "I Want To Hold Your Hand," "She Loves You" and "Please Please Me," while the albums *Meet The Beatles!* and *Introducing The Beatles* were selling strong.

Upon their return to London on February 22, the Beatles were greeted as conquering heroes. But there would be no rest for the boys. They were back at EMI Studios in St. John's Wood (now known as Abbey Road) on February 25 to record songs for their next project, a feature-length film. But this would not be the typical plotless musical showcase or teen exploitation film in which pop stars were frequently featured. Just as the Beatles had broken the norms in the music business, the boys would soon do the same in their first venture in the movie industry. Their patience and desire to do something different and meaningful would lead to popular and critical success on the silver screen.

After "Please Please Me" and "From Me To You" became big hits in England, the Beatles were approached to appear in pop musical films, but turned them down. In the June 15, 1963 Melody Maker, John explained why the Beatles were not interested. "We have been offered scene parts in a package show sort of film where about twenty different pop stars all appear with no story and no meaning. We prefer to wait until we find a film with a good plot that will hold the interest of the teenagers. Otherwise it might do us more harm than good." Fans would have to wait over a year before being able to see the Beatles in the movie theaters. It would be worth the wait.

The October 12, 1963 Disc ran an article titled "Film plans for Billy J and The Beatles" which reported that Billy J. Kramer and the Dakotas were in line for a big film role. Manager Brian Epstein told Disc: "[T]here have been several film offers for Billy, and we are studying the script of one particular film at the moment. All I can say is that it will include an acting role and that The Dakotas will also be in it." The magazine further reported on the possibility of a Beatles film, with Epstein telling Disc: "We think that we may have found the right story. There is a distinct possibility that the boys will be making a film early next year."

Although the Billy J. Kramer film never happened, the November 2 Disc informed its readers of sensational news. "That Beatles film is definitely ON–and it will be made by one of the biggest film companies in the world, United Artists. It will be produced by Walter Shenson and is scheduled to go before the cameras next February." The magazine reported that the official announcement was made on Tuesday evening [October 29] by Mr. Shenson, Brian Epstein and United Artists' George ["Bud"] Ornstein.

Disc added that award-winning Liverpool scriptwriter Alun Owen had been hired to write an original story for the film. Owen had written several television scripts, including the 1959 TV play *No Trams To Lime Street*, which was set in the Beatles home town of Liverpool. Filming for the Beatles movie was expected to take six weeks and would be shot in black and white. The Beatles, who were on tour in Sweden, had yet to be told of the plans. However, a spokesman for Brian Epstein's NEMS Enterprises Ltd. told Disc: "The boys will be delighted. They were thrilled when we told them there was a possibility of a film being made. And the news will really knock them out."

The November 2 NME also reported on the exciting plans for the Beatles first film, set to go into production in February for summer release. The film would be produced by Walter Shenson for his own production company and be distributed by United Artists. Brian Epstein would assist Shenson, an American living in London and responsible for Peter Sellers' highly successful film *The Mouse That Roared*. Beatles recording manager George Martin would supervise the musical work for the film and the recording of its soundtrack consisting of a batch of new John Lennon-Paul McCartney compositions.

The screen play was assigned to Alun Owen, one of Britain's top writers, who was Lionel Bart's collaborator on the forthcoming musical *Maggie May*. [Owen wrote the book for the play, based on the song about a Liverpool prostitute. In Owen's story, Maggie becomes involved with a Liverpool dockworker who attempts to sabotage a stash of weapons set for shipment to police in apartheid South Africa. The show opened on September 22, 1964, at London's Adelphi Theatre and ran for 501 performances. *Maggie May* won the 1964 Novello Award for outstanding score and the Critics' Poll as Best New British Musical of 1964. The Beatles later recorded the song "Maggie May" (spelled as "Maggie Mae") during their *Get Back/Let It Be* sessions.] Owen told NME: "I aim to create the story around 90 minutes of their own fantastic lives at the top of the music profession. But it will be fictional, despite the fact that the things which happen to them in the film are probably the sort of things that happen to them in reality. I aim to utilize their fantastic personalities and sense of humour." Shenson added: "I don't want to make this a conventional film because the Beatles are not conventional. In an exciting musical I want to capture them on the screen as they really are." The untitled film would be shot over six weeks in black and white CinemaScope at a British studio.

The November 2 New Record Mirror ran a brief story on the news from Brian Epstein that the Beatles would be making a "major film" early next year. The movie would be made by United Artists and feature all four of the Beatles. The full-length major production would be written by ace scriptwriter Alun Owen and directed by Walter Shenson. It would be the Beatles first film appearance. The script and title had not yet been decided on.

Two weeks later the magazine shortened its name to Record Mirror and featured color photographs for the first time. The cover to its November 16 issue featured a color portrait of the Beatles and "More news about that film." Record Mirror reported that because the Beatles movie had the potential to be "the biggest money-spinning attraction in years," scriptwriter Alun Owen was working closely with the group and its manager. Before flying to join the boys on tour in Ireland, Owen said: "It's most important to get to know the Beatles, to find out exactly what makes them tick. And also to ascertain which things cause those fantastic crowd receptions." The 90-minute film would be based on the hectic lives led by the Beatles. John and Paul were busy working out possible song ideas for the film. The pair were going to handle the entire score and that could lead to a dozen new compositions.

The December 7 Disc reported that the Beatles would start their film upon their return from America, with Brian Epstein telling reporter Alan Walsh: "Alun Owen is working hard on the script for the film at the moment." Walsh believed that United Artists, with their vast American company, would heavily promote the film in America. Brian agreed, adding: "It looks as though it will get terrific exposure."

During January and February 1964, the music weeklies ran several articles on the Beatles in Paris and America. The February 1 Melody Maker mentioned that George Martin had traveled to Paris to record a new Beatles single and songs for the group's upcoming film. That issue also ran an interview with John and Paul on how they write their hits. John said that they never consciously write B-sides to their records, adding: "Quite a few of our B sides could have been A sides, I suppose, but something has to go on the back, so we just choose." At first he thought "From Me To You" was "too way out." Paul chimed in: "I played it on the piano and thought, 'No, no one's going to like this,' so I played it for my dad and he thought it was a lovely tune and that's how it was. You value other people's opinions."

Record Mirror

THE 'SHADOW' WHO QUIT

by BRIAN BENNETT

FULL STORY PAGE SIX

No. 140 WEEK-ENDING NOVEMBER 16, 1963 EVERY THURSDAY PRICE 6d. Registered at the G.P.O. as a newspaper

More news about that film

AS the Beatles' movie is, potentially, the biggest money-spinning attraction in years, script-writer Alun Owen is working specially closely with his stars and with their manager, Brian Epstein.

Before flying out to join the boys in Ireland, Liverpudlian writer Owen said: "It's most important to get to know the Beatles, to find out exactly what makes them tick. And also to ascertain which things cause those fantastic crowd receptions."

The film, a 90-minute first feature, starts production in February. It will be based on the hectic lives led by the Beatles—but it hasn't yet been decided whether it will be fact or fiction.

BUSY TIME

Meanwhile, John Lennon and Paul McCartney are having an extra-busy time working out possible song ideas for the film. They will handle the complete score — and this could run to a dozen new compositions.

And the latest Beatle sensation, following hard on the incredible advance orders for their new L.P. "With The Beatles" and the single (due out November 29) "I Wanna Hold Your Hand," is that all four boys will almost certainly appear together on "Juke Box Jury" on BBC TV., December 7.

The Colourful Beatles

THE Beatles are undoubtedly the big success of 1963. We are very proud of the fact that the Record Mirror gave them their first write-up in a national record paper.

It is therefore fitting that we choose this top team to launch our colour programme.

Practically every possible honour has been heaped upon John, Paul, George and Ringo as far as the entertainment world goes. This year has seen them star on "Sunday Night At The London Palladium", shatter box office records throughout the country, and take part in that show of shows the "Royal Variety Performance".

The picture was taken by the Record Mirror's brilliant cameraman Dezo Hoffmann.

RECORD MIRROR CHART SURVEY P.11

NEXT WEEK—ELVIS, RICK NELSON, R&B, BRENDA LEE

The February 13 Mersey Beat featured a long interview with George Harrison, who was getting ready to depart for New York. He was keeping up with how the group's records were doing in America. "We're number one and number three now. It's great being on the top of the American charts, and one LP record [*Meet The Beatles!*] topped the LP charts in two weeks. It's a funny thing, 'I Saw Her Standing There' is the B side of the single and it's on Capitol, and the same number is on the Vee-Jay label on an LP [*Introducing The Beatles*] which has also got into the charts." George talked about future and recent recording sessions. "When we get back from the States, we'll spend a whole week recording. Germany is the next biggest market after America and Britain, and we've recorded 'I Want To Hold Your Hand' in German. There had to be a literal translation and the nearest to the name was 'Come Give Me Your Hand.' In German, the numbers are 'Komm Gib Mir Deine Hand' and 'Sie Liebt Dich.'"

The February 22 Melody Maker contained Paul's comments that the Beatles would start shooting their film at Pinewood Studios beginning on March 2. The script, which covered a day in the life of the Beatles, was finished, and the group was looking forward to making the film. John added: "We can't act but we'll have a go."

The February 29 Disc informed readers that the Beatles next single would be another John Lennon-Paul McCartney original, probably one written for their film, *Beatlemania*, and likely to be released by the end of March. The magazine reported that the boys started recording music for the film on Tuesday [February 25] and would spend the rest of the week in the studio. Brian told Disc: "They will make five or six recordings for the film and an LP will be released around August, when we expect the film to be ready for showing." The Beatles would start shooting the film on Monday [March 2]. The movie would be filmed on location, but not in Liverpool. That same week Melody Maker reported that the group's next single would be either one of the tracks recorded in Paris or one from their current recording sessions. George Martin added that the Beatles new single would most likely be a song from the film and would definitely be a Lennon-McCartney composition. The group would spend the week recording, with filming to start the following week at Pinewood Studios. The title for the film was still being discussed, with a spokesman from NEMS denying that it would be titled *Beatlemania*. The February 28 NME reported that the Beatles next single would be issued on March 20 and feature two Lennon-McCartney songs, "Can't Buy Me Love" and "You Can't Do That."

RECORD MAIL

A MONTHLY REVIEW AND DETAILS OF THE LATEST 'POPULAR' RECORDS ISSUED BY E.M.I RECORDS LTD.
H.M.V, Capitol, Columbia, Parlophone, Encore, Stateside, M-G-M, Liberty, United Artists, Verve

Vol. 7. No. 4. (Published on the first Friday of each month) April, 1964

BEATLEGOLD

ANOTHER Beatle Gold Disc it certainly is—for once again the fabulous Beatles have achieved the astonishing feat of selling 1,000,000 records here in advance orders before release. It happened only recently, of course, with their new Parlophone 'single' "Can't buy me love" (R5114). This exclusive page 1 picture was taken in E.M.I's St. John's Wood, London, studios, at the "Can't buy me love" session, and there are more exciting—and exclusive—pictures on pages 4 and 5.

EXCLUSIVE! BEATLES RECORDING SESSION: Pictures, pages 4-5

The April 1964 edition of EMI's Record Mail featured photos of the Beatles recording "You Can't Do That" on February 25, 1964. Although the magazine identified the pictures as being from the "Can't Buy Me Love" session, the single's A-side was actually recorded in Paris, France on January 29, 1964, at EMI Pathé Marconi Studios. Additional pictures from the session for "You Can't Do That" are shown on the second following page.

The March 14 Disc reported that "Can't Buy Me Love" was going to be the Beatles most fantastic disc ever, with combined advance sales in America and Britain of over 2,500,000. The record was set for March 16 release in the U.S., where advance orders might top 2,000,000, and in the U.K. on March 20, with orders already at 900,000. The single would begin receiving air play on March 15 on BBC radio's Pick Of The Pops and on Radio Luxembourg. Don Nicholl, who interviewed music publisher Dick James about the Beatles recent recording session, mixed up the songs and incorrectly reported that the Beatles recorded the backing for "You Can't Do That" in Paris and that "Can't Buy Me Love" was written in Miami and recorded in London. James told him that George was "having a ball...twanging and incorporating different effects" on his new 12-string guitar. In the March 13 NME, Chris Hutchins got the facts right by interviewing the group. John told Hutchins that Paul and he wrote and recorded "Can't Buy Me Love" in Paris during their January French session with George Martin. Paul was the only one who sang on the track. Harrison added: "For the first time ever on record I play a twelve-string guitar on 'You Can't Do That,' which is much wilder! I had the guitar given to me in America and will be featuring it in some of the numbers we do on stage in the future."

Reviews of the single were mixed. The March 11 Record Retailer found the disc disappointing, saying that it lacked the real Beatles sound. "It has a quality of growing on one, but the voice-blending gives it a rather unreal quality." The flip side was described as "a bluesy, routine beater...and possibly the stronger offering." The March 14 Record Mirror mirrored those sentiments, with its Pop Disc Jury finding that "Can't Buy Me Love" was: "Not their best disc, but the backing is probably the best for them for a long while. It builds up to a climax, and is totally different from their previous sides." While admitting the song was catchy and commercial, the magazine preferred "You Can't Do That," calling it "bluesy and well-performed." That same week in Disc, Don Nicholl described "Can't Buy Me Love" as a "large noise, a thumping good side with Paul leading the vocal on a forceful chant." George's 12-string lead was "exciting and often new." Nicholl observed: "There is one short burst of screaming but none of the old trademark of falsetto 'oohs' and 'yeah-yeahs,' which is probably wise." He thought that John's singing on "You Can't Do That" had a "rough'' quality that was interesting, though the song itself wasn't up to the group's usual songwriting standard. Nicholl noted: "One of the penalties of success is that people will be watching for the group to falter–BUT THERE IS NO SIGN OF IT HERE!" The Beatles were headed back to the Top Thirty charts.

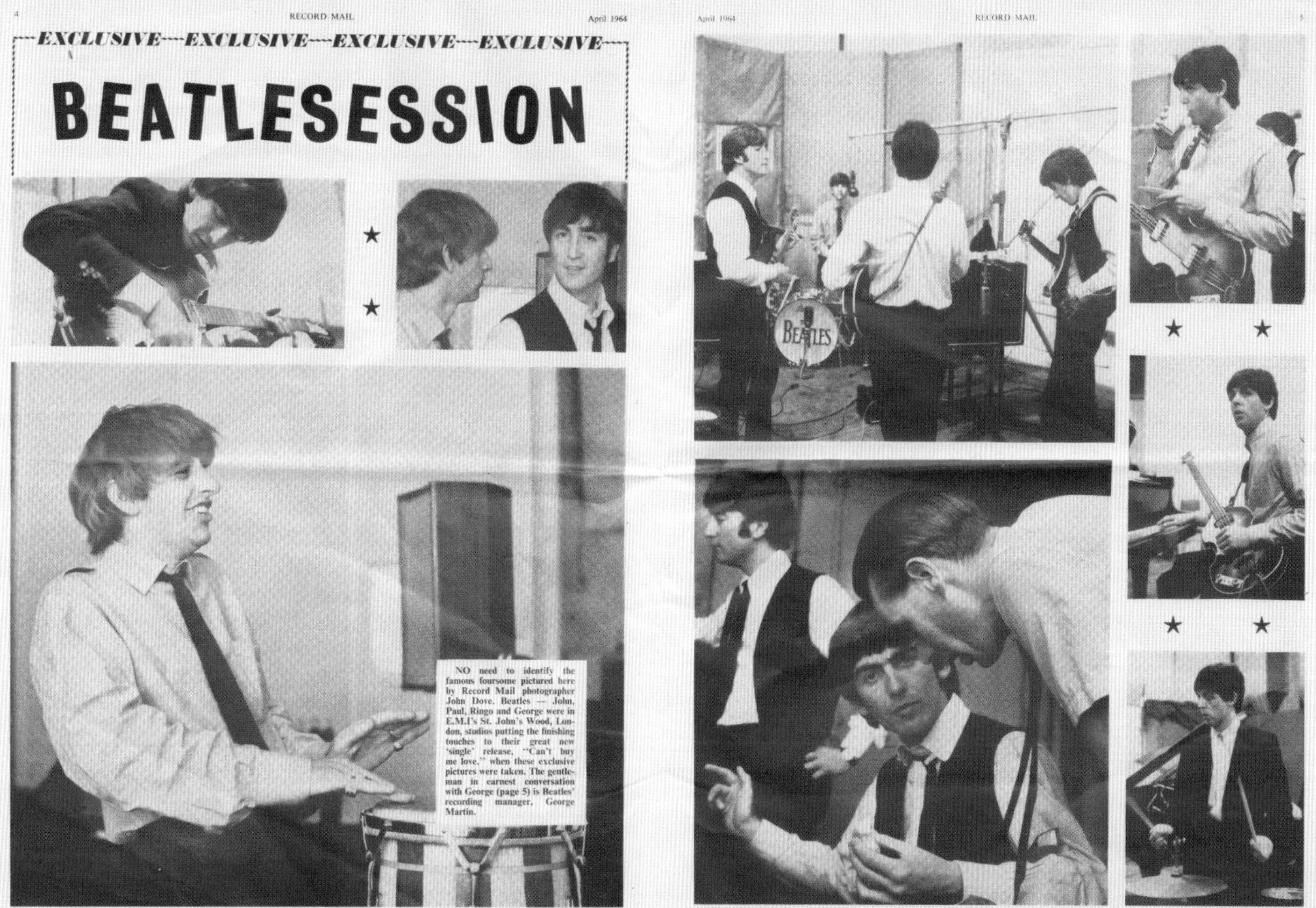

4 RECORD MAIL April 1964

EXCLUSIVE—EXCLUSIVE—EXCLUSIVE—EXCLUSIVE

BEATLESESSION

NO need to identify the famous foursome pictured here by Record Mail photographer John Dove. Beatles — John, Paul, Ringo and George were in E.M.I.'s St. John's Wood, London, studios putting the finishing touches to their great new 'single' release, "Can't buy me love," when these exclusive pictures were taken. The gentleman in earnest conversation with George (page 5) is Beatles' recording manager, George Martin.

April 1964 RECORD MAIL 5

e above interior two-page spread from the April 1964 Record Mail shows George on his new Rickenbacker 12-string ectric guitar (left page, top left), Ringo chatting with John (left page, top right), Ringo overdubbing conga drum on ou Can't Do That" (left page, bottom), the band ready to record (right page, upper left), George consulting with oducer George Martin (right page, bottom left) and Paul on bass, piano and drums (right page, right photos). Dick mes attended the session and provided information about the proceedings to Disc's Don Nicholl, which ran in the agazine's March 14, 1964 issue.

Derek Johnson wrote in the March 13 NME that it would be "invidious" for him to recommend readers buy the new Beatles single because, based on advance orders, most had already done so. "Can't Buy Me Love" was "another spine-tingling performance, which keeps your toes tapping, fingers snapping and heads nodding through many a dance session." He further described the song as a "pounding, vibrating, fast-medium twister in the r-and-b mould, with a fascinating trembling effect in the middle eight," but did not think it was as strong melodically as the group's previous singles as there was "rather more accent on beat." Johnson added that "for good measure, a few 'Twist And Shout' screams [are] thrown in." The flip side, "You Can't Do That," was slightly slower with a "heavier rumbling beat" and alternating vocals that had an "appealing plaintive quality."

Melody Maker solicited opinions from top disc jockeys on the new Beatles single. Alan Freeman didn't think "Can't Buy Me Love" was as strong as their other records. "It has not the depth, but again, on this new one, we have the Beatles epitomising that life is a ball, the world's a lovely place." He thought Paul sang "extremely well" on the record. Pete Murray also didn't think the new single was one of their best songs. He believed they were unselfish because they were giving their best songs to others, such as Peter and Gordon [referring to their "A World Without Love"]. He did, however, have no doubt that "Can't Buy Me Love" would top the charts. Jimmy Saville said: "If ever I don't like anything of theirs at first–very rare–I always do twenty-four hours later–but as it happens, I like this one a lot after one play." Jimmy Young thought it was "a very fine single" and that the Beatles make "a very fine noise." He added: "I think they have now set themselves a standard, and they always live up to it. I'm a Beatles fan. Who isn't?"

In the March 21 Pop Weekly, Peter Aldersley wrote that although the disc didn't have "quite the same immediate melodic appeal as some of their earlier platters," it grows on you after a few spins, having "all the old, and welcome, buoyancy and infectious enthusiasm to say nothing of the predominant beat which will drive all our feet and hands into a frenzy!" The single was "up to expectations with The Beatles' trademark stamped throughout." David Gell wrote in the April 1964 Beat Monthly that the new Beatles single was a "solid hunk of R 'n' B" with a "great driving beat, plus some clever George Harrison touches behind one of the keenest vocal efforts they have ever put out." The flip was "even further out," taking him several spins to get it all in. The new single was a "gold-plated smash!"

Ray Coleman interviewed George Harrison about the new single in the March 21 Melody Maker. Harrison liked both songs, but thought "You Can't Do That" (written in Miami Beach) was more interesting musically, while "Can't Buy Me Love" (written in Paris) was more instant and commercial. (He told Coleman that "This Boy" should have been the A-side to the previous single.) George described his new 12-string guitar as marvelous and gear. It sounded a bit like an electric piano and enabled him to "get a nice fat sound out of it." In the April 11 Disc, John answered critics of the new single as follows: "They must be joking. This is better than our other records. It's certainly the one we most enjoyed doing. This is a twelve bar number, which is what we always wanted to do. You might say our other discs led up to this one. People say this twelve bar stuff is easy, but it isn't, and we really like this disc." Dionne Warwick told Disc in its June 6 issue that she liked "Can't Buy Me Love" because "it is sort of a gospel thing–a real bluesy number."

British record buyers also liked the disc. "Can't Buy Me Love" entered the Record Retailer Top 50 singles chart at number eight on March 26. One week later, on April 2, the song replaced "Little Children" by Billy J. Kramer with the Dakotas at number one, where it remained for three weeks before giving way to Peter & Gordon's "A World Without Love," a song written by Paul and credited to Lennon-McCartney. "Can't Buy Me Love" spent 15 weeks on the charts, including five in the top five and seven in the top ten. Although Record Retailer was an industry trade magazine with modest subscription sales, its charts reached a larger audience through their publication in Record Mirror.

The single entered the Melody Maker National Chart, which also listed 50 songs, on March 28 at number one, where it remained for three weeks. The magazine charted the disc for 14 weeks, including six weeks in the top five and seven in the top ten. "Can't Buy Me Love" entered Disc's Top Thirty chart at number one on March 28 and remained there for three weeks. The record charted for ten weeks, including six weeks in the top five and seven in the top ten. The single performed similarly but slightly better in the NME Top Thirty, entering the chart on March 27 at number one, where it remained for four weeks. Its ten weeks on the charts also included six weeks in the top five and seven in the top ten. The BBC also reported the song at number one. Disc Weekly announced that "Can't Buy Me Love" had earned a gold disc award in its March 28 issue, indicating sales of one million units. While the March 28 Melody Maker reported that U.K. sales were closing in on two million, sales most likely stalled at just over 1,500,000.

Although the premiere of the Beatles film was several months away, some of the music weeklies began providing details about the movie shortly after filming began on March 2. The March 7 Disc ran the headline "IT'S ALL ABOARD FOR THE BEATLES FILM," which took up over half of the magazine's front page. The issue contained pictures and comments by the film's producer, Walter Shenson, on the magazine's front and back covers, plus an interior two-page spread with a report of the first few days on the set accompanied by additional photos. Shenson wrote that the film, which spanned a day-and-a-half in the life of the Beatles, would be finished in about eight weeks and that "when it arrives at your local cinema this summer you will see Paul, George, John and Ringo, not as 'film stars,' but as they REALLY are." His intent was to "present an entertaining version of The Beatles as you would like to see them and also to take you 'behind the scenes' to see how they work and how they play," adding: "They are such great personalties in their own right, it would be a great mistake to dress them up in the realms of fantasy, or to have them talk in any way other than their own Liverpool accents."

Shenson's comments made it clear that this would not be another cliché pop-star musical. "We are not attempting to make a musical in the usual sense of the word. There will be, of course, be a story-line and a plot–otherwise we would just be making a documentary. And a fictional character has been introduced in Wilfrid Brambell, who portrays Paul's grandfather. But, in the main, you will see the Beatles as you know them–and love them." The creative team behind the film would not be making any concessions for American audiences as British film makers had done in the past. Shenson was not concerned that some Americans "won't understand EVERY word" said by the Beatles. "We are going all out to make a true and honest film. We want it this way–and The Beatles themselves want it this way. And I'm convinced that's the way YOU want it too!"

The interior two-page spread was titled "All aboard the Beatles Special! Five days in their own train!" Readers learned that the Beatles were spending 11 hours a day for the entire week in a five-coach train supplied by British Railways for the opening sequences of their film. The train ran between Paddington Station and Minehead [though the train station shots shown in the movie would later be filmed at Marylebone London]. Publicity Director Tony Howard said: "The boys are real professionals and have taken their film directions in a willing and easy-going manner."

The back cover contained additional comments from Shenson, who said that when it came to delivering lines, "the boys are naturals, especially at making up their own!" He noted: "They are great at handling the press as they proved in America, and they are only too good at 'sending up' people. As I've found out to my cost!" It was important that the Beatles keep their identity in the film as that contributed to their success. They were nonconformists and a bit irreverent. He thought the Beatles were "going to make a great film, and...surprise a lot of people with their talent."

Chris Hutchins wrote about the first week of filming in the March 13 NME. Paul told him: "The film virtually opens with our departure from somewhere like Liverpool to somewhere like London, and that's how we come to be on the train. The snag is that my Irish grandfather is always interfering, telling everybody who manages us and so on–so we lock him up in the wire enclosure of the guard's van." George continued: "When we get to the big city we have to make our way to a television studio for a big show–and that's where the specialty acts like the Lionel Blair Dancers come in." Hutchins wrote that the film would have "a spectacular finish, with the boys being whisked away in a helicopter, disappearing into nowhere." As for the film's music, both sides of the group's latest single would be included. Ringo indicated that John played harmonica for the first time in ages on a song titled "I Should Have Known Better," which would be used in the guard's van scene. "And I Love Her" was another of the six numbers that would be "cleverly woven into the production...to keep the pace moving through this ninety minutes or so of virtually non-stop Beatles-as-they-are-in-real-life film." Hutchins assured readers that it was "going to be quite a picture."

Disc continued with reports on the film in its March 14 issue, informing readers of Tuesday's filming of solo scenes with Ringo in Turk's Head pub in Twickenham, where he wears a tattered raincoat and gets in trouble while drinking and playing darts. Tony Howard stated: "Ringo acted his part extremely well. Everyone was thoroughly satisfied." The March 21 Disc reported on the filming of the boys at Gatwick Airport for the movie's ending where they board a helicopter and the shooting of interior scenes at Twickenham Studios. Shenson commented on the rushes of the train scenes. "Dick [Lester] has photographed the scene in a very original way. Everything really moves along. Everyone of them has real star quality. Really, it's been a big bonus for all of us to work with them." In the March 28 Disc, Peter Thomson reported that his spies told him Paul had "written a really great ballad for THAT film."

The May 1964 issue of The Beatles Book (No. 10), which went on sale in early April, ran a story on the first two weeks of filming written by Billy Shepherd (actually Record Mirror reporter Peter Jones using a pen name). Shepherd wrote that during the early days of filming, the boys were knocked out by the friendliness of the production staff, but baffled at what they initially saw as a "waste of time" when they had to sit around and wait for the proper setting of the lighting, cameras and scenes. They also hated getting up so early in the morning to be on the set for 8:30 AM. The first week was spent entirely on the train. The cast included Wilfrid Brambell [of TV's Steptoe And Son] playing the part of Paul's grandfather as a "real old mischief-maker." Scriptwriter Alun Owen was often on set, rewriting some lines when the boys disagreed with words he had written. Walter Shenson's comments to Shepherd were similar to what he told Disc. "The vital thing here is not to do anything to damage the boys as they really are...We're certainly not going to build one of the boys bigger than the others. They complement each other." Dick Lester, who had directed Goon shows on television, said: "The Beatles, too, have a great off-beat sense of humour...in fact, they give the impression they don't even need their scripts. They could make it up as they go along."

Norman Rossington, who plays the group's road manager, thought Paul was the most self-conscious, while John and George didn't seem to worry too much. Ringo was made to be the dumb one, like Harpo Marx of the Marx Brothers, but he was doing very well. Rossington added: "'Course, when you get them all together, anything at all can happen."

Shepherd wrote of Ringo having his "own day of glory" in a scene in a public-house. Ringo admitted feeling a bit shaky being on his own, "but soon he was working like a star of long-standing." After a day off, the boys went to Twickenham Studios, which contained a maze of different sets. The first day of filming involved the guard's van scene where the group played a new song titled "I Should Have Known Better." The script had called for Paul's grandfather asking the boys: "Well, what can YOU do?," leading the boys to take out their guitars and play. The Beatles suggested they play cards and have the picture fade into them on their instruments. The next day they shot a scene in which Ringo found an old waiter in the closet of their hotel room. On Friday the 13th, it rained, causing a delay in filming outdoor scenes at and around Gatwick Airport, including the boys running to a helicopter and running around a field until they were "dead-beat, whacked, exhausted" causing them to realize "filming isn't ALL as easy as it looks."

FILMING with the BOYS IN

BEATLESCOPE

by Billy Shepherd

First Day

JOHN LENNON took a deep breath
and said: "Who's that little old
man over there." And Paul
McCartney queried: "What little old
man?" Dialogue which doesn't mean
much out of context . . . but
which were very important in
the fantastic Beatles. Becaus
the opening sentence fro
first-ever major movie.

The early days of filming were
the boys. They were knocke
friendly approach of all the te
production staff; but baffled
"waste of time", when they
sit around and do nothing
cameras and scenes were

And there was somethi
positively HATED. Gett
the morning. They us
the set by 8.30 a.m., a
would normally rega
middle of the night.
out of bed fell, as e
Neil Aspinall.

After the first fe
friends: "I'm wea
It means getting
the boys. They
try to get the

rhythm of the film studio's day.
Only once, in the first few weeks of
filming, were they late. And that was less
than half-an-hour.

The first week was spent entirely on a
train. They left from Paddington, went to
Minehead and back. And every newspaper
in the country wanted to get pictures of the
embarking. The fans? Well, film-
very expensive business, and
ld-ups. So, the boys,
Acton station
crowds

FIRST BEATL

THE PRIZES A
OF THESE FA
TRANSISTOR

PLUS

A PERSONAL
FROM ONE
BEATLES WI
PRIZE

TO ENTER:

Answer the followi

1. On what date was "
2. Name one school th
3. Which singer did Jo
4. In what month and
5. What is the name
6. Name two of the b

PRINT YOUR AN
COMP., 244 EDGW
six correct answers
John, Paul, George

Dick Lester directing Paul and Ringo in a scene with former Miss World, Rosemarie Frankland.

Rosemarie in

The Beatles MONTHLY BOOK

No. 10

MAY 1964

EVERY MONTH

Price ONE SHILLING & SIXPENCE

The April 4 Disc ran an article by Laurie Henshaw titled "Filming with the Beatles." George told of a scene with Lionel Blair and his girls in which they do the dancing and the Beatles "gag it up." The group made it clear that they had no plans to turn to acting. John pointed out the Beatles were playing themselves in the film, so they weren't really acting, they were just taking directions. Paul indicated that he loved music "much more." Walter Shenson praised a "marvelous" encounter between John and Anna Quayle in which the actress runs into John backstage and tells him that he looks like himself. John pretends he isn't a Beatle, but just looks like him. George said that there was an option for three films. That week Record Mirror reported that the film was going well, with the Beatles at the Scala Theatre completing interior shots. This included a special audience of 1,800 extras to provide the best atmosphere.

Peter Jones, who reported on the first two weeks of the film in the May issue of The Beatles Book as Billy Shepherd, wrote about his time with the Beatles for the April 11 Record Mirror. At Scala Theatre, the Beatles filmed indoor shots with "several hundred fans...being paid for the pleasure of screaming." The boys make suggestions about changing lines to screenwriter Alun Owen, who accepts their suggestions. "They know more about what they'd say in real-life than anybody else." Jones observes: "Filming is becoming fun. The Beatles are ALWAYS fun. But they're determined that this, their debut film, is going to be as good as it can possibly be. They are professionals. They know exactly when to gag around and when to be serious." Paul said the group was excited about the film, but did not consider themselves as actors. This was because they had recently seen Peter Sellers in *Dr. Strangelove*, which prompted Paul to say: "And you simply can't follow THAT!"

The April 10 NME reported that the Beatles film would premiere at the London Pavilion in Piccadilly Circus on Monday, July 6, with Royalty likely to attend the charitable event sponsored by the Variety Club of Great Britain. The Beatles would be there. A second premiere gala was expected to take place at the Odeon in Liverpool. The magazine added that Anna Quayle, co-star of Anthony Newley's *Stop The World*, had a small role in the film, featured in a "crazy conversation" sequence with John Lennon. The April 17 NME reported that Ed Sullivan had flown to London to interview the Beatles on the film set at Twickenham. Sullivan planned to broadcast the interview, along with excerpts from the film, prior to the film's U.S. premiere. The Beatles chose the title for their film, *A Hard Day's Night*.

NME's Chris Hutchins and American singer Roy Orbison were on set for the filming of the bath scene with John. George said about the film: "This whole thing should be quite funny by the time it is finished. Even if nobody else gets a laugh out of it we've had tremendous fun making it. In fact, they had to stop shooting numerous times because we couldn't stop laughing!" John added: "They wanted us to be natural so that's just what we are doing–being ourselves." Lennon acknowledged that the film had a gear script written by Alun Owen, who "agreed to re-write any bits we didn't think are us." George thought the film was going to be epic, adding that it had better be for all the mornings the group had to get up early. During the bath scene, John sang a verse of "Rule Britannia" as the submarine he was playing with sank to the bottom of the tub. Orbison observed: "This is something America has got to see!"

The May 2 Record Mirror reported that the Beatles film was over, with technicians saying that "the finished product will be a wow!" The film's score was complete, with John and Paul writing a title song to go over the credits. While the entire group did a grand job, "Ringo will come across as the most off-beat character." No one tampered with the "zany characters of the Beatles," allowing them to come across as they really are–"an unpredictable batch of guys whose sense of humour can't be suppressed." Director Dick Lester was impressed with the way the boys have worked: "They're 'naturals.' Sure they sometimes forgot their lines–but they're completely professional all the time." The May 16 Disc included an 8-page special on the film with lots of pictures and a summary of the film's plot.

Billy Shepherd opened his report on the film in June 1964 Beatles Book (No. 11) with: "WOW! WHATTA FILM!" While there was a script, the boys added "so much ad-libbed stuff...that the whole structure of the story has changed." There were "a load of Beatle-situations that could end up putting the Marx Brothers to shame!" After rejecting "Moving On," "Traveling On," "Let's Go" and "Beatlemania," the group selected one of Ringo's strange wordings as the title. After a long day's work had gone late into the evening, "Ringo said casually: 'Boy, this has been a hard day's night.'" Producer Walter Shenson had special praise for the drummer: "They're all good and very funny. But Ringo has surprised everybody by the confident way he copes with the cameras and the quick-witted way he dreams up a new approach to any incident." After recounting some of the film's zaniest moments, Shepherd advised: "Get early in the queues! Because just about everybody in the Beatles-conscious world will want to see it."

In the Post Bag letters section of the June 6 Disc, A.M. Purdom of Newlands, Harrow-on-the-Hill, Middlesex wondered if fans would ever be lucky enough to buy an original Beatles EP, pointing out that the group's four current EPs had album cuts and singles. Purdom reasoned: "Since the Beatles LPs have been long-term residents at the top of the LP charts and the EPs from them sell remarkably well, surely the group could make even more money–and give their fans more enjoyment on disc–by recording some special tracks for EP release." Purdom would not have to wonder for long. That same week, NME reported that, after tremendous demand, EMI would be releasing a Beatles EP featuring Paul McCartney's version of "Long Tall Sally" on June 19. The disc would also include Ringo singing the Carl Perkins song "Matchbox," the Lennon-McCartney number "I Call Your Name" and "Slow Down" [by Larry Williams]. Record Mirror also wrote about the rush release of a new Beatles EP consisting entirely of songs yet to be released in the U.K. Record Mirror provided additional information about the disc in its June 13 issue (shown right). Side One featured Paul on "Long Tall Sally" and John singing "I Call Your Name," the only Lennon-McCartney composition on the EP. Both tracks were recorded in London shortly after the Beatles return from America and were intended primarily for the U.S. market. [In fact, both songs were on the Capitol disc *The Beatles' Second Album*, issued on April 10.] Side Two contained John as vocalist on "Slow Down" and Ringo singing "Matchbox," the old Carl Perkins rocker. The magazine reported that both songs were recorded the previous Monday [June 1] with Perkins in attendance.

In the June 12 NME, John was asked what his favorite Beatles disc was. He replied: "The one with 'Long Tall Sally' on it. I always like the latest record we have best, for obvious reasons. But 'Sally' is a good 'un. It's basic rock 'n' roll and you can't beat that." The *Long Tall Sally* EP features Robert Freeman's October 25, 1963 photo of the group standing on a wall beside the Stadshuset (Town Hall) in Stockholm, Sweden, and liner notes by Brian's personal assistant, Derek Taylor. His opening salvo: "A new release by John, Paul, George and Ringo is more than a disc...it is a national event." He describes the title track as "wild and reckless but beautifully phrased and pure Beatle music," adding that Paul "has never done anything better." John's "Slow Down" is a "moody rocker, note-perfect product of the Beatles' early performances in Liverpool's Cavern." As for "Matchbox" and Ringo's vocal, Taylor humorously writes: "He sings little, but well, which is better than rotten and often." After predicting that the EP would sell millions to the world, he gave the following advice: "Dip it in gold and give it to your grandchildren. Or just simply wear it out."

● An early shot of the BEATLES with LITTLE RICHARD, the original recorder and writer of "Long, Tall Sally."

BEATLES LP, EP AND SINGLE

Top EMI executives met in secret conference last week to discuss the **Beatles'** forthcoming LP "A Hard Day's Night."

And as a result, there will now be 12 tracks on the record. Incidental music and informal dialogue on the album has been scrubbed, and there will either be six or eight tracks from the film **plus** either four or six completely new ones.

EMI are to issue the EP, "Long, Tall Sally," as forecast by the RM last week, on Parlophone.

The record is now being rush released on Friday, June 19.

Side one is "Long, Tall Sally," featuring Paul McCartney, and "I Call Your Name," the only Lennon-McCartney number on the disc, featuring John Lennon. Both numbers were recorded in London shortly after the Beatles returned from America, and their release was intended primarily for the U.S.

Both the numbers on side two were recorded on Monday last week. They are "Slowdown," featuring John Lennon, and "Matchbox," the old Carl Perkins' rocker, sung by Ringo Starr.

Carl Perkins attended the recording session last week.

The Beatles next single "A Hard Day's Night" will be issued on July 10. The title song of their new film will be coupled with "Things We Said Today", a folk flavoured number. "A Hard Day's Night" is to be issued in America on June 27 on Capitol.

BILLY FURY
I Will
c/w Nothin' Shakin' (but the leaves on the trees)
F 11888 45 rpm

Diary Dates

THURSDAY

The Kinky Kinks, with the **Bluesounds**, Seaton Town Hall; **Manfred Mann**, Bishop's Stortford; **King Size Taylor** and the **Dominoes**, Great Yarmouth; **Millie**, Prestatyn; **Yardbirds**, **Animals**, Brighton Dome; **Merseybeats**, Worthing Assembly Hall; **John Lee Hooker**, Southsea; **Swinging Blue Jeans**, **Merseybeats**, **Mojos**, **Mark Wynter**, **Andee Silver**, and **Miar Davies** on "For Teenagers Only" ATV; **Petula Clark**, **Billy J. Kramer** and **Dakotas**, **Lulu**, **The Strangers and Mike Shannon**, "A Swinging Time," BBC-1.

FRIDAY

The Mojos, **Joe Loss Pop Show**, BBC Light; **Bobby Shafto**, "Five O'Clock Club," Granada TV; **Dave Clark Five**, **Dusty Springfield**, **Peter and Gordon**, **Jimmy Powell and the Five Dimensions**, "Ready Steady, Go"; **Helen Shapiro** commences 10-day Irish tour; **King Size Taylor** and the **Dominoes**, Dunstable; **The Applejacks**, Cardiff Capitol; **Mike Cotton Sound**, Manchester; **Merseybeats**, Pembroke Palladium; **John Lee Hooker**, Liverpool Cavern; ... **Blue Jeans**, Stoke-on- ... **Berry** and the ... ickly and the ... stronaires, ... Shrews-... Boyle, "Thank Your Lucky Stars"; **Manfred Mann**, Wellington; **King Size Taylor** and the **Dominoes**, Boston; **The Applejacks**, Morecambe Floral Hall; **Mike Cotton Sound**, Woodford; **Millie**, Northwich Memorial Hall; **Merseybeats**, New Brighton Rugby; **Swinging Blue Jeans**, Sheffield; **John Lee Hooker**, Manchester; **Downliners Sect**, Nottingham; **Heinz**, Cambridge.

SUNDAY

Vernon Girls commence one week at Darlington La Bamba; **King Size Taylor** and the **Dominoes**, Southall; **Merseybeats**, Westbury Victor; **Dave Clark Five**, **Applejacks**, Leicester De Montfort Hall; **John Lee Hooker**, Stoke-on-Trent; **Swinging Blue Jeans**, Great Yarmouth.

MONDAY

Millie and the Five Embers, **The Mojos**, **Dave Clark Five**, **Applejacks**, Croydon Fairfield Hall; **Merseybeats**, Bradford Majestic; **Francoise Hardy**, **Mark Wynter**, **Dave Berry**, **Bob Miller** and his **Millermen**, "Disc A Gogo," TWW.

TUESDAY

Mike Cotton Sound, Wood Green; **Dave Clark Five**, **Applejacks**, Guildhall, Portsmouth; **John Lee Hooker**, Aylesbury; **Brian Poole and the Tremeloes**, Clacton Blue Lagoon; **Downliners Sect**, Greenwick Town Hall.

WEDNESDAY

Manfred Mann, Bristol; **Mersey-**... Edinburgh Palais; **The** ...s, Clacton Blue Lagoon.

PRELIMINARY POLL RESULTS

IT'S a neck-and-neck battle between The Beatles and The Rolling Stones. Either of the two groups, both of whom are now out of this country on nation-wide tours, could emerge from the RM POP POLL as the best vocal group in the British section.

Five tellers working day and night have been counting the thousands of poll forms that have flooded the RM's offices in London during the past fortnight.

The Beatles are also prominent in the best male group (World Section) and "She Loves You" looks like being the best disc of 1963 or 1964.

There are some startling surprises in the sections for favourite DJ, individual group member, and most promising new singer. All the results will be revealed in next week's bumper issue of the Record Mirror, increased to more than twice its normal size to present ten years of pop in pictures. There'll be colour and black and white pictures galore, featuring Elvis, Cliff, The Beatles, Rolling Stones, and many of the forgotten popsters of years ago.

The Record Mirror edition next week will be a copy to keep. As a souvenir of ten years of pop—"Rock Around the Clock + 10"—it will be something not to be missed.

Storyville label releases

First waxings on the Storyville label to be released in Britain for two years will be in the shops via Transatlantic Records next month.

Nine LPs and four EPs of Sonny Boy Williamson, Big Joe Williams, Bill Broonzy, Leadbelly, Sidney Bechet, Memphis Slim, Snooks Eaglin, Lonnie Johnson, and Otis Span, will be selling for 29s. 9d. and 12s. 3d. respectively.

Fifteen further items from Storyville will be issued in **September**.

Managing director of Transatlantic, Nathan Joseph, refused to disclose details of material for release in August on a new jazz and folk label called "Xtra."

A GREAT NEW DISC!

KARL DENVER

Love me with all your heart

F 11905 45 rpm

DECCA

The Decca Record Company Ltd Decca House Albert Embankment London SE1

...RY CRY CRY CRY

...1964 !

CRY CRY CRY CRY CRY CRY CRY CRY CRY CRY CRY CRY CRY

mono

THE BEATLES

LONG TALL SALLY

PARLOPHONE

Allen Evans reviewed the *Long Tall Sally* EP for the June 26 NME, stating that the Beatles were "sure to do well" with the disc. Paul sang the title track "hysterically, backed by torrid guitar-drums music." Ringo's vocal on "Matchbox" was echoed and double-tracked "to a beaty backing." "I Call Your Name" had "the familiar Beatles sound, and the best singing." Although "Slow Down" wasn't sung with the same unison, its backing was tops. Disc reviewed the EP in its June 27 issue. "Long Tall Sally" was "a real raver with the McCartney voice yelling out the lyrics and throwing in some squeals for good measure." The magazine thought that John was the best solo singer in the band, proving it with his two vocals. "I Call Your Name" was a Lennon-McCartney composition with "typical Beatle mixture of melody and beat," while "Slow Down" was a "vintage rock opus" written by Larry Williams. Disc stated that "Matchbox" by Carl Perkins "gives Ringo a chance to show off his voice. And show it off he does." The August 1964 Record Mail contained a write-up on the disc informing readers: "This is another EP from the fabulous four that has made the charts in a big way, proving beyond doubt that they are one of the most popular groups ever." The magazine described each of the songs, giving extra praise for the title track, "Long Tall Sally," calling it "one of the greatest rockers in history" and adding that "Paul sings it, and the excitement he generates is terrific."

The *Long Tall Sally* EP was scheduled for release on June 19, although the disc most likely did not reach shops in significant numbers until a week or so later. The June 27 Record Mirror listed the EP's release date as July 10. The disc entered the Record Retailer EP chart on July 2 at number two. One week later, on July 11, it replaced the Rolling Stones' first EP at number one for its first of seven straight weeks at the top of the chart. On August 30, it was bumped from the top by the new Rolling Stones EP, *Five By Five*, to number two, where it remained for 12 straight weeks. The *Long Tall Sally* EP charted for 37 weeks, including 23 weeks in the top five and 29 in the top ten.

The Beatles new EP entered the Melody Maker singles chart on July 4 at number 20, peaking at number 14 on July 18 during its 13-week run. NME charted the *Long Tall Sally* EP in its singles chart for six weeks, with the disc entering the chart on July 3 at number 13 and peaking the following week at 11. Disc reported the EP in its singles chart for seven weeks, with the record debuting on July 4 at number 13 and peaking at 11 a week later. *Long Tall Sally* was awarded a silver disc by Disc on February 23, 1965, in recognition of sales of 250,000 units.

Readers of the May 2 Record Mirror learned that John and Paul had written a title song to go over the credits to their film *A Hard Day's Night*. The May 23 Melody Maker reported that the Beatles next single would probably be "A Hard Day's Night," which featured a John solo vocal. The disc would most likely be released in late June or early July to coincide with the premiere of the film, set for July 6 in London. Publicist Derek Taylor noted that the Beatles didn't particularly like their next single being the title of their film, finding it a bit obvious, but it was difficult to see how it could be avoided. The soundtrack LP would also be linked to the release of the film. The June 13 Record Mirror confirmed that the Beatles next single would be "A Hard Day's Night," set for release on July 10. The title song of their new film would be coupled with "Things We Said Today," a folk-flavoured number. The June 19 NME reported that although the single would not be on sale until July 10, EMI was making it available for broadcast on June 26.

In the weeks leading up to the single's release there was talk that the Beatles were slipping in popularity. The June 20 Melody Maker played up the "Beatles versus the Rolling Stones" angle, noting that the Beatles new single was set for release just as the new Stones' disc was ready to start up the charts. This was a departure from the past when the groups avoided issuing their singles at the same time, instead waiting to release a new disc until the other's last record was falling down the charts. Those questioning the Beatles appeal and abilities would soon be silenced.

In his review of "A Hard Day's Night" in the June 27 Disc, Don Nicholl noted that the song was deliberately "tailored for the screen." It opened with a "tremendous guitar chord" played by George on his 12-string. It was necessarily "loud and hard...to make its impact over the noise of screaming fans and other sound-effects." Nicholl added that the opening chord's impact was equally effective away from the screen, leading into a "steady stamping number." John handled most of the vocal work, forcefully barking out the song's simple words, assisted in some places by Paul. The song contains a "fascinating instrumental break" blending piano and guitar that has a "delicate charming effect." Paul sings lead on "Things We Said Today," a "more subdued ballad which flows pleasantly and on a good melodic line." Nicholl closed by assuring readers that "A Hard Day's Night" was going to "hammer itself into our brains throughout the summer." Record Retailer agreed. "Exciting Beatles performance, lots of John Lennon vocal work and some intricate George Harrison guitar stylings. Silly to predict anything other than a chart-topper."

In the July 3 NME, Derek Johnson conceded that he need not recommend that readers purchase the long-awaited title song from the Beatles film because he was sure that every NME reader already had a copy of the disc on order. Johnson added: "The only way which my words will come as a revelation is if some square happens to read them, while eating his fish and chips out of this NME!" But going through the motions, he described the song as a "bouncy finger-snapper, with a pounding beat and catchy melody...plus the group's usual distinctive wistful feel." John takes the spotlight, joined by Paul in a few passages. George provides an intricate guitar solo. "Things We Said Today" did not have a crashing beat, but rather was a "melodic, almost plaintive, medium pacer" sung by Paul.

Dave Clark, drummer for the Dave Clark Five, reviewed the single in the July 4 Melody Maker. He thought that "A Hard Day's Night" was an unusual title for a Beatles song, but added that "you've got to like it." Clark commented that the song's instrumental sound was very unusual and different from the Beatles other hits. He liked the number "very much" and stated it would definitely reach number one. Clark thought there was a touch of the Everly Brothers about "Things We Said Today." He did not like the song, but said it was the A-side that counts. In the July 11 Pop Weekly, Peter Aldersley said that, based on first hearing alone, he liked "A Hard Day's Night" even more than "Can't Buy Me Love." However, the latter song grew on him the more he heard it. The new disc had "all the bite and impact" expected from the Beatles and "sizzles with their zest and personality." Although the song was a powerful offering, Aldersley suspected that it wouldn't be as durable as some of John and Paul's earlier compositions.

"A Hard Day's Night" quickly topped the Record Retailer chart. After debuting on July 16 at number three behind the Rolling Stones' "It's All Over Now" and the Animals' "House Of The Rising Sun," the new Beatles single took only one week to move into the top position, where it remained for three weeks before being replaced by Manfred Mann's "Do Wah Diddy Diddy." The song charted for 12 weeks, including six in the top five and eight in the top ten. The new Beatles single debuted at number one in NME (July 17), Melody Maker (July 18) and Disc (July 18), topping the charts for four weeks in each magazine. The song charted for 15 weeks in Melody Maker, 13 in Disc and 11 in NME. The single also topped the BBC chart. "A Hard Day's Night" had advance sales of over 500,000 and sales of 800,000 within two weeks of release. The cover of the July 18 Melody Maker summed it up: "BANG! BEATLES ARE BACK!"

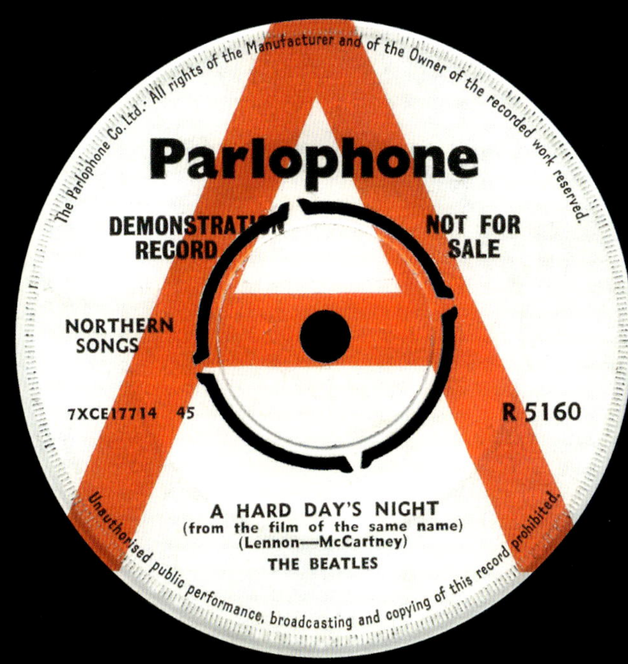

EMI initially planned on marketing the disc as a double A-side single as evidenced by an ad in the July 2 Record Retailer. Demonstration records prepared for the single have a large red A on both sides. The July 9 Record Retailer reported EMI had changed plans and would be "concentrating on the film theme as the top side."

As recounted above, fans first read about the Beatles film album in the February 29 Disc, with Brian saying that the boys "will make five or six recordings for the film," with an LP to come out around August contemporaneously with the film's release. An article about the movie appearing in the March 13 NME indicated that film would have six songs, which was not enough for an album. Titles included "I Should Have Known Better" and "And I Love Her." The April 24 NME reported that the Beatles had recorded the title song for the film on the previous Thursday [April 16]. There would now be an LP from the film that would include "the eight songs [recorded for the film] and soundtrack music." The album would be issued around the end of June. [Although the concept for the British LP would change, the United Artists album issued in the States would have eight Beatles songs plus four tracks of soundtrack music.]

Two weeks later, the May 9 Record Mirror ran a report on the "New Beatles L.P." that differed from the NME description. The magazine indicated there would be only six [Beatles] tracks on the album, with the remainder including incidental music from the film and "informal conversation between the Beatles and their A & R man, George Martin." EMI had yet to decide on the album's title, but it most likely would be the same as the film title. The album's release was expected for June 25, less than two weeks before the film's July 6 premiere. While all the group's previous records had been on Parlophone, it was "strongly rumoured" that the new LP would be on United Artists.

The prospect of a Beatles album with only six Beatles songs did not sit well with the magazine's readers. In the letters page of the May 23 Record Mirror, Charles Knapp of West Norwood wrote: "I think the decision to make the next Beatles L.P. as half sound-track, half-song is terrible. Surely they do not have to put six songs from the Beatles on an L.P. to sell the theme music from a film. It would have been better to release the six songs with some more tracks separate from the film. A lot of the young fans will be doubtful about paying the price of an L.P. for nothing more than an E.P." Letters Editor James Craig added: "Several other letters have reached us on the same line."

Apparently rumors surfaced that the Beatles album might consist of the film songs mixed with dialog from the film. In the June 12 NME, Andy Gray wrote that John had told him that the idea of an LP half of humour and half of the film songs was "a soft rumour." Lennon added: "We'll put more songs with the film songs to make a fully singing LP."

That same issue provided the names of seven new songs that would be included on the album: "A Hard Day's Night," "I Should Have Known Better," "And I Love Her," "If I Fell," "Tell Me Why," "I'll Cry Instead" and "I'm Happy Just To Dance With You." The LP was likely to have five former hits: "She Loves You," "I Wanna Be Your Man," "Don't Bother Me," "All My Loving" and "Can't Buy Me Love." The June 27 Disc stated these five songs were in the film.

The June 13 Record Mirror reported that a secret meeting of top EMI executives resulted in a change of plans for the Beatles upcoming album, *A Hard Day's Night*. The initial concept of including incidental music and informal dialog on the album had been scrubbed. The LP would now contain a dozen tracks, with six or eight from the film plus four or six completely new ones. The June 13 Disc had even more information about the new album in an article by Nigel Hunter, who had interviewed George Martin. The LP was set for release on July 10, along with a single of the title song for the film. Martin said the album had seven new songs plus "Can't Buy Me Love," adding: "The boys started writing them when they were in Paris and continued in America during their first visit." After stating that the order of the songs on the album had yet to be determined, Martin described the new tracks. On "Tell Me Why," they "all sing strident harmony...over a shuffle rhythm which is almost Blue Beat [U.K. term for Ska/Jamaican R&B]." "And I Love Her" is a "beautiful melodic ballad" sung solo by Paul in a mood similar to that of "Till There Was You." George plays a "very good solo on Spanish guitar" on the song. "I Should Have Known Better" is used during the "luggage-van scene on the train." "If I Fell" is played to an audience towards the end of the film and is "very much a Beatle song, with unusual harmony and voice playing." "I'm Happy Just To Dance With You" is a "lively up-tempo number with a definite Latin-American feel." Martin said that "Can't Buy Me Love" was originally going to be featured twice in the film, but he thought that a new song would be better for the second spot. The boys came up with "I'll Cry Instead," which was a "good up-tempo number" that features George on his 12-string guitar.

The June 19 NME gave an update on the new album, correcting information from the prior week. The plan to include several old songs on the soundtrack album had been dropped as the group had "recorded four new titles specifically for the album." The disc would contain the seven new songs listed in the previous week's issue, "Can't Buy Me Love" plus the four new songs. "I'll Cry Instead" had been cut from the film, but would still be on the album.

Billy Shepherd's article on the movie appearing in the June 1964 edition of The Beatles Book stated that there would definitely be an LP featuring the songs from the movie, all of which were written by John and Paul. John said: "There were times when we honestly thought we'd never get the time to write all the material. But we managed to get a couple finished while we were in Paris, during our stay at the Olympia. And three more were completed in America, while we were soaking up the sun on Miami Beach." Paul added: "The only real panic was over the title number. For a long time there wasn't a title at all. So that had to be a rush job." Shepherd mentioned that George had "another stab at composing" and that "his song will probably be on the album, though it is not in the film." The song Shepherd refers to is very likely "You Know What To Do," which was recorded in demo form at EMI Studios on June 3, 1964, the day before the Beatles departed to Denmark for the start of their 1964 world tour. Because Ringo became ill that morning, he does not play on the song. It is quite possible that "You Know What To Do" would have been recorded as the fourteenth song for the album had Ringo not taken ill. The Beatles never returned to the song, which was finally released on *Anthology 1* in November 1995.

The June 27 Record Mirror accurately reported that the Beatles *A Hard Day's Night* album, set for release on July 10, would have 13 tracks, all written by John Lennon and Paul McCartney. Only two of the songs had been previously released, "Can't Buy Me Love" and "You Can't Do That."

Melody Maker editor Jack Hutton wrote an extensive article on the *A Hard Day's Night* LP in the magazine's June 27 edition, informing readers that he had been given a preview of the new album on Monday [June 22]. As George Martin and the EMI engineers did not finish mixing all of the album's songs until that day, it is not known if he heard the final mixes of all of the tracks. While it is also not known if he heard the mono or stereo version of the album, his comments suggest he heard stereo mixes. Hutton interviewed George Martin, who commented: "For a single, it's simple to have a rave, use a harmonica and yell your head off. But albums are a different story. You've got to be different. I think this album stacks up against their previous discs." Hutton was told that most of the tracks were completed in two to three takes after the arrangements were worked out. Nine of the numbers were completed in three days. Hutton thought that the group had "been touched up a bit," with "voices added and a bit more cymbal."

NO MORE HARD DAY'S NIGHTS

waiting for

THE BEATLES'

great new LP

IT'S ON SALE HERE NOW!

SIDE ONE

A HARD DAY'S NIGHT
I SHOULD HAVE KNOWN BETTER
IF I FELL
I'M HAPPY JUST TO DANCE WITH YOU
AND I LOVE HER
TELL ME WHY
CAN'T BUY ME LOVE

From the Soundtrack of the
United Artists Film 'A HARD DAY'S NIGHT'

SIDE TWO

ANY TIME AT ALL
I'LL CRY INSTEAD
THINGS WE SAID TODAY
WHEN I GET HOME
YOU CAN'T DO THAT
I'LL BE BACK

Words and Music:
JOHN LENNON AND PAUL McCARTNEY

TRADE MARK OF
THE PARLOPHONE Co. Ltd.

PARLOPHONE RECORDS

PCS 3058 (stereo LP) **PMC 1230** (mono LP)

E.M.I. RECORDS LTD.
(Controlled by Electric & Musical Industries Ltd.)
EMI HOUSE
20 MANCHESTER SQUARE · LONDON W.1.
Printed in Great Britain

G2770 PSL

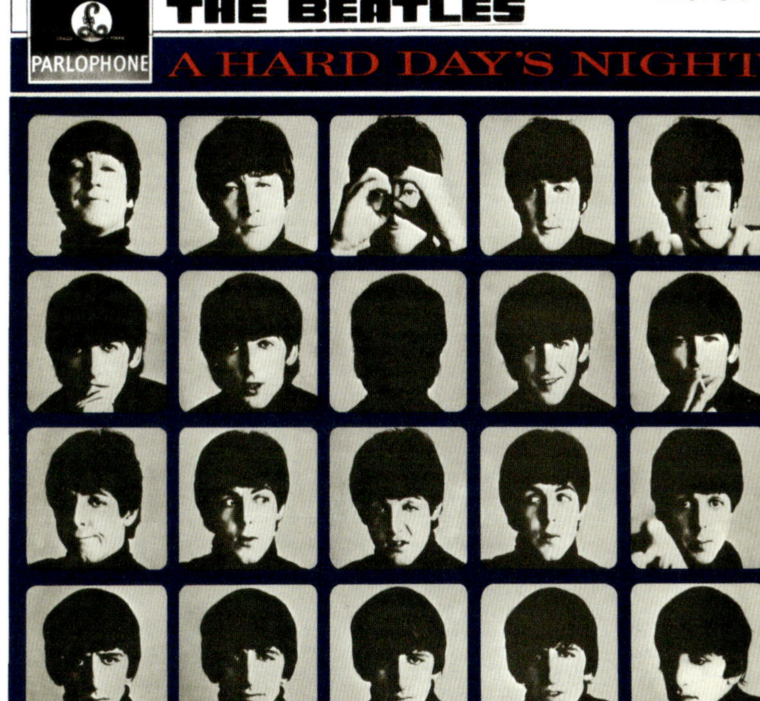

Hutton described "A Hard Day's Night" as a "great curtain opener for the LP" and the disc's most commercial track. It would be an "outstanding hit." The hard-swinging song featured excellent guitar by George and an odd effect in the middle eight with two Beatles and George Martin creating a sound like an organ. "I Should Have Known Better" had gutsy drumming by Ringo and swinging harmonica by John. Double tracking allowed for John to sing over his harmonica playing. "If I Fell" was a slowish quiet number with a nice melody. Oddly, Hutton did not think the song was commercial. He thought that "I'm Happy Just To Dance With You" had one of the best lyrics of the album's songs. The track's "weird sound" was a special drum from the studio's effect department [a loose-skinned Arabian bongo drum]. "And I Love Her" was one of Hutton's favorite tracks on the disc. He correctly identified Paul as the song's solo vocalist, but incorrectly stated that the others joined him on the chorus when, in fact, Paul's voice was double-tracked on parts of the song on the stereo mix. The song had an "unusual beat"with Ringo playing bongos and George playing claves. George played an excellent acoustic guitar solo. "Tell Me Why" was sung by John, with the others coming in with "good harmonies." Hutton was impressed by the song, saying that it was the "most polished Beatles number I've heard." Side One ended with "Can't Buy Me Love." All of the songs on the first side were featured in the film.

None of the songs on Side Two were featured in the film, though some were written for it. "Any Time At All" was "sung with great gusto" and had George playing "an interesting figure in the background." "I'll Cry Instead," which had been cut from the film, had a "good melody." "Things We Said Today" had a minor feel to it, with the boys approaching it in a "folky way" that made it "almost like a folk song." "When I Get Home" was another track with "excellent lyric and melody." Hutton thought that "You Can't Do That" was "considerably improved" and a "much better version" [than the mono single]. This seems to indicate that he heard the stereo mix of the song. The album's closing track, "I'll Be Back," was a "slower number, very well played, which demonstrates clearly the instrumental lead the Beatles have over nearly every other group."

Allen Evans reviewed the Beatles new LP in the July 3 NME. As for the seven movie tracks on Side One, Evans thought the first and last tracks were the best. The title song was "a sure-fire hit, a driving Merseysider, with good unison singing and a lyric with appeal, about a girl making a hard day's work all worth the while in the evening." The song started "with a big twang, then bursts into unison singing, and ends with a quiet twang tone-pattern." The last song on the side was an old favorite, "Can't Buy Me Love." In between were: "I Should Have Known Better" (a plaintive song with a John double-tracked vocal); "If I Fell" (a quiet, slowish song "with expert vocal merging by Paul McCartney and John, a bit one-note tunewise, yet not without fascination"); "I'm Happy Just To Dance With You" (a fast and bright song with "a lot of noise" behind George's solo vocal); "And I Love Her" (Paul singing, in the style of "Till There Was You," a "tender love ballad with a Latin-American backing with bongos and claves"); and "Tell Me Why" ("good harmony singing in the big-sound Beatles tradition, though the high notes are a bit half-hearted").

Two of the songs on Side Two have "John belting out the solo, and the others chiming in." Evans describes "Any Time At All" as a "shouter" and "When I Get Home" as "up-beater about a chap going home after work." "You Can't Do That" is a "raving number," while "I'll Be Back" is a "slower tune, with laboured playing," that gets better on a second hearing. John and Paul share vocals on "I'll Cry Instead," a "fast-moving hand-clapper," while Paul sings solo on "Things We Said Today," which "sounds like a folk group, soft and monotone." Although Evans did not think the album had the "uninhibited, joyous drive" of the group's prior albums, the disc was "way out ahead of rivals."

Disc ran Nigel Hunter's review of the LP in its July 4 issue. Hunter observed that the fab foursome's latest album would keep record pressmen working overtime. The first seven tracks were from the film, and the remainder were all new. He incorrectly stated that "Can't Buy Me Love" was the only track that had been heard before, failing to recognize that "You Can't Do That" was that single's B-side. John and Paul wrote all of the disc's songs, and "their gift for simple and attractive melody and words" was the "outstanding feature of the set." The title song was a "medium beater" with "memorable lyric and tune." John's vocal was double-tracked, and George added "some nimble guitar work." "I Should Have Known Better" was another "medium beater" that moved well behind the voices and John's harmonica. "If I Fell," with John and Paul sharing vocals, was "one of the highlights of the album, a slow, wistful ballad with pleasant harmonies." George sang lead on "I'm Happy Just To Dance With You," with Ringo "rattling the cymbals all the way." Paul sang solo on "And I Love Her," a tuneful ballad that was the closest on the LP to being "a departure from the usual Beatle sound." The medium beat returns with "Tell Me Why," which has a John and Paul vocal and a "typically Beatle falsetto gimmick." "Can't Buy Me Love" was a solid song that still sounded good.

"Any Time At All" was a "heavy medium beater, and a typical Beatle production, full of vim and vigour," with John on lead vocal. "I'll Cry Instead" was an up-tempo track with John and Paul joining forces on the vocals. "Things We Said Today" was a powerful medium-tempo track. Hunter incorrectly identified John, rather than Paul, as the lead vocalist. "When I Get Home" is an interesting track with blues singing by John. "You Can't Do That" is another song with a medium beat, sung by John with Ringo adding cowbell. The album closer, "I'll Be Back," is a "hefty, full-blooded" medium-paced track with John on lead vocal.

Record Mirror reviewed the LP in its July 11 issue. The album's opening track, "A Hard Day's Night," was "already passing into pop history." "I Should Have Known Better" was "just fine." "If I Fell" was a "slow ballad, with a stack of compulsive charm." George does a good job with his lead vocal on "I'm Happy Just To Dance With You." He "swings amiably," and the song is pushed along with Ringo's "persuasive percussion." Paul sings lead on "And I Love Her," which "is not typically Beatle in sound." "Tell Me Why" is "unmistakably Beatlish" with "all the falsetto highlights." As for "Can't Buy Me Love," reviewer Peter Jones said "oh, what's the use of saying anything more about this one!"

"Any Time At All" is a "medium-paced thumper" with a "throaty" Lennon vocal and solid piano. "I'll Cry Instead" is an "up-tempo bit" that is "mostly John, vocally...with Paul interjecting enthusiastically." "Things We Said Today" featured Paul on a "plaintive sort of number." "When I Get Home" was "right back to true Beatle-ism" with "John apparently dislodging his tonsils as he blows the blues through the microphone." "You Can't Do That" was a mid-tempo track with John as the main singer. The closing song, "I'll Be Back," was "delicately sung" with "rather pleasant harmonies all the way, but the melody line isn't as strong as most of the other tracks."

Richard Attenborough reviewed the new Beatles album in the August 1964 Record Mail. Side One was a "lively, rocking collection, mainly of up-tempo numbers" sung primarily by John and Paul. The styles range from the "big-sounding" "Tell Me Why" to the quiet ballad "And I Love Her," with Paul backed by acoustic guitar. "I'm Happy Just To Dance With You" was a "beat-ballad" featuring George. Attenborough ranked "If I Fell" as the side's best, describing the song as "very harmonious" and "the most pleasant ballad to stem from the collective pen of John and Paul." Side Two was "more bluesy than beaty," although beat was still a strong factor. "Any Time At All" and "When I Get Home" were fast numbers "with strong blues leanings." "I'll Cry Instead" was more rock 'n' roll, with "an accompaniment very much like those in vogue years ago." Attenborough called the album the best recorded by the boys, "who once again demonstrate the range of their talent." He hoped that they would "make many more of this high standard."

The album entered the Record Retailer chart on July 16 at number three. The following week it moved up to number one, where it remained for 21 straight weeks before being replaced by *Beatles For Sale*. The LP charted for 34 weeks, including 31 in the top five. The LP debuted in Melody Maker on July 18 at number one, remaining there for 21 straight weeks. The record charted for 34 weeks, including 31 in the top five. The new Beatles album entered the NME Best Selling LPs chart on July 17 at number one, where, as on the other charts, it remained for 21 straight weeks. The album charted for 30 weeks on the ten-position chart, including 28 in the top five. NME also reported the LP on its singles chart for six weeks, including three weeks at its peak position of number 22. Disc did not run an album chart until late 1965, but reported the LP on its singles chart for nine weeks with a peak at number 16. Sales exceeded 250,000 units by mid-July and were at 970,000 within six months of the album's release.

After a 10:30 AM press screening at the Leicester Square Theatre on July 6, *A Hard Day's Night* premiered that evening at the London Pavilion on Piccadilly Circus. All of the music weeklies praised both the film and the boys. In the July 10 NME, Andy Gray opened his review with: "The Beatles are a hit all over again–as comedians!" In their debut film, the Beatles "emerge as most successful wacky gagsters, way-out pantomimists and a great new comedy team, reminiscent of the Marx Brothers and the Goons." And while the band's "on-beat singing" is terrific, it's their "off-beat comedy that lifts the picture to hit proportions." There is John's sarcasm, Paul's wit, George's hifalutin, intricate phrases, and Ringo "proving he can say most by staying silent." In addition to the verbal barrage, the film has many sight gags such as John's foam bath scene, where he's "playing submarines and warships, and in the end giving the impression he's gone down the plughole!" Paul has fun with the schoolgirls on the train and shows warmth towards his trouble-making grandfather. George shines in a scene with a weirdie fashion trend-setter. But if anyone steals the picture, it's Ringo, who shows "definite Chaplin qualities." The train scene with a pompous old traveler and the Beatles rude responses "won't please elders, but for the most part adults will enjoy the picture as much as youngsters." The press reception scene is "a riot, as they deal with silly questions with silly answers," and the police chase scene is "reminiscent of Keystone cop days." Gray also has praise for Wilfrid Brambell as Paul's grandfather, Victor Spinetti's hilarious portrayal of a way-out TV producer, Dick Lester's flair for comedy and the film's razor-sharp editing. Gray ends his review with more plaudits. "The Beatles have come through with flying colours. Whereas many pop stars sound unreal and even horrible when given lines in films, the Beatles really punch them over with a naturalness that is refreshing and they look good throughout. Hail the Beatles, the screen's latest comedy team!"

Jack Hutton's review of the film in the July 11 Melody Maker was titled "FAB! FAB! FOUR!" Hutton wrote that if the Beatles were not already millionaires, their new film "would put that right" for it is "a smash hit if ever there was one." He observed that the Beatles don't try to act. "They are just themselves. Witty. Cheeky. Impertinent. Human. Animated. Deadpan. Natural. And-if-you-don't-like-it-lump-it sort of thing." While each Beatle is a star in his own right, "Starr is an extra special star." Hutton describes some of Ringo's finest moments, including the scenes where he "doffs his coat in a Walter Raleigh act for a smashing bird who promptly disappears down a muddy hole" and has his camera fall into the water. Ringo "does it all with a feel for tragi-comedy that belies his nil screen experience."

LONDON PAVILION PICCADILLY CIRCUS

ROYAL WORLD PREMIERE

in the gracious presence of
HER ROYAL HIGHNESS THE PRINCESS MARGARET and THE EARL OF SNOWDON
to aid THE DOCKLAND SETTLEMENTS and THE VARIETY CLUB HEART FUND

on MONDAY, 6th JULY 1964 at 8.30 p.m. (DOORS OPEN 7.30. SEATS MUST BE TAKEN BY 8.20 p.m.)

RINGO STARR GEORGE HARRISON PAUL McCARTNEY JOHN LENNON

THE BEATLES

IN "A Hard Day's Night"

Directed by RICHARD LESTER Produced by WALTER SHENSON Screenplay by ALUN OWEN

WILFRID BRAMBELL NORMAN ROSSINGTON

SEAT No. 21 15 gns.

DRESS CIRCLE ROW A MAIN ENTRANCE PICCADILLY CIRCUS

The Dress Circle ticket to the July 6, 1964 Royal World Premiere of *A Hard Day's Night* at the London Pavilion shown left was used by a member of George Harrison's family. It was obtained by the author from George's sister, Louise Harrison.

Hutton also calls out "one hilarious, goon-like running-and-jumping bit on a piece of open ground and a glorious send-up of non-with-it reporters at a press conference." Lennon "scores heavily with his cheeky witticisms and his confidence at the camera." Hutton praises the "deft documentary type photography" and writes that all of the Beatles and the strong Lennon-McCartney compositions make *A Hard Day's Night* a "jumbo sized hit."

In the July 11 Disc, Laurie Henshaw called the film a winner all the way, describing it as: "Terrific! Stupendous! Tremendous!" Henshaw added: "There just aren't enough adjectives around to do justice to this colourful, riotous, rip-roaring, tearaway saga of 36 hours in the life of The Beatles." She praised the film's inspired production and direction and witty script, attributing its success to producer Waler Shenson, director Dick Lester and writer Alun Owen, who have "cleverly contrived to not to be too clever at putting The Beatles on film." The film's brilliant camera work is imaginative, with several special sequences including the "bird's-eve view of the boys on a helicopter launching pad, fooling around in 'silent movie' fashion." Henshaw also praised the music, with the title tune sure to be a hit. She advised readers to listen to the gorgeous ballad "If I Fell," suggesting "you'll fall, hook, line and sinker." The film is "practically a documentary, packed with witty, tongue-in-cheek situations in which The Beatles poke fun at The Establishment–and themselves," as well as would-be hipsters, advertisers, "with-it" girl interviewers and the press at pop receptions. *A Hard Day's Night* "just about crowns those Beatles as the True Kings of the Pop World." Music publisher Dick James said that seeing the film was a tremendous thrill, with the opening title song hitting him like an explosion. "This is a marvelous musical documentary of the Beatles–a worthy record of their position in the entertainment world." Disc jockey David Gell called it a "fabulous film," with the boys being "natural actors." He loved the scene with Ringo wearing the old raincoat and called the film a "refreshing change" from the corny pop movies "we have all suffered in the past."

Peter Jones reviewed the film in the July 11 Record Mirror, informing readers that it was "every bit as good as expected" with "no concessions to the usual run of musicals." It's just the Beatles behaving like the Beatles, displaying "all the earthiness of their humour." John shows a "distinctly acid touch," while Ringo "displays all the basic attributes of a sad-eyed clown." Jones writes of the scene where Ringo is enticed away from the group by Paul's grandfather

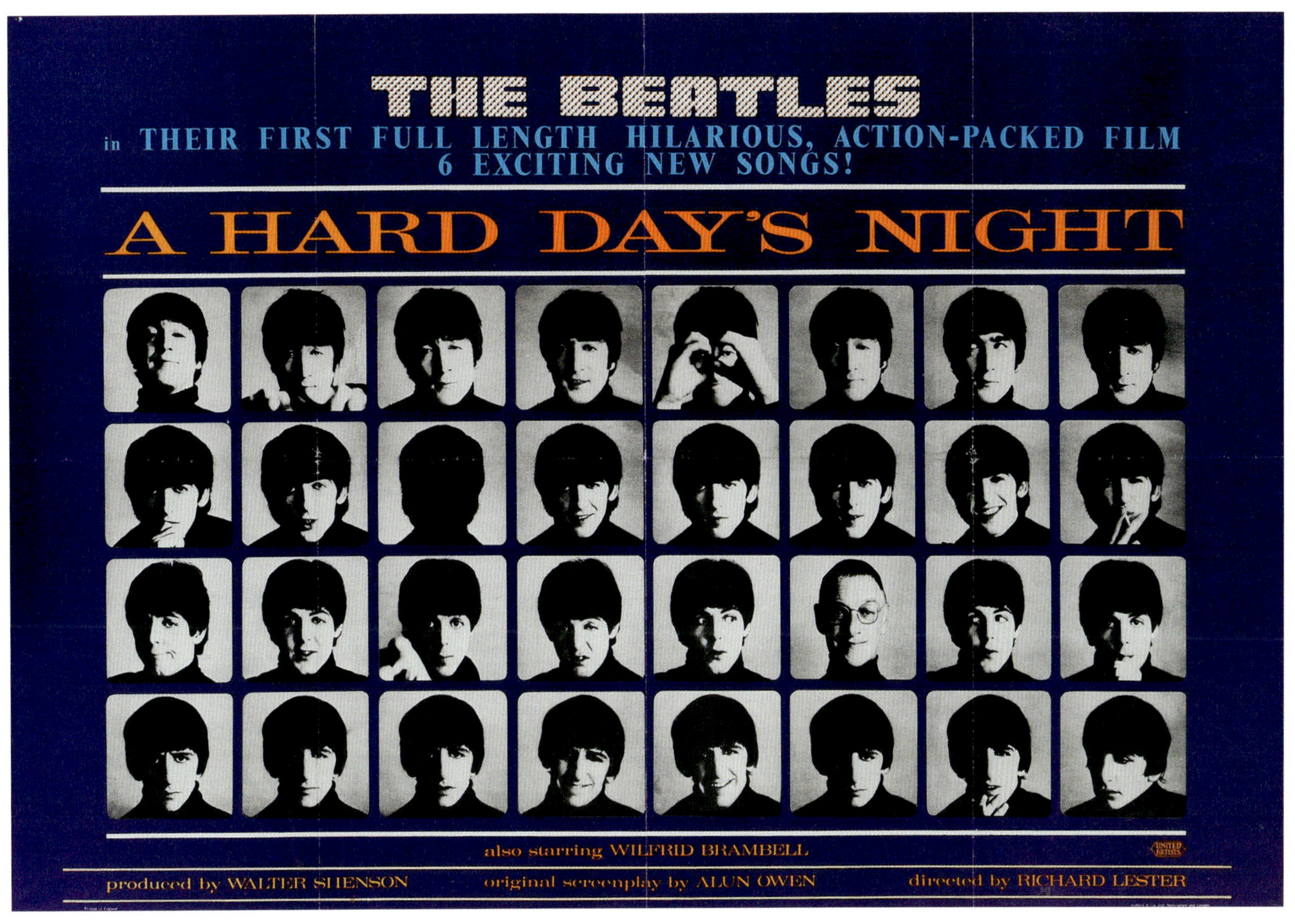

and leaves to "start living." George has a funny scene when he is mistaken for a male model. Director Dick Lester goes for a musical with realism in an almost-documentary approach with "fast-moving camera work" and "superbly controlled cutting and editing." The film buzzes with action. Jones praises the film's "black-and-white shooting technique," believing that the movie would have been "far less effective in 'glorious colour.'" As for the songs, "If I Fell" and "I Should Have Known Better" are "destined to be whistled round the world." At the end of the film, "one really feels one knows what makes the Beatles tick." Jones is certain that the film will be a "huge success" and will "take its place in film history because of its different approach in the musical field." Jones notes that the group swore they would "not fall for the usual old corny routines...and they haven't." The Beatles come "across as comedians, musicians and all-around good blokes. But not 'goody-goody'...just GOOD!"

But it wasn't just the British music press that praised *A Hard Day's Night*. While the critics for the British newspapers normally panned musicals filmed in Britain that featured British stars, the Beatles debut film received glowing reviews as summarized in the August 1964 edition of The Beatles Book (No. 13). Robert Ottoway of the Daily Sketch wrote that the Beatles film "makes other British musicals relics from a stiff-jointed past." The movie was a "pell-mell string of zany happenings" that was "endearing" and "crackles with imagination." In the Daily Herald, Ann Pacey observed that the film "has nothing whatever in common with the standard British pop musical." The Beatles were "zany and funny and witty and sharp with a script" and "have arrived with the force of a left hook from a heavyweight champion." Patrick Gibbs wrote in the Daily Telegraph that "The Beatles have repeated their success of night-clubs, theatre and television." Although the script was hardly original, Alun Owen "exploits the Beatles cleverly in their public image, which is to personify a defiance of convention." As for the group's acting, Gibbs said: "Paul tends to be regarded romantically and Ringo is seen as the comic butt, largely on account of his smaller size. Actors they may not be, but personalities they certainly remain, engagingly provocative and wonderfully photogenic."

In the Daily Mail, Cecil Wilson described the Beatles as: "Merseybeat Marxes...four adenoidal young anarchists from Liverpool. As crazily inconsequential, as endearingly insolent, as infectiously pleased with themselves–as funny as the Marx Brothers." Wilson wrote that the group exhibits a "zest for life that exhilarates and exhausts you by turns" and added: "At times the straining after a laugh at all costs is too hard, but for the most part...with glorious bursts of slapstick mime and machine-gun wisecracking...It all comes naturally." Leonard Mosley of the Daily Express only had words of praise. "What gorgeous fun! It's a mad, mad, mad, mad film, man [referencing the late 1963 comedy film *It's A Mad, Mad, Mad, Mad World*]. Nothing like it since the Goons on radio and the Marx Brothers in the 'thirties. Delightfully loony. Palpitating cinema. It sends up everyone, publicity agents, pretentious TV producers, newspaper columnists, dizzy pop-fans, even the Beatles themselves. It never flags." The Daily Mirror's Dick Richards admitted that he "was never a founder member of the Beatles' admiration society." Nonetheless, when asking if the film clicked, he responded with a resounding "Yeah, yeah, yeah." Richards noted that the Beatles "have not been presented as a kind of four-headed monster," but rather the boys are "cheeky, irreverent, funny, irresistible" with a "thumb-on-the-nose sense of the ridiculous."

Alexander Walker of London's Evening Standard described the film as a "splendid pop musical and far more besides," being the "first inside report on the Beatles" and a "vivid, newsreel-like documentary on Beatlemania." As for their acting abilities, Walker writes: "The Beatles prove themselves as actors, not of John Barrymore stature yet...but they'll never have to play any characters but themselves. Paul comes over as the Beatle with the mostest in the way of charm and sex appeal...but that's because he's the Beatle with the leastest in the way of hair. Who knows what goes on under the others' thatch?" He concludes: "Not the greatest movie since Edison's camera started to turn. Their inexperience shows...but a hit it deserves to be." Even The Times [of London] had some kind words for *A Hard Day's Night*: "One nice thing about this film to star the Beatles: it is not, by any manner of means, the usual sort of thing British film makers come up with to exploit the latest show business sensation...Mr. Richard Lester has had a real go, and a lot of his bright ideas come off very well; the way, for instance, that several of the numbers are treated as contrapuntal sound track accompaniments to screen action of quite another sort; the outbursts of Goonish visual humour; the freshly observed London locations and the vivid glimpses of backstage (or in this case behind the screen) show business life."

Penelope Gilliatt reviewed the film for The Observer. She observed that the Beatles "accept one another with stoicism of clowns" and "behave to one another with the kind of unbothered rudeness that is usually possible only between brothers and sisters." She believes that "this feeling that you are looking at an enviable garrison of a family that is at the root of the Beatles charm." Although the film has no plot, it has plenty of "invention, good looks and a lot of larky character." The Beatles situation is "pure comedy: four highly characterised people caught in a series of intensely public dilemmas but always remaining untouched by them, like [comedian actor and filmmaker Buster] Keaton, because they cart their private world around everywhere. Gilliatt praises lighting cameraman Gilbert Taylor, noting that "the grainy blacks and glowing whites and free-wheeling camera work are a minor revolution in a British pop film." Although the film lifts from cinéma vérité, it is not a real piece of camera truth-telling like the Maysles Brothers film of the Beatles in America. It is best described as a "piece of feature journalism" that was produced under pressure, yielding "something expressive and alive." Ringo emerges as a "born actor" and is like a "silent comedian, speechless and chronically underprivileged, a boy who is already ageless with a mournful loose mouth."

Four months after the release of the album *A Hard Day's Night*, EMI issued an EP featuring four songs from the album and film of the same name. At the time the EP was issued on November 6, 1964, the album was still firmly entrenched at the top of the charts. The EP's complete title was *Extracts From The Film A Hard Day's Night*. The front cover is nearly identical to that of the album. Tony Barrow's back cover liner notes give a brief synopsis of the film and describe the four songs appearing on the EP. John's driving "I Should Have Known Better" appears early in the film when the boys are playing cards in the guard's van of the train. John and Paul sing "If I Fell," a "wistful ballad" featured in the theater sequences that show the boys rehearsing and performing in a TV spectacular. "Tell Me Why" is a "lively fast-rocking piece" sung by John and Paul. "And I Love Her" is a gentle romantic ballad with Paul's "persuasive voice thread[ing] its way through the lyrics smoothly and appealingly."

The EP entered the Record Retailer EP chart at number 11 on November 12. After three weeks at number two, it replaced the Rolling Stones' *Five By Five* EP at the top on December 10. During the next two months, the Beatles and Stones' EPs swapped places five times. The Beatles disc spent six weeks at number one and seven weeks at number two. Its 30-week chart run included 16 weeks in the top five and 24 weeks in the top ten. The EP entered the Melody Maker singles chart at 48 on November 28 and peaked at 34 the following week during its four weeks on the charts. Because so many fans had already purchased the album, the EP failed to reach sales of 250,000 for a silver disc.

The second EP containing songs from the album *A Hard Day's Night* features four songs not appearing in the film and thus is fully titled *Extracts From The Album A Hard Day's Night*. Based on when it entered the charts, the EP was most likely issued in late December 1964. The front cover of the jacket features eight of the twenty mini-head shots from the album cover and has an orange rather than blue background. Tony Barrow's back liner notes explain that after it was realized that John and Paul had written too many compositions of excellent quality for the film, but not enough for a separate album, the decision was made to record all the material and place the extra titles on the second side of the soundtrack album. This EP draws from the non-film side of the album. Barrow brags that any one of them could have been a highlight of the film and made the top of the charts as a single. He states that the group records nothing but the best and correctly points out that "there are very few 'Beatle people' who will have had cause to claim that any track by John, Paul, George and Ringo has ever fallen short of the fabulous foursome's fantastically high standard of composition and presentation." John is the dominant voice on "Any Time At All" and "When I Get Home," while Paul handles the lyrics of "Things We Said Today" and duets with John on "I'll Cry Instead."

The second *A Hard Day's Night* EP made its debut on the Record Retailer EP chart at number 11 on January 7, 1965, while the first EP was in its third of six weeks at number one. Two weeks later it reached its peak at number seven. After nine weeks it had dropped from the chart, but the EP reappeared for two weeks in April, two weeks in May and the four weeks from July 29 through August 19. Although the disc was in the top ten for five of its 17 weeks on the EP chart, it never appeared on any of the singles charts published by the British music magazines. While the EP was certainly not a failure, it sold fewer copies than any of the previous Beatles records issued by EMI in the U.K. Its relatively poor performance was due in part to the large number of fans who had already purchased the album and the lack of promotion on the part of EMI.

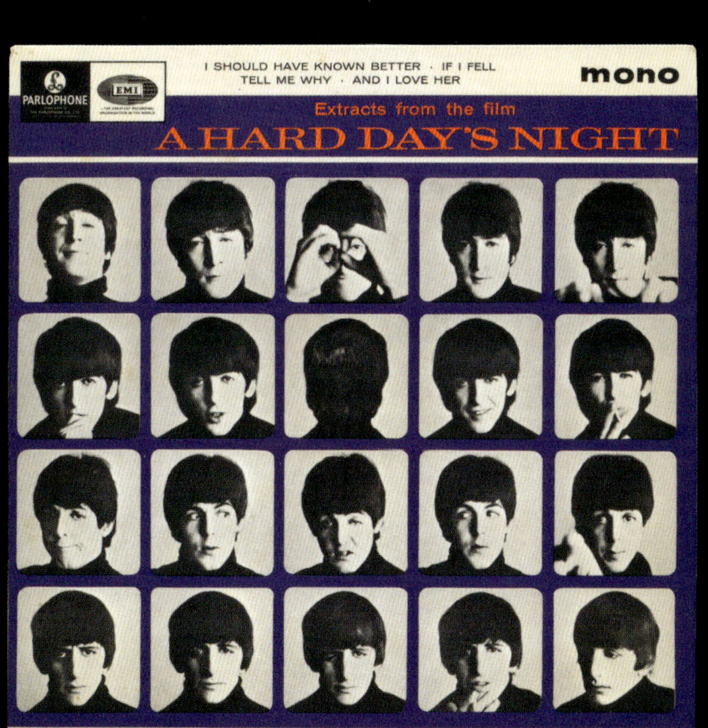

Over a million and a half albums sold and delivered- and still going strong!!!

Stereo UAS 6366, Monaural UAL 3366

Number One in the nation!!!
The fastest-selling album ever!!!
The best-selling soundtrack in history!!!

A Hard Day's Night in America

By the time the Beatles movie *A Hard Day's Night* made its America debut in August 1964, American Beatles fans were already familiar with the songs featured in the film. United Artists Records had rush-released its soundtrack album in late June, over a month ahead of the movie hitting American cinemas. Capitol Records responded with three singles featuring songs from the film and its own album with four tracks from the film. Despite the competition from Capitol, the United Artists ["UA"] soundtrack LP reigned supreme. The company's advertisements bragged: sales of over a million and a half albums; the number one album in the nation; the fastest-selling album ever; and the best-selling soundtrack in history. United Artists' gambit of signing the Beatles to a film deal at a time when the group was virtually unknown in America had paid off well beyond the company's most optimistic forecasts and wildest dreams.

It all started in September 1963 with a plan devised by the music publishing division of the American film company's London office. But that was only possible because of United Artists' decision to enter the music industry six years earlier. According to the October 14, 1957 Billboard, the film company formed United Artists Records Corporation and United Artists Music Corporation because of its desire to diversify into "other sphere[s] of the entertainment business" and its "recognition that music and films have allied interests." UA had previously entered into discussions with a number of independent labels such as Imperial and Liberty, but had decided against purchasing existing labels because the price was too high. United Artists Records later merged with Liberty and its by-then subsidiary Imperial in 1969. Capitol purchased United Artists Records in 1978. The company hoped that the "added lure of disk profits and music rights" would "induce more properties to come to UA." Recognizing that the Beatles popularity in England could spread to the United States, Noel Rogers, an employee of the London office of UA's music division, proposed signing the Beatles to a film deal to obtain the American record and publishing rights for the group's soundtrack music. The goal was simple–produce a low-budget film with the Beatles and release a soundtrack LP. George "Bud" Ornstein, European head of production for UA, explained it to film producer Walter Shenson: "Our record division wants to get the soundtrack album to distribute in the States, and what we lose on the film we'll get back on the disc."

At the time the plan was conceived in early fall of 1963, the Beatles had yet to achieve any meaningful recognition or success in the States. After Capitol refused to issue the group's records in America, three of its singles, "Please Please Me," "From Me To You" and "She Loves You," had been issued on smaller labels (Vee-Jay for the first two, and Swan for the third). All three sold poorly. Because EMI's contract with the Beatles did not specifically cover film soundtracks, United Artists was able to negotiate directly with Beatles manager Brian Epstein for the American rights for both the film and its soundtrack album. The company also obtained a split publishing interest in the songs used in the film for its subsidiary, Unart Music Corp. Under the deal, UA also got an option for two additional films and one more American soundtrack album. An essential element of the company's strategy was to begin production on the film in early 1964 so that the motion picture would be in theaters by July. The company wanted a quick release because it was concerned that the Beatles popularity might decline by summer's end.

The November 24, 1963 New York Times ran an article on British films that contained a few paragraphs about the Beatles, who writer Stephen Watts described as a "social phenomenon...wearing floor-mop haircuts which remind one of nothing so much as an adolescent version of the Three Stooges." Watts reported that Walter Shenson would be producing a Beatles film. The December 28, 1963 Cash Box and Music Vendor magazines reported that producer Walter Shenson and United Artists had entered into an agreement with the Beatles for a feature film to be shot in London in early 1964. Cash Box added that Shenson and UA, who recently worked together on the comedy film *The Mouse On The Moon*, had picked playwright Alun Owen to write the script and Richard Lester to direct. The February 1, 1964 Billboard reported that the group would start their first film, *The Beatles*, on March 2. The February 8 Billboard informed readers that the Beatles had recorded a new song in Paris that most likely would be included in their film. That same week Cash Box reported that the film was set for summer U.S. release and that the resulting soundtrack LP would "probably be in the hands of the flick company's disk affiliate, United Artists Records."

United Artists sent out invitations to a Beatles press conference at the Plaza Hotel scheduled for February 10, the day after the group's Ed Sullivan television debut. The Beatles and Brian Epstein were photographed with UA's David Picker, Vice-President for Production and Marketing (shown on next page surrounded by the boys and their manager).

The invitation announced that the Beatles would "soon be making their motion picture debut for United Artists." UA distributed a press release titled "The Beatles Biographical Feature," which began with: "A new show business phenomenon is sweeping the world—Beatlemania, which is also the tentative title of a new United Artists motion picture. Beatlemania is marked by mobs of hysterical teenagers, theaters packed to the rafters with screaming, fainting youths wearing mop-like haircuts, and the most exciting new musical sound since the era of Elvis Presley."

On February 23, 1964, Ed Sullivan presented the Beatles for a third straight week. Although the group had departed New York two days earlier, Sullivan implied that the Beatles were appearing live on the show, telling his audience: "You know all of us on the show are so darn sorry, and sincerely sorry that this is the third and thus our last current show with the Beatles because these youngsters from Liverpool, England, and their conduct over here not only as fine professional singers, but as a group of fine youngsters will leave an imprint with everyone over here who has met them. And that goes for all of us on our show. Let's bring them on. The Beatles." Sullivan's last words were drowned out by the screaming leading into the group's powerful rendition of "Twist And Shout." The exciting rocker, which was then only available in America on Vee-Jay's *Introducing The Beatles* album, had not been previously heard by most watching the show. But Americans would soon become very familiar with the song.

In early January 1964, Vee-Jay Records had released a single featuring "Please Please Me" and "From Me To You" in addition to its truncated version of the British *Please Please Me* LP, *Introducing The Beatles*. With the Beatles now signed to Capitol Records, Vee-Jay knew it would not obtain any additional Beatles songs for release. The company would have to make due with the 16 Beatles masters it had previously received from EMI. In anticipation of issuing a series of singles, Vee-Jay had each of the 12 songs on *Introducing The Beatles* separately mastered at Universal Recording Corporation in Chicago and sent to Audio Matrix, Inc. in the Bronx, New York for preparation of masters and mothers. By having the first two of the three metal parts needed for the manufacture of records, Vee-Jay could quickly order the metal stampers used to press the singles. Vee-Jay documents indicate that the company was preparing to issue six singles with songs from its Beatles album. In mid-February, Vee-Jay decided that its first of these singles would pair "Twist And Shout" with "There's A Place."

Ludwig
THE

“Twist And Shout” was released on or about February 27, 1964. However, the single was not issued on Vee-Jay, but rather was the debut record on Tollie, a Vee-Jay subsidiary label named after Calvin Tollie Carter, who served as Vee-Jay’s primary A&R (artists and repertoire) man, signing acts and producing sessions. Calvin was the brother of Vivian Carter, who founded Vee-Jay with her husband James Bracken in 1953. In the March 7, 1964 Billboard, Vee-Jay executive vice-president Jay Lasker explained that Tollie was started to give Vee-Jay another label to vie for air play and to offer an outlet for new talent. At the time “Twist And Shout” was released, Vee-Jay’s “Please Please Me” was still receiving heavy airplay. In addition, disc jockeys were busy spinning Beatles singles on Capitol, Swan and MGM. Perhaps Vee-Jay was concerned that another Beatles record on Vee-Jay would confuse radio programmers, so Vee-Jay issued its next entry into the saturated Beatles market on a new label. This meant that “Twist And Shout” would be identified as the Tollie single, ready to do battle with the Capitol, Swan, Vee-Jay and MGM Beatles singles.

“Twist And Shout” entered the Billboard Hot 100 on March 14 at number 55 while the top three songs were “I Want To Hold Your Hand,” “She Loves You” and “Please Please Me.” The Tollie single charted for 11 weeks, peaking on April 4 at number two, where it remained for four weeks behind “Can’t Buy Me Love.” Cash Box charted “Twist And Shout” for 13 weeks, including one week at number one on April 4, when the Beatles held down the top five positions in the Cash Box Top 100 along with seven other songs on the chart. The other songs in the top five were, in order, “Can’t Buy Me Love,” “She Loves You,” “I Want To Hold Your Hand” and “Please Please Me.” The Tollie single also topped the Music Vendor chart on April 4 during its 12-week run. The magazine changed its name to Record World on April 18. Cash Box published a weekly Radio Active survey of key radio stations in all important markets throughout America to determine, by percentage of those reporting stations, which releases were being added to their playlists for the first time. The survey kept a cumulative total. The March 14 Cash Box reported that as of March 4, 29% of its reporting stations had added “Twist And Shout” to their playlists. The following week the song was added by 67% of the stations, meaning that by March 11 the total percentage of reporting stations playing the Tollie single was up to 96%. February orders for the single exceeded 428,000 copies. By the end of March, Vee-Jay had shipped 938,848 units. Total sales exceeded 1,200,000. The single was certified gold and platinum by the RIAA (Recording Industry Association of America) on July 24, 2014, utilizing Vee-Jay sales information provided by the author.

NOT EVERY NEW RECORD COMPANY CAN START WITH

*

A MILLION SELLER AS tollie RECORDS HAS.

WE AREN'T DELUDING OURSELVES THAT EVERY RECORD TOLLIE PUTS OUT WILL SELL A MILLION...

HOWEVER WE EXPECT TO GET MORE THAN OUR SHARE.

FOR EXAMPLE WE THINK THAT OUR NEXT RELEASES OF

T-9002
ALL MY LOVING
BY THE DOWLANDS
&
T-9003
BACKFIELD IN MOTION
B/W
BAD MOTORCYCLE
BY THE ANGELOS

MAY NOT SELL A MILLION BUT IT WILL SELL A LOT OF RECORDS AND MAKE US ALL A LOT OF MONEY.

OUR BIG BROTHER (YOU KNOW THAT LABEL THAT SAYS IT IS ONLY #9 IN SALES–VEE JAY) CONSIDERS US RATHER BRASH FOR A YOUNG PUNK THAT IS PROBABLY #799 IN SALES AT THIS MOMENT.

WATCH US GROW... OUR FIRST THREE RELEASES ARE ALREADY GONE.

VJ is only #~~12~~ 9 in sales ...but here is why you should go with us

#1

INTRODUCING THE BEATLES VJLP 1062

#2

THE BEATLES & FRANK IFIELD VJLP 1085

& THE HOTTEST SINGLE VJ 581

#3 PLEASE, PLEASE ME & FROM ME TO YOU

V-J's NEW HOME · 9056 SANTA MONICA BLVD. · LOS ANGELES 69, CALIFORNIA · CR 3-5800

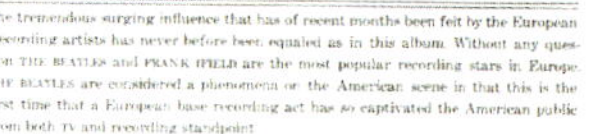

The tremendous surging influence that has of recent months been felt by the European Recording artists has never before been equaled as in this album. Without any question THE BEATLES and FRANK IFIELD are the most popular recording stars in Europe. THE BEATLES are considered a phenomena on the American scene in that this is the first time that a European base recording act has so captivated the American public from both TV and recording standpoint.

It is with a good deal of pride and pleasure that this copulation has been presented.

SIDE ONE	SIDE TWO
PLEASE, PLEASE ME — THE BEATLES	I REMEMBER YOU — FRANK IFIELD
ANY TIME — FRANK IFIELD	ASK ME WHY — THE BEATLES
LOVESICK BLUES — FRANK IFIELD	THANK YOU GIRL — THE BEATLES
I'M SMILING NOW — FRANK IFIELD	THE WAYWARD WIND — FRANK IFIELD
NOBODY'S DARLING — FRANK IFIELD	UNCHAINED MELODY — FRANK IFIELD
FROM ME TO YOU — THE BEATLES	I LISTEN TO MY HEART — FRANK IFIELD

Shortly before the release of the Tollie "Twist And Shout" 45, Vee-Jay ran a full-page ad in the February 22 issues of Billboard and Cash Box promoting its *Introducing The Beatles* LP and "Please Please Me" single, along with a new album *The Beatles And Frank Ifield On Stage*. (Vee-Jay's claim that it was now #9 in record label sales was a dubious marketing ploy with no basis in fact.) The front cover (shown on previous page) features a drawing of a mustached English statesman holding a pair of spectacles. A Beatles wig has been placed on his head. The top of the cover has the phrase "Jolly What!" in an attempt to give the album the proper British atmosphere. The jacket proudly bills the Beatles and Frank Ifield as "England's Greatest Recording Stars," which at the time wasn't quite as misleading as one might think. Between July 1962 and early 1964, Ifield had amassed four number one hits plus two Top 10 hits in the U.K. But that doesn't mean that the combination was a match made in heaven for American Beatles fans. Ifield's crooning style and yodeling was the antithesis of the Beatles high-energy rock 'n' roll. The album's "on stage" billing is misleading as all 12 songs on the album are studio recordings, not live versions of the songs as the title implies.

The back cover reveals that only four Beatles songs are included in the package: "Please Please Me," "From Me To You," "Ask Me Why" and "Thank You Girl." These songs were released on a pair of Vee-Jay singles in 1963. The album's eight Ifield tracks were previously issued on Vee-Jay singles. Although "I Remember You" peaked at number five in the Billboard Hot 100, few Americans today remember Frank Ifield. Of his three other Vee-Jay singles, only "Lovesick Blues" made the national charts, peaking at number 44 in Billboard, 50 in Cash Box and 32 in Music Vendor.

The back cover's liner notes stretched the truth a bit by proudly proclaiming: "Without any question, THE BEATLES and FRANK IFIELD are the most popular recording stars in Europe." While Ifield had a string of pop hits in England, he was not currently in the same league as the Beatles. Put simply, there was no Ifieldmania infecting Europe. The liner notes conclude with Vee-Jay stating: "It is with a good deal of pride and pleasure that this copulation has been presented." This humorous reference to the Beatles and Ifield compilation LP as a "copulation" appears to have been an innocent misuse of the English language. However, for Beatles fans purchasing the LP and expecting to get live performances of Beatles songs, it may have seemed like a "copulation" album in that they were getting screwed as the disc only contained four previously released studio recordings of the Beatles.

The album's creation resulted from legal rather than marketing considerations. After all, if Vee-Jay really thought that the public wanted an LP with both Beatles and Frank Ifield songs, it would have had more Beatles songs than Ifield songs. You didn't have to be a rocket scientist for Project Mercury to figure that one out in 1964. Corporate minutes from early January 1964 indicate that attorney Walter Hofer advised Vee-Jay that it had the right to issue the four Beatles songs previously released on singles during 1963, but probably did not have the right to release additional Beatles material. Realizing it might be limited to those four songs, Vee-Jay developed a fallback plan. It would release an album pairing the four Beatles songs with eight songs that originally appeared on four singles by Vee-Jay's other British act, Frank Ifield. Thus, if Vee-Jay was prohibited from selling its *Introducing The Beatles* album, the company could still market a Beatles album, albeit one with two-thirds of the songs by another recording artist.

As detailed in the author's book *The Beatles Records on Vee-Jay*, Capitol and Vee-Jay were involved in multiple lawsuits over the U.S. rights to the Beatles. This litigation adversely affected Vee-Jay's ability to get its Beatles records into stores. On January 15, 1964, Capitol obtained a temporary injunction prohibiting Vee-Jay from manufacturing or distributing Beatles recordings. Although the injunction did not stop stores from selling their Vee-Jay Beatles records already on hand, it prevented Vee-Jay from meeting the huge demand for additional Beatles product. On February 5, the appellate court entered an order staying the injunction, thus allowing Vee-Jay to resume pressing and selling Beatles records. However, on March 19, the appellate court issued a confusing opinion that returned matters to the status quo, meaning that the temporary injunction was once again in force. This pressured Vee-Jay into reaching a settlement with Capitol signed on April 1 under which Vee-Jay's rights to the Beatles ended on October 15, 1964.

Vee-Jay's fallback album, identified as *Jolly What!* by "Beatles & Frank Ifield," debuted in the Billboard Top LP's chart at number 135 on April 4. The album peaked at 104 during its six weeks on the chart. *Cash Box* showed the debut of *The Beatles & Frank Ifield* at number 90 on March 14, with the LP peaking at 70 during its six-week run. Although *Jolly What!* by "Beatles/F. Ifield" failed to make the Music Vendor Top 100 LP's chart, it got to number 107 during its six weeks in the magazine's Looking Up Long Play Albums chart. Vee-Jay shipped over 51,000 copies of the album by the end of March, but with a return rate of 55%, final net sales were under 25,000 units.

By mid-February, "I Want To Hold Your Hand" was no longer the only Capitol Beatles single being sold in America. Several record stores, particularly in the North, began carrying a disc containing two songs unavailable in America, "Roll Over Beethoven" and "Please Mister Postman." This was soon followed by another record featuring one of the more popular songs from *Meet The Beatles!*, "All My Loving," with "This Boy" on the flip side. These singles had the familiar Capitol orange and yellow swirl labels but were not issued by the Hollywood-based company. They were pressed for Capitol of Canada and imported into the States in mass quantities (estimated at 350,000 copies each). According to Billboard, retailers who were first in their market to stock the singles could "sell them for anything from $1.25 to $1.75" [at a time when singles normally sold for 69¢ to 99¢]. New York City's WMCA began charting "Roll Over Beethoven" in its February 12 survey, showing a debut at number 25. Both singles entered the national charts in March, with "Roll Over Beethoven" charting in Billboard for four weeks, peaking at 68, in Cash Box for seven weeks, peaking at 30, and in Music Vendor for six weeks, peaking at 35. "All My Loving" charted in Billboard for six weeks, peaking at 45, in Cash Box for eight weeks, peaking at 31, and in Music Vendor for seven weeks, peaking at 32.

When distributors began asking Capitol about "Roll Over Beethoven" in mid-February, the label considered releasing the song as its next Beatles single. After word of this reached EMI, George Martin, who was in the U.S. with the Beatles, flew to Hollywood and persuaded Capitol to wait a few weeks to release the newly recorded "Can't Buy Me Love" instead. Capitol issued a statement that "Beethoven" was not characteristic of the group's present sound.

The trade magazines reported in their March 14 issues that the next Beatles single would be a pair of John Lennon-Paul McCartney compositions, "Can't Buy Me Love" and "You Can't Do That." Capitol began taking orders for the disc without even disclosing the titles of the songs. By March 3, Capitol already had 1,700,000 orders on the books. Capitol explained that it decided not to rush-release the disc, instead holding back its release until March 16 to allow sufficient time to complete its initial pre-run target of two million copies. To achieve this goal, Capitol had the disc pressed by three outside plants [RCA, Decca and Savoy] in addition to its Scranton and Los Angeles factories. "Roll Over Beethoven" would be included on the group's next Capitol album, which was being prepared for a late March or early April release. Cash Box quoted Capitol A&R Vice-President Goyle Gilmore saying: "There was tremendous pressure on us to release the 'Beethoven' side as a single, but we and the Beatles agreed that the new tunes would be far better." Cash Box and Music Vendor reported that both songs were written by John and Paul a few weeks ago while the Beatles were in Miami Beach and were recorded in London upon the group's return from its U.S. visit. [This was only half correct as "Can't Buy Me Love" was written and recorded in Paris, France.] Billboard informed readers that both songs on the new single would probably be included in the Beatles film, which went into production the week before. The movie was still untitled, though it would "bear the title of a song to be included in it."

Capitol originally planned on releasing "Can't Buy Me Love" on March 30, 1964, as evidenced by the 3-304 release code on the label. (The "3-30" means March 30 and the "4" indicates 1964.) The logistics of manufacturing and distributing two million singles in time for the new release date meant that Capitol could not wait for picture sleeves to be printed prior to starting the pressing of the records. For most of the initial production run, singles were placed in generic Capitol sleeves. Due to the limited time for Capitol's art department to design a picture sleeve for "Can't Buy Me Love," the company used the same film as its "I Want To Hold Your Hand" sleeve, merely changing the song titles and record number in the box above the photo. Four days after the single's release, Dave Dexter sent a memo to Capitol's Production Department and to Queens Litho informing them that no additional sleeves were to be printed. Dexter reasoned that the sales of the single were so strong that no additional visibility was required. He was also concerned that the similarities between the two Capitol sleeves could cause confusion at the retail level. Thus, the "Can't Buy Me Love" sleeve is the rarest of the standard Capitol Beatles picture sleeves.

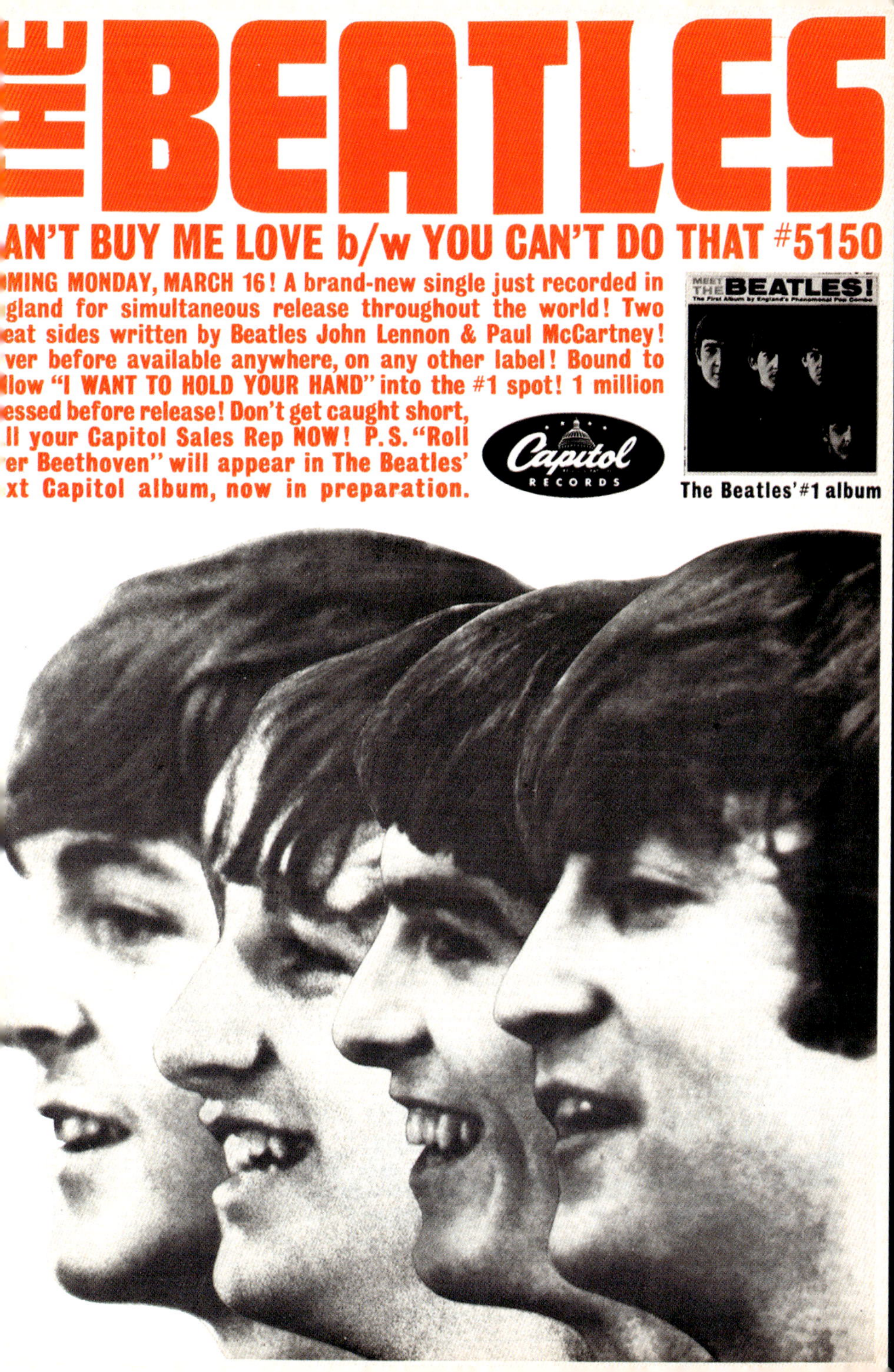

THE BEATLES

AN'T BUY ME LOVE b/w YOU CAN'T DO THAT #5150

MING MONDAY, MARCH 16! A brand-new single just recorded in gland for simultaneous release throughout the world! Two eat sides written by Beatles John Lennon & Paul McCartney! ver before available anywhere, on any other label! Bound to llow "I WANT TO HOLD YOUR HAND" into the #1 spot! 1 million essed before release! Don't get caught short, ll your Capitol Sales Rep NOW! P. S. "Roll er Beethoven" will appear in The Beatles' xt Capitol album, now in preparation.

Capitol
RECORDS

The Beatles' #1 album

The March 21 Music Vendor reported that New York's WMCA had prematurely played "Can't Buy Me Love" over the weekend [of March 7]. The station claimed it acquired the single from England [although that is unlikely as the single was not issued in the U.K. until March 20, making it more probable that it was covertly obtained from RCA's Rockaway, New Jersey pressing plant]. Cash Box's Radio Active chart indicates that 81% of its reporting stations had added the single by March 18. The next week 18% more stations added the disc, bringing its air play up to 99%. The trade magazines reviewed the new single in their March 21 issues. Billboard kept it brief: "Two more from the British group that are solid senders. Both are hard rockers and both are moving as they leave the plant." Cash Box said the single was a "can't miss" with orders having "zoomed past the million mark." The A-side, misidentified as "You Can't Buy Me Love," was called a "driving, beat-filled rocker that sports the foursome's famed 'Liverpool' sound." "You Can't Do That" was called a "pulsating stomper bound for chartdom." After writing that the Beatles new disc had supposedly already passed the million sales mark, Music Vendor added: "It's a good side and worthy of all the attention it will get. The boys continue producing their seductive beat, and the lyric will captivate teen listeners, too."

"Can't Buy Me Love" began its ten-week run in the Billboard Hot 100 at number 27 on March 28, 1964. The following week it leaped to number one, replacing "She Loves You" and heading an incredible chart (shown on the next page) dominated by the Beatles, who held the top five spots and placed seven other songs in the Hot 100. The top five songs were "Can't Buy Me Love," "Twist And Shout," "She Loves You," "I Want To Hold Your Hand" and "Please Please Me." The other charting songs were: "I Saw Her Standing There" (#31); "From Me To You" (#41); "Do You Want To Know A Secret" (#46); "All My Loving" (#58); "You Can't Do That" (#65); "Roll Over Beethoven" (#68); and "Thank You Girl" (#79). The Beatles also had the top two albums. The next week, "There's A Place" and "Love Me Do" joined these songs, giving the Beatles a record 14 songs in the Billboard Hot 100. "Can't Buy Me Love" remained at number one for five straight weeks before falling to number five on May 9. "Can't Buy Me Love" also charted at number one in Cash Box (for five of its 11 weeks) and in Music Vendor/Record World (for four of its 13 weeks). The single's flip side, "You Can't Do That," spent four weeks in the Billboard Hot 100, peaking at 48. Cash Box charted the song for three weeks with a peak at 77. Music Vendor charted the B-side at 138 on March 28. The single was certified gold on March 31, 1964. Although not RIAA certified for additional sales, the disc sold over 2,000,000 units.

For Week Ending April 4, 1964

Billboard HOT 100

★ STAR performer—Sides registering greatest proportionate upward progress this week.

This Week	1 Wk. Ago	2 Wks. Ago	3 Wks. Ago	TITLE Artist, Label & Number	Weeks On Chart
1	27	—	—	CAN'T BUY ME LOVE Beatles, Capitol 5150	2
2	3	7	55	TWIST AND SHOUT Beatles, Tollie 9001	4
3	1	1	2	SHE LOVES YOU Beatles, Swan 4152	11
4	2	2	1	I WANT TO HOLD YOUR HAND Beatles, Capitol 5112	12
5	4	3	3	PLEASE PLEASE ME Beatles, Vee Jay 581	10
32	35	38	47	HEY JEAN, HEY DEAN Dean & Jean, Rust	7
33	43	50	63	TELL IT ON THE MOU... Peter, Paul & ...	
34	46	59	66	WHITE ON ...	

MAKE ME FORGET Bobby Rydell, Cameo 309 — 2

Compiled from national retail sales and radio station airplay by the Music Popularity Dept. of Record Market Research, Billboard.

THE BEATLES
I WANT TO HOLD YOUR HAND
I SAW HER STANDING THERE
5112 Capitol Records

"SHE LOVES YOU"
THE BEATLES

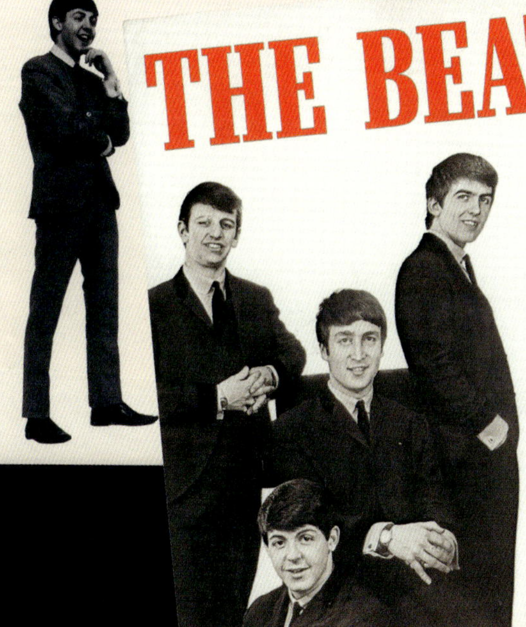

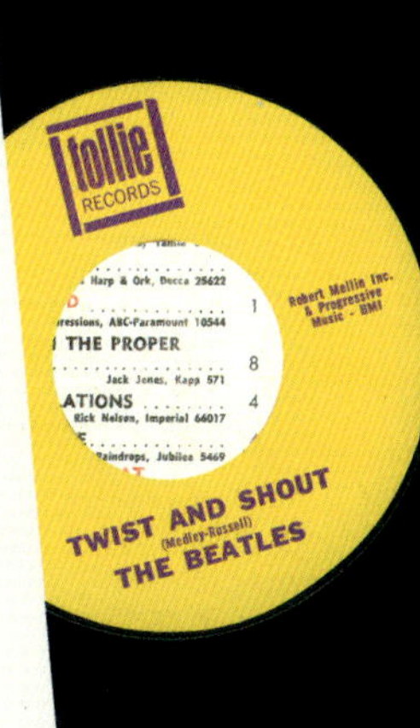

Vee-Jay announced two new Beatles releases in a full-page ad appearing in the March 21 editions of Billboard and Cash Box. The ad was a parody of a Tareyton cigarette commercial that used the tagline "Us Tayerton smokers would rather fight than switch!" and showed its actors with black eyes. Vee-Jay paired "Do You Want To Know A Secret" from its *Introducing The Beatles* album with "Thank You Girl," which had previously been released by Vee-Jay in May 1963 as the B-side to "From Me To You" on VJ 522. The company also issued an Extended Play (EP) disc with four tracks pulled from *Introducing The Beatles*. Both of these records were issued on or about March 19.

Once again, Vee-Jay was on target with its selection of the A-side. Although the Beatles did not release "Do You Want To Know A Secret" as a single in England, Billy J. Kramer with the Dakotas took the song all the way to number two on the British charts in May 1963. It was blocked from the top by the Beatles "From Me To You." The Vee-Jay disc marked George Harrison's first lead vocal on a Beatles single officially released in England or the United States, although he was the lead vocalist on the Capitol of Canada 45 "Roll Over Beethoven." For its third Beatles single in as many months, Vee-Jay returned the Beatles to its primary label, releasing the record as VJ 587. The single was issued in a picture sleeve featuring the same Jim Johnson drawing of the Beatles four faces as the ad for the disc.

"Do You Want To Know A Secret" entered the Billboard Hot 100 at number 78 on March 28. It quickly shot up the charts, reaching the number two spot on May 9, blocked from the top by Louis Armstrong's "Hello Dolly!" It was the first time a non-Beatles song topped the Hot 100 since February 1, bringing the Beatles 14-week monopoly at number one to an end. Cash Box charted "Do You Want To Know A Secret" for 12 weeks, including three weeks at three. Music Vendor/Record World also charted the song for a dozen weeks, with a peak at three for two weeks. Cash Box's Radio Active chart indicates that 16% of its reporting stations had added the single by March 18. Two weeks later this had increased to 49%. "Thank You Girl" charted in Billboard for seven weeks, peaking at 35, in Cash Box for nine weeks, peaking at 38, and in Music Vendor/Record World for eight weeks, peaking at 39. Vee-Jay began taking orders for the single on March 11. By the end of the month, Vee-Jay had shipped over 500,000 copies. Sales for the second quarter were brisk, adding another 468,000 units. Based on sales information provided by the author, the RIAA certified sales of over 925,000 on July 24, 2014, giving the Beatles yet another gold record.

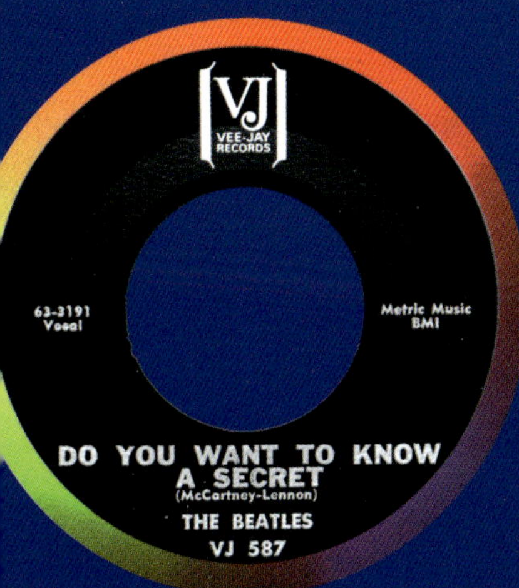

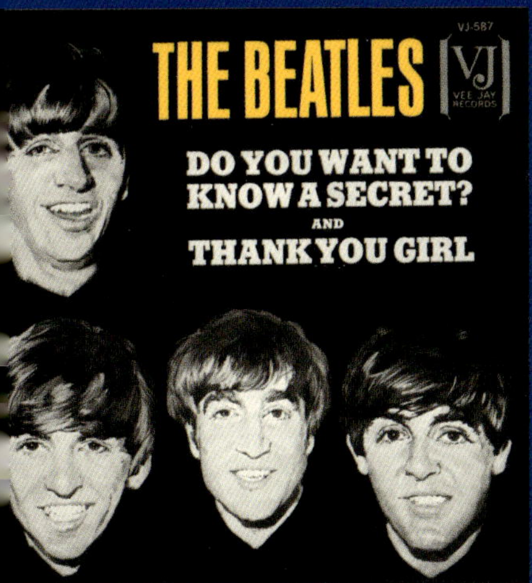

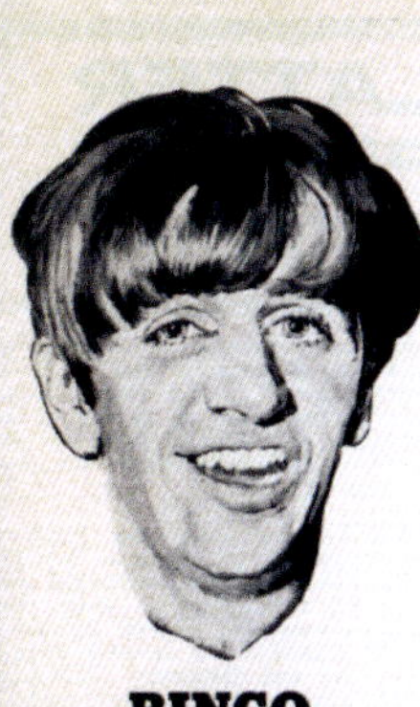

RINGO STARR

PAUL McCARTNEY

JOHN LENNON

GEORGE HARRISON

US VEE-JAY PEOPLE WOULD RATHER FIGHT ...THAN ADMIT WE ARE ONLY #9 IN SALES

2 NEW BEATLES RELEASES

NEW BEATLES SINGLE

IN SPECIAL SLEEVE

VJ 587

DO YOU WANT TO KNOW A SECRET

AND

THANK YOU GIRL

VJ
VEE-JAY RECORDS

NEW BEATLES E.P.

Beautiful new four color Beatle paintings front and back. Four Great Songs never released as singles. Each a Hit in its own right.

MISERY

TASTE OF HONEY

ASK ME WHY

ANNA

THE E.P. (ECONOMY PACKAGE) OF THE CENTURY

VJ EP 1-903

With the Beatles February arrival in America and their appearances on The Ed Sullivan Show fresh in everyone's mind, Vee-Jay marketed its EP as a "Souvenir of Their Visit to America" even though none of the four songs were performed by the Beatles during their initial U.S. visit. The four tracks, "Misery," "A Taste Of Honey," "Ask Me Why" and "Anna," were pulled from Vee-Jay's *Introducing The Beatles* LP. Vee-Jay packaged the EP in a colorful cardboard jacket with the same layout and faces as its "Do You Want To Know A Secret" picture sleeve.

Vee-Jay began taking orders for the EP on March 16. By month's end, the company had shipped 35,000 copies, leading Cash Box to chart "Beatles E.P." for one week at 130 on its March 28 Looking Ahead singles chart. An additional 24,500 were sold during the second quarter. This was considerably less than the massive sales of its Beatles singles. In response, Vee-Jay developed a new marketing strategy under which it would sell the EP for the price of a single and promote "Ask Me Why" as if it were a single. Vee-Jay ran ads in the July 4 editions of Billboard and Cash Box announcing the plan and admitting the company was crazy for doing so. Subsequent production runs of the disc were pressed with labels emphasizing "Ask Me Why," which was printed in larger letters than the other songs (as on the revised promotional copy of the EP shown right). To further plug "Ask Me Why" to disc jockeys, Vee-Jay issued an extremely limited number of promotional discs in a one-sided black and white title sleeve listing only "Ask Me Why" and describing the record as "an E.P. that is selling like a single...at single record prices" (shown on page 197). Cash Box reviewed the single-priced EP in its July 11 issue, stating it was likely that the EP would "soar up the singles charts" and described the songs as: "Ask Me Why" ("an infectious, rhythmic cha cha-like affair"); "Misery" (a "tearful jumper"); Arthur Alexander's "Anna" (a "slow rock-a-cha cha"); and "A Taste of Honey" ("haunting, waltz-styled"). Cash Box re-charted the "Ask Me Why EP" for two weeks with a peak at 139 on August 1. Record World charted "Ask Me Why" for three weeks in August on its Singles Coming Up chart with a peak at 132. The EP sold 78,000 copies.

In addition to marketing the EP as a single and lowering its price, Vee-Jay resorted to promotional tie-ins with various food products to generate sales and liquidate inventory. Purchasers of Perky Pies could mail in 12 wrappers or one wrapper and a dollar to receive a "free" EP. Laura Scudder printed a coupon on its potato chip bags (shown right) that enabled purchasers to buy the "Special Souvenir Record Album" for a dollar, which was no cheaper than retail sales.

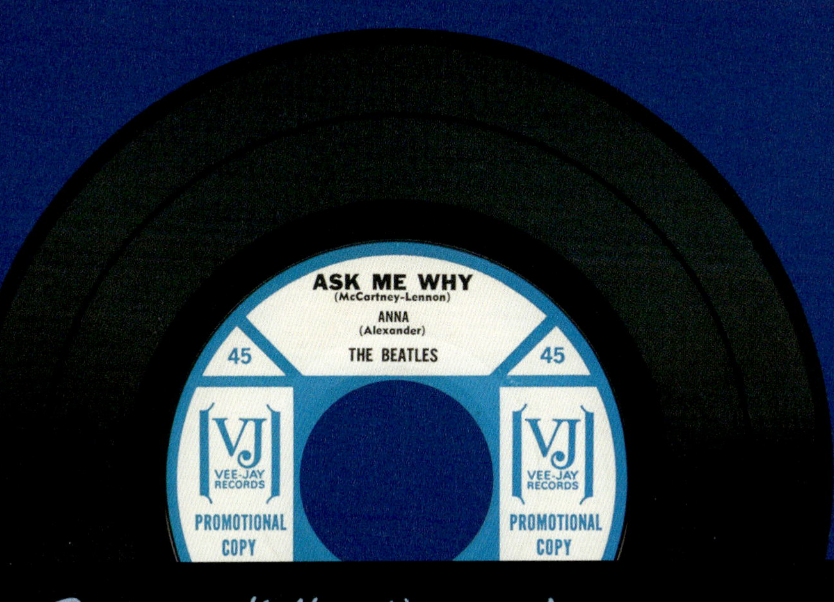

Souvenir of Their Visit to America

VJEP 1-903

THE BEATLES

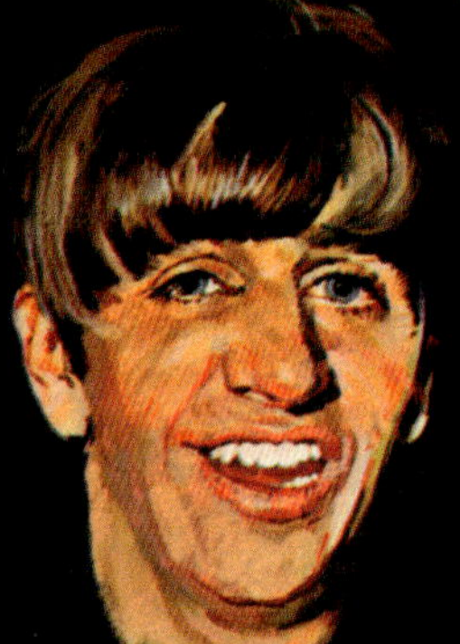

MISERY / TASTE OF HONEY
ASK ME WHY / ANNA

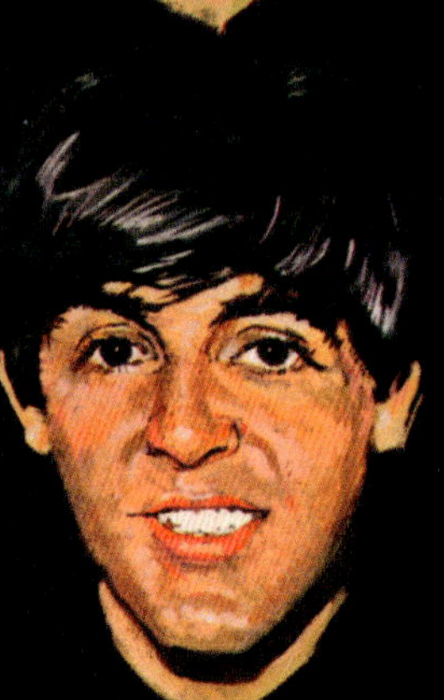

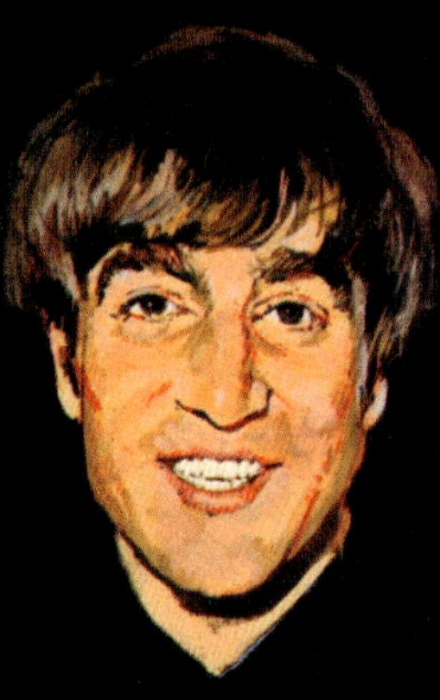

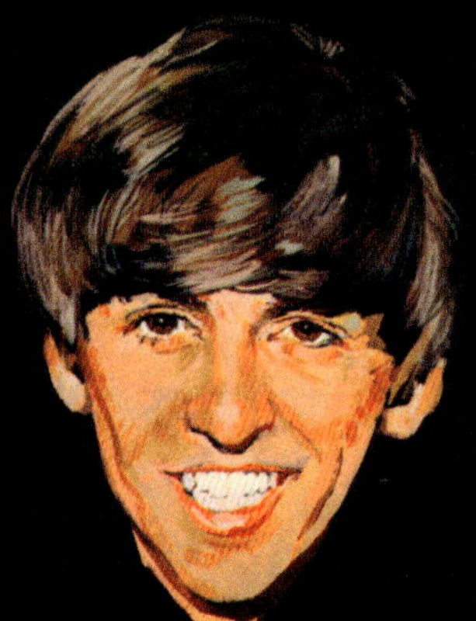

While "She Loves You" was still topping the charts, Swan attempted to get additional mileage out of the 45 by promoting its B-side. The March 28 Cash Box reported that Swan was re-servicing the flip side, which the label felt had been "neglected in the triumph of the topside." Swan was hoping radio stations would add "I'll Get You" to their playlists, thus encouraging those who had not already purchased the record to buy the disc. To prompt DJs to play "I'll Get You," Swan issued white label promo singles with "I'll Get You" on one side and a blank label on the other. There are multiple variations of this rare promotional disc. Music Vendor was not aware of this ploy and reviewed "I'll Get You" in its March 28 issue as if the song was a brand new Beatles single. "The voices of The Beatles will be heard throughout the land in a big way with this new one that has them cocksure they'll win their girlie. The song has the Beatle beat and the pleasing singing to match. Undoubtedly a smasheroo for them." Unfortunately for Swan and the Beatles, most disc jockeys and program directors were not impressed, and "I'll Get You" failed to chart nationally. It was a rather silly plan because over two million Beatles fans had already bought the single for "She Loves You."

At the time Capitol released its follow-up album to *Meet The Beatles!* on April 10, 1964, the top two albums on the charts were *Meet The Beatles!* and Vee-Jay's *Introducing The Beatles*. In an attempt to divert attention from and to trivialize the Vee-Jay disc, Capitol boldly named the record *The Beatles' Second Album*. While the LP was Capitol's second Beatles album, it was the third album consisting entirely of Beatles songs to be released in the United States. Capitol's trade magazine ad for the Capitol album let record stores and distributors know the album was "ALL Beatles!!!," a dig a Vee-Jay and MGM, who had each released albums with just four songs involving the Beatles.

It's Here!
It's on Capitol!!
and It's ALL Beatles!!!

(S) T 2080

For the first time on any album their smash, number one single "She Loves You" and "Roll Over Beethoven." PLUS other great tunes ALL by the fantastic Beatles. Their first Capitol Album broke all sales records everywhere. And this one's going to break even THOSE records. THE Beatles albums are on Capitol.

And THE Beatles singles are too. "Can't Buy Me Love" b/w "You Can't Do That" (#5150) is an unprecendented hit, just released on Capitol. Within 2 weeks of release "Can't Buy Me Love" was #1 on the Billboard Chart — and your #1 money maker!

#5150

HAVE YOUR BUYER CALL CRDC AND ORDER IMMEDIATELY.

The Beatles' Second Album was compiled by Dave Dexter, Capitol's head of International A&R who had previously turned down the Beatles four times. Dexter drew from a variety of sources. The new disc contains the five songs from the U.K. album *With The Beatles* that were left off *Meet The Beatles!* All of these tracks are cover versions of songs originally recorded by American artists. The quality of these "leftovers" is astounding. Also included are both sides of Swan's "She Loves You" single. Because Swan's licensing agreement was limited to the singles format, Capitol was free to place these songs on its album. Capitol also added the B-side to its current Beatles single, "You Can't Do That." In a somewhat strange move, Dexter selected "Thank You Girl," which had previously been released by Vee-Jay, for the LP. In all likelihood, he was not aware of Vee-Jay's rights to the song. Because the publishing to the song was with Vee-Jay's publishing subsidiary, Conrad Music, Vee-Jay received royalties for each copy of the album sold. The remaining two tracks on the album represented a coup for Capitol as the Beatles recordings of "Long Tall Sally" and "I Call Your Name" had yet to be released anywhere in the world. To save money on song publisher's royalties, which were calculated in America on a per-song basis, Capitol limited the number of songs on the album to eleven, one less than on Capitol's first Beatles LP. The names of the members of the group appear on the labels

The album gets off to a rousing start with George Harrison singing lead on Chuck Berry's "Roll Over Beethoven." This is followed by the thumping opening to "Thank You Girl," an upbeat Lennon-McCartney composition that was the B-side to "From Me To You," the Beatles third Parlophone single and second Vee-Jay 45. The song was also placed on the B-side to Vee-Jay's "Do You Want To Know A Secret" single. After two rockers, the album's pace gracefully slows with a cover version of "You Really Got A Hold On Me," which was written by Smokey Robinson and recorded with his group the Miracles. George handles the lead vocals on "Devil In Her Heart," a cover version of "Devil In His Heart" by the Donays, a little-known girl group from the Detroit area. The song has a Latin American flavor. Then it's back to rock 'n' roll with John leading the group through a cover of Barrett Strong's "Money (That's What I Want)." The first side ends with another strong John lead vocal on the rocking Lennon-McCartney song "You Can't Do That."

Side Two opens with a pair of recordings making their worldwide debut. First up is the Beatles high-spirited rendition of Little Richard's "Long Tall Sally." The track is one of the group's hardest rockers featuring Paul's powerful lead vocal. This is followed by John's reinterpretation of the Lennon-McCartney composition "I Call Your Name," which was previously recorded and released as the B-side to the Billy J. Kramer with the Dakotas' single "Bad To Me" (another Lennon-McCartney song). During the song's instrumental break, George's guitar solo is played over a ska beat. These two songs would later appear in the U.K. on the group's *Long Tall Sally* EP (as detailed on pages 18-20). The pace picks up again with another John lead vocal on an exciting cover version of the Marvelettes "Please Mister Postman." The album ends with both sides of the Beatles fourth British single, "I'll Get You" and "She Loves You."

Although *The Beatles' Second Album* is a pieces-parts collection bearing no resemblance to any British LP, it is a great rock 'n' roll album full of incredible songs and performances. John provides scorching lead vocals on "Money" and "Please Mister Postman," two of the group's finest cover songs. John and Paul's vocal harmonies are spot on for the entire disc. On "Long Tall Sally," Paul beats Little Richard at his own game. George plays solid guitar throughout and provides fine lead vocals on "Roll Over Beethoven" and "Devil In Her Heart." Ringo is at the top of his game, with exciting precision drumming on tracks such as "Thank You Girl," "She Loves You" and "Long Tall Sally," particularly at the end. And with songs and performances like that, you know that can't be bad. Yeah, Yeah, Yeah.

Music Vendor reviewed *The Beatles' Second Album* in its final issue (April 11) before its re-branding the following week as Record World. The LP was one of a "Golden Dozen" designated with an "Award of the Week." The magazine stated that Capitol was putting "another sure thing on the market" with "only a matter of short time before this one is lodged in the #1 spot." The group's performances of the songs were described as "galvanically big-beat," with a prediction that "teens will be dancing by the hour to them within days." The other trade magazines reviewed the disc the following week in their April 18 issues. Billboard made the album a Pop Spotlight Pick and included its review on the back cover. "The boys are back with the big stomping, stamping sound. This is the long-awaited album that contains 'Roll Over Beethoven,' 'She Loves Me' [sic] and a flock of newer material. Everyone is getting played, but look for 'Long Tall Sally' to step out of the set." Cash Box designated the album as one of its Pop Picks. After stating that the Beatles had amassed "a plethora of best-selling singles and LPs running rampant on the charts," the magazine predicted that the new album would quickly top the charts. "The lads lash out with 'Roll Over Beethoven,' and follow thru with such chart-riders as 'She Loves You' and 'Thank You Girl.' Still the hottest group around, there's loads of loot to be made with this one." Capitol prepared a huge 42" x 54" promotional poster that told store customers that "The Beatles on Capitol are the Greatest!"

The Beatles' Second Album made its debut in the Billboard Top LP's chart (150 listings) at number 16 on April 25. The following week it replaced *Meet The Beatles!* as the top album on May 2, remaining number one for five weeks. The Beatles monopoly of the number one spot on the album charts ended on June 6, when the album slipped to number four behind three adult-oriented albums: the original Broadway cast album *Hello, Dolly!*; the original Broadway cast album *Funny Girl*; and *Hello, Dolly!* by Louis Armstrong. *The Beatles' Second Album* remained on the Billboard charts for 55 weeks, including 11 weeks in the top ten. Cash Box published both Monaural (top 100 albums) and Stereo (top 50 albums) charts up until mid-January 1965. The LP topped the Monaural chart for four weeks during its 28 weeks on the charts, including 12 in the top ten. The album was on the Stereo chart for 12 weeks, with a peak at number four. Record World reported the album on its Top 100 LP's chart for 28 weeks, including four weeks at number one and 13 weeks in the top ten. It was certified gold by the RIAA on April 13, three days after its release, and sold over two million copies. The RIAA awarded the album 2x Multi-Platinum status on January 10, 1997.

THE BEATLES' SECOND ALBUM

ELECTRIFYING BIG-BEAT PERFORMANCES BY ENGLAND'S
Paul McCartney, John Lennon, George Harrison and Ringo Starr

featuring
SHE LOVES YOU
and
ROLL OVER BEETHOVEN

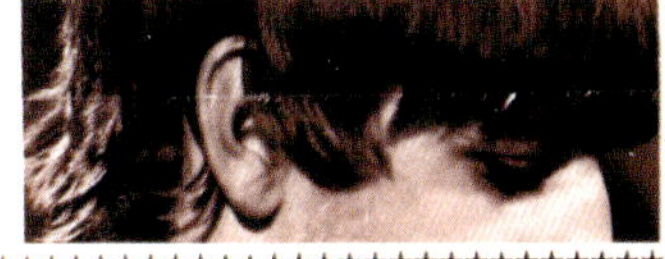

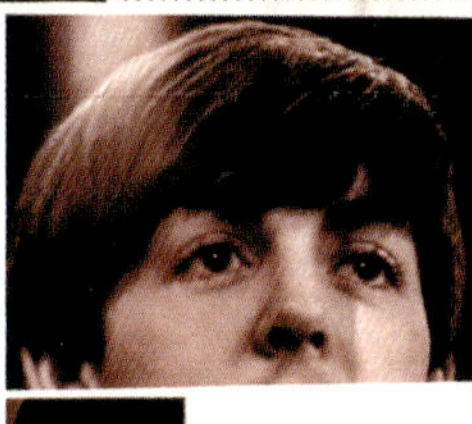

(S)T-2080

LONG TALL SALLY ✯ YOU CAN'T DO THAT ✯ YOU REALLY GOT A HOLD ON ME ✯ PLEASE MR. POSTMAN
THANK YOU GIRL ✯ DEVIL IN HER HEART ✯ MONEY ✯ I CALL YOUR NAME ✯ I'LL GET YOU

MEET THE BEATLES!
The First Album by England's Phenomenal Pop Combo

(S) T 2047

THE BEATLES ON CAPITOL ARE THE GREATEST!

THEIR NEW SINGLE HIT
YOU CAN'T DO THAT
AND
CAN'T BUY ME LOVE

Although Capitol of Canada did not issue any of its 1963 and 1964 Beatles singles in picture sleeves, it is believed that a U.S. distributor handling the imported "All My Loving"/"This Boy" single had a limited number of sleeves prepared for the disc, using the same layout and picture as the "I Want To Hold Your Hand" sleeve.

While "Love Me Do" and "P.S. I Love You" were on the initial pressings of Vee-Jay's *Introducing The Beatles* album, Vee-Jay was forced to remove the songs from the LP after the U.S. publisher for the songs (Capitol's Beechwood Music Corporation subsidiary) obtained an injunction prohibiting Vee-Jay from distributing the songs in America. In mid-February, Vee-Jay began pressing copies of *Introducing The Beatles* with "Please Please Me" and "Ask Me Why" as replacements for the prohibited songs. This created a void in America for "Love Me Do," which by late March was being filled by distributors importing the Capitol of Canada single that matched the Beatles first British single. The April 4 Cash Box charted the import "Love Me Do" single at 77. That same week Billboard reported that "Love Me Do" was "getting hot air play across the country," although the breakdown of a pressing machine in Canada was limiting the single's availability. Despite this handicap, "Love Me Do" (Capitol of Canada) began moving up the charts.

As part of Vee-Jay's April 1 settlement with Capitol, Vee-Jay was allowed to issue a single with "Love Me Do" and "P.S. I Love You." On April 10, Vee-Jay notified its distributors that it would soon be releasing the single as Tollie 9008, urging them to notify their customers to prevent them from ordering the Canadian single "at a much higher cost." Once the Tollie single began appearing in stores around April 24, it effectively put an end to sales of the Canadian single as it was cheaper, easier to obtain and came packaged in an attractive picture sleeve. While the Canadian 45 was dubbed from the U.K. single and contained the September 4 version of "Love Me Do" with Ringo on drums, the Tollie single pulled its tracks from *Introducing The Beatles*, meaning that it had the September 11 recording of "Love Me Do" with Andy White on drums and Ringo on tambourine. Billboard charted the single for 14 weeks. On May 30, "Love Me Do" replaced Mary Wells' "My Guy" at number one for one week before falling behind the Dixie Cups' "Chapel Of Love." Cash Box and Record World also charted the single for one week at number one. The flip side, "P.S. I Love You," reached number 13 in Record World and ten in Billboard and Cash Box. Total sales exceeded 1,100,000. The single was certified gold and platinum by the RIAA on July 24, 2014, utilizing information provided by the author.

BRAND NEW FROM

tollie RECORDS

THE BEATLES

LOVE ME DO

*

P.S. I LOVE YOU

T-9008

Capitol ran an ad in the May 23 Billboard promoting the Beatles upcoming performance of "You Can't Do That" on the May 24 Ed Sullivan Show and plugging the label's entire Beatles catalog, including its brand-new EP, *Four By The Beatles* [which was released on May 11], and an album of "sing-along, play-along" orchestrated instrumental arrangements of Beatles "greatest hits" by the Hollyridge Strings. The ad stated that "You Can't Do That" was featured in the Beatles forthcoming motion picture, *A Hard Day's Night*, and was "bound to be a hit in its own right after all the TV and movie exposure!" [Although the Sullivan Show aired a clip filmed for the movie's Scala Theatre concert of the group performing "You Can't Do That," the song was cut from the film.] Readers were told not to forget the group's earlier Capitol releases. In an article in the same issue, Billboard wrote: "With disk jockeys reportedly turning over the Beatles single of 'Can't Buy Me Love' to expose 'You Can't Do That,' Capitol is restocking the single in anticipation of new sales activities when the group sings the tune May 24 on The Ed Sullivan Show. Meanwhile, label reports the biggest EP sales ever on 'Four by the Beatles,' which contains two tracks from their first two LPs."

That same week Cash Box reported that Capitol was back in the EP business with a new Beatles release. Capitol indicated that the EP had not received full distribution until the week's end [May 15] and would be the largest EP seller in the firm's history. A Capitol executive said that the disc was selling like a "very good, not Beatles' single." Capitol claimed that track selection was made after a survey of a portion of the two million plus pieces of Beatles fan mail received by the label. [In all likelihood, Capitol just decided to feature the four songs from the two imported Capitol of Canada singles, "Roll Over Beethoven," "Please Mister Postman," "All My Loving" and "This Boy."] Cash Box reported that Capitol would have no new Beatles single until the release of the film's title song. The magazine reviewed the EP in the same issue as a Pick of the Week. The disc contained two songs that had already charted as Canadian singles plus a "tantalizing revival" of the Marvelettes' "Please Mr. Postman" and an inviting slow beat-ballad lover's lament, "This Boy." The phenomenal English group's EP was "a cinch to move out in the pattern of their smash singles" and "be all over the charts in the coming weeks." This prediction failed to materialize. The EP, which came in a full-color cardboard sleeve, entered the Billboard Hot 100 at number 97 on June 13. After an additional week at 97, the EP peaked at 92 in its third and final week on the charts. Cash Box reported the disc for three weeks with a peak at 86, while Record World charted the EP for two weeks with a peak at 97.

SEE THE BEATLES

perform YOU CAN'T DO THAT

on the ED SULLIVAN SHOW (CBS-TV), Sunday May 24! It's the flip side of The Beatles' current million-selling CAPITOL smash, CAN'T BUY ME LOVE (#5150)... It's featured in The Beatles' forthcoming United Artists' motion picture, A HARD DAY'S NIGHT ...and it's bound to be a hit in its own right after all the TV and movie exposure!

HEAR THE BEATLES

sing four of their top sides on one brand-new CAPITOL EP!

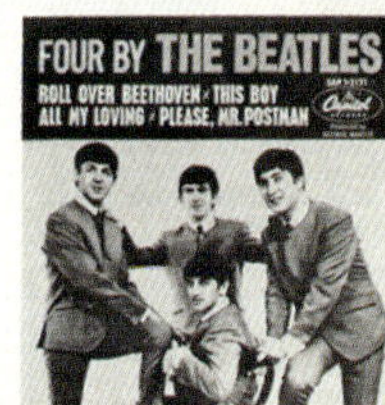

EAP-1-2121

ENJOY THE BEATLES'

greatest hits as performed in sing-along, play-along instrumental arrangements by the Hollyridge Strings!

(S)T-2116

And if you want still more of The Beatles, don't forget their first great CAPITOL album, MEET THE BEATLES (S)T-2043, THE BEATLES' SECOND ALBUM (S)T-2080, and their first fantastic single (now approaching the four-million mark!), I WANT TO HOLD YOUR HAND b/w I SAW HER STANDING THERE #5112.

The March 7 Billboard reported that Electrola [on its Odeon label] was releasing the first record made by the Beatles in a foreign language: "Komm, Gib Mir Deine Hand" ("I Want To Hold Your Hand") and "Sie Liebt Dich" ("She Loves You"), both sung in German. The initial 100,000 pressings would go on sale March 5 in Hamburg, Munich, Frankfurt and Cologne. [The record charted at number one and sold 350,000 copies in Germany.] The May 9 Cash Box wrote that WWDC's Carroll James had obtained the German disc and was playing both sides of the single. Perhaps one of these articles alerted Swan to the existence of the German-language version of "She Loves You." The company obtained a copy of the Odeon disc and dubbed "Sei Liebt Dich" for release as a single paired with "I'll Get You." The record was issued on or about May 21, with Swan hoping that the novelty of hearing the Beatles sing in German would be enough to obtain radio air play and sales. It wasn't. The single entered the Billboard Bubbling Under The Hot 100 chart at number 108 on May 30. After bubbling for four weeks, "Sie Liebt Dich (She Loves You)" by "Die Beatles" moved into the Hot 100 on June 27 at 97 before disappearing from the charts. Record World listed "She Loves You (Sie Liebt Dich)" in its Singles Coming Up chart for four weeks starting on June 6 at 126, with a peak at 121.

Swan knew it was taking a chance releasing "Sie Liebt Dich" without the approval of EMI or Transglobal. Its reasoning that its contract with Transglobal for the U.S. rights to "She Loves You" and "I'll Get You" gave it the rights to any recorded versions of the songs by the Beatles was clearly flawed. Swan had the rights to the specific master recordings, but not the songs themselves. After being sued by Capitol, Swan quickly settled the case, agreeing to stop production and distribution of the single, effectively killing any chance of "Sie Liebt Dich" becoming a hit in the U.S.

Although the *Four By The Beatles* EP and the "Sie Liebt Dich" single failed to light up the charts, the Beatles chart success during the first half of 1964 was unprecedented. On April 4, the Fab Four held down the top five spots in both the Billboard Hot 100 and the Cash Box Top 100, placing 12 songs in each. The group also dominated local surveys. The Beatles had the top 12 songs in the March 7 Official Request Survey of WORC in Worcester, Massachusetts. Boston's WMEX gave the group the top 15 on March 23. Both included album cuts and had "All My Loving" at the top. Pittsburgh's KQV survey of April 6 showed ten Beatles songs tied at number one: "Can't Buy Me Love," "Twist And Shout," "Do You Want To Know A Secret," "She Loves You," "All My Loving," "This Boy," "Please Please Me," "I Want To Hold Your Hand," "I Saw Her Standing There" and "Roll Over Beethoven." The next week's survey added "Thank You Girl," "Devil In Her Heart" and "Long Tall Sally" (from *The Beatles' Second Album*) as part of eight Beatles songs tied at the top. Boston's WBZ charted "Long Tall Sally," "I Call Your Name" and *The Beatles' Second Album* at number one on its singles chart in April. WLCY in Tampa had the Beatles holding down the top five spots, while San Diego's KGB and Providence's WPRO had the Beatles in the top six places. KXOA in Sacramento, California charted the *Meet The Beatles!* album at number one on its singles chart, with the Canadian import single "Roll Over Beethoven" at two.

The May 16 Cash Box reported that the Beatles first feature film, *A Hard Day's Night*, had just been completed in England. The English team's Paul McCartney and John Lennon had written nine new songs, including the title track, for the movie [of which seven would actually appear in the film]. United Artists only had album rights to the score and was prohibited from issuing any Beatles singles from the LP. Capitol, however, would issue a single of the film's title song. Capitol could also release songs from the soundtrack on an LP, but was "prohibited from merchandising the album as a soundtrack package." Cash Box reported that the movie would get a royal sendoff with a benefit premiere in July, sponsored by the Variety Clubs of Great Britain and attended by HRH Princess Margaret and the Earl of Snowden. The American premiere was set for New York in August. The Beatles, who would be in America in August for a month-long cross country tour, were to attend both premieres. [The group would only make the London and Liverpool premiers of the movie.] The film, shot in and around London, was a fictional account of 36 eventful hours in the lives of the boys. The movie also featured Anna Quayle, star of the stage production of "Stop the World . . ." [though she is limited to a brief but funny hallway encounter with John] and British TV comedy star Wilfrid Brambell.

The July 4 Billboard reported that United Artists Records and Capitol would be "locking horns" over the songs from *A Hard Day's Night*. UA had the rights to the original soundtrack album, which would have seven songs [actually eight] plus instrumental music by George Martin, "but Capitol was going all-out to buck the soundtrack set with singles and an LP by the Beatles singing the seven songs from the picture as well as five new songs." Capitol's *Something New* LP was set for release on August 1. UA had rushed advance copies of its album to disc jockeys towards the end of the previous week [ending Friday, June 26]. That weekend, the American Records Manufacturers and Distributors Association ("ARMADA") held its sixth annual convention at the Eden Roc Hotel in Miami Beach. UA planned to introduce its soundtrack album at its distributors meeting set for June 26 at 2:00 PM. Britain's Melody Maker reported that New York radio stations received their copies of the LP mid-week, with WMCA and WINS (with Murray the K Kaufman) battling to see who could get the most songs on the radio the fastest. In Miami, WQAM received a tape of the album from an undisclosed New York source on late Thursday [June 25] and began playing the songs shortly after 1:00 AM that Friday morning, catching WFUN off guard. The station immediately dispatched disc jockeys Dick Starr and Bill Holley to rectify the situation. The pair headed to Harry's American Bar at the Eden Roc and located UA vice president Si Mael, who gave them a copy of the LP. By 4:00 AM, WFUN began playing tracks from the actual album, boasting an exclusive as rival WQAM only had a tape! Such was sixties radio with the Beatles.

In an article titled "Beatles' LP: 4 Days That Shake Industry," the July 11 Billboard reported that the UA soundtrack album had become "one of the fasting selling LPs in the history of the record business," selling 1,000,000 copies within four days of its introduction at the ARMADA convention. The other trades ran similar articles. After nine days, sales neared 1,500,000, quickly leading to chart success. The LP debuted in Billboard on July 18 at number 12 while the top albums were *Hello Dolly!* by Louis Armstrong and the original cast albums *Hello Dolly!* and *Funny Girl*. On July 25, the UA album spent its first of 14 straight weeks at the top of the charts. Finally, on October 31, the UA soundtrack was overtaken by Barbra Streisand's *People* and *Everybody Loves Somebody* by Dean Martin. Billboard charted the UA album for 51 weeks, including 28 in the top ten. The LP topped the Cash Box Monaural chart for 14 weeks during its 37-week run, with 25 in the top ten, and peaked at number two in the Stereo chart during its 26 weeks on that chart. Record World charted the LP for 46 weeks with 13 at one and 26 in the top ten. Total sales would exceed 4,000,000.

At the time UA compiled its soundtrack album, the film was to feature eight new Beatles songs, counting "Can't Buy Me Love" and "I'll Cry Instead." The remaining four tracks were instrumental versions of film songs recorded by the George Martin Orchestra. Side One opens with the Beatles recording of "A Hard Day's Night," with its attention-grabbing opening chord. The disc keeps on rocking with "Tell Me Why" and the country-flavored "I'll Cry Instead." The latter song ended up being cut from the film and is misidentified on the initial record labels and back covers as "I Cry Instead." Next up is a swinging instrumental of "I Should Have Known Better," followed by George's lead vocal for the film and album, the upbeat "I'm Happy Just To Dance With You." The side closes with an instrumental version of "And I Love Her." Side Two opens with three straight Beatles recordings. "I Should Have Known Better" is a catchy rocker featuring John's lead vocal and harmonica. This is followed by two slower numbers, "If I Fell," with exquisite vocal harmonies by John and Paul, and one of Paul's best ballads, "And I Love Her." Next is "Ringo's Theme (This Boy)," a instrumental version of "This Boy." Unfortunately, the album has a lush orchestrated version of the song that is inferior to the George Martin arrangement appearing in the film. The final vocal track on the album is "Can't Buy Me Love," which is featured twice in the film. The album closes with a swinging jazzy instrumental of the title track.

Songs from the album immediately received saturation air play. WORC in Worcester, Massachusetts listed "A Hard Day's Night," "And I Love Her" and "If I Fell" at one, two and three for three straight weeks beginning on July 4.

Cash Box reviewed the *A Hard Day's Night* soundtrack album in its July 11 issue, noting that the Beatles were "probably one of the most phenomenally successful vocal-instrumental groups to come out of any country" and indicating that it was a foregone conclusion that the film and the album would be "blockbusters in the coin-making department." The record was "destined for chartdom with such slick tracks as 'A Hard Day's Night,' 'I Should Have Known' and 'If I Fell.'" Billboard listed the Beatles soundtrack LP as a National Breakout Album in its July 18 issue.

The July 11 Record World featured the jacket to the United Artists soundtrack album and the label to the Capitol single "A Hard Day's Night" on its front cover as "Number One Picks." The write-up proclaimed: "It's Beatle week, which means much action for two companies—United Artists and Capitol." United Artists had the soundtrack of "the moptops' new UA film," which was "due very soon." Capitol was releasing a single with the title tune and "I Should Have Known Better," also from the flick. The magazine added: "The score for the film was written by the redoubtable Lennon-McCartney team, and the foursome gives its wailing all to the projects. Land office sales are already being made, proving The Beatles' popularity is still phenomenal." That same week Cash Box predicted that "the English sensations should find it extremely easy chart goin' with their new Capitol single," which was the title tune from the group's "soon-due pic bow." The song was described as a "pulsating driver that's sure to flip the teeners in no time flat." The review added that "the thumpin' undercut, from the flick, can also step way out," and noted both tunes were penned by Lennon and McCartney. Billboard, which did not review the UA soundtrack album, took a different tone by limiting its review of the single to a short sarcastic statement: "Nice try for these newcomers."

Although the Capitol single's official release date was July 13, it was most likely in stores a week earlier. Radio stations were quick to add the new disc from "these newcomers" as evidenced by Cash Box's Radio Active chart. The July 11 issue reported that as of July 1, "A Hard Day's Night" had been immediately been added by 78% of the stations. One week later the song was being played by 20% more of the stations, bringing the total to 98%.

"A Hard Day's Night" entered the Billboard Hot 100 on July 18 at number 21. It spent a week at number two before topping the charts the next week on August 1, displacing the Four Seasons' "Rag Doll." After two weeks at the top, the tune dropped to number three, giving way to Dean Martin's "Everybody Loves Somebody" and the Supremes' "Where Did Our Love Go." During its 13-week run, "A Hard Day's Night" spent eight weeks in the top ten. Cash Box charted the song for 14 weeks, including three at number one and ten in the top ten. Record World charted the song for 15 weeks, including three at number one. Most radio stations took more time to add the single's excellent flip side, "I Should Have Known Better," to their playlists. By July 8, only 25% of the stations were playing the song. More got on board in the following weeks, with 30% of the stations adding the tune the next week, bringing the total to 55%. By July 29, this had grown to 80% of the reporting stations. This impressive air play did not, however, lead to comparable success on the charts due to the A-side's dominance. Billboard charted "I Should Have Known Better" at number 53 during its all too brief four-week run. The song did slightly better in Cash Box, which charted the song for five weeks, with a peak at 43. Record World reported the song for two weeks, with a peak at 84. The disc quickly gave Capitol its third straight million-selling Beatles single. By summer's end, it had sold over 1,210,000 copies.

3 BRAND-NEW BEATLES SINGLES!

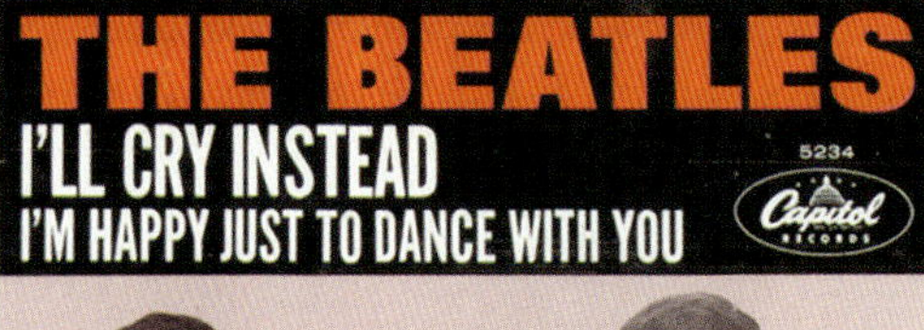

A BEATLES BONANZA! 6 FABULOUS NEW SIDES FROM THE BEATLES' FIRST MOTION PICTURE (A United Artists Release), A HARD DAY'S NIGHT! CONTACT YOUR CAPITOL SALES REP TODAY!–AND WATCH FOR THE BEATLES' GREAT NEW CAPITOL ALBUM, "SOMETHING NEW," COMING SOON!

(S)T-2108

Capitol continued its attack on the United Artists soundtrack album with the release of two additional singles. The company also moved up the release date for its competing album, *Something New*. Capitol promoted its film-related releases in a color ad appearing on the back cover of the July 11 Billboard. The ad displayed the picture sleeves for the three singles, although the rectangles containing the titles of the later two singles would be modified. The ad also previewed the cover to the *Something New* album prior to the addition of the text and song titles. A two-color version of the ad ran in the July 11 Record World and the July 18 Cash Box.

The decision to schedule the two additional Beatles singles on a rush basis was communicated to Capitol's Engineering Department in a memo from Dave Dexter dated June 26, 1964. This was shortly after United Artists introduced its film soundtrack album at the ARMADA convention attended by distributors in Miami Beach. Dexter requested the immediate preparation of 45-RPM reference dubs for two new singles: "And I Love Her" b/w "If I Fell" and "I'll Cry Instead" b/w "I'm Happy Just To Dance With You." The memo stated that the recording level was to be "the hottest possible on these four sides." This was in keeping with Capitol's policy that Beatles singles should be mastered to provide a radio-friendly, booming big beat sound. Dexter concluded the memo with "WE MUST GET THEM IN PRODUCTION SOONEST!" Less than a month later, both singles were in the stores.

Although Capitol initially planned on releasing its second and third singles featuring songs from the film on July 20, the records were actually issued a week apart. First out of the box was a disc with "I'll Cry Instead" and "I'm Happy Just To Dance With You," which most likely was available for sale on Friday, July 17. "I'll Cry Instead" bubbled under the Billboard Hot 100 at number 115 on July 25 before moving up to 62 on August 1. During its seven-week run on the charts, the song peaked at 25, making it the least successful of the three A-sides issued by Capitol in July 1964. Cash Box debuted "I'll Cry Instead" at number 74 on July 25, charting the song for nine weeks, with a peak of 22. The single entered the Record World 100 Top Pops chart at number 52 on August 1, charting for a total of six weeks with a peak of 28. Radio stations were anxious to give the new single multiple spins. The Cash Box Radio Active chart indicated that "I'll Cry Instead" was being played by 35% of its reporting stations by July 15. The next week 45% more of the stations added the track, bringing it up to 80%. By July 29, this had grown to 98% of the stations.

The record's flip side, "I'm Happy Just To Dance With You," also made its debut in the Billboard Hot 100 on August 1, 1964, but its appearance was limited to one week at number 95. It did, however, spend six weeks Bubbling Under The Hot 100. The song entered the Cash Box Looking Ahead chart at number 124 on August 1, broke into the Top 100 at 91 the following week, but fell to 97 in its second and final week in the Top 100. The B-side entered the Record World Singles Coming Up chart at Number 124 on August 1 before moving up to 110 the next week and entering the 100 Top Pops chart for one week at 94 on August 15. These weak chart performances, as well as the song's absence from Cash Box's Radio Active chart, indicate that the Harrison-sung "I'm Happy Just To Dance With You" was largely ignored by program directors.

Cash Box reviewed the single in its July 18 issue, describing the disc as "Two-sided sales dynamite from the boys," and observing, "once again it's money-in-the-bank for all concerned." "I'll Cry Instead" was called a "driving rocker," while "I'm Happy Just To Dance With You" was a "stomp-a-rhythmic delight." That same week Record World noted: "both [songs] gallop along in good rock and roll fashion and will delight The Beatles fans. There can be little doubt that this is a potent disk on the current market." Billboard chose not to review this latest release by the Beatles.

The single's relatively poor performance is not that bewildering considering that neither song matched the high quality of the previous Beatles singles or the other songs recorded for *A Hard Day's Night*. There was also little incentive for fans to purchase the single as both songs were on Capitol's latest Beatles album, *Something New*, which was released simultaneously with the 45, and on the United Artists film soundtrack album, which had gone on sale nearly a month earlier. Even the sleeve had little to offer as it featured the same photo used for Capitol's first two Beatles singles. And if that weren't enough, "I'll Cry Instead" wasn't even in the film. Still, the record sold over 450,000 copies by the end of August.

By Friday, July 24, Capitol's third and final single featuring songs from *A Hard Day's Night* went on sale. The disc paired "And I Love Her" with "If I Fell." The three Capitol singles contained all the new songs recorded for the film except "Tell Me Why." "And I Love Her" debuted in the Billboard Hot 100 on July 25 at number 80 and peaked at 12 for the weeks of September 5 and 12 during its nine-week stay on the charts. The song entered the Cash Box Top 100 on August 1 at number 67, charting for nine weeks with a peak of 14. "And I Love Her" entered the Record World Singles Coming Up list at Number 101 on August 1 before jumping up to 47 on August 8 and peaking at 16 during its eight weeks in the 100 Top Pops chart. Radio stations gave "And I Love Her" saturation air play, with Cash Box's Radio Active chart indicating that 42% of its reporting stations were playing the song as of July 22. A week later 41% more of the stations added the track, bringing it up to 83%. By August 5, 98% of the stations were playing the song.

Billboard charted "If I Fell" at number 53 during its nine-week run. Cash Box reported the flip side separately for four weeks, with a peak of 64. Record World charted the song for five weeks, with a peak of 59. "If I Fell" got more radio air play than the previous B-side, "I'm Happy Just To Dance With You," but was no where near as popular with stations as "And I Love Her," with only 14% of the Cash Box reporting stations playing "If I Fell" as of July 29.

There were, of course, exceptions, with WSPR in Springfield, Massachusetts listing "If I Fell" at the top ahead of "And I Love Her" at three and "A Hard Day's Night" at four on August 5. The following week "If I Fell" remained at number one, while "And I Love Her" moved up to two. Springfield's other pop station, WHYN, reported "And I Love Her"/"If I Fell" at number three on August 8. Seattle's KJR reported "If I Fell" at number one on July 31.

The July 25 Cash Box noted: "This is the 3rd Beatles release in as many weeks from Capitol and it looks (and sounds) like another very big winner from the group's debut pic, *A Hard Day's Night*." "And I Love Her," called the side to watch, was described as an "extremely pretty, soft beat cha cha opus...that the boys wax in soft and tender fashion." The magazine alerted readers not to overlook "If I Fell," an "easy beat cha cha" that could also "step out." The July 25 Record World noted that these were two of the slower tunes from the film, and that, of course, "the ditties are by John Lennon and Paul McCartney and they incorporate the L-McC trademarks of soft, subtle harmonies and simple lyrics." Once again, Billboard failed to turn its spotlight on the Fab's latest slab of plastic. But while Billboard ignored the disc, record buyers did not, as evidenced by sales of over 500,000 records by the end of August even though both songs were on the United Artists soundtrack LP and Capitol's *Something New* LP.

Here come 6 new Beatles songs, plus 5 great hits from their first movie, all in one great new album:

(S)T 2108

Millions of Beatlemaniacs are waiting for *Something New,* right now! It's got 6 great new songs that aren't available on any other album, and it's got the best songs from the Beatles new movie, *A Hard Day's Night,* including "And I Love Her" and "I'll Cry Instead"!

("And I Love Her" #5235 and "I'll Cry Instead" #5234 are both on the charts right now, along with "A Hard Day's Night" #5222.)

So cash in on *Something New,* and take advantage of something new in Beatles prices. See your CRDC rep for Capitol's new one price to everybody: $2.02 mono, $2.53 stereo. (Album available beginning July 20.)

Then open the door, and stand back!

(Note: if you tear this ad out, and cut it along the dotted line, the top makes a great poster for your window. Let everybody know you've got the Beatles newest album!)

The July 4 Billboard reported that Capitol had scheduled a Beatles LP titled *Something New* for release on August 1. The album would contain the seven songs from *A Hard Day's Night* and five new tunes, but would not be marketed as a soundtrack album. Capitol's initial plan was to issue its new Beatles album in close proximity to the Beatles film arriving in theaters; however, when United Artists rush-released its soundtrack LP in late June, Capitol decided to push its release date up to July 20. Recognizing that Beatles fans were aware that the UA soundtrack album was in stores weeks ahead of its new LP, Capitol prepared an in-store promotional poster assuring record buyers that its *Something New* LP would be "worth waiting for." The company also slightly altered the album's contents.

Capitol ran an ad in the July 25 issues of all three trade magazines plugging its third Beatles album of 1964, informing distributors and stores that: "Millions of Beatlemaniacs are waiting for *Something New,* right now!" Capitol stressed that the album had six great new songs not available on any other album plus five great hits from the Beatles first film. Dealers were advised to trim the ad on the dotted line and place the top part in their store windows as a poster letting customers know they had the Beatles latest album in stock. Record World ran an article on the album in its July 25 issue, proclaiming that *Something New* lives up to its name with six tunes never before released in America. The magazine added that these songs were recorded after the Beatles completed their first film. Stanley Gortikov, President of Capitol Records Distributing Corp., indicated that pre-release sales had been fantastic, with over a half-million shipped. These orders were keeping Capitol's Scranton and Los Angeles plants at full capacity, with the label adding outside sources to press the disc. Gortikov said that initial demand was amazing, demonstrating that "dealers have as much enthusiasm today as they did six months ago when we put out the first Beatle album." He attributed the excitement for the LP to the Beatles upcoming American tour and the UA motion picture, factors that could make *Something New* one the biggest selling albums in Capitol history. The album has 11 tracks, including the German-sung "Komm, Gib Mir Deine Hand," better known in the U.S. as "I Want To Hold Your Hand," the first Capitol Beatles single. [The inclusion of "Komm, Gib Mir Deine Hand" was most likely influenced by the favorable response to the track from air play by WWDC's Carroll James, who previously had played a British copy of "I Want To Hold Your Hand," leading Capitol to rush-release that single.] All of the songs on the album were written by Lennon and McCartney, with the exception of "Slow Down" and "Matchbox." Cash Box ran a similar article.

Something New opens with "I'll Cry Instead," which was still being promoted as a film song. Although the words to this rocker are a bit of a downer, Capitol probably chose the song to open the album because it was the A-side of the Capitol Beatles single released simultaneously with the album. This is followed by three Lennon-McCartney songs from Side Two of the British *A Hard Day's Night* LP. "Things We Said Today" is a wistful ballad beautifully sung by Paul. John returns as the lead vocalist on the rockers "Any Time At All," which contains an interesting guitar and piano duet during its instrumental break, and "When I Get Home," with its memorable "Whoah-ho-ho-I, whoah-ho-ho-I" vocal hook. The first side closes with two rocking covers from the British *Long Tall Sally* EP: Larry Williams' "Slow Down" with a scorching lead vocal by John; and Carl Perkins' "Matchbox" showcasing Ringo on lead vocal. Side Two features the album's four songs from *A Hard Day's Night*. It opens with John and Paul singing the rocking "Tell Me Why" before turning mellow with Paul's pretty ballad, "And I Love Her." George then sings lead on the upbeat "I'm Happy Just To Dance With You" followed by John and Paul harmonizing on the ballad "If I Fell." The album closes with the familiar hard-rocking introduction to "I Want To Hold Your Hand," but sung in German. To Beatles fans, "Komm, Gib Mir Deine Hand" was not only something new, it was something weird.

Capitol originally planned on issuing a 12-song LP with all of the film songs. The album most likely would have matched the 13-track British LP but without "You Can't Do That," which was on *The Beatles' Second Album*. The reconfigured album leaves off three songs from the film, "A Hard Day's Night," "I Should Have Known Better" and "Can't Buy Me Love." The album fails to include "I'll Be Back," the closing track on the British *A Hard Day's Night* LP. The song would later appear on the Capitol LP *Beatles '65*. It may have been dropped to make room for "Komm, Gib Mir Deine Hand."

Cash Box and Record World reviewed the album in their August 1 issues. Cash Box described the Beatles as "England's most successful export since wool, who are currently dominating the Top 100 with a plethora of best-selling singles." The disc spotlighted a "flock of tunes from their new UA flick." Selections include "I'll Cry Instead," "And I Love Her" and "an interesting rendition of 'I Want To Hold Your Hand' sung in German." Cash Box predicted that the disc would "develop into a sales-monster." As the magazine had done three weeks earlier, Record World featured the new Beatles LP on its cover as its Number One Album Pick. It predicted that some of the album's songs could be up for Oscar and Grammy recognition and said: "Most of these ditties were written by The Beatles for their...film." After choosing not to review the United Artists soundtrack LP and Capitol's past two Beatles singles, Billboard made *Something New* one of its Pop Spotlight Picks on the back cover of its August 8th issue. The magazine listed some of the selections and added that the album included five vocals from the Beatles first motion picture.

Something New entered the Billboard Top LP's chart on August 8 at number 125. The following week it rocketed to number six before moving up to the second spot for nine weeks, unable to get past the United Artists *A Hard Day's Night* soundtrack album. The Capitol album charted for 41 weeks, including 18 weeks in the top ten. Cash Box reported the album on its Monaural chart for 29 weeks, including nine weeks at number two and 21 weeks in the top ten. The magazine listed the LP on its Stereo chart for 23 weeks with a peak position of six. Record World charted the Capitol album for 32 weeks, including seven weeks in the second spot and 17 weeks in the top ten. Although the album was out-performed by the United Artists soundtrack LP and did not meet the lofty expectations sought by Capitol, it was still quite successful. *Something New* was certified gold by the RIAA on August 24, 1964. The album sold over two million copies, with the RIAA awarding it 2x Multi-Platinum status on January 10, 1997.

The July 18 Record World reported that the Beatles *A Hard Day's Night* film was a hit in London, having its world premiere there on July 7 "before an appreciative, $42-a-seat audience that included Princess Margaret and her husband, Lord Snowden." The British critics were "almost unanimous in their praise for the film" with some calling the boys the "new Marx Brothers;" however, the Beatles were "curiously unimpressed and self-effacing about their first screen credit." Paul told Princess Margaret: "I don't think we are very good, ma'am, but we had a very good producer [Walter Shenson]." The film was expected to have the "largest world-wide saturation bookings with initial prints numbering well into the hundreds" and the boys' popularity "certain to translate into flick crowds." The July 25 Billboard indicated that business for the Beatles film showing at the London's Pavilion was astonishing, with afternoon lines equal to evening ones. Producer Walter Shenson said the Beatles movie was the first in film history to have sufficient revenue to cover its production costs before its opening due to UA's album sales in America. United Artists had prepared a record 800 copies of the movie for the United States.

Doug McClelland reviewed the film in the July 25 Record World, immediately answering the question: "How good can the *movie* be? Very, that's how." McClelland noted that the Beatles were unique, and so was their movie. It was a "melding of Europe's New Wave filmmaking with Sam Katzman's quickie American film production, plus more than a smattering of TV's Huntley-Brinkley Report [NBC's evening news program]." [Katzman specialized in "B" pictures, whose productions included the *Jungle Jim* film series (starting in 1948), *Superman* (1948), a *Batman And Robin* serial (1949) and the teen movies *Rock Around The Clock* (1956) and *Don't Knock The Rock* (1957) with Bill Haley and His Comets, *Twist Around The Clock* (1961) with Chubby Checker, *Kissin' Cousins* (1964) and *Harum Scarum* (1965) starring Elvis Presley, the Hank Williams biopic *Your Cheatin' Heart* (1964), the Herman's Hermits' film *Hold On!* (1966), *The Fastest Guitar Alive* (1967) with Roy Orbison, and *Riot On Sunset Strip* (1967).] McClelland praised the "dizzyingly virtuoso camerawork," the "expert documentary-like reporting" and the "superb pace sustained by director Richard Lester and the dexterity and flair with which cinematographer Gilbert Taylor literally composes each scene." Lester and Taylor capture the "barely controllable frenzy of fan adoration." McClelland states: "It's all here on film for the ages and incredulous Late, Late Show eyes of the year 2000." He writes of the "undeniable amiability" of the Beatles and each member's image, particularly Ringo, who "has the audience with him *regardless*."

After noting that the London press compared the lads to the Marx Brothers, he understands the similarities. Some of John's dialog is Groucho-like and Ringo wears a Harpo-like coat, which he takes off and places over a mud puddle for a pretty young girl who promptly falls into a manhole. He notes that Wilfrid Brambell, in his role as Paul's grandfather, serves as a foil for the Beatles the way Margaret Dumont was ravaged by Groucho. McClelland's biggest complaint is the difficulty in understanding the Beatles thick Liverpool accents even without the audience squealing sure to accompany showings of the film. He concludes that the film is: "a brisk 83 minutes long, giving adults little time for criticism of any nature and should also keep children enthralled. But it's the teens, mostly, who, in the words of a supporting player, will find the film 'fab and all the other pimply hyperboles.'"

Cash Box reported in its July 25 edition that *A Hard Day's Night* would get "heavy saturation dates right from the start," opening simultaneously on August 11 at 18 theaters in the metropolitan New York area, with Cleveland, Los Angeles and Miami soon to follow. However, prior to the film's premiere in New York City, *A Hard Day's Night* played in a few selected markets. The movie had a special Saturday screening on August 1 at the Hollywood Theatre, not in California, but on 410 W. 71st Street in Fort Worth, Texas. According to the August 2 Fort Worth Star-Telegram, girls started lining up for good seats early on Friday evening. Columnist Elston Brooks described the screening: "It was like a silent movie. The girls on the film sound-track screamed. The girls in the audience screamed–for 90 minutes! No one heard anything, but no one complained. They wept tears of delight for all of those closeups of Ringo, John, George and Paul." He added that *A Hard Day's Night* was "an imaginatively shot motion picture, using overhead helicopter scenes, stop-motion photography, slow motion for better views of the unbarbered quartet and speeded-up frames for laughs. Playing themselves, the boys chose to weave a plot around their 11 songs, six of which are new for the film. It has chases, laughs, fair dialog if you can decipher the Liverpoolese." When asked about the film for a taped interview by local KFJZ's hot disc jockey Mark Stevens, Brooks replied: "I was pleasantly surprised. They gave us a picture, as well as the Beatles. They could have just gone before the cameras and hung those 11 songs on a clothesline, but they made it an entertaining movie. I liked it." The film opened its regular run at the Hollywood Theatre on Wednesday, August 5, playing for one week before being replaced by Alfred Hitchcock's latest film, *Marnie*, on August 12.

The Bradley Theater in Columbus, Georgia had two special Saturday showings of *A Hard Day's Night*. The August 2 Columbus Ledger ran a picture of some of the 1,500 youngsters who attended the previous morning's screening (shown lower right on the following page). The Bradley also had a late show of the film on August 1, with the movie's regular run starting on Wednesday, August 5. The August 3 TV Amusements Guide of The Atlanta Constitution announced that *A Hard Day's Night* was opening at four neighborhood and 11 drive-in theaters on August 5.

The July 12 Philadelphia Inquirer reported that the Beatles film would have a saturation opening in the Philadelphia area on August 5. By July 26, theaters were advertising advance ticket sales. The August 6 Philadelphia Inquirer ran an article on the film's local debut (shown upper right on the next page). "The Beatles and their young–very young–devotees whooped and hollered at each other for 87 minutes of devastating decibels in more than 60 area movie theaters Wednesday [August 5]." Reporter Henry T. Murdock attended the matinee at the 69th Street Theater along with 1,800 youngsters, mostly girls under 16, "shrieking in unison under one roof." Murdock wrote that the non-stop screaming "produced a paradox," with *A Hard Day's Night* coming "as close to being a silent film as any we have reviewed in years." He had to do a bit of guessing as to the plot, with the Liverpool accents "rendering things even more cryptic." He speculated that when the film was shown "some years hence on the late, late show, we may figure it to be pretty good entertainment." Overall, Murdock found the premiere to be "an interesting experience" and "a little awesome," adding: "If the super-charged energy released Wednesday could have been channeled through a dynamo, President Johnson would never have to go around turning off the White House lights."

The film also opened on August 5 in theaters and drive-ins in the St. Louis, Missouri area, in Camden and Atlantic City, New Jersey, Lancaster, Pennsylvania, and Newport News, Virginia, with the latter city having an August 4 preview. Some of the smaller towns in Louisiana were also ahead of the film's normal August 12 opening date. Frank's Theatre in Abbeville advertised an "Area World Premier!" for its Special Preview on Friday Night, August 7 (see ad on next page). Patrons were advised: "Be one of the FIRST in the State of Louisiana to see it! (Before New Orleans and New York City)." Other early bird Louisiana towns and cities included: Crowley (August 8); Shreveport (August 8 preview before its August 12 opening); Ferriday (August 9); and Hammond (August 9).

THE ATLANTA CONSTITUTION
August 3, 1964

TV Amusements Guide

MOVIES RADIO THEATER NIGHT CLUBS RESTAURANTS

FRED TAYLOR

Weep On, Grown-Ups, Beatles Now In Film

The mop-top quartet, alias the Beatles, appear in their first full-length motion picture, "A Hard Day's Night," which opens here Wednesday at four neighborhood and 11 drive-in theaters. It is a fictional account in a day in the life of the Beatles, George Harrison, Paul McCartney, John Lennon and Ringo Starr, and they sing six new songs in the epic.

PHILADELPHIA INQUIRER, THURSDAY MORNING, AUGUST 6,

See The FABULOUS BEATLES "A Hard Days Night"

Eager-faced Beatles fans jam entrance to 69th Street Theater awaiting admission to the singing group's first full-length film, "A Hard Day's Night."

At Area Theaters

Beatles Outshouted At 'Hard Day's Night'

The Beatles and their young — very young — devotees whooped and hollered at each other for 87 minutes of devastating decibles in more than 60 area movie theaters Wednesday

...made by the Liverpool larks with the homegrown fright wigs.

SOUTHERN PREMIERE–STARTS TODAY

Starring in their first full-length, hilarious, action-packed film!

The Beatles

A Hard Day's Night

new songs! ★ A Hard Day's Night ★ I Should Have Known Better ★ I'm ★ Tell Me Why ★ She Loves You ★ All My Loving ★ Bother Me ★ Can't Buy Me Love

UNITED ARTISTS

FRANK'S THEATRE ABBEVILLE

STARTS SAT. AFTERNOON, AUGUST 8
(Special Preview Friday Night, August 7)

LAFITTE DRIVE-IN ABBEVILLE

STARTS SUNDAY, AUGUST 9

AREA WORLD PREMIERE!

Be one of the FIRST in the State of Louisiana to see it! (Before New Orleans and New York City).

Special advance sale of tickets for the Friday Night preview now on sale. (These tickets guarantee you a seat for Friday night advance showing).

The BEATLES

Starring in their first full-length, hilarious, action-packed film!

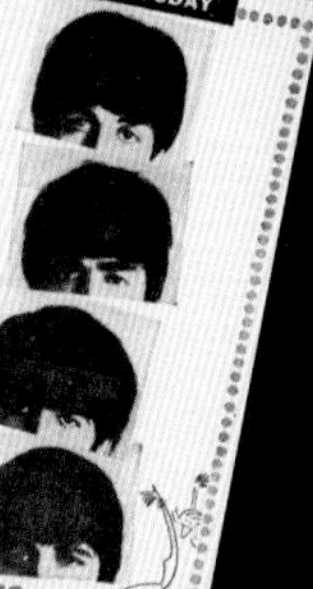

BEATLEMANIA . . . Shown above are some of the 1,500 or so local youngsters who crowded into the Bradley Theater Saturday morning for a special showning of the Beatles' new movie, "A Hard Day's Night." Many of the mophead quartet's enthusiasts are displaying sweaters, membership cards, dolls and other assorted Beatlefan products. The British singing group's movie will start a regular run Wednesday at the Bradley.

A Hard Day's Night had its New York premiere on Tuesday, August 11, a day ahead of most of the country. The Daily News started spreading the news in its August 2 edition courtesy of columnist Wanda Hale: "STOP THE WORLD! United Artists has a universe-shaking announcement to make. On Aug. 11 (my birthday, goody, goody!) the Beatles are coming to town in their first feature-length film, 'A Hard Day's Night.'" Hale quoted producer Walter Shenson extensively, including: "They are four likable young men, full of pep, enthusiasm and contagious humor. And they are intelligent." She informed readers that London critics were comparing the Beatles to the Marx Brothers and that the picture was a "fictional 36 hours in the lives of the Beatles...[with] a good many musical numbers, ending up with a big evening before a live audience." Hale concluded with: "This information ought to hold you Beatle fans until they get here! Those who are groaning at the prospect of the invasion can take to the hills."

Kate Cameron reviewed the film for the August 12 Daily News, opening with: "Well kids, the great day has finally arrived. The Beatles are here performing on a number of screens all over town...Thank goodness their showmanship is being distributed all over the map instead of a single theatre. For if all those shrieks, yells, signs and hollers were concentrated in one spot, I don't think we adults could stand the noise." After praising Shenson, Lester and Owen, Cameron writes that the "picture adds up to a lot of fun, not only for teenagers but for grownups as well." Rather than limiting comparisons to the Marx Brothers, Cameron describes the Beatles as "mixture of all the oldtime slapstick comedians with a dash of up-to-date slickness" and adds that there is "honest good humor throughout the film." Cameron concludes by saying: "The Beatles are not just another singing-swinging team, they are unique in their power of attraction." In the New York Times, a previously skeptical Bosley Crowther wrote: "This is going to surprise you...but the film with those incredible chaps, the Beatles, is a whale of a comedy" with "so much good humor... that it is awfully hard to resist." The film is a "wonderfully lively and altogether good-natured spoof on the juvenile madness called 'Beatlemania'" and a "fine conglomeration of mad-cap clowning in the old Marx Brothers style, and it is done with such a dazzling use of camera that it tickles the intellect and electrifies the nerves." He observes that the "commercially sure-fire film...is much more sophisticated in theme and technique than its seemingly frivolous matter promises." As for the music, he writes: "To ears not tuned to it, it has moronic monotony." As for screen appearance, "they're all good–surprisingly natural in the cinema-reality style that Lester expertly maintains."

7-11 STORES OKLAHOMA PREMIERE
Starting Wednesday, August 12, 1964
THE BEATLES
In their First Feature-Length Motion Picture
"A HARD DAY'S NIGHT"
ALL SEATS $1.00
THIS TICKET IS GOOD ONLY AT THE
CENTER THEATRE
Civic Center - 415 Couch Drive
Oklahoma City, Oklahoma
First Come - First Served -
Good Only Wed. Aug. 12, 1964
7-11 STORES
SOUVENIR ADVANCE SALE TICKET
Starring in their first full-length, hilarious, action-packed film!
The BEATLES
"A Hard Day's Night"
UNITED ARTISTS

RESERVED
Starring in their first full-length, hilarious, action-packed film!
The BEATLES
"A Hard Day's Night"
UNITED ARTISTS

THE BEATLES
Starring in their first full-length, hilarious, action-packed film!
The BEATLES
"A Hard Day's Night"
UNITED ARTISTS

I'VE GOT MY BEATLES MOVIE TICKET
HAVE YOU?
SPECIAL PREVIEW-ADMIT ONE
THE BEATLES
Wed. Aug. 26th - 2:00 P.M.
In their First Feature-Length Motion Picture
"A HARD DAY'S NIGHT"
Admission $1.
THIS TICKET IS ONLY GOOD AT THE
BOULEVARD THEATRE
HAMPTON BLVD.
NORFOLK, VA.
NO REFUNDS
No 61

Starring in their first full-length, hilarious, action-packed film!
The BEATLES
"A Hard Day's Night"
6 BRAND NEW SONGS
PLUS YOUR BEATLES FAVORITES!
also starring
WILFRID BRAMBELL
produced by WALTER SHENSON
screenplay by ALUN OWEN
directed by RICHARD LESTER
released thru UNITED ARTISTS
Hear the Beatles on the one, the only, the original sound track album from United Artists Records!

A Hard Day's Night officially opened in Boston on Wednesday, August 12, at the Mayflower and 20 neighborhood and eight drive-in theaters in the Boston area. Radio station WBZ, with its popular DJ Jefferson Kaye, sponsored a pre-screening (flyer shown on the next page). Marjory Adams' review of the movie appeared in the August 13 Boston Globe where she pontificated on the screaming girls that dominated the Mayflower audience: "The Beatle worshipers prove their love and admiration by weird, loud screams which might be Indian war cries, or could be African voodoo rituals. Actually, it is the American teen-age manifestation of vitality, youth, and a desire to expend love on somebody who is more romantic than the boy next door." She also offered an explanation for the group's success. "The secret of the Beatles as entertainers is that they put the same zany unconventionality into their performances as the Marx Brothers once did. They are like catnip to the teen-ager. Just as felines act silly when plied with the stimulating weed, so do young people when the Beatles start their antics and their songs." Adams thought the ending concert sequence was way too long "except for a true Beatle admirer." Her overall verdict was less than glowing: "'A Hard Day's Night' is scarcely a great picture, nor are the Beatles actors in any sense of the word. They are personalities who at this moment are the idols of the younger generation. Eventually they will separate–as did the Marx Brothers, alas–but meanwhile the money rolls in."

The film opened in Miami on Friday, August 14. Columnist Herb Kelly of the Miami News warned in the newspaper's August 9 edition: "It'll Be A Hard Day's Night For Ushers, Too." Kelly predicted that local theater lobbies would be "jammed with squealing youngsters" on Friday morning, with ushers standing guard over posters and photos of the Beatles, probably to no avail. Ushers would also take immediate action should anyone "leap on stage just to touch the image of Ringo or the others." Off-duty policemen might also be hired to keep patrons in line: "Shrieking and squealing are all right; vandalism and mischief are out." The theaters will have a "one-show-for-each-ticket policy...for the first few days until the epidemic slackens" and sell souvenir programs and pillows with the faces of the Beatles. After seeing the film, Kelly wrote a column titled "Beatles' Movie Funny Once The Shrieking Stops." He was impressed that Beatles management had avoided the pitfall of throwing the group into a cheap movie with disastrous acting to make a fast buck. "The four boys...are themselves and act naturally. The dialog they have is simple...and it is comical. Most of the comedy is of the sight variety like that of Mack Sennet and the Marx Brothers."

MATINEE TICKET
SPECIAL PREVIEW ADMIT ONE
Tues. Sept. 1 at 2:00 p. m.
THE BEATLES
in their First Feature-Length Motion Picture
"A HARD DAY'S NIGHT"
ALL SEATS $1.00
THIS TICKET IS GOOD ONLY AT THE
2:00 P. M.
MATINEE
RIALTO THEATRE

I'VE SEEN THE BEATLE'S MOVIE
WHY DON'T YOU?

DOORS OPEN
One Half Hour Before Showtime
DATE
PERFORMANCE
THE BEATLES
in their First Feature-Length Motion Picture
"A HARD DAY'S NIGHT"
ALL SEATS $1.00

...ES (in their first feature-length motion picture) "A HARD DAY'S NIGHT"
...cial Preview -- Admit One -- Thursday, Aug. 27th at the Mode Theatre
...1.00.
This Souvenir Ticket Courtesy of The Music Shop.
Do Not Detach. Present Entire Ticket to Doorman

THEY'RE JUMPING WITH EXCITEMENT
OVER JEFFERSON KAYE'S
WBZ RADIO
BEATTLE MOVIE PARTY!

Learn how you can be one of fifteen lucky listeners to take your guest to the exclusive pre-screening of

FOR DETAILS
LISTEN HERE!

The Beatles A Hard Day's Night
RELEASED THRU UNITED ARTISTS
WBZ RADIO 103 GROUP W

JEFFERSON KAYE

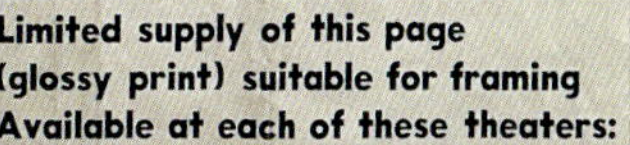

Limited supply of this page (glossy print) suitable for framing
Available at each of these theaters:

Community — Dedham
Oriental — Mattapan
Dedham Drive-In
Strand — Dorchester
Hancock Village
(W. Roxbury)

EXCLUSIVE !
2968
29c
THE BEATLES
STARRING IN
A HARD DAY'S NIGHT

With a special foreword by The BEATLES themselves

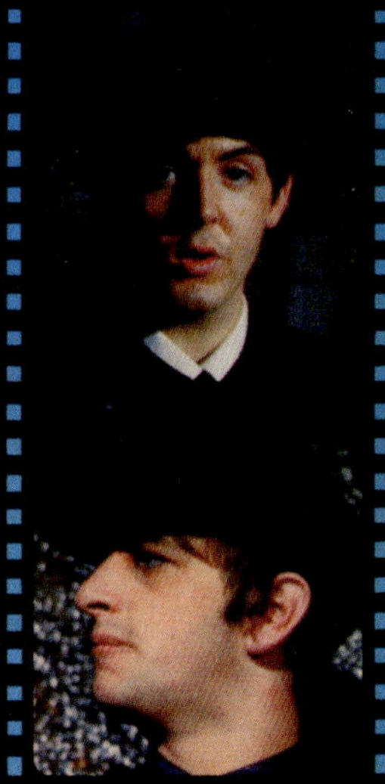

THE OFFICIAL UNITED ARTISTS' PICTORIAL SOUVENIR BOOK
★ Candid cameras behind the scenes
★ Stories you won't see on the screen
THE WHOLE CRAZY MAKING-OF-THE-FILM STORY — FROM START TO FINISH

A Hard Day's Night debuted on the West Coast on August 12. The August 9 San Francisco Examiner ran an article on the movie based on reporter Phyllis Seidlin's interview with former San Francisco resident Walter Shenson, the film's producer. Shenson indicated that the movie cost under $750,000 to make and was already profitable due to sales of the soundtrack album. He spoke glowingly of the Beatles: "The boys are very, very professional and very talented. They don't think they can act, but they can and they have a fantastic ability for comedy. And one thing the picture shows is that they have fun when they work." After comparing John to Groucho and Ringo to Harpo and Chaplin, Shenson emphasized that the Beatles are "four individuals, and we tried not to treat then as a four-headed monster."

Stanley Eichelbaum titled his review in the August 12 San Francisco Examiner: "How About That New Beatles Movie! The Lads From Liverpool Aren't Half Bad." Eichelbaum wrote that his eyes and ears had only just recovered from the film, describing it as "an 83-minute, rough-and-tumble carousel of Beatlemania, which serves to introduce those four scraggly and adenoidal folk-singers from Liverpool to the screen." After calling the film a "jerky, glaring and largely improvised assemblage of home movies" with a "quasi-documentary look," he added that "there is also camera surrealism to enhance the film's mood of comic lunacy and social revolt, which remind me of those mad old flicks with the Marx Brothers or the Three Stooges." The film has a "brisk and nervous tempo...a New Wave canter," with the Beatles "allowed to wisecrack, preen, frolic and clown with what appears to be extemporaneous relish." Some of the nonsense, such as the smart-aleck answers to reporter's questions, is "engaging," while some is on "an inane level that only a child or Jerry Lewis could appreciate." The lad's "Liverpoolese speech...makes many of the gags incomprehensible." Ringo Starr is given star status as a "brooding, mischievous drummer," while the others come across as "happy-go-lucky rebels" though Paul is described as a "baby-faced worrier." The group sings "with boyish and bleating verve."

Eichelbaum saw a preview of the film at a small screaming room on Hyde Street with two dozen female members of the Beatles Fan Club present. The girls "shrieked and moaned and wept for joy...pounded their fists and bounced deliriously in their seats." He ended his review by advising potential viewers: "The movie will assuredly amuse you more than irritate you; fascinate you more than frighten you; and relax you more than oppress you."

The August 12 Los Angeles Times issued the following alert: "As loud as electronics can make it, the sound of the Beatles' beat will fill some 30 Los Angeles theaters today in their first full-length movie, 'A Hard Day's Night.'" The next day, Times Motion Picture Editor Philip K. Scheuer had words of praise: "It's crazy and far out, man, and what will seem its filmie virtues to some may seem vices to others. The main surprise, at least to a square like me, is that the Beatles not only aren't monsters, they aren't even faintly grotty (grotesque). And while their sense of humor is unabashedly zany, there's an underlying gentleness–I won't go so far as to say sensitivity, though that could be–about their behavior which is hard to resist." Scheuer wasn't quite as enthusiastic about the music: "And if their singing and the musical sound they make are awful, at least they're characteristic, outgoing and spontaneous. Besides, the squeals of the girls–on-screen as well as off–all but drown them out anyway." On the technical side, he said: "Spontaneity is the keynote of the picture's technique, which has been shot a la New Wave in documentary or newsreel style, but with an impishness that reflects great credit on the skill of the cameraman, Gilbert Taylor." He added that comparisons to "Mack Sennett (visual gags) and the Marx Brothers (verbal) are not so far fetched, after all."

Writing in the August 30 Chula Vista [California] Star-News, Ernest Mandeville advised adults as well as teenagers to go see *A Hard Day's Night*, calling it "one of the most promising comedies since the glorious days of Charlie Chaplin and the Marx Brothers" and "a lively, well-directed film based on the madcap antics of the Beatles (especially Ringo Starr) ably assisted by a wonderful droll Irish comedian, Wilfrid Brambell." Mandeville added: "The dialog gives the impression of being spontaneous remarks on the now well-known Beatlemania hysteria. These boys do not take themselves seriously. They are intelligently aware of the absurdity of the teenage screamers." At the time of the film's release, many theaters, particularly those in suburban and rural areas, as well as nearly all drive-is, ran two films for the price of one. Teenagers anxious to see their heroes in *A Hard Day's Night* would often have to first sit through a second-bill feature that varied among locations. These movies ranged from Westerns to horror to comedies (such as Jerry Lewis and the Three Stooges) to Elvis to musicals like *Bye, Bye Birdie*. In Chula Vista, the theater ran an Elvis film second on the bill. According to Mandeville, this prompted "the whole mob of teenagers [to] yell, 'We want the Beatles!' and 'Elvis, you're so old-fashioned. Drop dead!'" Mandeville thought the "shaggy haired boys" had proved they were "not a flash in the pan" and were "here to stay–on films at least–as inspired comics."

Beatles fans in Chicagoland had to wait a couple of extra weeks to see the Beatles film, which made its solo debut at the Woods Theater on August 28. Mae Tinee reviewed the movie in the September 3 Chicago Tribune, indicating that she was advised by theater management to see the film during the evening to avoid the "screamies" who attend the film in droves during the day and whose squeals make it hard to hear the dialog. The later shows are more satisfactory because "the lines are well worth catching." Tinee further advised: "Even if you don't care for their music, you'll find them entertaining and full of a kind of irrepressible humor and exuberance and a refusal to take anything seriously, especially themselves." With a script that "makes fun of everything," the Beatles "seem completely natural and unactorish; they mug and wisecrack and clown whenever their impish spirits move them...aided and abetted by Wilfrid Brambell, an expert comic." Her verdict: "The action is chaos from start to finish and really pretty good fun."

Bob Thomas of the Associated Press wrote that *A Hard Day's Night* was surprisingly good. In his August 1 by-line, Thomas pointed out that "movies designed to cash in on the curiosity value of headline personalities have traditionally been slapdash affairs." So while one might expect "little more than a tape recording of an orgiastic Beatle concert," the film shows that the group may be around for a long time, "not as freaks but as qualified entertainers." Thomas applauds the creative team's decision to portray the quartet "as what they are: Beatles." Paul's rake grandfather, skillfully played by Wilfrid Brambell, impels the film along, with his mischief adding "to the travails suffered by the Beatles at the hands of their fanatical fans." The movie's ending TV concert "pours forth enough of their twangy chantings to satisfy any Beatlemaniac." The Beatles banter "flies at a rapid clip," but sometimes the wisecracks are "too fast–and occasionally too British–to comprehend." Thomas' assessment: "The comedy follows the pattern of vintage Marx Brothers or vintage Three Stooges, though not as hilarious as either. But then, the Beatles are new at it."

The August 14 Time wrote that *A Hard Day's Night* was "one of the smoothest, freshest, funniest films ever made solely for exploitation" with the Beatles proving themselves "disarming personalities." It had "enough mad puns and sight gags and individual comedy bits to throw any Beatlemaniac into spasms of joy." Although the reviewer preferred the Maysles Brothers' *What's Happening!–The Beatles In The U.S.A.* documentary (see page 189), the film "fills the gap with Beatlesong, frothy fiction, and an air of high-spirited improvisation almost as amusing as life itself."

The August 24 Newsweek proclaimed: "The legitimacy of the Beatles phenomenon is finally inescapable...Sight gags and documentary realism, semi-abstract, Antonioni-ish chases, a Fellini helicopter at the end, the meagerest possible plot line–all contribute to making 'A Hard Day's Night' a truly fresh, lively length of film." In The New Yorker's August 22 issue, Brendan Gill stated that he did not understand what made the Beatles "so fascinating to so many scores of millions of people," but admitted: "I feel a certain mindless joy stealing over me as they caper about uttering sounds." In the August 27 Village Voice, Andrew Sarris, who indicated he had resisted the Beatles as long as he could, wrote: "'A Hard Day's Night' has turned out to be the 'Citizen Kane' of jukebox musicals, the brilliant crystallization of such diverse cultural particles as the pop movie, rock 'n' roll, cinema-verite, the nouvelle vagua, free cinema, the affectedly hand-held camera, frenzied cutting, the cult of sexless sub-adolescent, the semi-documentary and studied spontaneity." He opined that "the movie works on every level for every kind of audience."

Perfect timing for profits! A smash new Beatles single combining two of the top hits from their smash album, "SOMETHING NEW!"

MATCHBOX b/w SLOW DOWN

(Ringo lead vocal) (John Lennon vocal)

As the summer of 1964 drew to a close, Capitol believed that the Beatles were invincible. Having no new Beatles recordings available, Capitol decided to issue something old, pulling the tracks "Matchbox" and "Slow Down" from its *Something New* album for release as a "new" Beatles single. While this choice of two cover songs over Lennon-McCartney gems such as "Any Time At All" and "Things We Said Today" seems strange, both songs are undeniably great rockers. The Beatles recording of Carl Perkins' arrangement of "Matchbox" was most likely selected as the A-side because it featured a lead vocal by Ringo, whose ranking as the most popular Beatle in America was further cemented by his attention-grabbing performance in the film *A Hard Day's Night*. "Slow Down" featured John's lead vocal on a Larry Williams song. Capitol ran an ad for the single in the August 29 Billboard.

The trade magazines reviewed Capitol's latest Beatles record in their August 29 issues. Billboard made the disc one of its Hot Pop Spotlight singles, writing: "No doubt this group will make some sort of impression during their forthcoming tour of the Colonies that may effect the sales of this recording." Cash Box made the single a Pick of the Week, announcing: "The fabulous smash-makers serve up two more rockers that should take the wax mart by storm." "Matchbox" was described as a "contagious steady-beat pounder," while "Slow Down" was called a "sizzling, high-speed affair...that puts heavy emphasis on the instrumentation."

The September 5 Cash Box Radio Active chart indicated that as of August 26, 60% of its reporting stations immediately added "Matchbox" to their playlists. The next week 38% more stations added the song, bringing its air play to 98%. "Slow Down" was initially added by 30% of the stations as of August 26, with increases of 34% and 16% in the following weeks, bringing its total to 83% as of September 9. "Matchbox" entered the Billboard Hot 100 at number 81 on September 5, peaking at 17 on October 17 during its eight-week run on the charts. Cash Box, which charted the song for eight weeks, also showed a peak at 17, while Record World charted the song for seven weeks, with a peak of 22. "Slow Down" sneaked into the Billboard Hot 100 at number 99 on September 5, peaking at 25 on October 10 during its seven-week run on the charts. Cash Box also charted the B-side for seven weeks, but with a peak at 34. Record World, which charted "Slow Down" for only six weeks, gave the song its highest position in the three trades at number 23. The single sold a respectable 415,000 units.

As per its settlement with Capitol, Vee-Jay's rights to the Beatles were set to terminate on October 15. With no new product possible, Vee-Jay had to make due with what it had. The company decided to repackage its *Introducing The Beatles* LP with a fancy gatefold cover. When Vee-Jay showed EMI the new cover's sample artwork on May 22, EMI told Vee-Jay that the new package violated the settlement. Two weeks later, Capitol sent Vee-Jay a letter stating that the re-release of *Introducing The Beatles* in the new "magazine type" jacket with new artwork, text and photos along with a new and different title and record number violated the settlement. Vee-Jay went to court and was victorious as the judge ruled that Vee-Jay had the right to promote its Beatles master recordings in any cover, jacket or package which Vee-Jay deemed appropriate. Shortly thereafter, Vee-Jay began distributing *Songs, Pictures And Stories Of The Fabulous Beatles* in late July; however, the album's strongest sales did not occur until the last quarter of 1964.

While Vee-Jay did not bother to print new record labels for the album, it went all out on its cover, giving it the appearance of a teen magazine that came with a record. The jacket has a gatefold cover whose front flap is two-thirds of the full jacket's size. The front panel has text above the same Dezo Hoffmann photo used on the picture sleeve for "I Want To Hold You Hand" with autographs below. The exposed white inside right flap has the same four faces previously appearing on Vee-Jay sleeves and ads. The open gatefold has color-tinted pictures of the Beatles and personal information on the group's members. The back cover leaves no doubt that the LP was aimed at young girls. Below Ringo's color-tinted picture is the phrase "Ringo Loves" and a blue dash-bordered heart containing the phrase "Picture Here." The other Beatles are given the same treatment. Girls are told: "Paste your picture with your favorite Beatle and your friends with their favorite and for you fellows tough luck!!" Some later front covers were customized by adding names of concert locations from the Beatles 1964 American tour on banners proclaiming: "Souvenir of Their Appearance at [Venue, City . Date]." Nine concert locations have been confirmed.

Songs, Pictures entered the Billboard Top LP's chart at number 121 on October 31. It peaked at 63 on December 5 during its 11 weeks on the charts. After landing in Cash Box's Looking Ahead Albums chart for four weeks, the LP charted at 100 for one week on November 21 in the Top 100 Albums Monaural chart. *Songs, Pictures* peaked at 79 in Record World's Top 100 LP's chart on December 12. The LP sold an estimated 384,150 mono and 7,375 stereo copies.

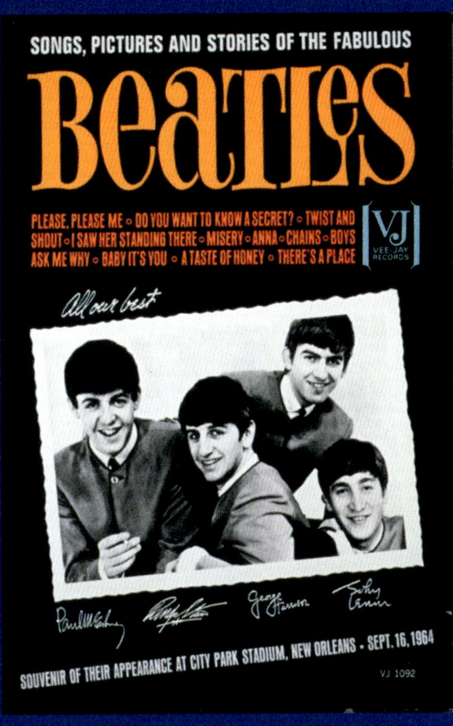

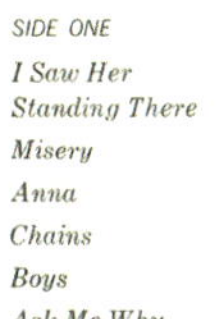

SIDE ONE

I Saw Her Standing There
Misery
Anna
Chains
Boys
Ask Me Why

SIDE TWO

Please, Please Me
Baby It's You
Do You Want To Know A Secret?
A Taste Of Honey
There's A Place
Twist And Shout

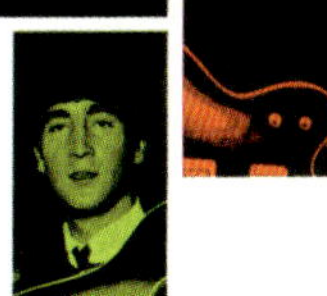

PAUL McCARTNEY

Paul is sometimes called the "Nut Beatle" or "Beatle Nut" because he is the zaniest of the group—he has the quickest wit—loudest laughter and craziest sense of humor and is a habitual practical joker. • Paul is the only Beatle with jet black hair—he has a strong straight nose and full lower lip and gleaming white teeth. He hates to shave and calls it the curse of mankind. He favors tight clothes and in case you'd like to shop for him his collar size is 15" and his waist size 30". He is indifferent to what he eats and can make do with very little sleep—he loathes pajamas and prefers to sleep raw—hates tub baths and loves showers. Oh yes and one more thing, he hates jelly beans.

JOHN LENNON

Although he was reluctant to allow himself to be called the Chief Beatle, John Lennon still refuses to accept the title of 'Leader'. "We've always been a group, not anyone of us worked any harder than the other." John is a natural born leader but none the less fun loving than the other Beatles. He is nearsighted and off stage wears glasses. As a child he lived a life of uninterrupted calm and cannot recall any childhood sadness—his mother died after his 14th birthday and this event remains the greatest tragedy of his life. • After John met Paul McCartney they both began to teach themselves the guitar and after school they would "rush through their tea and practice the guitar." They called themselves the Nurk Twins—although they had no way of knowing it at that time. John and Paul had laid the foundation for what was to become in an astonishingly short time a group known as The Beatles.

GEORGE HARRISON

George plays the lead guitar, the one with the deadpan face working in the middle between John and Paul—he is also probably the best musician, having taken lessons which makes him the only one in the group with formal musical training. George is more introverted than the rest and an interviewer would most likely get a lot of yes and no answers from George. George is the quietest of the Beatles and he is also the youngest of the group. His interests cover a wide spectrum and he secretly nurses a desire to become a serious guitarist one day and would love to play a Spanish guitar unamplified. He is a devotee of the great guitarist Andres Segovia. • George was the only one of the Beatles who had been to the United States before the group came here in February and he had the privilege of meeting President Kennedy at that time. • The most striking thing in George's appearance is his lean face highlighted by large hazel eyes shadowed by his hair worn in the shaggy Beatle cut. Lamb chops are his favorite food although he is not very much concerned with food. His collar size is 14", chest 38", waist 30"—he is one of four children and was a better than average student in school.

RINGO STARR

Ringo is the most easily identified of all the Beatles—for one reason or another most people can pick him out from the group. He is the shortest Beatle and the only one with blue eyes and although John Lennon looks like the oldest Beatle this dubious distinction belongs to Ringo. When the spotlight falls on Ringo the clamoring shouting and squealing becomes deafening—why is not easily discernible—he only sings occasionally and of course is known as the drummer of the group. He is not the best looking and in fact has a nose that rivals Jimmy Durante and Danny Thomas—but he has a sad little boy lost look and this could possibly be the key to his charm. • Ringo is the newest member of the group joining them in August '62—his nickname of Ringo came about because he wears a lot of rings—he is never with less than three or more than five—he is not only the shortest Beatle but the lightest weighing only 136 lbs.—his hair is brown and he is the only one with grey streaks in his mop and the grey is natural. • Ringo's father is a house painter and his mother works as a barmaid to augment the family income—and whenever he can he rushes home to visit his family. He is very fond of good food and will send back his steak if it is not blood red. He can't stand girls who wear jeans "when they're not built for it," loves blue silk shirts, big brassy cuff links, leather coats and suede boots—as he himself admits, in a clothing store he's like a drunken sailor.

PAUL McCARTNEY

Real Name: Paul McCartney
Birthplace: Liverpool, England
Birthdate: June 18, 1942
Height: 5'11"
Weight: 160 lbs.
Hair: Jet Black
Eyes: Brown
Education: Liverpool Institute
Marital Status: Single
Plays: Guitar, piano, drums, and banjo
Favorite Singers: Ray Charles, Peggy Lee
Favorite Actress: Ann Margaret
Instrument he plays most: Guitar

JOHN LENNON

Real Name: John Lennon
Birthplace: Liverpool, England
Birthdate: October 9, 1940
Height: 5'11"
Weight: 150 lbs.
Hair: Brown
Eyes: Brown
Education: Quarry Bank High School & Liverpool Art College
Marital Status: Married – One child
Plays: Guitar, harmonica, piano and Banjo
Favorite Color: Black
Instrument he plays most: Guitar
Work before becoming a singer: Poet
Favorite Singing Group: Shirelles
Type of Music he likes most: Traditional jazz
Favorite Food: Steak & Chips
Favorite Actress: Brigitte Bardot

GEORGE HARRISON

Real Name: George Harrison
Birthplace: Liverpool, England
Birthdate: February 25, 1943
Hair: Dark Brown
Eyes: Hazel
Education: Liverpool Institute
Marital Status: Single
Plays: Guitar & one finger piano
Favorite Instrument: Guitar
Favorite Hate: Having his hair cut
Dislikes Most: Traveling on buses
Favorite Actress: Elizabeth Taylor

RINGO STAR

Real Name: Richard Starkey
Birthplace: Liverpool, England
Birthdate: July 7, 1940
Height: 5'8"
Hair: Brown
Eyes: Blue
Education: St. Salas & Dingle Vale Secondary Modern School
Marital Status: Single
Plays: Drums
Favorite Singers: Dinah Washington, Ray Charles
Dislikes Most: Riding a scooter
Favorite Cartoon: Donald Duck
Favorite Actress: Brigitte Bardot

The Beatles weren't the only popular group of four white male singers to appear on Vee-Jay before moving on to another label. The Four Seasons had three number one singles on Vee-Jay ("Sherry," "Big Girls Don't Cry" and "Walk Like A Man"). Vee-Jay Executive Vice-President Jay Lasker, the mastermind behind the *Jolly What!* combination of the Beatles and Frank Ifield, conceived the idea for an album of hits by the Fab Four and the Four Seasons. In a March 30, 1964 interoffice memo, Lasker advised compiling an "International Battleground" LP featuring the Beatles and the Four Seasons immediately upon the settlement of its Beatles litigation with Capitol. Because the settlement limited Vee-Jay to issuing its Beatles songs in the same record configurations, it needed to ask permission from EMI to prepare such an album. By letter dated April 24, EMI President L.G. Wood replied: "George Martin and I have given very close thought to...the possible release of an album of the Beatles coupled with the Four Seasons but we very much regret that for a variety of reasons we cannot go along with you on it." Although this prevented Vee-Jay from compiling a newly configured record with the two groups, Vee-Jay devised a plan to issue a gatefold two-record set containing its existing *Introducing The Beatles* and *Golden Hits Of The Four Seasons* records in separate pockets.

The deluxe set, titled *The Beatles vs. The Four Seasons*, has a boxing theme. The front cover touts "The International Battle of the Century" with "each delivering their greatest Vocal Punches." The back is a score card enabling listeners to assign points to 12 rounds of Beatles songs pitted against Four Seasons' songs. The open gatefold has several color-tinted pictures of each group. Its left panel recycles the Beatles bio from *Songs, Pictures*, while the right has a "4 Seasons Biography." The set included an 11" x 23" poster with the often-used Jim Johnson-drawn faces of the Beatles.

The September 5 Record World reported that Vee-Jay had rushed out a double LP to capitalize on the "popularity of The Beatles and The Four Seasons, the two best-selling groups of their countries." The set contained "score cards, biographies, pictures and stories." The package's relatively high list price and lack of new songs by either group adversely affected sales. Billboard charted the album for three weeks with a peak at number 142 on October 17. Record World reported the album in its LP's Coming Up chart for five weeks starting on October 10, including three weeks at 103. Cash Box, which did not publish a Looking Ahead Albums chart until November 14, 1964, did not chart the album. *The Beatles vs. The Four Seasons* sold an estimated 18,700 mono and 725 stereo copies.

TWO RECORD SET

THE INTERNATIONAL BATTLE OF THE CENTURY

VJ VEE-JAY RECORDS

THE Beatles vs THE FOUR SEASONS

EACH DELIVERING THEIR GREATEST VOCAL PUNCHES

INSIDE: SCORECARDS, BIOGRAPHIES, PICTURES, STORIES OF ALL THE CONTESTANTS
PLUS: FREE BONUS 8" X 15" FULL COLOR BEATLE PICTURE SUITABLE FOR FRAMING

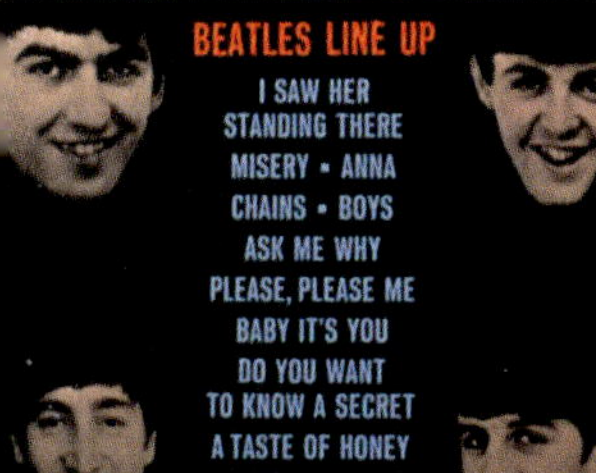

YOU BE THE JUDGE AND JURY!

DX 30

YOU BE THE JUDGE / KEEP SCORE BY ROUNDS!

RULES OF CONTEST: The most points for any Round is 10. Thus should you judge the Round is even you give Beatles 5 points and Four Seasons 5 points. Should you judge Four Seasons decisively win a Round, you might give Four Seasons 9 points and Beatles 1 point. Total points given for each Round must never exceed 10. So – *Ring the bell and set the Battle of the Century going.*

SCORE BY ROUNDS	THE BEATLES GREATEST HITS	ROUND	FOUR SEASONS GREATEST HITS	SCORE BY ROUNDS
	I SAW HER STANDING THERE	1	SHERRY	
	MISERY	2	I'VE CRIED BEFORE	
	ANNA	3	MARLENA	
	CHAINS	4	SOON	
	BOYS	5	AIN'T THAT A SHAME	
	ASK ME WHY	6	WALK LIKE A MAN	
	PLEASE, PLEASE ME	7	CONNIE-O	
	BABY IT'S YOU	8	BIG GIRLS DON'T CRY	
	DO YOU WANT TO KNOW A SECRET	9	STAR MAKER	
	A TASTE OF HONEY	10	CANDY GIRL	
	THERE'S A PLACE	11	SILVER WINGS	
	TWIST AND SHOUT	12	PEANUTS	
TOTAL	THE WINNER			TOTAL

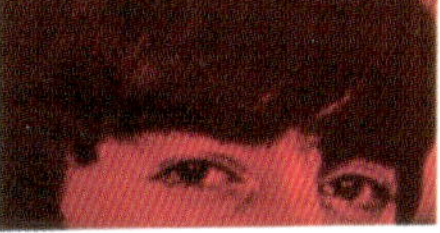
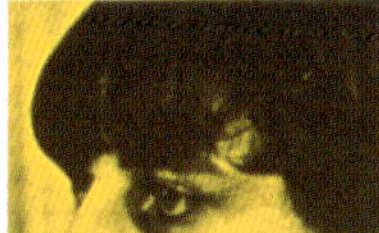
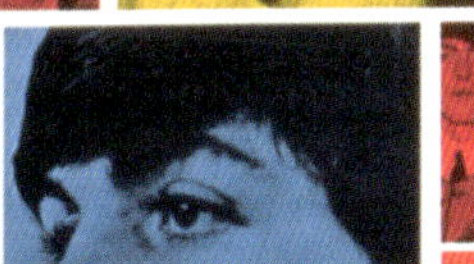

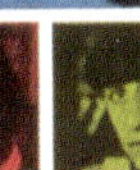

PAUL McCARTNEY

JOHN LENNON

GEORGE HARRISON

RINGO STARR

4 SEASONS BIOGRAPHY

Within four weeks after their release of "Sherry," the Four Seasons became the No. 1 best selling American vocal group. Their name today has become a household word among record buyers of all ages.

The group consists of Frank Valli, whose voice you associate most with the "sound" of the group, Bob Gaudio, the youngest member of the Four Seasons, Nick Massi and Tommy DeVito. Except for Bob Gaudio, who joined the group after leaving the Royal Teens, the other three boys had been working together for about six years as the "Four Lovers." Their smash hits such as "Walk Like A Man," "Sherry," "Marlene," "Big Girls Don't Cry," "Candy Girl," "Rag Doll," etc., have earned for them a position as one of the all time best sellers in the history of the record business.

During August 1964, Vee-Jay reissued its four 1964 Beatles singles on its Oldies subsidiary label. While it may seem strange to consider a song an oldie when it was issued only a few months before, this marketing ploy proved effective. With sales of the four Beatles singles grinding to a halt, Vee-Jay was able to get new life out of these records by having them placed in the oldies section of record stores. Initial sales in August and September averaged about 4,500 copies per Beatles Oldies disc for a total of 18,086 units. With the October 15 deadline looming, Vee-Jay made a final push to get as much Beatles product into the pipeline as possible. To further entice shoppers to buy Beatles singles on the Oldies label, Vee-Jay ordered 200,000 special center-die-cut Beatles Christmas picture sleeves. Vee-Jay advised distributors and stores: "Beatles Singles Make Wonderful Christmas Gifts." Apparently, many teenagers agreed as total sales for the Beatles Oldies singles in October exceeded 112,000 copies.

After repackaging its *Introducing The Beatles* album as *Songs, Pictures And Stories Of The Fabulous Beatles* and including the disc in the deluxe two-record set *The Beatles vs. The Four Seasons*, the only remaining Beatles album for Vee-Jay to repackage was the Beatles/Ifield LP. This posed quite a dilemma for the company as by August 1964, the album was being returned in "record" numbers due to poor sales. Vee-Jay would need to repackage *Jolly What!* in a way to focus on its strengths and downplay its weaknesses. *Jolly What!* had eight things going for it, namely John, Paul, George, Ringo, "Please Please Me," "Ask Me Why," "From Me To You" and "Thank You Girl." It also had eight things going against it, namely the eight Frank Ifield songs, which were unwanted intrusions for most Beatles fans. Vee-Jay replaced the silly English statesman *Jolly What!* cover with an attractive blue background cover featuring the striking Jim Johnson painting of the Beatles previously used on the *Love Me Do* picture sleeve (see page 67). The portrait was based on a Dezo Hoffman color photograph of the group. The titles to the four Beatles songs are prominently featured. It is believed that this portrait cover version of the Beatles/Ifield LP was issued in September 1964. Based on the album's scarcity, it probably sold only a few thousand mono and few hundred stereo copies.

The October 17 Cash Box announced that the current best-selling LP, *A Hard Day's Night*, would be available to record stores with a special Christmas wrapper on November 1. United Artists hoped to entice shoppers to buy the album as a Christmas present. Although the year still had two months to go, 1964 was clearly **The Year of the Beatles**.

ORIGINAL MOTION PICTURE SOUND TRACK
THE BEATLES
WISHING YOU A HAPPY BEATLES HOLIDAY

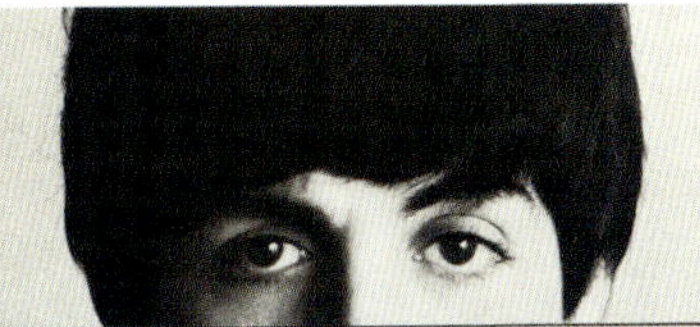

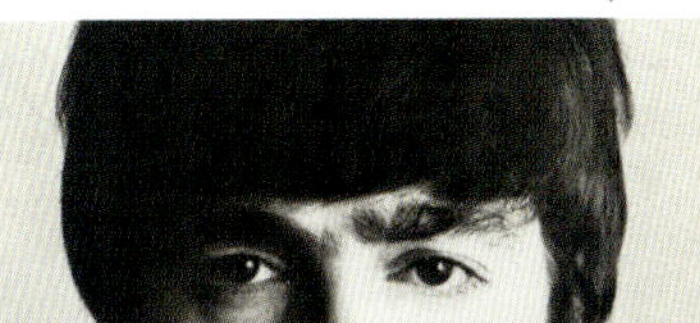

The Beatles

with tony sheridan

beatles bop – hamburg days

once upon a time in germany

Records from the 1961 Hamburg Sessions

Prior to the Beatles becoming Parlophone recording artists, the band signed a recording contract with Bert Kaempfert Produktion company during its 1961 residency at the Top Ten Club in Hamburg, Germany. This led to the Beatles first professional recording session on June 22, 1961. The Beatles recorded five songs backing British singer Tony Sheridan plus two songs performed exclusively on their own. An eighth backing track recorded on May 24, 1962, was later given a Sheridan vocal. All mono and stereo versions of these eight songs are included on the CD box set *Beatles Bop - Hamburg Days*. The cover (shown on the preceding page) depicts Paul on piano, Pete Best on drums, Stuart Sutcliffe on bass and George and John on guitars. The July 20, 1961 second issue of Mersey Beat reported on the Beatles recording sessions with producer Bert Kaempfert in Germany. The group backed singer Tony Sheridan on “Why,” “My Bonny” [sic] and “The Saints,” and recorded two tracks on their own, the instrumental “Cry For A Shadow” and the John Lennon vocal “Ain’t She Sweet.” The first recordings issued from the Hamburg sessions were “My Bonnie” and “The Saints,” released in Germany as Polydor NH 24 673 on October 23, 1961, credited to Tony Sheridan and the Beat Brothers (actually John, Paul, George and Pete Best). Original pressings described the songs as “Rock.” Kaempfert and Polydor tried to take advantage of the Twist craze by pressing later copies of the record with labels describing the songs as “Twist.” “My Bonnie” peaked at number four in the chart of popular twist records published in the Hamburg newspaper Bild-Zeitung on May 21, 1962. It reportedly sold 100,000 copies in Germany.

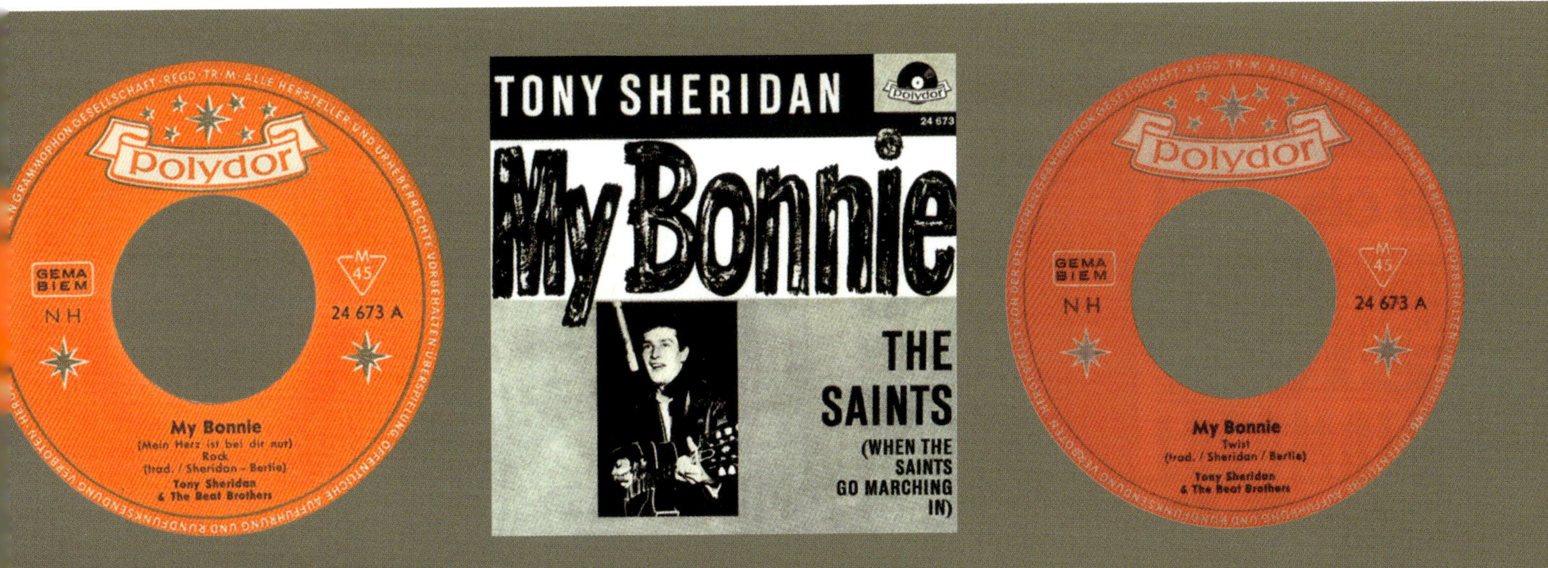

Future Beatles manager Brian Epstein initially imported 75 copies of the German single for his NEMS record store in Liverpool. Legend has it that Raymond Jones entered NEMS on October 28, 1961, and asked for a record called "My Bonnie." After much investigation, it was determined that the disc was on the Polydor label in Germany and that the band performing on the single was actually a Liverpool group called the Beatles. This prompted Brian to see the Beatles perform at the Cavern Club on November 9, 1961. He became the group's manager shortly thereafter.

In early December 1961, Epstein sent the German "My Bonnie" single, along with a copy of the Beatles contract with Bert Kaempfert Produktion, to Ron White, General Marketing Manager of EMI. White had the contract translated into English and forwarded the record to two of EMI's pop labels, Columbia and HMV. By letter dated December 18, 1961, White informed Brian that neither label was interested in signing the Beatles to a recording contract. That month, representatives of the British branch of Deutsche Grammophon Gesellschaft ("DGG"), owner of the Polydor label, met with Brian Epstein and the Beatles to discuss the release and promotion of the "My Bonnie" single in the U.K. Because the Beatles had a strong following in the Liverpool area, the company decided to change the name on the label from "Tony Sheridan & The Beat Brothers" to "Tony Sheridan & The Beatles."

The British "My Bonnie" single was released as Polydor NH 66833 on January 5, 1962. That same day, Keith Fordyce reviewed the disc in NME, describing Tony Sheridan and the Beatles as a "young British group who display a welcome amount of imagination in their treatment of 'The Saints.'" Fordyce added that both sides of the disc were "worth a listen for the above-average ideas." Don Nicholl reviewed the single in the January 13 Disc, describing Sheridan as a "Norwich boy who sings and plays a guitar." Nicholl said he had been told that Sheridan has been "going great guns" in Germany. The German Polydor label placed him "on disc with the British rock instrumental group The Beatles." [Nicholl was not then aware that the Beatles were a vocal/instrumental beat group from Liverpool.] He concluded: "Both sides are good old stand-bys." The January 27 Melody Maker praised both sides of the disc and, like NME, assumed Tony Sheridan and the Beatles were an actual group: "We should be hearing a lot more of them." The World's Fair called "My Bonnie" a "real gone rocker which will please the youngsters" in its January 6 issue. Despite these favorable reviews, the record failed to generate interest outside of Liverpool and did not make the U.K. charts.

Meanwhile, the December 16, 1961 Cash Box reported in its Germany column that "My Bonnie" and "The Saints" by a "Twister from England" named Tony Sheridan would soon be released in America with six top U.S. record companies fighting over the master. The American and Canadian rights to the single went to [American] Decca Records, which then had a reciprocal licensing agreement with DGG. The single was released on April 11, 1962, naming "Tony Sheridan and the Beat Brothers" as the artist. Cash Box reviewed the single in its April 28 issue, informing readers that the disc was an import from Europe with both sides in English. "The Saints" was described as "an Americanized, build-up blues romp for the famed piece" with "some off-beat rock touches." "My Bonnie" had a "deceptive slow start" leading into a "rapid-fire rock take-off on the traditional tune." That same week, Billboard gave both sides of the single 3 out of 4 stars in its Moderate Sales Potential listings. With virtually no promotion or air play, the single was ignored.

After the Beatles first two singles of 1963 topped the charts in England, Polydor reissued the "My Bonnie" single in late May. Peter Jones wrote an article in the June 1 Record Mirror asking: "Can this disc harm the Beatles?" Tony Barrow did not think it would harm "the boys' good name in the business," but found it a shame that such "obviously inferior material should be available for the fans." The June 22 Melody Maker ran the cover headline "Beatles Blast Own Hit Disc!" John explained: "It's just Tony singing with us banging in the background. They're flogging it but I wish they would shut up. It's terrible. It could be anybody. I wouldn't buy it." Record Retailer charted "My Bonnie" at number 48 on June 8. Melody Maker listed the song for two weeks in June with a peak at 38.

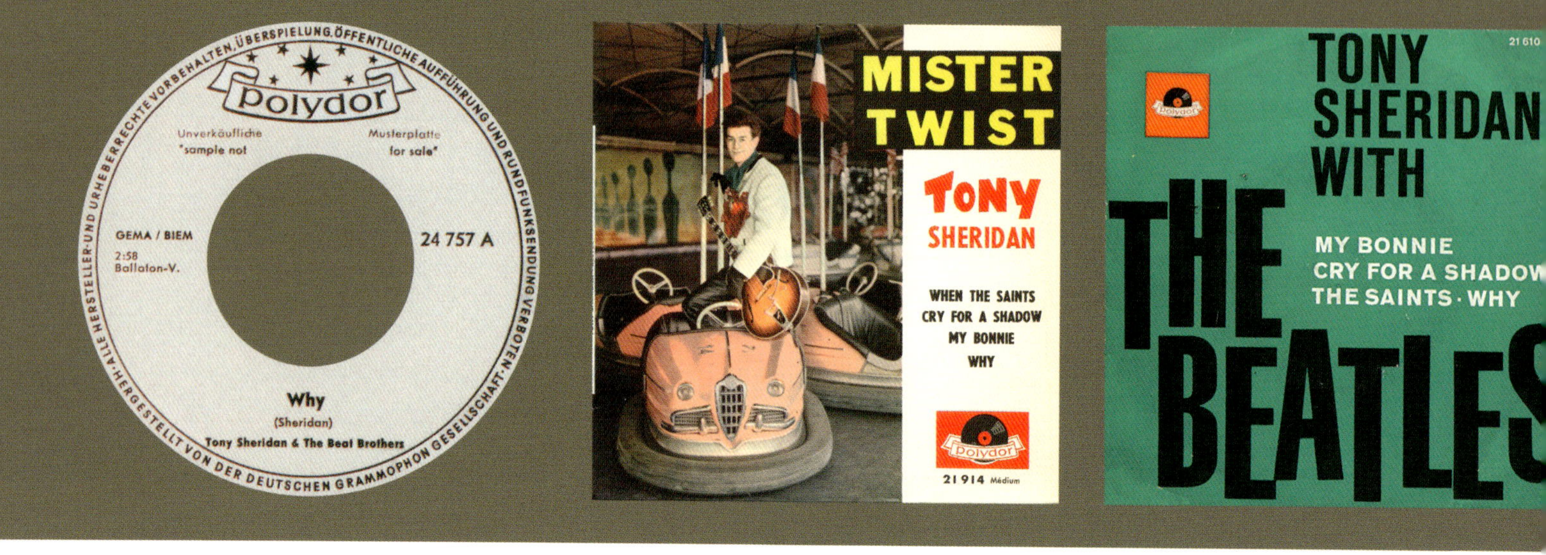

In late 1961, Deutsche Grammophon considered issuing a German follow-up disc to "My Bonnie." The company pressed promotional copies of a new single (Polydor 24757) by Tony Sheridan & The Beat Brothers in December 1961 with "Why" as the A-side and "Cry For A Shadow" as the flip side. However, the record was canceled before any stock copies were pressed. The label gave songwriter credit for "Why" to Tony Sheridan, who does his best to sound like Elvis, particularly on the bridge. The Beatles provide the instrumental backing, and John, Paul and George supply doo-wop-style backing vocals. "Cry For A Shadow" was written by the one-time-only songwriting team of George Harrison and John Lennon. Although the instrumental track was a Beatles-only recording, Polydor credited the song to Tony Sheridan & The Beat Brothers.

The four songs on the issued and canceled Tony Sheridan singles, "My Bonnie," "The Saints," "Why" and "Cry For A Shadow," were released together on a French EP in April 1962. The disc (Polydor 21914) was packaged in a picture sleeve featuring Tony Sheridan standing in a bumper car. The EP was titled *Mister Twist* to take advantage of the Twist craze. There is nary a mention of the Beat Brothers or the Beatles on the sleeve or labels, although "Cry For A Shadow" lists "G. Harrison-J. Lennon" as the songwriters. When the Beatles began their rise to fame, Deutsche Grammophon pressed an EP in Germany (Polydor EPH 21610) with the same four songs for export to the U.K. The disc was packaged in a green background title sleeve that gave more prominence to the Beatles than Tony Sheridan. The Polydor EP was overshadowed by Parlophone's *Twist And Shout* EP, issued at the same time in mid-July 1963.

As interest in the Beatles continued to grow, Polydor searched for additional Hamburg recordings in which the group participated. "Sweet Georgia Brown" was first released on Sheridan's German *Ya Ya* EP (Polydor 21 485 EPH) in October 1962. Although the instrumental track for the song was arranged by Paul and recorded by the Beatles with Roy Young on piano in May 1962, Polydor may not have initially known of the Beatles involvement. Sheridan's vocal was recorded separately that June. Hoping to cash in on current trends, Sheridan's new producer had the singer record a different vocal on January 3, 1964, with new lyrical references to the Beatles, the twist and a DJ, including the line: "In Liverpool she even dared to criticize the Beatles hair with their whole fan club standing there." This updated version of "Sweet Georgia Brown" was paired with Sheridan's recording of "Nobody's Child" on a German single (Polydor NH 52906). The label lists the artist as Tony Sheridan. The "Sweet Georgia Brown" side has the following credit below Sheridan's name: "Vocal backed by „?"." The label to "Nobody's Child" states "accompanying himself on his Guitar," although the track also includes Paul on bass and Pete Best on drums.

The single was rush-released on January 31, 1964, and exported into the U.K. Polydor advertised that the disc was by "Tony Sheridan with George Harrison, John Lennon, Paul McCartney, etc." The January 30 Record Retailer stated: "Almost a swing version of the standard from beatster Tony, who uses plenty of improvisation on this goodly release." In the February 8 Disc, Don Nicholl wrote: "You'll be finger-snapping" to his update of "Sweet Georgia Brown." The single was largely ignored and did not chart despite its reference to the Beatles and their hair.

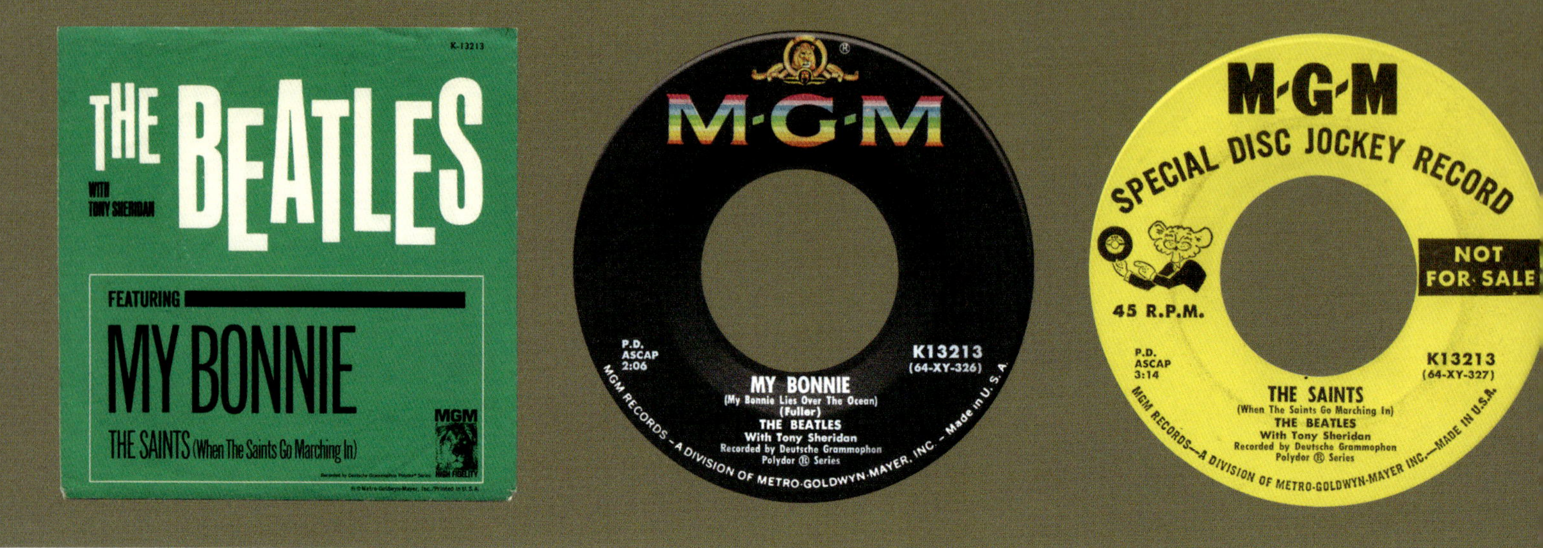

Shortly after Beatlemania exploded in America, MGM Records entered into a leasing agreement with Deutsche Grammophon giving MGM the American rights to four Tony Sheridan and the Beatles songs, including the two issued by Decca nearly two years earlier. While "My Bonnie" by "Tony Sheridan and the Beat Brothers" was ignored in 1962, the same recording of "My Bonnie" by "THE BEATLES With Tony Sheridan" became a hit in 1964 shortly after its January 27 release. It was all a matter of timing and marketing. Because its contract with DGG was for Tony Sheridan masters, MGM did not have the right to market the disc with images of the Beatles. Instead, it modified the green background sleeve for the 1963 German EP (shown on page 108) by minimizing "Tony Sheridan."

The music trades reviewed the single in their February 1 issues. Billboard stuck to the facts: "The Beatles do their thing in this chestnut standard and Tony Sheridan is the lead singer. The disk was originally recorded for the German DGG firm." Cash Box predicted that the "sizzling, MGM rock refitting of 'My Bonnie Lies Over The Ocean' could turn to gold simply because it bears the name the Beatles." It added that the "featured singer is Tony Sheridan, who's not a member of the group" and that the flip side "has the fellas zipping through a romping up-dating of another oldie." Music Vendor stated: "Another entry in the Beatles market, and there's room for plenty of coin. Sure to do well." Cash Box's Radio Active chart showed that 30% of its reporting stations were playing "My Bonnie" as of February 19. The single entered the Billboard Hot 100 on February 15, charting for six weeks with a peak of 26. Cash Box reported the disc for eight weeks with a peak of 29. Music Vendor showed a peak of 31 during its nine weeks on the charts.

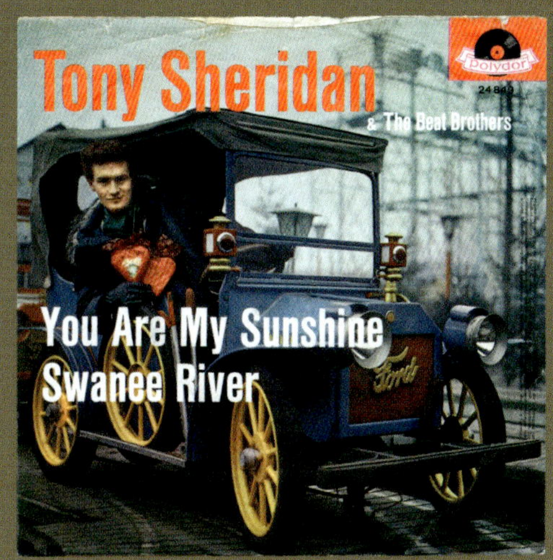

One week after issuing its first "Beatles with Tony Sheridan" single, MGM released an album containing all four of the Beatles Hamburg tracks available to MGM through its five-year leasing agreement with DGG on February 3. *The Beatles With Tony Sheridan And Their Guests* was padded with two additional Tony Sheridan recordings without the Beatles and six instrumentals by the Titans. The two Tony Sheridan tracks, "You Are My Sunshine" and "Swanee River," came to MGM's attention through their release on a German Polydor single issued in January 1962. These tracks were credited to Tony Sheridan and the Beat Brothers. (The musicians backing Sheridan were called the Beat Brothers regardless of who they were.) These six German recordings were paired with six selections by the "rocking, socking" Titans, who were further described in the album's liner notes as "a group musically related to their English cousins." Although this implied that the Titans were a hip, young American rock 'n' roll band, they were actually a group of New York session musicians assembled by MGM staff producer Danny Davis. The Titans included Davis on trumpet, Billy Mure on guitar, Dick Hickson on trombone, jazz great Milt "The Judge" Hinton on bass and Don Lomand on drums. Their six selections were pulled from the Titans' second album, *Let's Do The Twist For Adults*.

Music Vendor reviewed the MGM album in its February 8 issue, noting: "Not since Elvis has there been a sensation comparable to the British foursome. Everything they do sells like wildfire and the market never seems to become saturated." After describing the Titans as "rocking instrumentalists" and Sheridan as "one of Blighty's most popular male vocalists," Music Vendor wrote: "Together the three acts make for an extremely potent package."

The February 15 Billboard ran the following review: "Here's an album that is bound to attract some attention despite the fact that the Beatles are present on only four of the tracks and that these are the Beatles of two years ago appearing as a back-up group to soloist Tony Sheridan.... On name value, sales can result. But it is surely not the Beatles sound present on their other disks." That same week Cash Box reviewed the MGM album, calling out "Cry For A Shadow," "Why" and "My Bonnie" and noting: "Beatlemania is 'in' and the set should score at the marketplace." Billboard charted the LP for 14 weeks with a peak at number 68, while Cash Box reported the LP for 10 weeks with a peak at 43, and Music Vendor/Record World charted the disc for 12 weeks with a peak at 48.

After "My Bonnie" began falling down the charts, MGM issued a second "Beatles" single on March 27. This disc featured the Tony Sheridan vocal "Why" as the A-side with the Beatles instrumental "Cry For A Shadow" on the flip. The single was issued in a red background title sleeve with the same layout as the "My Bonnie" sleeve. Cash Box ran this review in its March 28 issue: "The Beatles with Tony Sheridan clicked with 'My Bonnie,' and this second MGM entry...should be headed up the same success path. Sheridan takes the vocal lead on this rhythm ballad with the Beatles coming in for some close-harmony chanting and big beat instrumentation. Strictly instrumental on the other end with the crew dishing up a pulsating dance delighter. Another solid coin-puller." Billboard charted "Why" for one week in its Hot 100 at number 88 on April 18. Cash Box reported "Why" for two weeks in its Looking Ahead list with a peak at 129, while Music Vendor listed "Why" for one week in its April 4 Looking Up chart at 138.

The February 28 NME reported the surprise release that day of an instrumental recorded by the Beatles two years earlier. "Cry For A Shadow" was written by George Harrison and John Lennon. The flip side featured Tony Sheridan singing "Why," a song he co-wrote with Bill Crompton, backed by the Beatles. [The songs had previously been available in the U.K. on the German export EP issued the previous July and would be released on a German single a few weeks later in a picture sleeve.] A Polydor ad in the February 27 Record Retailer ridiculously claimed "over 1/4 million sold."

The single was reviewed in the February 29 Record Mirror by its Pop Disc Jury. "Cry For A Shadow" was "a good enough tune and performance" that sounded like it was "recorded while the Beatles were under the influence of [the] Shadows." The Jury's verdict: "Must sell well." The flip-side was judged "none too hot." In the March 6 NME, Derek Johnson described the Beatles first-ever instrumental as a "hangover from their Hamburg days" that was a "pretty impressive showcase for George Harrison." The track "generates a rumbling twist beat and a riotous sound, even if the recording is a trifle tinny." Johnson thought the song would be a hit if the Polydor record was "accessible to sufficient fans." The Sheridan side, "Why," was an "attractive rockaballad...with the Beatles harmonizing in the background." Don Nicholl admitted in the March 7 Disc that the 1961 tracks cut by Sheridan and the Beatles in Germany were tricky to access. Sales would depend largely on "how much the group's name means." If fans wanted everything Beatles, then the "twangy beater" instrumental might be "massive;" however, the record didn't have the current Mersey sound. Although "Cry For A Shadow" did not chart in the U.K., it was a number one hit in Australia.

Towards the end of May, news broke that Polydor had rush-released a "New 3-Years-Old Beatles' Disc." Peter Jones revealed in the May 30 Record Mirror that the "new" disc was "Ain't She Sweet" featuring a John Lennon solo vocal backed by "If You Love Me, Baby" with Tony Sheridan singing lead backed by the Beatles. Jones wrote that John "sings the old Ager-Yellen standard with a rather restrained attack and the boys fill in comfortably enough behind him." The track has Pete Best on drums. Record Retailer reviewed the disc in its May 28 edition: "John Lennon takes solo vocal on the old standard, with the boys chugging away on this three-year-old release. Must cause a lot of interest, though it's hardly the Beatles sound of today." The May 30 Melody Maker ran a page-one story announcing: "Another 'early Beatle' storm was building up this week over Polydor's release of John Lennon's first recorded solo vocal–'Ain't She Sweet,' with the original Beatles, taped in Hamburg in 1961." The single was released on Friday, May 29, with advance orders of 15,000. A Polydor spokesman claimed: "Some people have said that it is as good, if not better, than today's Beatles numbers." Brian Epstein told the magazine that he was not pleased with the record's release, noting that it would "in no way reflect the Beatles as they are today." Despite his misgivings, Brian, according to the June 6 Disc, went to a West End record shop on Saturday [May 30] and bought five copies of "Ain't She Sweet."

The May 29 NME described the single as: "John Lennon takes the solo in a raucous, uninhibited styling of 'Ain't She Sweet.' Pleasant listening and dancing material, but no trace of the Mersey sound that was to follow." Don Nicholl gave the single three stars out of five in the May 30 Disc, writing: "John Lennon takes solo vocal on the oldie 'Ain't She Sweet' while the others back him up with firm rhythm work. The vocal is hoarse and deliberately rough-edged–the guitars crisp." He speculated that sales could be high due to the disc's "curiosity value" and collectors wanting to ensure "their collections are fully comprehensive." In that same issue, Nicholl wrote that Polydor had forgotten about the coupling but hunted through its vaults after a newspaper story mentioned the song. Polydor rushed it out so that the record could register during the present gap in the group's Parlophone releases. One week later, Penny Valentine interviewed Tony Sheridan about the record in the June 6 Disc. Sheridan told her that "Ain't She Sweet" was recorded at the same sessions as "My Bonnie" and "Cry For A Shadow." Sheridan thought the disc was not all that terrific, but added, "it IS John exactly as he used to sound." The single entered the Record Retailer chart on June 11 at number 45. It charted for six weeks, peaking at 29. Melody Maker, NME and Disc all reported the disc at 24.

Record Mirror

Week ending May 30, 1964

No. 168
Every Thursday 6d. Registered at the G.P.O. as a newspaper

INSIDE: CLIFF & THE SHADOWS IN EUROPE

BUDDY HOLLY L.P. EXCLUSIVE, ELVIS, DIONNE, YARDBIRDS, BEATLES, POP POLL.

Peter AND Gordon

THE NEW 3-YEARS-OLD BEATLES' DISC

by PETER JONES

TONY SHERIDAN

HERE we go again! Another Beatle disc comes on sale—a disc that was made back in the pre-"Love Me Do" era. Which means that it is controversial . . . and also extremely saleable. It also happens to be a "new" sort of Beatle-disc.

Polydor have released "Ain't She Sweet," featuring John Lennon on solo vocal. Flip features "If You Love Me, Baby," with Tony Sheridan doing the lead bit and with the Beatles as accompanying group.

NOT ACCEPTED

Obviously the basis is there for a lot of interest, pop-wise. Top side has earned a Top Fifty Tip from our Disc Jury this week but personally I'm not so sure. This "Ain't She Sweet" side came from a session in Polydor's Hamburg studios some three years back . . . in the days when the Beatles were wowing them in the clubs but not really accepted back in Britain.

There was, of course, a whole lotta argument when Polydor re-released the original "My Bonnie," which had the Beatles working with Tony Sheridan. It made the charts in a small way in Britain — and was a very much bigger hit in the States.

THE BEATLES may not be pleased at this disc release ! (R.M. Pic. Dezo Hoffman)

The argument was simply this:

Was it right and proper to release a Beatles' disc from so far back? Was it fair to the boys, who had certainly developed musically in the years between that lone German session and their current top-of-the-charts form, to bring out something that they did purely as a backing group to Tony Sheridan?

This is no dig at Polydor. They paid for the session and they're entitled to do whatever they like with the discs made there. It should be remembered that the Polydor company DID record the boys in the days when nobody else wanted to know.

RESTRAINED

Me? I feel that Polydor would be failing as a commercial concern if they didn't bring out whatever Beatle material they had on file. But I can also see the Beatles' view that they don't particularly want to be reminded of the sort of thing they did in years gone by!

However, "Ain't She Sweet" is out now. John Lennon sings the old Ager-Yellen standard with a rather restrained attack and the boys fill in comfortably enough behind him. It's not Ringo Starr on drums for this was the era when Pete Best filled the drum chair.

UNIQUE

As to how the disc was found . . . well! Johnny Francis, of Polydor, read a line about the other material the company had on tape—the writer asked why it wasn't released. So he checked. And out came this particular release.

Says Johnny: "We feel that it is a unique sort of disc, with John Lennon singing the whole thing by himself. It's got the right sort of beat and there's some good guitar work on it." Both he and publicity man Ken Barnes felt that Polydor were right to bring it out, as the company had contracted the boys in the first place.

DOUBT

Of course, this is NOT a Beatle composition . . . and the Liverpool four have always insisted on doing their own material for single releases. And their sound has changed a lot in the time since EMI's George Martin first got hold of them.

It is, then, a disc of great interest . . . and commercial appeal. That there will be arguments is beyond doubt.

But I do know of two big-name disc jockeys who are anxious to give the disc all available air-time.

We simply have to wait and watch the charts.

THE BLUESWAILERS WITH THE MOD APPEAL

spell with various groups he joined the Yardbirds. Now the very interesting thing about Eric is that he hap- ... but after a while he developed a liking for R & B, and soon joined up with the Yardbirds. ... graph readers are interested in this group, the name isn't the Yardsticks. It's Y-A-R-D-B-I-R-D-S . . .

THE PICKWICKS

WELCOME

PRESS PRESENTATION LTD.
7 DENMARK STREET, W.C. 2

as their sole Press, Public Relations and Publicity Representatives

Meanwhile, back across the Pond, Atlantic Records obtained the American rights to the four remaining Beatles songs from the Hamburg sessions when it replaced MGM as the American distributor for Deutsche Grammophon's Polydor subsidiary. Atlantic entered into a five-year leasing agreement for "Sweet Georgia Brown," "Take Out Some Insurance On Me Baby," "Ain't She Sweet" and "Nobody's Child." As detailed in *The Hamburg Sessions* chapter (see pages 230-231), Atlantic was not satisfied with the quality of the masters, adding extra instruments to three of the recordings and editing the fourth. Apparently, this was done without the knowledge or permission of Deutsche Grammophon, Tony Sheridan or the Beatles. Atlantic released these recordings on its Atco subsidiary.

The first single, Atco 45-6302, featured the standard "Sweet Georgia Brown," complete with the new lyrics referencing the Beatles. The B-side was the blues song "Take Out Some Insurance On Me Baby," previously misidentified by Polydor as "If You Love Me Baby" and falsely credited as "Trad./arr. Sheridan" (see Polydor U.K. B-side above). Apparently, Polydor was unaware of Jimmy Reed's recording of the song. The disc, issued in early June, was reviewed in the June 13 Cash Box. "Atco has latched onto a master that has the Beatles backing up Tony Sheridan's vocal–a la their MGM clock date, 'My Bonnie.' This one's another oldie, 'Sweet Georgia Brown,' that Tony and the fabulous foursome belt out in sizzling rock-a-twist fashion. The kids'll love it. Undercut's a bluesy, up tempo shuffler." The kids didn't love it, realizing that "THE BEATLES With Tony Sheridan" meant a non-Beatles vocal, non-Merseybeat recording. The disc sold poorly, being listed for one week at 147 on Record World's Singles Coming Up chart on July 4.

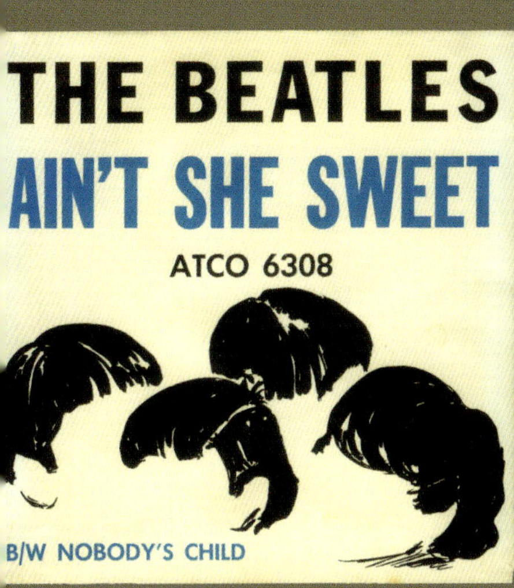

One month after issuing its first "Beatles" single, Atlantic released a second pairing of Beatles Hamburg recordings as Atco 45-6308 on July 6. The new disc featured the only song from the Hamburg sessions with a Beatle lead vocal. "Ain't She Sweet," with "Vocal by John Lennon," was coupled with Tony Sheridan's performance of "Nobody's Child." To further stimulate sales, Atlantic prepared a picture sleeve showing four featureless heads with Beatles-style hair.

The June 13 Billboard reported that "Polydor had its highest-ever advance orders for the Beatles' 'Ain't She Sweet,' recorded in Hamburg in 1961 and issued [in London] last week." The magazine mistakenly added that the disc would soon be released in the U.S. on MGM. The July 11 Record World reported that DJs in California, Atlanta and Miami obtained European copies of "Ain't She Sweet" and had "built up a tremendous demand for the record in their areas." Cash Box reviewed the single in its July 11 issue. "There's Beatles product all over the place this week and chances are Atco will make a solid impression with their entry that has John Lennon in the featured vocal slot. It's the oldie, 'Ain't She Sweet,' that the artists rock out with an infectious glee. Tony Sheridan's the solo songster on the heart-rending, slow paced folk-updated undercut, 'Nobody's Child.'" Cash Box's Radio Active chart indicated that 31% of its reporting stations had added "Ain't She Sweet" as of July 8. This grew to 71% as of July 15. Atco claimed sales of 250,000 copies in four days. Billboard charted the single for nine weeks with a peak of 19, while Cash Box reported the disc for nine weeks with a peak of 14, and Record World charted the single for ten weeks with a peak of 13. Considering the competition from 45s with songs from *A Hard Day's Night*, the single did remarkably well.

ATCO 33-169 STEREO

ain't she sweet THE BEATLES

& OTHER GREAT GROUP SOUNDS FROM ENGLAND

SIDE ONE

1. THE BEATLES
   AIN'T SHE SWEET
2. THE BEATLES WITH TONY SHERIDAN
   SWEET GEORGIA BROWN
3. THE BEATLES WITH TONY SHERIDAN
   TAKE OUT SOME INSURANCE ON ME BABY
4. THE BEATLES WITH TONY SHERIDAN
   NOBODY'S CHILD
5. THE SWALLOWS
   I WANNA BE YOUR MAN
6. THE SWALLOWS
   SHE LOVES YOU

SIDE TWO

1. THE SWALLOWS
   HOW DO YOU DO IT
2. THE SWALLOWS
   PLEASE PLEASE ME
3. THE SWALLOWS
   I'LL KEEP YOU SATISFIED
4. THE SWALLOWS
   I'M TELLING YOU NOW
5. THE SWALLOWS
   I WANT TO HOLD YOUR HAND
6. THE SWALLOWS
   FROM ME TO YOU

The incredible success of The Beatles is the most important event in popular music since Elvis Presley. The ecstatic response of teenagers to The Beatles music has opened the floodgates to an unending flow of hit recordings and hit singing groups from overseas. Known variously as the English Sound, the Liverpool Sound, or the Mersey Beat, this music has dominated our record scene for many months. Sometimes it almost seems all that is necessary to become a hit singing group is to hail from England (preferably the Liverpool area), adopt a style of dress introduced by Lord Fauntleroy, and have no contact with barbers whatsoever. But these things are only the frosting on the cake. Beneath The Beatles highly distinctive appearance are truly extraordinary talents.

The Beatles have created the sound of *today*—a sound which is unmistakably theirs, and which has inspired countless other successful groups. The impact of The Beatles has been so enormous that teenagers have learned the words to every song in The Beatles repertoire by heart. Among the many international hit recordings produced by The Beatles *Ain't She Sweet* ranks high. As a single, the recording became one of America's best-selling records.

The Beatles have been lauded time and time again for the excitement, the freshness, the vitality of their singing. Yet, no-one should overlook an equally important contribution—the great songs they have written. In this album another well-known English group, The Swallows are featured in a number of tunes written by John Lennon and Paul McCartney of The Beatles. Some of them were initially made famous by The Beatles' recordings of the tunes: *I Want To Hold Your Hand, Please Please Me, She Loves You, I Wanna Be Your Man, From Me To You. How Do You Do It* became a hit through the famous version by Gerry and The Pacemakers and Billy J. Kramer had an enormous hit with *I'll Keep You Satisfied*. Without the phenomenon of The Beatles the sound of music today would indeed be very different.

ATCO RECORDS 1841 BROADWAY, NEW YORK 23, NEW YORK

33-169

The September 26 Record World reported that Atlantic was rush-releasing a Beatles album titled after the group's "Ain't She Sweet" single. The album was released on October 5, with the music trades reviewing the LP in their October 10 issues. Record World wrote: "The Beatles are heard on four tracks and are aided and abetted by the Swallows, another crackerjack English group. The famous clan's 'Ain't She Sweet' is danceable fun. The Swallows sing a group of Lennon-McCartney tunes, and the package is jolly good." Cash Box described the album as an "ultra-commercial set featuring the famous lads from Liverpool plus the Swallows, another British crew." The magazine added that "the Beatles' legions of fans should really dig the group's top-draw renditions of such fine vintage items such as 'Sweet Georgia Brown,' 'Nobody's Child' and 'Take Out Some Insurance.'" Billboard wrote: "Four sides by the Beatles, including their hit single 'Ain't She Sweet,' 'Sweet Georgia Brown,' 'Take Out Some Insurance on Me, Baby' and 'Nobody's Child.' Add in eight songs, six of them written by Beatles Lennon and McCartney, done by another group from England, the Swallows, and you have the picture of an album that should have lots of appeal to the teens, subteens and Beatle fans of all ages."

Despite these glowing reviews, the album performed poorly, with Billboard and Cash Box ignoring it completely. Record World listed the album for nine weeks in its LP's Coming Up chart with a peak at the equivalent of number 114. The album's back liner notes on the "incredible success of The Beatles" end with a statement as true today as it was then: "Without the phenomenon of The Beatles the sound of music today would indeed be very different."

CANADIAN RELEASES

A Hard Day's Night in Canada

by Piers Hemmingsen

Early 1964 was a confusing time for disc jockeys (and record buyers) in Northern America. Although Capitol Records of Canada had been issuing Beatles records from the start, its American parent company had declined to do so, resulting in the Beatles first few singles appearing on other labels in the States. Additional confusion was caused by the release on MGM of the group's Hamburg recordings backing singer Tony Sheridan on tracks such as "My Bonnie." Paul White, national promotion manager for Capitol of Canada, attempted to set the record straight in the January 24, 1964 edition of the company's weekly promotional flyer, The Sizzle Sheet: "We notice MGM have dug up an old waxing by The Beatles, and that the group's original EMI (England) recordings are split up between Swan- Veejay, etc., etc., etc. Don't worry about matters in Canada. The Beatles best discs are only on Capitol Records up here!!"

White made sure he was putting the fans (and profits) first when it came to singles released in Canada. In addition to issuing the same discs as its parent company, Capitol of Canada copied the unique American pairings on Vee-Jay, Tollie and Swan. In The Sizzle Sheet dated March 13, 1964, White wrote: "On its way to you- the BRAND NEW Beatles single 'CAN'T BUY ME LOVE'-- It's headed right into No.1 spot...and 'TWIST AND SHOUT' as a single will be on release over the next week. We have had such a demand for this as a single release that we couldn't refuse." The latter single, issued on Capitol of Canada 72146, had "There's A Place" on the B-side as did Tollie 9001 [see page 46]. Sandy Gardiner, who two years earlier became the first North American journalist to review a Beatles disc in March 1963 with "Love Me Do," wrote about the Beatles new worldwide release in the March 21 Ottawa Journal: "Bound for the No. 1 spot in one week flat...That's THE BEATLES' new single, 'Can't Buy Me Love.' It's a twistin' R and B beater with a catchy quivering effect throughout. It'll bug you. The flip, 'You Can't Do That,' is more of a foot-stomper with Paul and John alternating vocally. The top side was recorded in Paris and the flip waxed after the boy's return from the U.S."

THE SIZZLE SHEET

FAST TALK ABOUT HOT Capitol SINGLES

From The Desk Of Paul White

Dateline: Week Ending January 24,1964 NO: 67

CLIFF REMAINS CHAMP!

Cliff Richard makes it five Canadian hits in a row with his new release. We reported last week that it had taken off faster than any previous release of Cliff's --- Here are the chart listings reported for "DON'T TALK TO HIM"........ No. 18 CFUN-Vancouver; 28 CKCM-Grand Falls; 29 CHOW-Welland; 30 CHUM-Toronto; 30 CKPT-Peterboro; 31 CFPL-London; 31 CKLB-Oshawa; 32 CKEY-Toronto; 32 CKBB-Barrie; 33 CHIQ-Hamilton; 37 CFCO-Chatham; 39 CKCK-Regina; 43 CKLC-Kingston; 43 CHNS-Halifax; 44 CHWK-CFVR-Fraser Valley; 44 CKY-Winnipeg; 45 CFRS-Simcoe; 49 CKWS-Kingston; 53 CHEX-Peterboro; 55 CFCH-North Bay; and 78 CHAB-Moose Jaw. PICK HIT WITH CKOM-Saskatoon; CJCA-Edmonton; CHOK-Sarnia; CFAC-Calgary and CKYL-Peace River.

***

BEATLEMANIA SPREADING LIKE WILDFIRE!

There isn't really much to add in this column. You read "Billboard" and "CashBox" I know, and by now you've noticed "She Loves You" and "Please Please Me" are starting to move like crazy and "I Want To Hold Your Hand" is No. 1 after three weeks.

We notice MGM have dug up an old waxing by The Beatles, and that the group's original EMI (England) recordings are split up between Swan - Veejay, etc., etc., etc. Don't worry about matters in Canada. The Beatles best discs are only on Capitol Records up here!! There hasn't been anything so exciting around here since Cliff Richard crashed the Canadian scene . . . . , To say that everyone at Canadian-Capitol HQ are "Beatles Mad" is a SLIGHT understatement!

We feel The Beatles are more than 9 day wonders. Teenagers all over the World have joined the 'CULT' - people keep referring to them as "four Elvis P's" - but we think the Beatles represent more to teenagers in that they reflect something of themselves.. . . mischievous rebels, enjoying themselves. The hero worship has spread to the States and by the time the boys arrive in New York for their Ed Sullivan Show we expect their fans will have purchased all the tickets for the Carnegie Hall concert on February 13th. "I Want To Hold Your Hand" is climbing onto Canadian charts in a hurry, while "She Loves You" and "Roll Over Beethoven" continue to dominate the top chart positions here. For instance, "She Loves You" is No. 1 at CHUM-Toronto; CKY-Winnipeg; CKLC-Kingston; CHIQ-Hamilton; CFOS-Owen Sound; CFRS-Simcoe; CHEX-Peterborough; Gene McCormick Show CHUB-Nanaimo. "Roll Over Beethoven" is No. 1 with CKEY-Toronto - No. 2 CHUM-Toronto and 2 CKPT-Peterboro.

The Beatles, this week, held down No. 1 and 2 positions with singles and their "Beatlemania" album in Toronto. This is the only time in Toronto's history that an artist or group has had the top two singles and top album at the same time.

CHUM-Toronto's chart capitalized on the Beatle craze in Toronto with a front page photo of the group and a back page spread of four CHUM deejays complete with wild Beatle wigs painted on by the CHUM artist. The CHUM chart now has an 108,000 weekly circulation!

-OVER-

THE SIZZLE SHEET

FAST TALK ABOUT HOT Capitol SINGLES

Dateline: Week Ending March 13/64 NO:74 From The Desk Of Paul White

TWO NEW BEATLE RELEASES

On its way to you - the BRAND NEW Beatles single "CAN'T BUY ME LOVE" -- It's headed right into No. 1 spot . . . and "TWIST AND SHOUT" as a single will be on release over the next week. We have had such a demand for this as a single release that we couldn't refuse.

"ALL MY LOVING" is turning out to be the giant of all Beatles discs. It's the biggest chart jumper with all of you and both teenagers and adults are buying the 45. BOB WOOD writing from CKCK REGINA says the station has had no choice but to chart "Loving" at No.1 due to the sides popularityover the last few weeks - this was No.4 then,No.1 at CKCK!

FROSTY FORST AT CFUN-VANCOUVER reports the side clicking at No,1 also after two weeks; and the group at CKYL-PEACE RIVER also show "Loving" as No.1 (with 4 more Capitol hits-Beatles) - at CHUM-Toronto it jumped from 30 to No.4.....

In closing this weeks gab about the Beatles, I just want to say that there has been NO let up on Beatle sales on any of their singles .... it's a fantastic situation!

****

ALSO BIG -- BIG -- BIG !!

E DAVE CLARK FIVE and "GLAD ALL OVER" -- after last weeks successful Ed Sullivan pearance the calls and letters started to pour in for fan clubs, pics, etc. "Glad All r" is now one of our top ten best sellers.

"HIPPY HIPPY SHAKE" by THE SWINGING BLUE JEANS is our next bet for the Top 10. It's on surveys like:- 9 CKYL-Peace River; 10 - CFUN-Vancouver; 31 - CFCN-Calgary; 34 CHSJ-St. John; 34 CHNS-Halifax; 36 CFAC-Calgary; 36 CJCA-Edmonton; 43 CKY-Winnipeg; 43 CFCO-Chatham; 46 CHEX-Peterborough; 47 CKWS-Kingston; 50 CKLC-Kingston 77 CHAB-Moose Jaw; Pick Hit - CFGP-Grande Prairie; Pick To Click at CJME-Regina; Extra at CKLB-Oshawa; Wax To Watch CKCK-Regina; . . . It's all the rage in the States -- now No.50 in "CashBox" and No. 61 "Billboard".

ONE TO WATCH . . . as reported in last weeks "Sizzle" - "HE WALKS LIKE A MAN" by JODY MILLER is getting ... attention -- and deservedly so. Showing up at 3... land; 50 CFUN-Vancouver; 51 CKWS-Kin... Regina; and extra at CKLB-Osh...

CAN'T BUY ME LOVE
(John Lennon–Paul McCartney)
Capitol RECORDS
RECORDED IN ENGLAND
Northern Songs Music, Ltd. ASCAP–2:12
5150
(45–X44914)
THE BEATLES

YOU CAN'T DO THAT
(John Lennon–Paul McCartney)
Capitol RECORDS
RECORDED IN ENGLAND
Northern Songs Music, Ltd. ASCAP–2:33
5150
(45–X44913)
THE BEATLES

"Can't Buy Me Love" sold a respectable 91,369 copies in Canada in 1964 following its March 13 release. It topped the surveys issued by CFPL in London, Ontario, CJSP in Leamington, Ontario, CKGM in Montreal, CKRC in Winnipeg and CFRA in Ottawa. However, the single stalled at number two on Vancouver's CFUN chart and at three on Toronto's CHUM Hit Parade. This relatively poor performance was due to being sandwiched between the chart-topping Canadian 45 "All My Loving," released on March 9, and "Twist And Shout," issued on March 16. It was also competing with several other Beatles singles. The March 23, 1964 CHUM Hit Parade shows the competition that "Can't Buy Me Love" was facing when it debuted at number 14. That week the top three records were "All My Loving"/"This Boy," "I Want To Hold Your Hand"/"I Saw Her Standing There," and "She Loves You." It was also competing with the first three Beatles singles, "Love Me Do" (at #8), "Please Please Me" (at #7) and "From Me To You" (at #10), all of which had flopped upon their initial 1963 release in Canada but were now selling strong and receiving considerable air play.

As for the "Twist And Shout" 45, its sales were hampered by the previous and continuing strong sales of the *Twist And Shout* LP, which contained both sides of the single. Still, it sold an impressive 97,405 copies in 1964 and reached number five in the CHUM Hit Parade during its ten weeks on the chart. The single fared even better at Vancouver's CFUN (#2), Edmonton's CJCA (#3) and Ottawa's CFRA (#4). It was a Top Ten hit at Leamington's CJSP, Winnipeg's CKRC and London's CFPL.

By April 1964, Capitol Records' Hollywood headquarters had growing concerns over the large quantities of Capitol of Canada singles being imported into the United States. These discs included the Beatles first EMI single, "Love Me Do" b/w "P.S. I Love You," and even more problematic, two unique Canadian singles featuring "Roll Over Beethoven" b/w "Please Mister Postman" and "All My Loving" b/w "This Boy." The April 18 Cash Box reported that Capitol of Canada would no longer issue future Beatles releases that were not being made available simultaneously in the United States. Paul White later confirmed that the label discontinued preparing special Canadian records after being ordered by its parent company to conform all releases to the U.S. records. While "All My Loving" would be the last unique Canadian single, the company was allowed to copy U.S. releases on other labels. In addition, circumstances necessitated the modification of the next Beatles album issued by Capitol in the States.

CHUM HIT PARADE

this week | last week | week of MARCH 23, 1964

	Title	Artist	Label	Last week
1.	ALL MY LOVIN' /THIS BOY	The Beatles	Capitol	4
2.	HOLD YOUR HAND/SAW HER STANDING THERE	The Beatles	Capitol	1
3.	SHE LOVES YOU	The Beatles	Capitol	2
4.	DAWN (GO AWAY)	The 4 Seasons	Philips	3
5.	GLAD ALL OVER	Dave Clark 5	Capitol	11
6.	FUN FUN FUN	The Beach Boys	Capitol	10
7.	PLEASE PLEASE ME	The Beatles	Capitol	5
8.	LOVE ME DO	The Beatles	Capitol	9
9.	NAVY BLUE	Diane Renay	20th Cent.	7
10.	FROM ME TO YOU	The Beatles	Capitol	8
11.	HELLO DOLLY	LOUIS ARMSTRONG	KAPP	12
12.	BIRD DANCE BEAT	TRASHMEN	APEX	14
13.	YOUNG AND IN LOVE	CHRIS CROSBY	MGM	15
14.	CAN'T BUY ME LOVE	THE BEATLES	CAPITOL	—
15.	CALIFORNIA SUN	THE RIVIERAS	DELTA	6
16.	MY HEART BELONGS TO ONLY YOU	BOBBY VINTON	EPIC	17
17.	HI-HEEL SNEAKERS	TOMMY TUCKER	CHECKER	21
18.	THE WAITING GAME/THINK	BRENDA LEE	DECCA	33
19.	KISSIN' COUSINS/IT HURTS ME	ELVIS PRESLEY	RCA	18
20.	WHITE ON WHITE	DANNY WILLIAMS	U.A.	29
21.	ROLL OVER BEETHOVEN	THE BEATLES	CAPITOL	13
22.	TELL IT ON THE MOUNTAIN	PETER, PAUL & MARY	W. BROS.	28
23.	BLUE WINTER	CONNIE FRANCIS	MGM	25
24.	PENETRATION	THE PYRAMIDS	BEST	31
25.	BEATLE HAIRCUT	DONNA LYNN	CAPITOL	16
26.	YOU DON'T OWN ME	LESLIE GORE	MERCURY	20
27.	THE HIPPY HIPPY SHAKE	SWINGING BLUE JEANS	CAPITOL	38
28.	BROTHERHOOD OF MAN	THE CHUMINGBIRDS	QUALITY	24
29.	I ONLY WANT TO BE WITH YOU	DUSTY SPRINGFIELD	PHILIPS	22
30.	SANDY	JOHNNY CRAWFORD	DELFI	23
31.	SHANGRI-LA	ROBERT MAXWELL	DECCA	42
32.	DIANE	THE BACHELORS	LONDON	46
33.	FOREVER	PETER DRAKE	MERCURY	40
34.	WE LOVE THE BEATLES	THE VERNONS GIRLS	LONDON	34
35.	STAY	THE 4 SEASONS	REO	—
36.	NEEDLES AND PINS	THE SEARCHERS	PYE	35
37.	STARDUST	TEMPO/STEVENS	ATCO	27
38.	MILLER'S CAVE	BOBBY BARE	RCA	19
39.	WE LOVE YOU BEATLES	THE CAREFREES	LONDON	—
40.	FUNNY LITTLE CLOWN	BOBBY GOLDSBORO	U.A.	30
41.	WHO DO YOU LOVE	THE SAPPHIRES	REO	36
42.	BOOK OF LOV[illegible]	[illegible]AINDROPS	JUBILEE	—
43.	SUSPICION[illegible]	[illegible]FFORD	REO	44
44.	YOU WE[illegible]	[illegible]	VANGUARD	48
45.	PRIVA[illegible]	[illegible]EWS	TAMARAC	—
46.	UND[illegible]	[illegible]	COLUMBIA	41
47.	W[illegible]	[illegible]	TAMLA	50
48.	[illegible]	[illegible]	PHILIPS	—
49	[illegible]	[illegible]	[illegible]RKWAY	26
50	[illegible] HERE TON[illegible]	[illegible]	[illegible]SCENDO	—

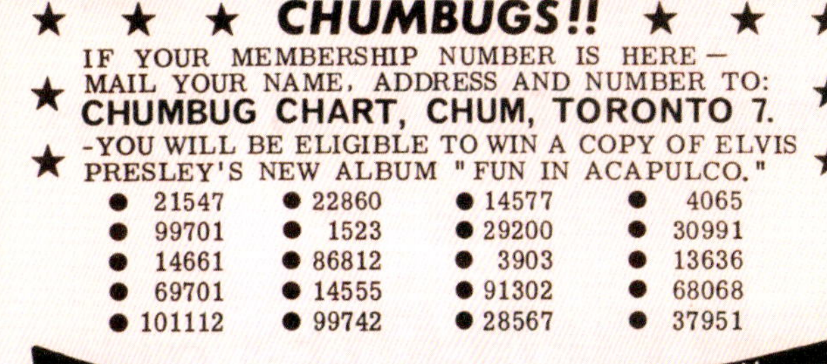

★ ★ ★ **CHUMBUGS!!** ★ ★ ★

IF YOUR MEMBERSHIP NUMBER IS HERE – MAIL YOUR NAME, ADDRESS AND NUMBER TO: **CHUMBUG CHART, CHUM, TORONTO 7.** -YOU WILL BE ELIGIBLE TO WIN A COPY OF ELVIS PRESLEY'S NEW ALBUM "FUN IN ACAPULCO."

21547	22860	14577	4065
99701	1523	29200	30991
14661	86812	3903	13636
69701	14555	91302	68068
101112	99742	28567	37951

CHUMDINGER #14

(THE RECORD THAT MADE THE BIGGEST JUMP THIS WEEK)

THE MOOSE PARADE

1. UNDERSTAND YOUR MAN — JOHNNY CASH
2. SAGINAW, MICHIGAN — LEFTY FRIZZELL
3. MILLER'S CAVE — BOBBY BARE
4. B.J. THE D.J. — STONEWALL JACKSON
5. MOLLY — EDDY ARNOLD

CHUM'S ALBUM INDEX

1. TWIST AND SHOUT — THE BEATLES – CAPITOL
2. BEATLEMANIA — THE BEATLES – CAPITOL
3. IN THE WIND — PETER, PAUL & MARY – W. BROS.
4. FUN IN ACAPULCO — ELVIS PRESLEY – RCA
5. HONEY IN THE HORN — AL HIRT – RCA

THERE'S A PLACE
(McCartney–Lennon)
Capitol
REG'D. TRADE MARK
RECORDS
RECORDED IN GREAT BRITAIN
W. Hofer
1:50
72146
(CC2–72146)
THE BEATLES

Confusion reigned supreme in Canada with the release in April 1964 of two different Beatles albums with nearly identical covers. Capitol in the States was preparing a Beatles LP featuring the five cover songs that were not included on *Meet The Beatles!*, along with four tracks previously issued on singles and two Beatles recordings that had yet to be released anywhere in the world, "Long Tall Sally" and "I Call Your Name." The album had an eye-catching cover and was named *The Beatles' Second Album*. This put Paul White in a quandary. The record could not be released in Canada with that title because this would be the Canadian label's third Beatles LP, not its second. White knew that a third Beatles album would be a good bet for his company and Canadian record buyers, and that he needed to modify the track line-up. He named the album *Long Tall Sally* after the group's dynamic recording of the Little Richard rocker. The album's 22" x 8¾" promotional poster noted that this was, in fact, "The Beatles Third Album" [in Canada].

The disc opens with the Canadian album debut of both sides of the single "I Want To Hold Your Hand" and "I Saw Her Standing There." The next three selections, "You Really Got A Hold On Me," "Devil In Her Heart" and "Roll Over Beethoven," had previously been issued on the *Beatlemania!* LP. The side closes with "Misery," a song that had yet to be released in Canada after being left off the *Twist And Shout* LP. As with the U.S. album, Side Two opens with "Long Tall Sally" and "I Call Your Name," followed by "Please Mister Postman," which was also on *Beatlemania!* The last three tracks, "This Boy," "I'll Get You" and "You Can't Do That," were B-sides making their Canadian album debut. Although only three of the record's 12 songs were new to Canada, an additional five had yet to appear on a Canadian LP. Inexplicably, White left off the B-side "Thank You Girl," which was on *The Beatles' Second Album* and had not been on any Canadian LP. It would have been a better choice than "Devil In Her Heart." By the time the *Long Tall Sally* LP was issued in mono only on April 27, record stores in Toronto and Montreal had been selling and were well stocked with imported copies of *The Beatles' Second Album*. As the two covers had the same photos, fonts and layout, this caused a "ball of confusion" for Canadian Beatles fans. Montreal's CKGM featured the cover of *The Beatles' Second Album* on the front page of its April 25 survey, naming the record its "LP of the Week." Radio station CFPL in London, Ontario listed the top three albums in its May 1 LP chart as *Long Tall Sally*, *Twist And Shout*, and *Beatlemania!* Toronto's CHUM charted *Long Tall Sally* for eight weeks on its album chart, including five non-consecutive weeks at number one. The album sold 88,689 units from 1964 through 1967, about half that of each of the first two albums.

THE BEATLES THIRD ALBUM

In compliance with its parent company's mandate to conform with all U.S. releases, Capitol of Canada issued the American *Four By The Beatles* EP on or about May 11. As the disc merely contained the two unique Canadian singles featuring "Roll Over Beethoven," "Please Mister Postman," "All My Loving" and "This Boy," there was little reason for Canadians to buy the record. Capitol of Canada did not bother to promote the disc. Nor did Paul White mention it in The Sizzle Sheet. It probably sold only a few thousand units, if that.

On March 23, Vee-Jay issued the single "Do You Want To Know A Secret" b/w "Thank You Girl" in the U.S. This led to air play of the A-Side by CKLW in Windsor, Ontario, whose listeners could also tune in to Detroit radio stations located across Lake Michigan. Canadian DJs did not need the single as they could pull the song from the *Twist And Shout* album. CKLW listed "Do You Want To Know A Secret" as a new entry at number 15 in its March 24 survey. The song peaked at number three on the April 14 chart. Other stations began to follow CKLW's lead, creating demand for a Canadian 45. In the May 15 Sizzle Sheet, Paul White wrote that the song would be released as a Canadian single, explaining: "We've had so many requests for this one on a 45 we've decided to release as soon as possible. Most of you have listed the song on your charts (from album Twist & Shout) anyway, so you won't be too excited." White duplicated the Vee-Jay single with the release of Capitol of Canada 72159 on May 26. As White had low expectations, he most likely had only 5,000 copies pressed, making it the one of the rarest Capitol of Canada Beatles singles.

Shortly after the May 21 release of the Swan single in America pairing "Sie Liebt Dich" and "I'll Get You," Paul White used the May 29 Sizzle Sheet to alert disc jockeys of the record: "We'll tell you-- SOON-- The Beatles singing She Loves You in GERMAN-- Don't smile there-- the disc (Sie Liebt Dich) is selling well in the States, in fact it will be on the Billboard survey next week!" After the disc was issued as Capitol of Canada 72162 on June 15, White informed readers of the June 19 Sizzle Sheet that the Beatles German disc was out and sure to be "a favourite with your listeners." The next week he wrote that the record "will be a real sizzler!" Although "Sie Liebt Dich" stalled at number 20 in the CHUM Hit Parade, it made CFUN's Top Ten in Vancouver, British Columbia, was a Top Five hit at CHSJ in St. John, New Brunswick, and topped the survey published by CKCK in Regina, Saskatchewan! Sales figures are not available for the record, but it probably sold under 5,000 units as did the "Do You Want To Know A Secret" single.

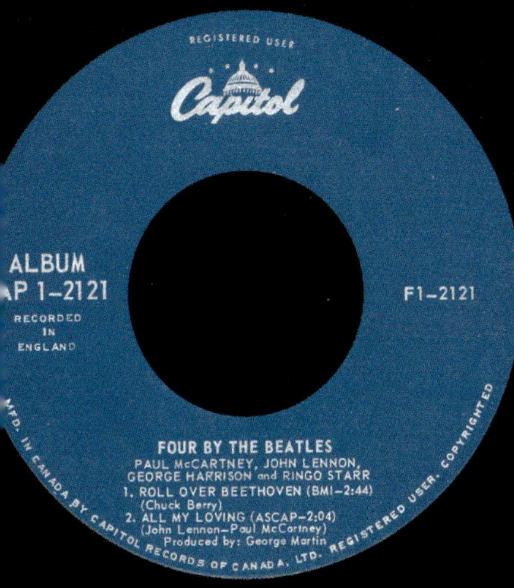
REGISTERED USER
Capitol
ALBUM
EAP 1-2121
RECORDED IN ENGLAND
F1-2121
FOUR BY THE BEATLES
PAUL McCARTNEY, JOHN LENNON, GEORGE HARRISON and RINGO STARR
1. ROLL OVER BEETHOVEN (BMI-2:44) (Chuck Berry)
2. ALL MY LOVING (ASCAP-2:04) (John Lennon-Paul McCartney)
Produced by: George Martin
MFD. IN CANADA BY CAPITOL RECORDS OF CANADA, LTD. REGISTERED USER. COPYRIGHTED

FOUR BY THE BEATLES
ROLL OVER BEETHOVEN × THIS BOY
ALL MY LOVING × PLEASE, MR. POSTMAN
EAP 1-2121
Capitol
Produced by GEORGE MARTIN

REGISTERED USER
Capitol
ALBUM
EAP 1-2121
RECORDED IN ENGLAND
F2-2121
FOUR BY THE BEATLES
PAUL McCARTNEY, JOHN LENNON, GEORGE HARRISON and RINGO STARR
1. THIS BOY (ASCAP-2:11) (John Lennon-Paul McCartney)
2. PLEASE MISTER POSTMAN (BMI-2:34) (Holland)
Produced by: George Martin
MFD. IN CANADA BY CAPITOL RECORDS OF CANADA, LTD. REGISTERED USER. COPYRIGHTED

DO YOU WANT TO KNOW A SECRET?
(McCartney-Lennon)
Capitol
RECORDS
RECORDED IN GREAT BRITAIN
W. Hofer
1:55
72159
(7XCE 17330A)
THE BEATLES

THANK YOU GIRL
(McCartney-Lennon)
Capitol
RECORDS
RECORDED IN GREAT BRITAIN
Conrad Pub. Co. Inc.
2:00
72159
(7XCE 17330)
THE BEATLES

SIE LIEBT DICH
(She Loves You)
(Lennon-McCartney-Nicolas-Montague)
Capitol
RECORDS
RECORDED IN EUROPE
Northern Songs Ltd.
2:24
72162
(7XBE 1506)
DIE BEATLES

I'LL GET YOU
(Lennon-McCartney)
Capitol
RECORDS
RECORDED IN GREAT BRITAIN
Northern Songs Ltd.
2:00
72162
(7XCE 17396)
THE BEATLES

By June of 1964, Canadian Beatles fans were well aware that the group would soon be starring in their own film. As early as mid-January of that year, Trudy Medcalf, president of the Ontario Beatles Fan Club, had been spreading the news of the Beatles first movie to members of the fan cub in print and to a larger audience with appearances via Toronto's CHUM on the Paunch & Trudy Show with disc jockey Dave Johnson. In addition, Canadians could read about the movie in issues of the weekly British music magazines flown in from England. In February, fans could see the Beatles on CBC-TV on The Ed Sullivan Show and on the February 21 edition of Telescope Portraits in Television with Fletcher Markle, which broadcast a half-hour edit of Maysles Brothers documentary of the Beatles first U.S. visit under the title "Stalking The Beatles." On March 14 and 15, fans in many cities could go to the theater to watch a closed circuit television replay of the Beatles being pelted with jelly beans at their February 11 concert at the Washington Coliseum. In April, some movie goers got to see the Pathé News color film short *The Beatles Come To Town*, which featured the group's November 20, 1963 concert at the ABC Theatre in Manchester, England. In Toronto, Calgary and other cities, it was an "added attraction" to the Yul Brynner film *Flight From Ashiya*.

United Artists conducted an experiment in Toronto by selling advance tickets to see *A Hard Day's Night* two months ahead of the film's release. On June 13, four Toronto theaters sold out a combined 3,028 tickets for special preview showings of the film in just 90 minutes. Based on this result, UA informed branch managers that it was launching a North American campaign to "duplicate the Toronto success in every city, town and hamlet" in which the movie would play. Although the film would not be in theaters until August, Canadians would hear the movie's music well before then. United Artists officially released its soundtrack LP on June 26, but it most likely did not appear in stores until early July. It had the same track listing as the U.S. album. The UA soundtrack LP topped CHUM's Album Index in its second week on the chart, July 13, and remained the number one LP for 18 weeks. The album was initially issued only in mono. The stereo version was not released until early 1965. The mono album sold between 200,000 and 250,000 units, while stereo sales were about 5,000. UA also released the same two George Martin singles that were issued in the States. Some pressings of the "Ringo's Theme (This Boy)"/"And I Love Her" 45 deceptively list the recording artist as THE BEATLES, causing some fans to buy it by mistake. All of the second singles with "A Hard Day's Night" and "I Should Have Known Better" list the artist as George Martin & His Orchestra. Neither disc sold very well.

the
PAUNCH & TRUDY
show

...week nights at 8 p.m., DAVE JOHNSON and TRUDY MEDCALF (president of the only official Beatle Fan Club in Ontario) present 30 minutes of BEATLE music and news !!

★★★★★★★★★★

CHUM Teen Product of the Week
Helps clear skin fast

Paul White used the July 3 Sizzle Sheet to explain why Capitol didn't have the soundtrack album to the Beatles film *A Hard Day's Night*. "Well folks the rights to this one were given to United Artists way back last year when the movie idea first came along.......it was sort of a package deal. We aren't too unhappy about the situation though because Capitol does have the rights to all the material for release as singles........still with us?.......So we've already in their [sic] pitching with our first one- the title song......'A Hard Day's Night'.....and there will be more to come very shortly." As was the case in the States, the lead single from the film had "I Should Have Known Better" as the B-side. CHUM listed both sides of the single at number one. "A Hard Day's Night" topped the charts throughout Canada, including Vancouver's CFUN, Montreal's CKGM, Winnipeg's CKRC, Edmonton's CJCA, St. John's CHSJ, Hamilton's CHIQ and the Ottawa Citizen Platter Poll. RPM Weekly, which debuted in February 1964 and ran its first national "Top Forty-5s" listing on June 21, charted the song for 11 weeks, including two at the top. The record sold 129,314 copies in 1964.

The July 10 Sizzle Sheet alerted DJs to two more 45s, "I'll Cry Instead" b/w "I'm Happy Just To Dance With You" and "And I Love Her" b/w "If I Fell," calling them "two more prospects for No. 1 position!" "I'll Cry Instead" peaked as follows: CHUM (#20); Vancouver's CFUN (#4); Sault Ste. Marie's CKCY (#9); Montreal's CKGM (#13); and RPM Weekly (#16). The Ottawa Citizen's Platter Poll charted "I Just Want To Dance With You" [sic] at number two. The disc sold 27,258 units in 1964. "And I Love Her" peaked as follows: CHUM (#15); Montreal's CKGM (#25); and RPM Weekly (#20). "And I Love Her"/"If I Fell" charted as follows: Vancouver's CFUN (#3); St. John's CHSJ (#21); and Winnipeg's CKRC (#22). CHNS in Halifax charted "If I Fell"/"And I Love Her" at number one. The single sold 40,936 copies in 1964.

White wrote about the new Capitol LP in the July 10 Sizzle Sheet. "We sure aren't wasting any time in releasing a NEW Beatles album. Next week the boys will be swinging your way with an LP entitled 'SOMETHING NEW'...it's packed with goodies - songs from the United Artists movie 'A Hard Day's Night,' plus SIX - SIX - NEW SONGS -- and they're dandies!! Watch us go on this one...and watch the way your listeners swing towards OUR ALBUM once they hear the fabulous songs!!" The next week, White added: "It's Out NOW! The latest and greatest LP by the fabulous foursome–and what a package." CHUM charted *Something New* for 23 weeks, including four weeks at number one and 11 weeks in the second spot. The album was initially issued only in mono and had sold 80,703 units by the end of 1967.

THE SIZZLE SHEET
FAST TALK ABOUT HOT Capitol SINGLES

Dateline: Week Ending July 3, 1964 From The Desk of Paul White

THE BEATLE MOVIE STORY:

We've been asked by a few people this week just how come we don't have the soundtrack album to the Beatles' "Hard Day's Night" movie. Well folks the rights to this one were given to United Artists way back last year when the movie idea first came along ....it was sort of a package deal. We aren't too unhappy about the situation though because Capitol does have the rights to all the material for release as singles ....still with us?.......So we're already in their pitching with our first one - the title song......"A Hard Day's Night".....and there are more to come very shortly.

BRITAIN REALLY DOES RULE THE CHARTS!!

Here's an interesting news item. Do yo
the U.K. charts for the first half of 1
Express" shows that only one American a
Top 10. The analysis was worked out on
week to a No. 1 spot, down to 1 point f
interesting - because it shows that art
label have dominated the survey.......t

1 - THE BEATLES........710 points:
4 - CILLA BLACK........467 points:
8 - GERRY/PACEMAKERS...412 points:

Look at that.....6 out of the Top 10 ar
of you have shown much interest in, are
to their "HERE I GO AGAIN" single (it r

THINGS ARE JUMPING!!!

Gazooks...we're really in their maintai
you should be charting that are HOT---H
really started this one moving!

NOBODY I KNOW/ PETER & GORDON have that

YOU DON'T KNOW/ NANCY WILSON - our top
1964. Initial reaction has marked this

I LOVE YOU BABY/ FREDDIE AND THE DREAME
then a rouser at CFUN, Vancouver, ----t
States.

THE COURT OF KING CARACTACUS/ Rolf Harr
sure can pick the hits!

YOU'RE MY WORLD/ CILLA BLACK--------Onta
......the Epstein stable scores again!!

SOMETHING NEW
THE BEATLES

I'LL CRY INSTEAD
TELL ME WHY
AND I LOVE HER
I'M HAPPY JUST TO DANCE WITH YOU
IF I FELL
THINGS WE SAID TODAY
ANY TIME AT ALL
WHEN I GET HOME
SLOW DOWN
MATCHBOX
KOMM, GIB MIR DEINE HAND

Needless to say this great Beatles album for Capitol is wonderful in the very special and exclusively marvelous Beatles way! Here are the latest, greatest new Beatles hits and all but two are written by those two busy Beatles, John Lennon and Paul McCartney. One of the most popular is "Komm, Gib Mir Deine Hand", the German-language version the boys made of their smash Capitol hit, "I Want to Hold Your Hand".

And now the Beatles are movie stars! You wouldn't think they could get any more famous, but now they've made a motion picture that's a box office sensation from Tokyo to Toledo. And here in this album are five hits from that movie, United Artists' "A Hard Day's Night". Now their fans can see John, George, Paul and Ringo giant-size on the screen and play the big hits from the picture on their HiFi and Stereo sets between trips to the movies.

Mono only (F2108, $4.20)

5076 produced by art bell press limited, montreal, que.

THE SIZZLE SHEET
FAST TALK ABOUT HOT Capitol SINGLES

Dateline: Week Ending July 10,1964 NO:91 From the Desk of Paul White

THE LABEL THAT NEVER STANDS STILL!

We sure aren't wasting any time in releasing a NEW Beatles album. Next week the boys will be swinging your way with an LP entitled "SOMETHING NEW" . . . it's packed with goodies - songs from their United Artists movie "Hard Days Night", plus SIX - SIX - NEW SONGS -- and they're dandies!!

Watch us go on this one . . . and watch the way your listeners swing towards OUR ALBUM once they hear the fabulous songs!!

BEATLE SINGLES
****

/A HARD DAYS NIGHT/has started off at a great rate . . . it's already charted by CHUM and CKEY Toronto; CJCA-Edmonton; CKY-Winnipeg; CHAB-Moose Jaw; CFUN-Vancouver and CKWS-Kingston.

Next week two more 45's will be on their way to you -- the couplings are I'LL CRY INSTEAD b/w I'M HAPPY JUST TO DANCE WITH YOU and AND I LOVE HER b/w IF I FELL --- two more prospects for No.1 position!

SIE LIEBT DICH is galloping along at a nice pace . . . it's a big chart item too - 20 CHUM-Toronto; 27 CKY-Winnipeg; 7 CHOW-Welland; 13 CHLO-St. Thomas; 51 CHAB-Moose Jaw; 7 CJCH-Halifax; 4 CHSJ-St. John; 20 CFPL-London; 3 CKCK-Regina; 30 CKPT-Peterboro; 47 CJSP-Leamington; 20 CKEY-Toronto; 30 CKBB-Barrie; 9 CFUN-Vancouver and 29 CKWS-Kingston.

***

+++++ HOLLIES STARTING TO MOVE +++++

getting a lot of attention now . .
GP-Grande Prairie; CKLB-Oshawa;
ifax; CKLY-Lindsay; CKCK-R

***

NANCY WILSON

YOU DON'T
with this s
Nancy's singl
49 CKPT-Peterbo
Hit at CKCK-Reg

happy
astic
ton;
n;

singer's cha
esponse. Stations
C-Quebec West; 42 CHUM-
S-Halifax; also . . Pick
Deer.

...over..

A HARD DAY'S NIGHT
(John Lennon–Paul McCartney)
From the motion picture "A Hard Day's Night"
A United Artists Release
Capitol REG'D. TRADE MARK RECORDS
RECORDED IN ENGLAND
Maclen Music, Inc.
BMI–2:28
5222
(45–X45035)
THE BEATLES

I SHOULD HAVE KNOWN BETTER
(John Lennon–Paul McCartney)
From the motion picture "A Hard Day's Night"
A United Artists Release
Capitol REG'D. TRADE MARK RECORDS
RECORDED IN ENGLAND
Maclen Music, Inc.
BMI–2:42
5222
(45–X45036)
THE BEATLES

The Beatles Greatest

SOMETHING NEW!

Songs From Their Movie
Plus 6 Other Hits

"MATCHBOX" "SLOW DOWN"
"I WANT TO HOLD YOUR HAND" (*Sung in German*)
"ANYTIME AT ALL" "WHEN I GET HOME"
"THINGS WE SAID TODAY"

from

PAUL McCARTNEY

GEORGE HARRISON

JOHN LENNON

RINGO STARR

A Hard Day's Night had its Canadian premiere at special 9:30 AM previews on Wednesday, August 5, at selected theaters in Vancouver, British Columbia, with regular showings starting the following day at five theaters and two drive-ins. Les Wedman of the Vancouver Sun reported that evening on the morning premiere at the Vogue (see ticket below), where youngsters began lining up at 5:30 AM. Most were girls with an average age of 12. Carolyn Beavington, aged 15, was one of the first in line. "We just have to get in the front row of the balcony. Then we're going to scream and scream." Equally thrilled was 71-year-old Elsa Baumann, an avid collector of Beatles records and literature. "They're such nice boys and I like the way they sing." The program began with a comedy short and a cartoon, both of which were met with screams of protest. And then the Beatles appeared on the screen. According to Wedman: "What had been a solid wall of noise turned to bedlam, sheer, utter, uncontrollable stupidity. A Hard Day's Night might just as well have been a silent movie. All you could hear were screams. Some of the girls burst into tears...The Beatles didn't have a chance against their howling fans to prove whether they're freaks or actors." Wedman walked out after 20 minutes–not because he wanted to, but for fear his eardrums would split. The headline of his article appropriately read: "New Beatles Movie Opens; Was It Good? Who Knows?"

In the August 11 Vancouver Sun, Wedman wrote that he was rested after "retreating from an impenetrable wall of noise," so he went back to "unfriendly territory [on] Sunday night [August 10] for a complete look" at the Beatle film in a half-empty and relatively quiet theater. This time, he knew the film was good. "Everyone knows The Beatles are this decade's show business phenomena, but until you see them in this film, there's no realizing that more phenomenally, they are the freshest, brashest bunch of natural comedians to hit the screen in years." The film was "easy-to-take entertainment" regardless of your view of their vocal and instrumental ability. "This is no cheap, shoddy attempt to capitalize on or perpetuate their popularity, but it is an honest–and mighty talented–job of movie making by Walter Shenson, Richard Lester and Alun Owen." The film "vividly portrays the pressures and problems that make John, Paul, George and Ringo prisoners of their own lucrative fame." The group's repartee, wisecracks and insults "have spontaneity that adds spark and zest to the proceedings." Wilfrid Brambell, as Paul's fictitious grandfather, is a "deceptive combination of helpless old man and troublemaker who bugs The Beatles but puts life into the comedy." Wedman concludes: "If A Hard Day's Night is an indication of what a breeze The Beatles can stir up in their first movie, it's a certainty we can expect an encore or two before their cock-eyed brand of fun goes stale."

Writing in the August 8 edition of a competing Vancouver newspaper, The Province, columnist Malcolm Turnbull was not overly impressed by the Beatles first film. Turnbull admitted that the 300 youngsters at the theater ("most of whom sat through two shows") were "ecstatic over the performance of their idols." However, the rest of his comments only played favor to the film's senior actor: "The producers have forgone any semblance of a plot and John, Paul, George, and Ringo just function in the manner we have come to know. What propels the flimsy craft along is the introduction of Paul's grandfather, an overage rake played with considerable skill by Wilfred Brambell."

Michael Kostelnue's review in the August 7 Winnipeg Free Press labeled the Beatles movie "a cinematic curiosity." Kostelnue found the film to be a missed opportunity: "A Hard Day's Night is many things but it is not an artistically successful movie." However, he did enjoy certain parts of the film, including some excellent slap-stick scenes such as the keystone cops sequence and John's bath tub segment. He also praised the high spirits and cheerful camaraderie of youth captured in the sequence where the Beatles cavort together in a field.

But Kostelnue complains that Alun Owen's comic dialog does not match the visual comedy. "It consists of smart-alecky wisecracks that are mostly of the intelligence level of Mad Magazine." [Considering that fictional road manager Shake is shown reading the *Son Of Mad* compilation paperback in the film's train scene, the Beatles would certainly consider that a compliment rather than a put down.] Kostelnue writes that the "low quality of the verbal humour" and the excessive time devoted to musical numbers prevents the film from rising to a level of excellence. As for the Beatles, they "appear to have a lively sense of some of the ridiculous aspects of our society, and a mocking irreverence that can extend even to them...[and] are not the bland, cautious, status-seeking youths that are all too prevalent in our society." He recommends the film for those "interested in how our youths maintain their high spirits in our perhaps too serious, over-planned society." But he warns: "you had better be prepared for the possibility of having one of those high-spirited youths screaming her head off in the seat next to you."

A Hard Day's Night opened in Toronto, Ontario at special night showings in four theaters on August 11, with its regular opening the following day in 11 theaters. Nathan Cohen opened his August 12 column in the Toronto Daily Star by telling readers that the film is "bright and breezy entertainment." Cohen attended the movie amongst "a swarm of jumping, swaying, sighing, hand-wringing, temple-clutching, ecstatic girls," which was "a test of nerves, as well as one's eardrums," but that he enjoyed it was "an indication that the film is made of worthwhile material." He thought the decision to make the movie a "half-documentary, half-fictitious day and a half in the life of the world's most adulated singing and playing quartet was inspired." Although he believed comparison to the Marx Brothers in their heyday was going too far, there was a "free-wheeling quality to the film, and in the conduct of the Beatles themselves, that bursts into honest comic inventiveness a number of times." He found a fine madness in John's bathtub scene and the police chase sequence. His favorite part of the film was the field scene where the Beatles run about and fly into the air. "The sense of joy with living and being on top of the world, is superbly evoked."

Cohen notes that "part of the film's charm is that the Beatles never take themselves seriously," as shown in John's hallway encounter with a woman over whether he is himself, the "ferociously funny press conference," and Ringo shying away from a beautiful beckoning woman on the train due to his fear of rejection and frustration. He praises the decision not to burden the movie with a plot, save for the conflict caused by Paul's fictional grandfather. This enables the film to make "amusing comments on the feverishness and harmlessness of teen-girl adulation." The film's TV concert climax was "cunningly photographed" with "close-ups of each alternating with group shots, and mixed in with the occasional glimpses of the happily convulsed audience in [the] theatre." Although the Beatles are treated as a group, each comes over as an individual figure, with John as the "droll anarchist," Paul as the best-looking with the "strongest family feeling," George as "the group's Hamlet," and Ringo as "both the flashiest and most vulnerable to success." He also praises the supporting cast. Cohen was skeptical of the group's staying power based on what he saw on The Ed Sullivan Show, thinking they were fated to go the way of Bill Haley and the Comets, and countless other rock and roll groups. But, "the Mersey sound turned out to be quite different from rock and roll," with the Beatles keeping their place with their fans on the charts. Their film proves: "they have more solidity than most adults imagined. It looks as if they are going to be with us for quite some time, especially if they continue to get movie scripts."

Gary McCarthy's review of the film in the August 15 Montreal Gazette opens with a Marx Brothers comparison: "Marx Brothers, move over. The Beatles are just as hairy. Maybe not as funny but every bit as hairy. But the Beatles... are witty in their own slapstick Merseyside way." Based on the "continuous screams of more than 2,000 teenagers who packed...the film's preview showing," he concluded that Paul and Ringo were the most popular "even though George and John gave very good performances." The zany antics of Paul's grandfather "give the Beatles just as rough a time as the screaming fans do." Although he found the humor to be corn, "when the Beatles deliver their lines, they somehow come out funny." His final verdict: "All in all, it is a good film, a typical rock 'n' roll film, but a good film."

In the August 21 Edmonton Journal, Pat Johnson described the scene at the Odeon Theatre for the first Edmonton screening of the film: "One thousand screaming, clapping kids–all with the same affliction...BEATLEMANIA." Kids began lining up at 5:00 AM, and by 8:00 AM, three hours before the start of the show, 400 youngsters were there, clutching Beatles pictures, records and magazines, and "chanting 'It's Been A Hard Day's Night.'" When the doors opened at 9:00 AM, "a thousand youngsters swarmed into the theatre, running for front row seats." The venue filled so quickly that management started the film 30 minutes early.

"Showtime, and the kids were clapping and screaming, rocking and hugging themselves for joy...the house was a sea of adoring fans," with one saying: "They're BEAUTIFUL, they've got EVERYTHING." With a week of six showings a day, management hired extra staff and stationed policemen outside to keep the youngsters in order. In the same edition, movie critic Barry Westgate's review was titled: "Not The Greatest...But It Sells." After lamenting he survived "85 minutes of frenzied teen-age hysteria," Westgate wrote: "But no matter that ALL adolescent girls appear to be mindless, howling morons...no matter that this very first movie by The Beatles is short on almost everything that counts...a theatre full of kids was delighted by 'A Hard Day's Night.'" After admitting that he "caught himself tapping toe," Westgate thought the film was "strictly a pitch for the box office...that hits the mark squarely." It was "go, go, go for the oddball foursome all the way," so youngsters were bound to be delighted." As for adults, the movie is a "delightful spoof on The Beatles by The Beatles" and a "telling putdown of a whole industry that seeks to manipulate and exploit adolescent tastes." He found the film to be "noisy, shot throughout with confusion, acted shoddily, and burdened with questionable sound recording," but acknowledged "it sells The Beatles, and does so with a vengeance."

Gordon Stoneham of The Ottawa Citizen reviewed the prior night's local premiere of *A Hard Day's Night* in the newspaper's August 25 edition. Stoneham praised the talented movie-makers for solving the problem of how to best present the Beatles to the vast motion picture audience. The result is "a lively romp" and surprisingly, "a fast, fresh and funny piece of business that should be easy for anyone to enjoy." The film is "charged with vitality and turned out with a slick professional polish." He credits Alun Owen for lacing the film's simple framework with "smart, sprightly dialog, an abundance of diverting incidents, and a subtle suggestion of the pressures and difficulties of which they work." He praises director Richard Lester's use of free cinema technique to create "an exciting visual style, splashing it with an array of madcap comedy sequences and sight gags, and giving it an air of irresistible spontaneity" and a "brisk and breezy" pace. Stoneham writes of the joyous mood of the "striking sequence in which [the Beatles] briefly escape their routine, and frolic in an empty field." The Beatles "take to their new medium with remarkable smoothness and apparent enjoyment," coming across "in spirited fashion, clowning delightfully and frequently projecting a refreshing zaniness." He also recognizes the supporting cast, calling them all "dandy." He concludes: "In fact, dandy is just the word for A Hard Day's Night. Who'd have thought it?"

Writing in the August 25 edition of The Ottawa Journal, Rick Lyons described the film's preview showing at the Rideau Theatre as "A Hard Day's Night" where close to 1,000 Beatles fans went wild, but not too wild. Although fans screamed and jumped up waiving their arms, none fainted or rushed the screen. Prior to the start of the film, a 14-year-old male high school student was mobbed by more than 50 girls because he had a Beatles haircut and looked like Ringo. He had to be rescued by two ushers and a security officer. Lyons thought the film was good and worth seeing. It had new and different photography and a number of side-splitting scenes.

When the film finally made its way to Hamilton, Ontario on Friday, September 18, youngsters were back in school, so only those attending their classes on the morning shift were able to catch the first showing that afternoon. According to the September 19 edition of The Hamilton Spectator, attendance was limited to a couple dozen fans. But that evening it was "a hard day's night" for the staff at the Palace Theatre as the movie "became a magnet for thousands of Hamilton teenagers who flooded into the theatre, turning a musical into a silent movie." The paper noted: "You could see the mouths moving. You could see the hands and fingers rippling over guitars and drums. And you couldn't hear a thing–except the ecstatic howl of fervent youth, the biggest symptom of Beatlemania. They yelled, they cried, they stupefied themselves with noise. And they'll be back, they said, to do it again." On Saturday, four 13-year-old girls, armed with blankets and sandwiches, arrived at the theater shortly after 5:00 AM, more than seven hours ahead of the first showing at 1:00 PM. They wanted the honor of being the first inside. By 8:00 AM, they had been joined by a hundred more teenagers, most of whom were glassy-eyed girls.

The film eventually reached St. Catharines, Ontario on Wednesday, September 30. Prior to its arrival, the Palace Theatre promoted *A Hard Day's Night* by running the following message to adult movie-goers in the September 26 edition of The Standard: "So that you may enjoy this excellent movie, the management will not allow any children under 14 to attend on Wednesday or Thursday nights unless accompanied by an adult who will be responsible for their good behaviour...This will enable grown-ups to enjoy the Beatles' movie which was acclaimed by all the critics as a terrific comedy." As was the case in the United Kingdom and the United States, *A Hard Day's Night* made adult Canadians realize the talent and staying power of the Beatles.

In plugging the *Something New* LP in the July 17 Sizzle Sheet, Paul White singled out two of the six tracks new to Canada: "One of them, a ditty written by Carl Perkins called MATCHBOX features RINGO on vocal-- and this fact alone assures the package of becoming a best seller! John Lennon really goes to town with song SLOW DOWN-- another tune set to become a hot request one!" White must have been delighted to announce in the August 7 Sizzle Sheet that the new single by the Beatles was coming soon and featured "Matchbox" and "Slow Down." After the disc was issued on or about August 24, White noted the disc in his list of "WHAT'S MOVING." Most stations listed the single as "Matchbox"/"Slow Down," with Toronto's CHUM and Montreal's CKGM showing a peak at number six. Vancouver's CFUN, which reversed the order on its survey, reported the disc at number four. The Ottawa Citizen's Platter Poll charted "Slow Down" at two and "Matchbox" at five. Montreal's CFCF listed "Matchbox" at three and "Slow Down" at 17. RPM Weekly reported "Matchbox" for four weeks with a peak at 17. The single sold 42,257 copies in 1964.

Canadians finally got to see the Beatles in person during the group's 1964 North American Tour. As the tour started on the American West Coast, Vancouver was the first Canadian city to see the boys in concert. The Beatles played an evening show on August 22 at Vancouver's Empire Stadium, attracting 20,621 fans at the outdoor venue. Under the headline "20,000 Beatlemaniacs pay so much for so little," Vancouver Sun music critic William Littler belittled the Beatles, adding that "the stuff shouted by these Liverpudlian tonsorial horrors left me particularly unimpressed." The group's next Canadian concert took place on September 7 at the Maple Leaf Gardens in Toronto where they played two sold-out shows of 17,000 fans each. Although Bob Pennington of the Toronto Telegram was disgusted with what he saw, describing the boys as "four Pied Pipers of our sick society," the Toronto Daily Star's Nathan Cohen had a favorable take: "They are energetic, good-natured, and robustly masculine. They have a sense of independence about them, of enjoying life to the fullest, which makes their appeal to the teenage generation easy to understand." The next day the Beatles played two concerts at the Montreal Forum [shown top left], with the afternoon show drawing 9,500 and the evening one a capacity crowd of 11,500. The Montreal Star's Beatles Bureau described the "Deafening Silence" to its readers: "The noise inside the Forum was unbelievable. As soon as the Beatles appeared... there was a burst of sound as if a hundred jet engines were being revved up at center ice. It made the Stanley Cup [hockey championship series] crowd sound like nightingales." Canada was no different than England and America.

MATCHBOX
(Carl Perkins)

Capitol
REG'D TRADE MARK
RECORDS
RECORDED IN
ENGLAND

Knox Music,
Inc.
BMI–1:37
5255
(45–X45052)

THE BEATLES

SEC. ROW SEAT
86 K 13
WEST
Retain Stub — Good Only
SERIES B
MON. SEPT. 7th
Davis Printing Limited
THE "BEATLES"
8.30 P.M. PRICE $4.00
ADMIT ONE. Entrance by Main Door or by West Door, Carlton St.
Maple Leaf Gardens
LIMITED
CONDITION OF SALE: Upon refunding the purchase price the management may remove from the premises any person who has obtained admission by this ticket.

ADULT ADMIT STUB
SERIES B
Not Good For Adult Admission If Detached

BEATLEMANIA!
CHUM

Paul McCartney greets Toronto with his camera at International Airport.

Paul McCartney talks to CHUM'S J. J. Richards & Dave Johnson.

Jungle Jay introduces the BEATLES to Toronto.

BEATLES pose with their fan club President Trudy Medcalf.

CHART

1964–The Year of the Beatles & More

by Al Sussman

For the youth of America and future music historians, 1964 was The Year of The Beatles. But it was so much more. As winter gave way to spring 1964, the Beatles were back in England from their conquest of America and shooting their first film. Over the past year, the Beatles had gone from second billing on tours headlined by British teenager Helen Shapiro and by Americans Tommy Roe and Chris Montez, to becoming the top entertainment act in the world.

During this time, America and the world also witnessed major changes on a number of levels. The leadership of West Germany, Great Britain, the Vatican, South Vietnam and the United States had changed, in the later two cases, violently. The drive for equal rights for black Americans had gained great momentum with the August 28, 1963 March on Washington for Jobs and Freedom, though it was soon followed by the bombing of a Birmingham, Alabama church that killed four young black girls. The first U.S. government-mandated report by the Surgeon-General on the effects of smoking put the brakes on several record years of cigarette consumption by Americans. The U.S. wrapped up its Mercury manned space program and transitioned towards the two-man Gemini program, the middle phase of the overall mission to put a man on the moon by 1969. But the man who had set that goal was murdered in the most shocking moment of change that many people had ever experienced. The assassination of President John F. Kennedy on November 22, 1963, set in motion a spiral of events that would resonate through the decades.

With the televised murder of the President's accused assassin, Lee Harvey Oswald, by Jack Ruby barely 48 hours after the rifle shots in Dallas' Dealey Plaza, it quickly became apparent that we might never find out exactly how and by whom President Kennedy was assassinated. A week after the shooting, the new President, Lyndon B. Johnson ("LBJ"), announced the creation of a commission to investigate it, headed by Earl Warren, the Chief Justice of the Supreme Court. The Warren Commission also included a future President, Michigan congressman Gerald Ford, who would first become Vice President and, some eight months later, President in another moment of national turmoil.

2035
PIANO/VOCAL $2.95
the FIRST
GOLDEN BEATLES
Album

OCTOBER 5, 1964 35c
Newsweek
THE ASSASSINATION
THE WARREN COMMISSION REPORT

Just a few weeks after the Warren Commission was established by executive order by President Johnson on November 29, 1963, former New York State assemblyman and frequent defense lawyer Mark Lane petitioned the Commission for defense representation of Oswald's interests, including his mother Marguerite and Russian-born wife Marina. This was the start of an adversarial relationship between Lane and the Commission that would culminate and continue after the Warren Report was released in September 1964. The Commission's lead finding was that Oswald was the lone assassin. Lane contended that the Warren Report was rushed so that LBJ could use the report to aid his presidential campaign. Lane documented his opposing viewpoint in his 1966 book *Rush To Judgment*, which launched a veritable industry in Kennedy assassination conspiracy theories that persists to this day.

Media attention towards the Kennedy assassination was intense from the beginning. With a bid of $150,000 (over $1,500,000 in 2023 inflation-adjusted dollars), Life magazine outbid CBS on the morning after the shooting for a 26-second silent 8mm color film taken by Abraham Zapruder of the President's limousine as it turned onto Elm Street heading into Dealey Plaza just as the shots were fired. Life first published still images from the Zapruder film in black and white in its November 29, 1963 issue and in color in its December 6, 1963 John F. Kennedy Memorial Edition and its October 2, 1964 issue covering the Warren Report. Life also ran a picture of Oswald holding the rifle used in the assassination on the cover of its February 21, 1964 edition. The photo was taken by his wife, Marina, in the back yard to the couple's residence in Dallas in the spring of 1963.

Jack Ruby went on trial for Oswald's murder in Dallas in February 1964, despite efforts by Ruby's attorney, Melvin Belli, to have the trial moved out of Dallas and then a move to have Ruby acquitted by reason of temporary insanity. On March 14, Ruby was found guilty, although his conviction was overturned in 1966. Ruby died of cancer in January 1967 while awaiting a new trial. With his death, it became even more likely that the full story would never be told.

On March 27, Radio Caroline ran a test broadcast from a ship anchored off British territorial waters near Felixstone, Suffolk. The pirate radio station, founded to circumvent the BBC's radio monopoly, was named after President Kennedy's daughter, Caroline. The station began its regular broadcasting schedule the next day.

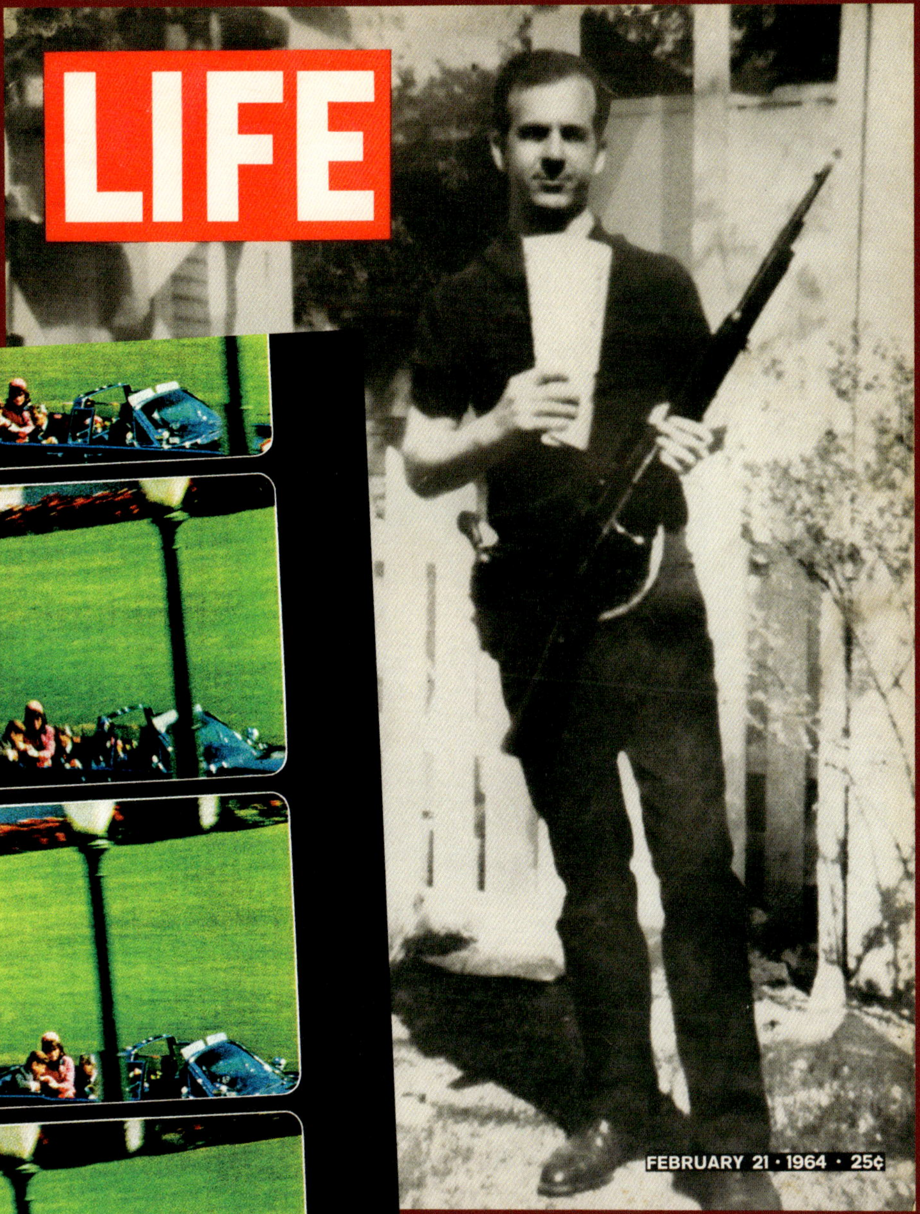

LIFE

FEBRUARY 21 · 1964 · 25¢

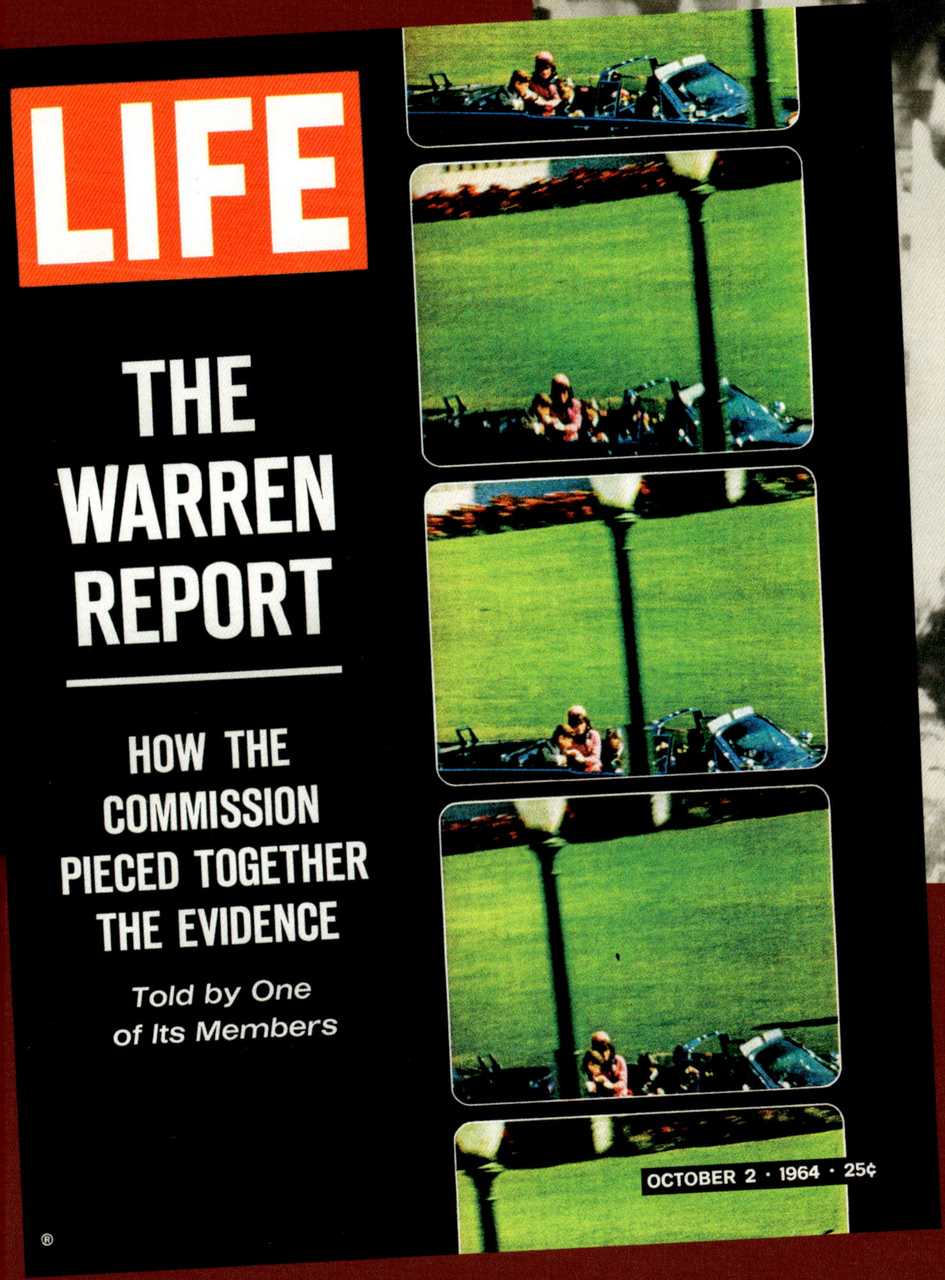

LIFE

THE WARREN REPORT

HOW THE COMMISSION PIECED TOGETHER THE EVIDENCE

Told by One of Its Members

®

On Good Friday, March 27, a 9.2 magnitude earthquake struck Anchorage and south-central Alaska. It was the most powerful North American earthquake and the second most powerful in the world since modern equipment began recording such quakes in 1900. The quake and resulting tsunamis claimed 131 lives, including five in Oregon and 12 as far south as Crescent City, California.

The Beatles first 1964 single of new recordings, “Can’t Buy Me Love,” was released in March and quickly hit number one in all of the British and American national charts. The group continued to cause seismic shifts in the music industry by holding down the top five spots on both the April 4, 1964 Billboard Hot 100 and Cash Box Top 100 charts.

Newly crowned heavyweight boxing champion Cassius Clay brought additional attention to the Black Muslim movement by confirming his membership in the Nation of Islam and changing his name, first to Cassius X and then to Muhammad Ali, the name bestowed on him by Black Muslim leader Elijah Muhammad. Malcolm X, who had largely been Clay’s mentor in converting him to Islam, became estranged from Elijah Muhammad and announced the formation of his Organization of Afro-American Unity at Harlem’s Audubon Ballroom on June 28.

During March, the strongest civil rights bill since Reconstruction, which President Kennedy sent to Congress the previous summer, reached the Senate floor after it had taken a circuitous route through the House of Representatives. The bill was brought up for debate before the full Senate on March 30. Almost immediately, a “Southern bloc” of 18 Southern Democratic senators and one Republican, Texas’ John Tower, began a filibuster that consumed all of April and May’s Senate business. Finally, a coalition of Minnesota Sen. Hubert Humphrey, Senate Majority Leader Mike Mansfield and, most importantly, Senate Minority Leader Everett Dirksen, were able to submit a compromise bill in hopes of breaking the filibuster. With Dirksen delivering enough Republican votes for cloture, Humphrey, the bill’s Senate manager, was able to craft a 71-29 margin to defeat the filibuster on June 10. Nine days later, the compromise bill picked up two more Democratic votes and passed the Senate 73-27. The final Senate-passed bill was approved by the joint conference committee and then sent back to the House, where the Civil Rights Act of 1964 was quickly voted into law and signed by President Johnson on July 2, just over a year after it was introduced in the House.

LIFE

In Color:
EARTHQUAKE
IN ALASKA

APRIL 10 · 1964

The New Hubert Humphrey

LBJ's Civil Rights Whip

But events in the South while the filibuster was ongoing in the Senate showed just how much work still had to be done, bill or no bill. On April 17, a second trial in Jackson, Mississippi, in the June 1963 murder of civil rights activist Medgar Evers ended in a second all-white hung jury. Evers' accused murderer, Byron De La Beckwith, walked free on $10,000 bond. It would be 30 years before he would finally be convicted in a third trial.

On June 15, the first 300 volunteers for the "Freedom Summer" campaign, consisting primarily of white northern college students, arrived in Mississippi to help black residents register to vote. These outsiders were resented for trying to change the state's customs and "Southern Way of Life." On June 21, three civil rights activists—24-year-old Michael Schwerner and 20-year-old Andrew Goodman, both white New Yorkers, and 21-year-old James Chaney, a black Mississippi resident—went missing after investigating the burning of a black church. The FBI became involved when their charred station wagon was found near Bogue Chitto Swamp three days later. Following a lead, the FBI found their buried bodies at an earthen damn site on August 4. They had been arrested and jailed on June 21 by Deputy Sheriff Cecile Price, a member of the Ku Klux Klan, for allegedly speeding within the city limits of Philadelphia, Mississippi. That evening, Price released the trio from jail, but followed their vehicle in his patrol car before pulling them over and driving them in his vehicle to a secluded area, where he turned them over to a group of fellow Klansmen who murdered and buried the three men. After the State of Mississippi refused to bring charges, those involved were later indicted under Federal law, with Price and others found guilty of conspiracy in October 1967.

Despite the passage of the Civil Rights Act, the summer of 1964 would be remembered as the first of a series of "long hot summers" in which black urban ghettos exploded in rioting, usually as a result of confrontations with police. It began in Harlem with six days of rioting in mid-July after the fatal shooting of a black teen by police, followed shortly thereafter by a disturbance in Rochester, New York after police attempted to make an arrest during a block party. In mid-August, there was rioting in Dixmoor, Illinois after a black woman was arrested for shoplifting. Later that month, Philadelphia, Pennsylvania exploded in looting and burning of white-owned businesses following a confrontation between a black woman and police. There would be larger-scale disturbances over the next three summers, culminating in the mass rioting in April 1968 following the assassination of Rev. Dr. Martin Luther King, Jr.

Newsweek

JULY 13, 1964

30c

MADISON
SHERIFF'S DEPT.
COUNTY

MISSISSIPPI

Summer, 1964

HARLEM: Hatred in the Streets

Meanwhile, in South Africa, a group of anti-apartheid activists were on trial for sabotage–a trial that had begun in October 1963. It took until April 20, 1964, for the defense team to present their case. The most high-profile of the accused, Nelson Mandela, gave a three-hour speech in which he spoke of the ideal of "a democratic and free society" in South Africa and proclaimed that "it is an ideal for which I am prepared to die." But on June 12, Mandela and seven other defendants were found guilty and sentenced to life imprisonment. Mandela would spend over 27 years in prison before being released in February of 1990 by order of South African President F.W. de Klerk. A little over four years after his release, Mandela would be elected President of South Africa.

Twenty-five years after the memorable 1939 New York World's Fair showed off the technology of tomorrow, including television, the Fair returned to the Flushing Meadows area of the New York borough of Queens. Along with the Fair grounds, a new stadium was about to open nearby. On April 10, demolition began on the Polo Grounds in northern Harlem, the longtime home of the baseball New York Giants (before moving to San Francisco) and football New York Giants, and the first home of the baseball Mets and football Jets. A week later, Shea Stadium opened, with a crowd of 48,736 turning out to see the Pittsburgh Pirates beat the Mets 4-3. In Shea's first year, the stadium would see the longest doubleheader in baseball history, a perfect game on Father's Day and the annual All-Star Game. Promoter Sid Bernstein, who had booked the Beatles into Carnegie Hall, was already thinking about a Beatles concert at Shea.

As for the Fair itself, it opened on April 22. Five students from St. Peter's College in Jersey City, New Jersey were first in line to gain admission, which cost $2 ($1 for children). Among the sites they would have seen, along with the huge Unisphere that was the Fair's symbol, was Michelangelo's Pieta on display at the Vatican pavilion. Many other pavilions looked to the future, including NASA's United States Space Park, General Motors' Futurama II, Bell System's Diorama and demonstrations of a Picturephone and a computer modem. Five days before the opening of the Fair, Ford Motor Co. introduced its new sports car, the Mustang, which would be one of the featured vehicles in Ford's Magic Skyway ride at the company's pavilion. The Mustang was an instant sensation. Priced at $2,368, Ford sold 418,862 Mustangs during 1964. A year later, the Pittsburgh Press proclaimed it "the most successful new car ever introduced." Wilson Pickett would bring the Mustang to the pop music charts in 1966 with "Mustang Sally."

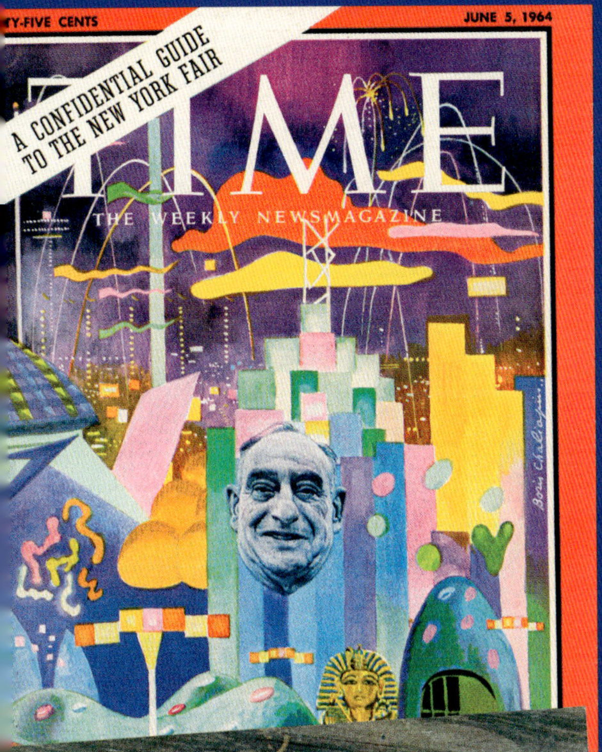

JUNE 5, 1964
A CONFIDENTIAL GUIDE TO THE NEW YORK FAIR
TIME
THE WEEKLY NEWSMAGAZINE

ADMIT ONE
CHILD
AT FAIR GATE
$1.00
NEW YORK WORLDS FAIR
1964
1965

admit one at fair gate
$2.00
NON-REFUNDABLE
ADULT
NEW YORK WORLDS FAIR
1964 - 1965
T 490050
UNISPHERE

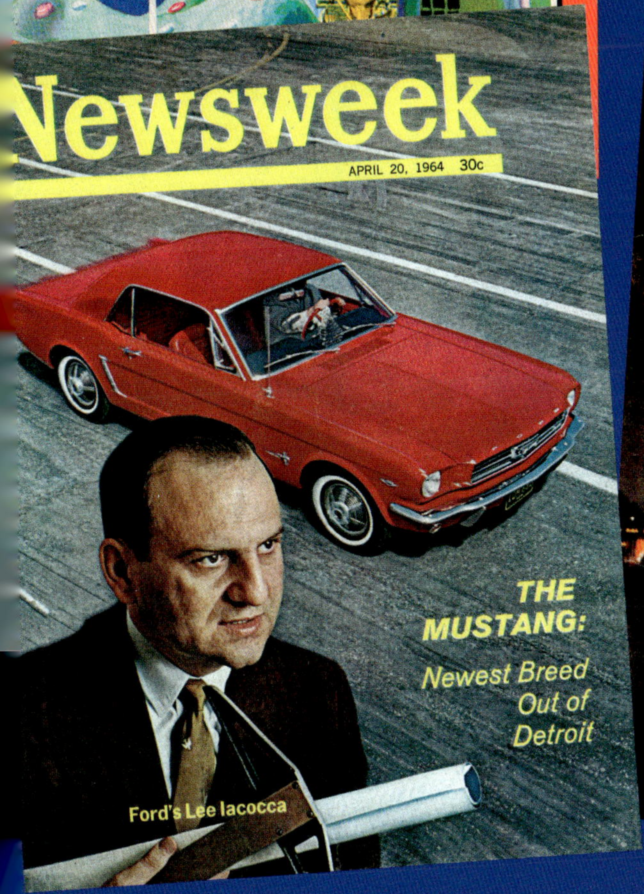

Newsweek
APRIL 20, 1964 30c
THE MUSTANG:
Newest Breed Out of Detroit
Ford's Lee Iacocca

LIFE
In Color
THE WORLD'S FAIR OPENS
MAY 1 · 1964 · 25¢

LIFE
in color
UGLY WAR
IN VIETNAM
U.S. officer
heads a patrol
JUNE 12
Newsweek
AUGUST 17, 1964 30c
Vietnam:
Widening
War?
202

Ten days after the opening of a World's Fair for which the theme was "Peace Through Understanding," the first major demonstrations against the American involvement in the war in Vietnam, known as the May 2 Movement, were held in New York, San Francisco, Boston, Seattle and Madison, Wisconsin. Two weeks later, at a War Resisters League demonstration in New York's Union Square, 12 young men burned their draft cards.

Although President Johnson wanted to hold off any large-scale escalation in Vietnam until after the November election, his Secretary of Defense, Robert McNamara, recommended a sharp increase in troop strength and the bombing of North Vietnam. Under what would be known as the "domino theory," McNamara contended that if North Vietnam remained under Communist control, "almost all of Southeast Asia will probably fall under Communist dominance." This view was shared by Richard Nixon, who believed that the U.S. needed to "take a tougher line toward Communism in Asia" and expand the war into North Vietnam and Laos. On June 6, Nixon's 1960 campaign running mate and U.S. Ambassador to South Vietnam, Henry Cabot Lodge, recommended to LBJ that American ground troop levels not be increased so that U.S. commitment would not "slide into a bottomless pit." But Barry Goldwater, the leading Republican candidate to take on Johnson, suggested on May 24 on ABC-TV's Issues And Answers that tactical nuclear weapons could be used as a deterrent against Viet Cong supply lines. On June 20, Gen. William Westmoreland succeeded Gen. Paul Harkins as head of the Military Assistance Command in South Vietnam. On July 1, Gen. Maxwell Taylor took over as U.S. ambassador, succeeding Lodge, who had won the Republican New Hampshire primary as a write-in candidate and was one of the hopes for the party moderates as an alternative to Goldwater. A week later, the Defense Department announced that 248 Americans had been killed "since American forces became fully involved in the jungle war in 1961." That number would soon increase precipitously.

On August 2, the destroyer USS Maddox was engaged by three Vietnam People's Navy torpedo boats in the Gulf of Tonkin. Two days later, the Maddox and USS Turner Joy reported that they were under fire, though there would be much debate over this. President Johnson used these incidents to order retaliatory air strikes on the North, a major escalation of the war. Six days later, Congress approved the Tonkin Gulf Resolution, authorizing the President to "take all necessary steps, including the use of armed force." Thus began America's full descent into The Big Muddy.

Johnson, who had made a belated effort to wrangle the Democratic nomination from Kennedy in 1960, began subtly campaigning for a term of his own in the weeks following his succession to the presidency but more overtly with his first State of the Union address on January 8. In that speech, LBJ announced the first of what he later dubbed his "Great Society" programs and a domestic "war on poverty," which he would detail for Congress in a message sent to Capitol Hill in March. On May 22, Johnson introduced his full slate of "Great Society" programs in a commencement address at the University of Michigan before turning his attention to passage of the civil rights bill and Vietnam.

Goldwater's candidacy for the Republican nomination energized the radical-right wing of the party, exposing a split from the party's moderate-to-liberal members. After losing the New Hampshire primary, Goldwater took command of the race, though New York Gov. Nelson Rockefeller won West Virginia and Oregon, and Pennsylvania Gov. William Scranton won his state. Goldwater then edged out Rocky in the California primary, with Rockefeller's divorce and marriage to a divorcee being a major issue. The Republican convention was held in mid-July at the Cow Palace in San Francisco (where the Beatles would open their North American tour a month later). Despite efforts to promote Scranton as a moderate alternative, Goldwater easily won the nomination. Political commentator Walter Lippmann observed in the July 20 Newsweek that Goldwater's views were "a denial of the historic traditions of the party." He expressed concern over the possible realignment of the parties, where one party was conservative and the other was liberal. He viewed the lack of sharp ideological differences between the parties as a safeguard to our democracy.

Despite a states' rights challenge from Alabama's segregationist Gov. George Wallace, LBJ had no obstacles in gaining the Democratic nomination. The only question was who would be his running mate, an issue since, in that pre-25th amendment era, the vice-presidency would be vacant until the following January. Despite their mutual personal dislike, Attorney General Robert Kennedy lobbied to be on the ticket with Johnson, but LBJ eliminated his entire Cabinet from consideration. Not long after, Kennedy decided to run for Republican Kenneth Keating's Senate seat in New York, despite having lived most of his life in Massachusetts. A Kennedy insider told Newsweek: "This is a marriage of necessity. They need a candidate and Bob wants to stay in government...They know he can bring in the votes. They don't give a damn where Bobby lives; they want to win." And win he did, becoming Senator Bobby.

Decision
By
Robert
Kennedy

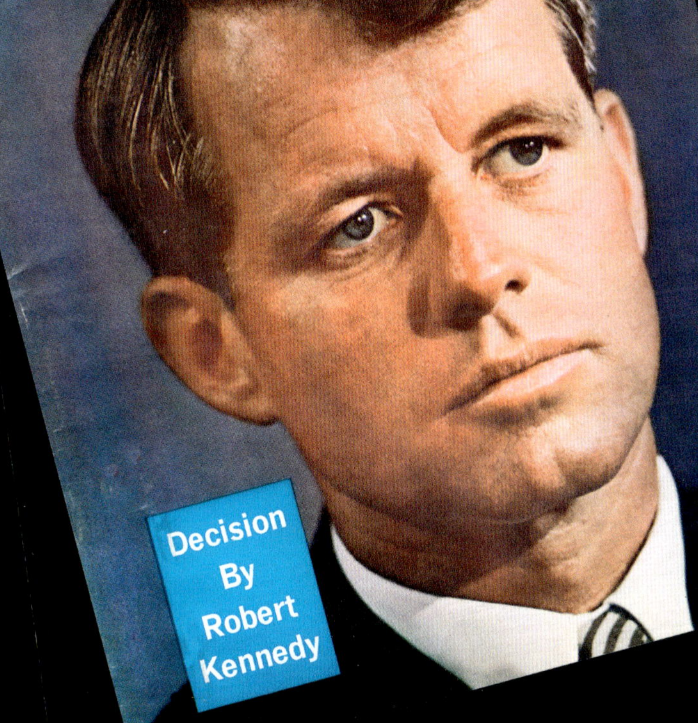

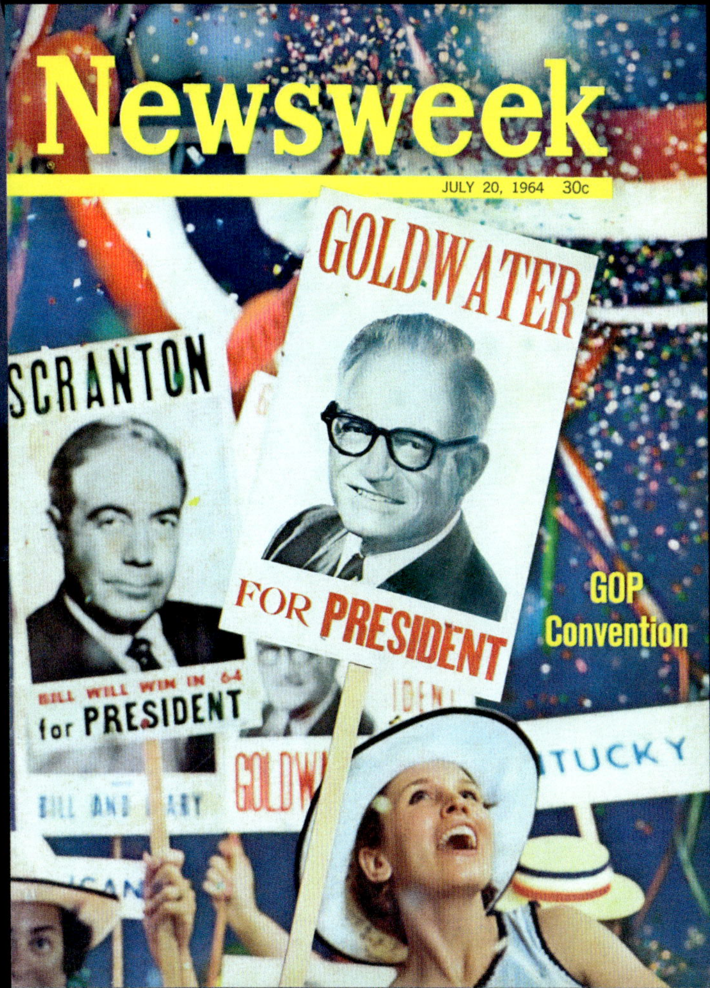

Newsweek
JULY 20, 1964 30c
GOLDWATER
FOR PRESIDENT
SCRANTON
BILL WILL WIN IN 64
for PRESIDENT
GOP
Convention

For his running mate, Johnson ultimately chose Hubert Humphrey, who had managed the effort in the Senate for passage of the Civil Rights Act and had been one of the Senate's liberal lions since before Johnson's days as Senate majority leader. The Democratic convention opened at the Convention Hall in Atlantic City just six days before the Beatles scheduled concert there. The Johnson-Humphrey ticket was easily nominated. But the convention's best-remembered moment came on its final night when Robert Kennedy came to the podium to introduce a film in tribute to JFK and was greeted with a long, emotional ovation, which, if it had happened before Humphrey was nominated as Johnson's running mate, might have led to a drive to draft RFK as the vice-presidential nominee.

On November 3, the campaign slogan "All the way with LBJ" became a reality, with Johnson winning a term of his own in a landslide, getting over 61% of the popular vote and 486 electoral votes. Goldwater won only his home state of Arizona and five Deep South states. LBJ was aided by the September release of the Warren Report concluding that there was no conspiracy and that Oswald was the lone gunman, his promise not to send American boys to do the job of the South Vietnamese, and Goldwater being labeled as an extremist war hawk. However, the Party of Lincoln's rightward lurch had begun, exemplified by the entrance into the political arena of an actor who narrated a film about Goldwater that had been shown at the Republican convention and gave a televised election-eve speech in support of Goldwater, a former Democrat named Ronald Reagan. Life magazine pictured Johnson and Humphrey celebrating the landslide victory at the President's Texas ranch, while Newsweek showed the Republican Party, represented by its elephant symbol, suffering a post-election hangover brought on by its selection of Goldwater, with the failed candidate's name in Periodic Table symbols, AuH_2O, on the label of an empty bottle.

Johnson was well on his way to going "all the way" in mid-October when the Soviet Union's Presidium and Central Committee each voted to accept Premier Nikita Khrushchev's "resignation," which turned out to be a peaceful coup led by Presidium Chairman Leonid Brezhnev, who was then elected First Secretary, with Alexei Kosygin installed as Premier. Two days later, Red China entered the nuclear sweepstakes with its first successful test of an atom bomb, as England saw another change in leadership, with Labor Party leader Harold Wilson installed as prime minister. The hopes for peace between the superpowers that seemed so bright just a year earlier had taken a major hit.

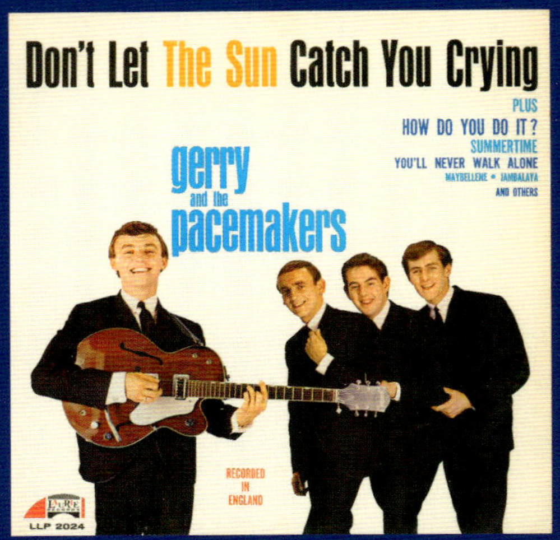

Gerry and the Pacemakers were the number two band in Liverpool behind the Beatles. The group was managed by Beatles manager Brian Epstein and produced by Beatles producer George Martin. During 1963, their first three U.K. singles, "How Do You Do It," "I Like It" and "You'll Never Walk Alone," all went to number one. "I'm The One" came close, stopping in the second spot in February 1964. After Capitol passed on "How Do You Do It" (a song that George Martin forced the Beatles to record in September 1962), the group was signed to Laurie Records. When the New York label released the first two singles in 1963 and the next two in early 1964, they were ignored. The group finally hit the American charts with the ballad "Don't Let The Sun Catch You Crying," written by the group's magnetic lead singer, Gerry Marsden. The single's success (it peaked in the U.S. at number four in early July and at six in the U.K.) prompted Laurie to reissue the earlier singles. "How Do You Do It" charted at number nine and "I Like It" at 17, but "I'm The One" wasn't the one, charting at an unimpressive number 82.

It was a similar pattern for another Epstein-managed/Martin-produced group, Billy J. Kramer with the Dakotas, who had the good fortune to record Lennon-McCartney compositions on four of their first five singles. Their three 1963 discs were big U.K. hits: "Do You Want To Know A Secret" (#2); "Bad To Me" (#1); and "I'll Keep You Satisfied" (#4). So were their first two singles of 1964, "Little Children" (#1 and the only non-Lennon-McCartney tune) and "From A Window" (#10). When Capitol declined to issue their records in America, the group was signed to Liberty Records, which released the first three singles to total indifference. When the British Invasion hit in 1964, Billy J. had four 1964 hits on Imperial: "Little Children" (# 7); "Bad To Me" (#9); "I'll Keep You Satisfied" (#30); and "From A Window" (#23).

The Searchers were the best of the non-Epstein-managed Liverpool acts. Their sound was full of tight harmonies and jangly guitars, presaging the sound of folk-rock. The group had five Top Five hits in the U.K. in 1963 and 1964, including three number ones. "Needles And Pins," written by Sonny Bono and Jack Nitzsche, and first recorded by American Jackie DeShannon, was the only one of their early British hits to score in the U.S., reaching number 13. The Swinging Blue Jeans' "The Hippy Hippy Shake" hit number two in the U.K., but stalled at 24 in the States. Peter & Gordon were based in London. With Paul McCartney dating Peter Asher's sister Jane and living in the Asher's home, the duo got to record three songs in 1964 penned primarily by Paul. The first, "A World Without Love," topped the charts on both sides of the Atlantic, becoming the first non-Beatles number one single of the British Invasion in late June. The others were "Nobody I Know" (#10 U.K.; #12 U.S.) and "I Don't Want To See You Again" (#16 U.S. only).

A diverse group of British female vocalists also made a considerable impression on the charts. The most stylish and successful was Dusty Springfield, who had a number 11 hit with "I Only Want To Be With You" (previously #4 in the U.K.) in early '64. She got to number six that summer with Burt Bacharach and Hal David's "Wishin' & Hopin'" before becoming one of the decade's most distinctive female vocalists. Millie Small, a Jamaican known as "The Blue Beat Girl" (blue beat was the Jamaican musical precursor to reggae), scored a number two hit in the U.K., U.S. and Canada with "My Boy Lollipop." This earned Millie a guest spot on Around The Beatles, a British TV special which also featured a guest appearance by the only female vocalist in the Epstein performing stable, Liverpool native Cilla Black. Although she became a big star in the U.K., Cilla's number one U.K. single "You're My World" stalled at 26 in America.

That spring, some of the American fan magazines that were covering the British Invasion began running stories about the "ugly" Rolling Stones, a blues/R&B-based band that had none of the cheery appeal of the Merseyside bands or the flash of the Dave Clark 5. And, unlike the Merseybeat bands and the DC5, when the Stones made their first trip to America, they made their network TV debut not with Ed Sullivan but on The Hollywood Palace, where guest host Dean Martin greeted them with a string of wisecracks and insults. The Stones didn't get a much better reaction from Top 40 radio or on the charts, despite a growing string of major hits in the U.K. in 1964: "Not Fade Away" (#3); "It's All Over Now" (#1); and "Little Red Rooster" (#1). Stones' manager Andrew Loog Oldham understood the differences between the British and American markets. The first two singles were issued in America, but "Not Fade Away" only got to number 48 and "It's All Over Now" stalled at 26. The band's cover of the Chicago blues number "Little Red Rooster" was not released as a U.S. single. Instead, the Stones other 1964 American singles were "Tell Me" (#24) and "Time Is On My Side" (#6), which was first recorded by New Orleans R&B/soul singer Irma Thomas.

Nonetheless, the Stones opened the door for more blues-based British bands. Two of these groups, the Animals and Manfred Mann, had their number one British hits top the American charts. These songs became the first non-Beatles or Lennon-McCartney-written number one singles of the British Invasion. The Animals' remarkable arrangement of the traditional folk song "The House Of The Rising Sun," with Hilton Valentine's arpeggio guitar notes, Eric Burdon's gritty, soulful vocal and Alan Price's ferocious organ part, topped the charts for three weeks in September, while Manfred Mann's cover of the Exciters' "Do Wah Diddy Diddy" was there for two weeks in October.

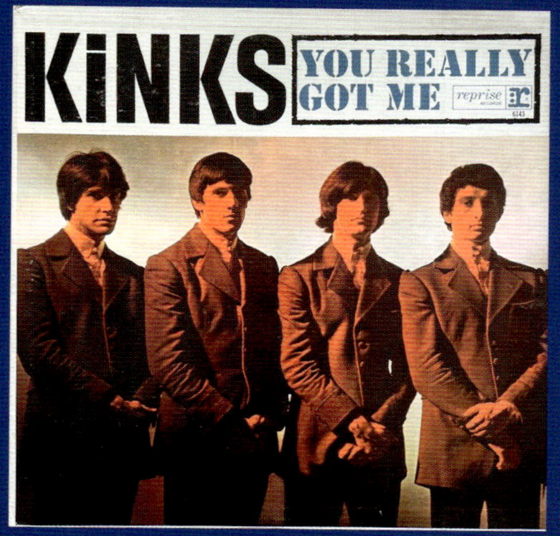

Other British groups included the Honeycombs, mainly remembered for their female drummer, with "Have I The Right" (#1 U.K., #5 U.S.), the Zombies with the distinctive lead vocals of Colin Blunstone on "She's Not There" (#12 U.K., #2 U.S.) and the Kinks with their debut hit, "You Really Got Me" (#1 U.K., #7 U.S.), much more hard-driving than their later Ray Davies-written work. The Honeycombs' recordings were leased to Vee-Jay's Interphon label.

Rock critics in the late '60s/early '70s created the myth that the period from 1958-59 until "I Want To Hold Your Hand" was a musical wasteland full of novelty songs, dance records and teen idols. Now, a younger group of self-proclaimed historians, most of whom weren't even born until the '70s, have decided that virtually all of that early '60s pop music was rendered passé by the Beatles and the British Invasion. Once again, nothing could be further from the truth. Take, for instance, the two best-selling American groups of 1963, the Four Seasons and the Beach Boys. In the last week of March, when the Beatles held the top four places on Billboard's singles chart, the Four Seasons were at number five with "Dawn (Go Away)" and the Beach Boys were at six with "Fun, Fun, Fun." Each spent two weeks at the top of the chart that summer with the Beach Boys' "I Get Around" followed by the Four Seasons' "Rag Doll," right in the middle of the British Invasion's first wave. Late in the summer, the Beach Boys' *All Summer Long* album spent five weeks stuck at number four while the *A Hard Day's Night* soundtrack LP and *Something New* monopolized the top two slots. And though Capitol was blocked from issuing the live Beatles album it recorded at the Hollywood Bowl in August 1964 [see page 216], the Hollywood label's *Beach Boys Concert* live album topped the LP chart for the last four weeks of the year. It would be the Beach Boys only number one album of the sixties.

How about the canard that traditional pop music was put out to pasture by the U.K. interlopers? Well, it was the legendary Louis Armstrong who broke the Beatles 14-week dominance of the top spot with "Hello Dolly." In early July, Barbra Streisand's showstopper from Funny Girl, "People," hit number five. After two weeks at the top in August, "A Hard Day's Night" was ousted by Dean Martin with what became his signature song, "Everybody Loves Somebody."

Did girl groups and girl singers, such a huge part of the sound of 1963, disappear from the charts? Nope. During the first three weeks "I Want To Hold Your Hand" topped the Billboard Hot 100, Lesley Gore's feminist anthem "You Don't Own Me" was at number two. And, while Phil Spector did little as a producer in 1964, the Dixie Cups' version of the Jeff Barry-Ellie Greenwich-Spector composition "Chapel Of Love" topped the chart for three weeks in June. The Shangri-Las spent the last week in November at number one with the melodramatic "Leader Of The Pack."

No one can deny that the Motown/Tamla/Gordy group of labels progressed to another level in 1964 with songs such as "Dancing In The Streets" by Martha & the Vandellas, a number two hit that summer. Much of Motown's success in '64 can be credited to the production and songwriting abilities of Miracles leader Smokey Robinson and the team of Eddie Holland, Lamont Dozier and Brian Holland. Smokey wrote and produced "My Guy" for early '60s Motown mainstay Mary Wells, a two-week chart-topper in May, and the Temptations' debut hit, "The Way You Do The Things You Do," which just missed the Top 10 that spring. Holland-Dozier-Holland took over writing/producing duties for the Four Tops, who also peaked at 11 at the tail end of the summer with "Baby I Need Your Loving."

But Holland-Dozier-Holland's most spectacular success came when they took over composing/production duties for a group that had been dubbed "the no hit Supremes" since they had a string of unsuccessful singles going back to 1961. But H-D-H's first single for the Supremes, "When The Lovelight Starts Shining Through His Eyes," reached the Top 25 in the early weeks of 1964. Their big break came that summer with the release of "Where Did Our Love Go," which hit the top of the charts for two weeks in August, followed by "Baby Love," a four-week number one that fall, the first two of six chart-toppers out of seven singles by the end of 1965. Motown's founder, Barry Gordy, tried to capitalize on the British Invasion by having the Supremes record an album titled *A Bit Of Liverpool*. The album has the girls singing four original Beatles songs, two original DC5 tunes, "How Do You Do It," "A World Without Love" and, ironically, two Motown songs covered by British bands, "You Really Got A Hold On Me" and "Do You Love Me."

A number of regular hitmakers in the early sixties either encountered hit record droughts during 1964 or disappeared temporarily or permanently from the upper reaches of the charts. Bobby Rydell reached number four with "Forget Him" just as "I Want To Hold Your Hand" was taking off in mid-January, but never saw the Top 40 again. Rick Nelson, a consistent hitmaker since the late fifties thanks to weekly TV exposure on The Adventures Of Ozzie & Harriet, reached number six in February with "For You." His next Top 40 single was a country-rock cover of Bob Dylan's "She Belongs To Me" late in 1969. Rick didn't reach the Top 10 again until 1972 with "Garden Party." Dion had reached number six on 1963's final Hot 100 with his cover of the Drifters' "Drip Drop." In the six decades since, Dion had only one Top 10 single, the post-assassinations lament "Abraham, Martin And John" in 1968.

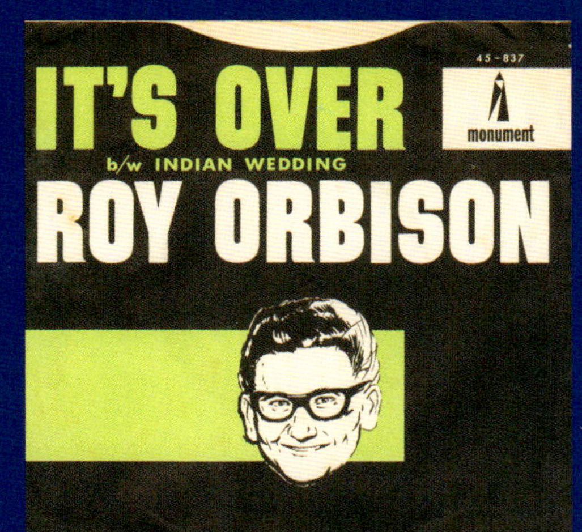

Others had much shorter spells between hits. Gene Pitney had Top 10 hits with "It Hurts To Be In Love" and "I'm Gonna Be Strong," his first since the fall of 1962. The popular doo-wop group Little Anthony & the Imperials reached the Top 15 with "I'm On The Outside Looking In" that fall and reached the Top 10 at year's end with "Goin' Out Of My Head," their first significant hits since their late fifties heyday. And Roy Orbison, a year after touring England with the Beatles, had his first Top 10 single since the previous autumn with "It's Over" and then knocked the Animals from the top of the charts in September with "Oh, Pretty Woman," though that would be his last number one hit.

Lost somewhat amidst Motown's successes and the British Invasion, 1964 was a big year for R&B, particularly the uptown variety. Betty Everett scored a number six hit with "The Shoop Shoop Song (It's In His Kiss)" and reached the Top Five with her duet with Jerry Butler, a cover of the Everly Brothers' "Let It Be Me." The Tams hit number nine with their "beach music" classic "What Kind of Fool (Do You Think I Am)." The Drifters got to number four with their summertime standard "Under The Boardwalk," featuring an impassioned Johnny Moore lead vocal, recorded the day after the sudden death of regular lead voice Rudy Lewis. The Impressions made quite an impression on the charts with five hits, including the civil rights anthems "Keep On Pushing" (#10) and "Amen" (#7), both written and produced by Curtis Mayfield. Dionne Warwick emerged as a first-line star with her work on Burt Bacharach and Hal David's "Anyone Who Had A Heart" (#8) and "Walk On By" (#6). Irma Thomas achieved her first national hit with "Wish Someone Would Care" (#17). After a four-year absence, rock 'n' roll pioneer Chuck Berry returned to the charts with "Nadine" (#23) and "No Particular Place To Go," his first Top Ten hit since "Johnny B. Goode" in 1958.

The Top Forty format left openings for all types of music despite the British Invasion. Country singer Roger Miller had two Top Ten novelty hits with "Dang Me" (#7) and "Chug-A-Lug" (#9). Actor Lorne Green spoke his way through "Ringo," a number one single about a Western outlaw whose title may have mistakenly led some to believe the song was about the Beatles drummer, who actually was a big Western fan. Other songs with a novelty slant included the Serendipity Singer's take on the traditional folk song "Don't Let The Rain Come Down (Crooked Little Man)" (#6) and the Newbeats' "Bread And Butter" (#2). Jan & Dean delivered the humorous "The Little Old Lady (From Pasadena)" (#3) and the car crash classic "Dead Man's Curve" (#8), while J. Frank Wilson & the Cavaliers' morbid "Last Kiss" took death in an automobile accident all the way to number two. Johnny Rivers scored with live recordings of two Chuck Berry songs, "Memphis" (#2) and Maybelline (#12). Although the quality of his songs declined, Elvis continued to sell records with movie themes such as "Kissin' Cousins" (#12) and "Viva Las Vegas (#29). Other songs getting considerable air play included Terry Stafford's "Suspicion" (#3), Jay & the American's "Come A Little Bit Closer" (#3), Gale Garnet's "We'll Sing In The Sunshine" (#4), Diane Renay's "Navy Blue" (#6), Bobby Goldsboro "See The Funny Little Clown" (#9), and British duo Chad & Jeremy's "Yesterday's Gone" (#21) and "A Summer Song" (#7).

Other R&B hits included Major Lance's "Um, Um, Um, Um, Um, Um" (#5), Bobby Freeman's "C'mon And Swim" (#5) and Shirley Ellis' "The Nitty Gritty" (#8). The biggest instrumentals of the year were the Marketts' "Out Of Limits" (#3) and trumpeter Al Hirt's rendering of Allen Toussaint's "Java" (#4). Stan Getz & Astrud Gilberto had a Top Five hit with "The Girl From Ipanema," with an airy vocal backed by a Brazilian blend of bossa nova and jazz sounds.

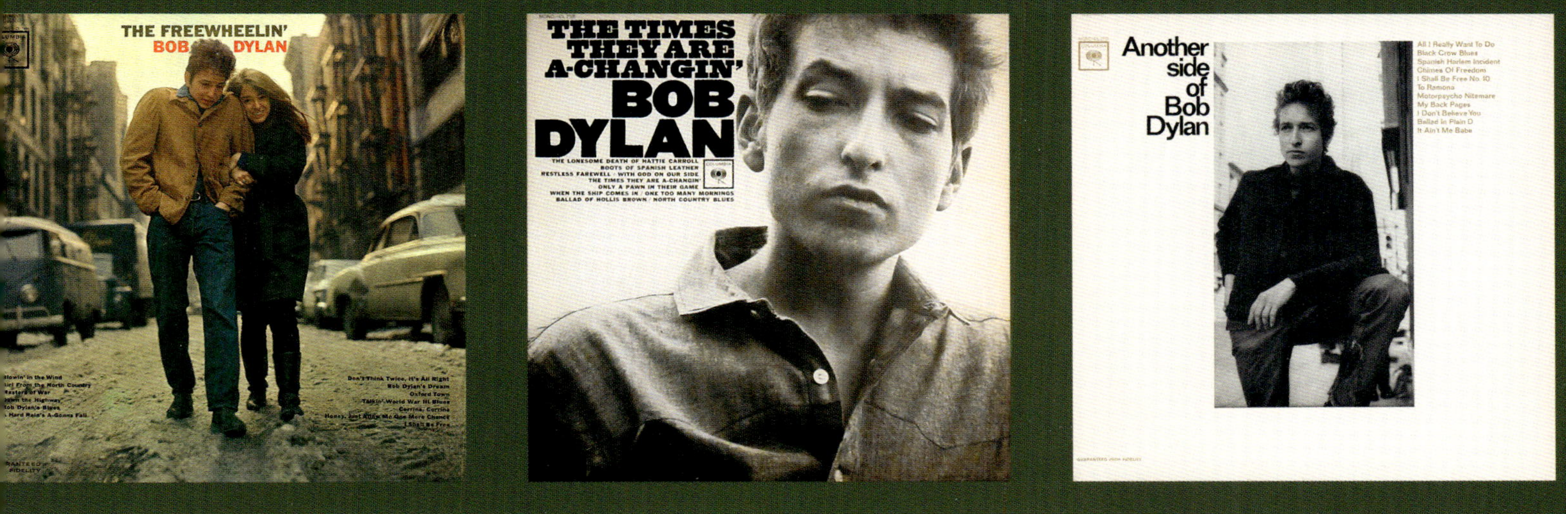

And then there was the man who would become arguably the single most influential musical figure of at least the second half of the sixties. When 1964 began, Bob Dylan was perhaps the fastest rising star in folk music. His song "Blowin' In the Wind" had been a Top Five hit single for Peter, Paul and Mary and a civil rights anthem in the summer of '63 which climaxed that year's Newport Folk Festival. By the beginning of 1964, Dylan's *Freewheelin' Bob Dylan* LP had come to the attention of the Beatles [who obtained a copy of the album while in Paris as detailed on page 238]. The Beatles came to Dylan's attention while he was traveling between cities on tour and first heard "I Want To Hold Your Hand" on the car radio. Dylan was touring to promote his third album, *The Times They Are A-Changin'*, which was full of the kind of protest songs that had made him famous, including the anthemic and oh-so-appropriate title song. But, in the wake of the JFK assassination and other events, Dylan was becoming uncomfortable with the "king of folk protest" role. In addition, there was turmoil in his personal life. In June, he recorded a batch of new songs that were more inward-looking than his "finger pointin'" songs, as Dylan termed them. Among these new songs were "Chimes Of Freedom," "All I Really Want To Do," "My Back Pages," "It Ain't Me Babe" and "Mr. Tambourine Man," though that latter song didn't make Dylan's next album. That LP, *Another Side Of Bob Dylan*, was released in early August and would have a profound influence on the blending of folk and rock in 1965. And not long after the album's release, Dylan and the Beatles had their first meeting where Bob turned the group on to pot. Dylan's musical influence on the Beatles continued as well. When the group starred on an early episode of Shindig in early October, John Lennon performed a new song of his called "I'm A Loser," which was highly Dylan-esque. Lennon even wore a Dylan-style harmonica holder. Indeed, the times they were a-changin'.

Proof of the musical changes of 1964 was on display at the Santa Monica Civic Auditorium on October 28 and 29 for the recording of a concert movie, *The T.A.M.I. Show* (for "Teen Age Music International."). It was shot using the "Electronovision" video system (a better version of kinescope) and was directed by Steve Binder, who would direct Elvis Presley's "comeback" TV special four years later. The finished product was released by American International Pictures, home of the "beach party" movies, and premiered in theaters during the 1964 Christmas break. The bill was a good sampling of the biggest pop/rock/R&B acts of the year. The concert was hosted by the "clown princes" of the Southern California surf/hot rod music scene, Jan & Dean, who sang the show's theme song "(Here They Come) From All Over The World," and the big kahunas of that scene, the Beach Boys, who played a four-song set. The British Invasion was represented by Gerry and the Pacemakers, Billy J. Kramer with the Dakotas, and the Rolling Stones. From Motown, there were the Miracles, Marvin Gaye and the Supremes, just coming off their first two chart-topping singles. Chuck Berry, recently back on the charts, participated in a medley of hits with Gerry. Lesley Gore was the lone female on the bill, and the Barbarians represented the early garage rock bands. But the most unforgettable set came from R&B veteran James Brown and the Famous Flames, especially his well-choreographed finale, "Please Please Please," which was such a sensation that the Stones delayed their set for a time. Phil Spector's resident arranger Jack Nitzsche was the show's music director. He utilized several members of the L.A. session players team known as the Wrecking Crew, along with the Blossoms, who were session singers that included Darlene Love. By then, the Blossoms had weekly TV exposure on Shindig. Like Shindig, The T.A.M.I. Show was a good representation of the pop world of 1964, demonstrating that, although the Beatles and the British Invasion dominated, the music scene of 1964 was so much more. Many of its featured performers would go on to greater success.

James Brown was on the threshold of his real breakthrough on the pop charts, gaining mainstream success between 1965 and 1968. The Rolling Stones would soon take their place as being second only to the Beatles. Lesley Gore would continue to have periodic hit singles. While not as spectacularly successful as, say, the Supremes, Marvin Gaye and the Miracles would continue to be important cogs in Motown's "Sound of Young America," especially with Smokey Robinson at his peak as a songwriter and producer. The Beach Boys would move further beyond their early surf/cars hits in 1965 and become one of the most influential of all American bands. The best was yet to come.

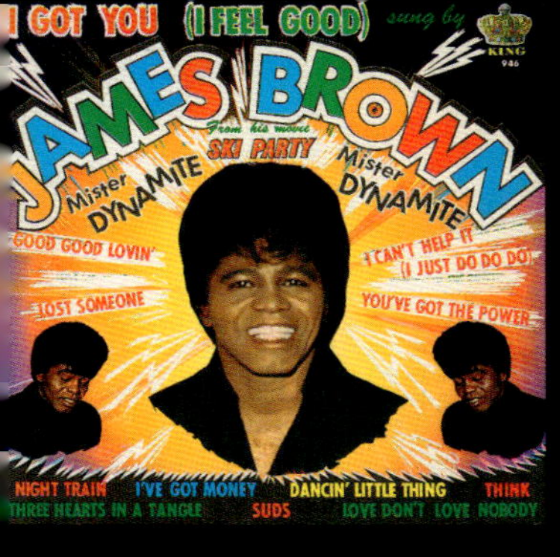

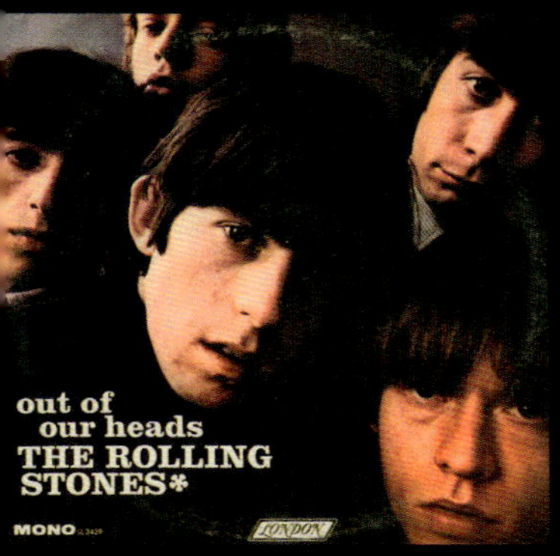

RECORDED LIVE
THE MOTORTOWN REVUE VOL. 2
MARVIN GAYE • THE MIRACLES • STEVIE WONDER
MARTHA & VANDELLAS • THE MARVELETTES
KIM WESTON • THE TEMPTATIONS • MARY WELLS

★★★★★★★★★★★★★★★★★★★★★★★★★★★★★★★★★★★★★★

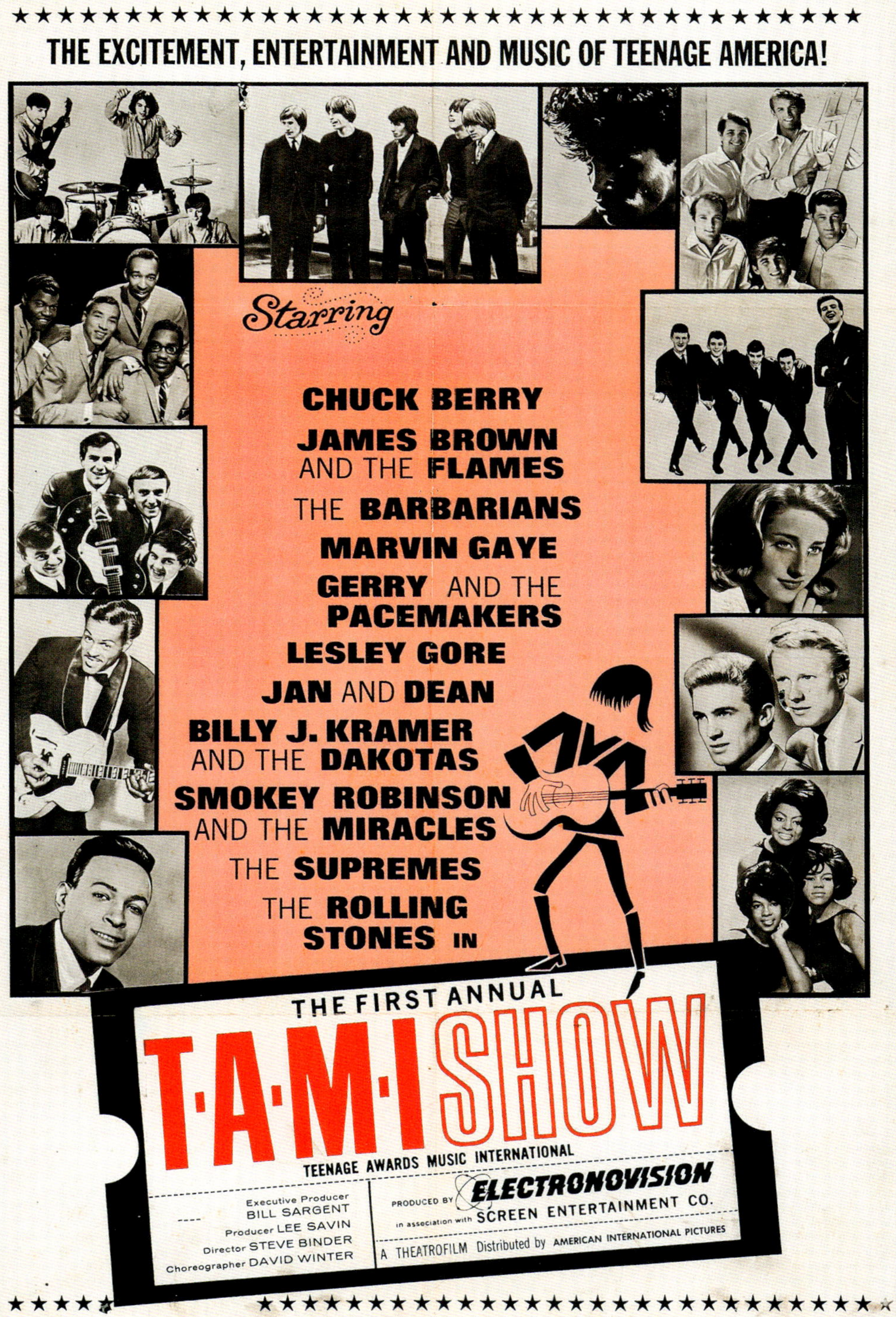

THE EXCITEMENT, ENTERTAINMENT AND MUSIC OF TEENAGE AMERICA!

Starring

CHUCK BERRY
JAMES BROWN AND THE **FLAMES**
THE **BARBARIANS**
MARVIN GAYE
GERRY AND THE **PACEMAKERS**
LESLEY GORE
JAN AND **DEAN**
BILLY J. KRAMER AND THE **DAKOTAS**
SMOKEY ROBINSON AND THE **MIRACLES**
THE **SUPREMES**
THE **ROLLING STONES** IN

THE FIRST ANNUAL

T·A·M·I SHOW

TEENAGE AWARDS MUSIC INTERNATIONAL

Executive Producer BILL SARGENT
Producer LEE SAVIN
Director STEVE BINDER
Choreographer DAVID WINTER

PRODUCED BY ELECTRONOVISION
in association with SCREEN ENTERTAINMENT CO.
A THEATROFILM Distributed by AMERICAN INTERNATIONAL PICTURES

★★★★★★★★★★★★★★★★★★★★★★★★★★★★★★★★★★★

How I Learned to Stop Worrying and Love the Movies

by Bruce Spizer

For young Beatles fans, it seemed that the only movie of any importance in 1964 was the Beatles debut film, *A Hard Day's Night*. But even the Beatles knew there were many magnificent films filling cinemas that year. In discussing the group's acting abilities during the filming of *A Hard Day's Night*, Paul said they didn't consider themselves actors. They had recently seen Peter Sellers in *Dr. Strangelove*, prompting Paul to proclaim: "And you simply can't follow THAT!"

And right he is. *Dr. Strangelove Or: How I Learned To Stop Worrying And Love The Bomb* is an amazing political satire black comedy produced, directed and co-written by Stanley Kubrick. Peter Sellers brilliantly plays three pivotal roles in the film: Group Captain Lionel Mandrake, an exchange officer from the British Royal Air Force who desperately tries to stop renegade (and quite insane) U.S. Air Force Brigadier General Jack D. Ripper and his order for an all-out nuclear bomber attack on the U.S.S.R.; President Merkin Muffley, who has to explain the situation to the drunk Soviet Premier, Dimitri Kissov; and Dr. Strangelove, a wheelchair-bound former Nazi who serves as the President's scientific advisor. General Buck Turgidson, brilliantly played by George C. Scott, is shocked when the President warns Kissov of the attack and orders his generals to assist the Soviets in taking down any bombers that do not get the recall order. But the ability of B-52 pilot Major T. J. "King" Kong to evade defenses and the Soviet's Doomsday Machine lead to a deadly ending for most of mankind. *Fail Safe* has a similar dark theme, but is not a comedy. When radar indicates that an unidentified plane (later determined to be civilian) has intruded U.S. airspace, a computer error sends orders to a group of bombers to execute a nuclear attack on Moscow. The President, played by Henry Fonda, comes up with a horrific but necessary plan of deadly sacrifice to avert an all-out nuclear war. In the event Moscow is destroyed, an American bomber on stand-by shall immediately drop a nuclear bomb on New York City, in effect trading the destruction of the largest American city for the unintentional leveling of the largest Soviet city.

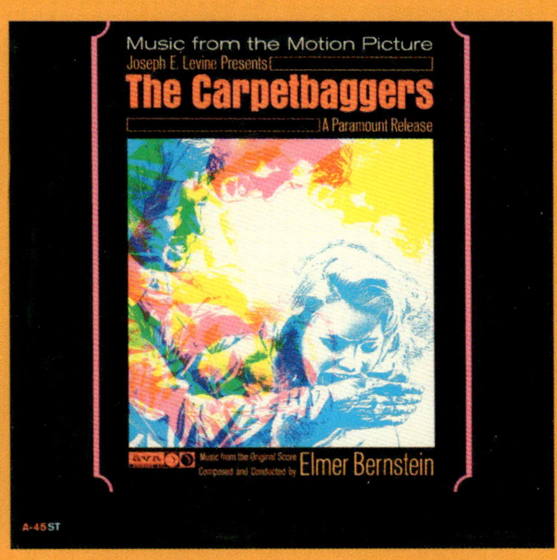

In *The Best Man,* Henry Fonda plays the part of an intellectual and former Secretary of State vying for the presidential nomination of his party against a ruthless populist and anti-Communist portrayed by Cliff Robertson. *Seven Days In May* is a cautionary tale of a planned military coup to remove the U.S. President (Fredric March) from office for entering into a disarmament treaty with the Soviet Union. A Marine colonel (Kirk Douglas) stumbles upon a plot by the Chairman of the Joint Chiefs of Staff (Burt Lancaster) to take the President into custody and install himself as head of a military junta ruling the nation. In the end, the President prevails and assures the nation that it gains strength through peace rather than conflict. *Four Days In November* is a documentary on the assassination of President Kennedy.

Although the second James Bond movie, *From Russia With Love*, premiered in England on October 10, 1963, it did not reach theaters in the United States until May 1964. America's growing infatuation with British pop culture helped further popularize the exploits of British secret agent 007, resulting in the film grossing $9,200,000 in North America. The next Bond extravaganza featuring Sean Connery, *Goldfinger*, did even better. It premiered in London on September 17 and hit U.S. cinemas that December 22. With its sexy Bond girls, including Honor Blackman as Pussy Galore, cunning villain Auric Goldfinger and his loyal Korean servant Oddjob tossing his deadly derby, and gadget-filled Austin Martin sports car, *Goldfinger* grossed $22,500,000. For movie-goers seeking overt sex and sadism, *The Carpetbaggers*, adopted from Harold Robbins' salacious novel, pushed the boundaries of American films of its day, although its nude scene was re-shot with Carroll Baker wearing a robe for U.S. audiences. It grossed $15,500,000.

Fans of Peter Sellers had much to rejoice for in 1964 beyond *Dr. Strangelove*. In the comedy-drama *The World Of Henry Orient*, he plays a New York City concert pianist who has an affair with a married woman and is stalked by two teenage girls. The film also features Paula Prentiss, Tom Bosley and Angela Lansbury. Bosley would rise to fame ten years later when he played the role of Howard Cunningham in the TV show Happy Days. In 1963, Sellers fell into the part of one of his most beloved characters, the inept French police Inspector Jacques Clouseau. Although *The Pink Panther* was released in Italy in December 1963, the Blake Edwards comedy did not open in America until mid-March 1964. David Niven plays the suave Sir Charles Lytton, who is secretly the infamous thief, The Phantom. It also features Robert Wagner as Sir Charles' ne'er-do-well nephew George, Capucine as Clouseau's adulterous wife, and Claudia Cardinale as Princess Dala. The film is aided by a great Henry Mancini score and a clever Pink Panther cartoon opening, but it is Sellers who steals the show with his slap-stick antics. Blake Edwards then adapted the play *A Shot In The Dark* to serve as the return of Sellers as Inspector Clouseau of the French Sûreté, this time in the lead role. Sellers continues with great physical comedy and develops his humorous pseudo-French accent. Elke Sommer plays a sexy murder suspect. The film introduces supporting cast members Herbert Lom as Commissioner Dreyfus, Graham Stark as Dreyfus' assistant Hercule, and Burt Kwouk as Clouseau's man-servant Kato. The trio would reappear in later films in the Pink Panther series. *The Pink Panther* grossed $5,935,000, while *A Shot In The Dark* did even better at $6,748,000. *Topkapi* is a thrilling fictional film about the heist of the emerald-studded Topkapi Dagger in Istanbul, Turkey. *The Pink Panther* and *Topkapi* each feature exciting theft scenes involving aerial skills.

A trio of musicals were big box office hits in 1964. *The Unsinkable Molly Brown* is a film adaptation with screenplay by Helen Deutsch of the 1960 Broadway musical with story by Richard Morris and song score by Meredith Willson (who wrote the score for *The Music Man* and its ballad "Till There Was You"). It stars Debbie Reynolds as Molly, who is rescued from the Colorado River as a child, becomes a saloon singer in Leadville, Colorado, marries a miner who sells his claim in a silver mine, travels to Europe, and survives the sinking of RMS Titanic. The film grossed $6,040,000. *Mary Poppins*, based on T.L. Traver's series of Mary Poppins' books, mixes live action and animation to tell the story of a magical nanny who arrives at the London home of George Banks to take care of his children, who are always getting into trouble. Julie Andrews stars in the title role along with Dick Van Dyke, who plays her close friend Bert. The film has several catchy songs, including "Supercalifragilisticexpialidocious," "A Spoonful of Sugar" and "Chim Chim Cher-ee." It was nominated for 13 Academy Awards, winning five, including Best Actress for Julie Andrews, best song for "Chim Chim Cher-ee," best score (by Richard M. Sherman and Robert B. Sherman) and best visual effects, and was the top grossing film of 1964 at $31,000,000. Not far behind at $30,000,000 was *My Fair Lady*, a comedy-drama film adaptation of the 1956 Lerner and Loewe Broadway musical based on George Bernard Shaw's *Pygmalion*. It stars Rex Harrison reprising his Broadway role of phonetics professor Henry Higgins and Audrey Hepburn as Eliza Doolittle, a poor Cockney flower-seller. The film won eight Academy Awards, including Best Picture, Best Director (George Cukor) and Best Actor. Memorable songs include "I Could Have Danced All Night," "Wouldn't It Be Loverly," "With A Little Bit Of Luck," "On The Street Where You Live" "The Rain In Spain" and "Get Me To The Church On Time."

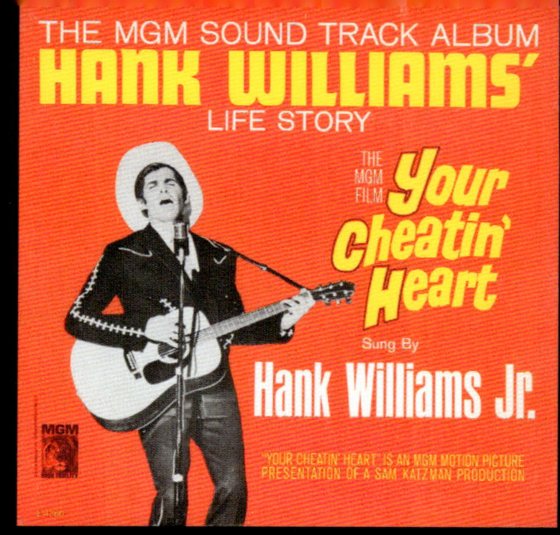

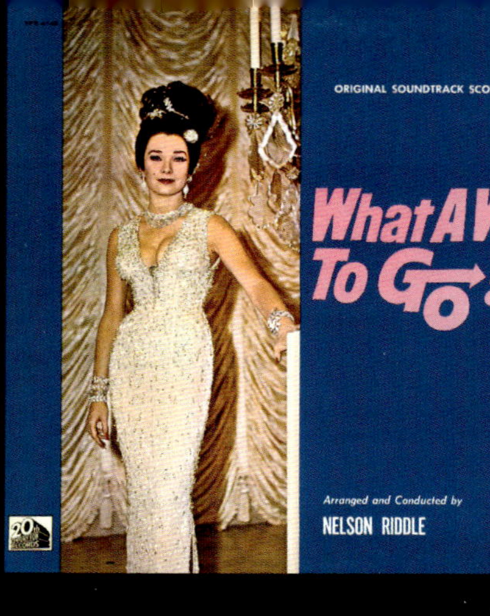

Less successful at the box office and with critics was the musical *Robin And The 7 Hoods*, which attempts to place the "rob from the rich, give to the poor" story of Robin Hood into Chicago's 1920s gangster scene. The picture stars Frank Sinatra, Dean Martin, Bing Crosby, Sammy Davis, Jr. and a pre-Columbo Peter Faulk. The film's centerpiece song, "My Kind Of Town," failed to make the Billboard Hot 100 when issued as a single by Sinatra. The critically acclaimed French musical *Les Parapluies de Cherbourg* (*The Umbrellas Of Cherbourg*) won top honors, the Palme d'Or, at the 1964 Cannes Film Festival. *Your Cheatin' Heart* stars George Hamilton in a biopic on the life of Hank Williams.

For those seeking laughs, the screwball comedy *Good Neighbor Sam* delivered. The film stars Jack Lemmon, who works in the art department of a San Francisco ad agency, and features a running gag of unsuccessful attempts to film the "Let Hertz Put You in the Driver's Seat" commercial. On the darker side is *What A Way To Go!* in which a woman, played by Shirley MacLaine, wants to give away her 211 million dollar fortune inherited from a series of husbands who start poor, get rich and die during their marriage to her. Other comedies included *Mail Order Bride* with Buddy Ebsen, then playing Jed Clampett on The Beverly Hillbillies, *The Patsy* with Jerry Lewis, and *The Incredible Mr. Limpet* starring Don Knotts, who turns into a talking fish and helps the U.S. Navy destroy Nazi subs. In *The Brass Bottle*, an architect, played by Tony Randall, buys an antique brass bottle and unintentionally sets free its imprisoned genie Fakrash, played by Burl Ives. Although well-meaning, the genie causes trouble for the architect and his relationship with his girlfriend, played by Barbara Eden, who would soon star as a genie in the TV show I Dream Of Jeannie.

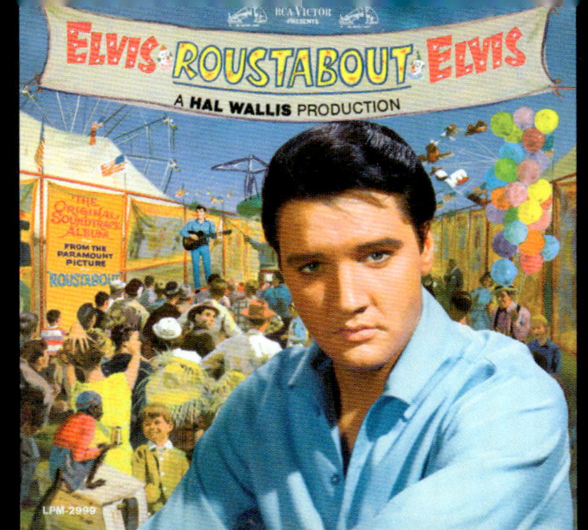

Historical films of 1964 included *The Fall Of The Roman Empire* and *Becket*, which follows the stormy relationship between King Henry II, played by Peter O'Toole, and the Archbishop of Canterbury, played by Richard Burton. Other notable films of the year included Alfred Hitchcock's psychological thriller *Marnie* starring Tippi Hedren, Sean Connery, Bruce Dern and Alan Napier, who, in two years, would be playing Batman's butler, Alfred. And speaking of the Batman TV show, Adam West, who portrayed the Caped Crusader, was in a cool science fiction movie, *Robinson Crusoe On Mars*, though West's character meets his demise early on. *The Time Travelers,* which inspired the 1966 TV show The Time Tunnel, follows a group of scientists as they travel through time. Hanna-Barbera's *Hey There, It's Yogi Bear!* was the first full-length animated film based on a TV cartoon show. Beach movies remained popular, with Frankie Avalon and Annette returning for *Muscle Beach Party* and *Bikini Beach* with Little Stevie Wonder. Others included *Surf Party, Ride The Wild Surf* and *For Those Who Think Young*. The latter film stars James Darren and Paul Lynde, with Bob Denver and Tina Louise, who would soon spend three years on Gilligan's Island as Gilligan and Ginger. Elvis kept cranking out films with *Kissin' Cousins*, *Roustabout* and *Viva Las Vegas*, which co-stars Ann-Margret and is one of his best.

United Artists, the company that had the foresight in 1963 to commit to making a film on the Beatles, had a fabulous year with five of the top ten grossing films of 1964: *Goldfinger* (#3); *From Russia With Love* (#5); *A Shot In The Dark* (#6); *The Pink Panther* (#9); and *A Hard Day's Night* (#10), which grossed a respectable $5,800,000 in North America. James Bond, Peter Sellers as Inspector Clouseau, and the Beatles. No wonder we love the movies!

Rock 'n' Roll Goes to the Movies

by Frank Daniels

Whenever movies appeared in the early history of rock and roll, they were usually exploitative attempts to sympathize with teenagers in order to attract them to the cinema. In fact, rock and roll's earliest years were not documented in film. For that to happen, we had to wait until the middle of the 1950s. "Rock Around The Clock" started out as an underrated pop song; it wound up being a snapshot of teenage life in the mid-1950s. Bill Haley and his Comets added it to their concert repertoire in July 1953, but it took Haley another nine months to record it. The song, issued as the B-side to "Thirteen Women" on Decca 29124, was reviewed in the May 15, 1954 issue of Billboard. "Big beat and repetitious blues lyric makes this a good attempt at 'cat music' and one which should grab coin in the right locations." This prediction came true when the song began being played on coin-operated juke boxes and, more important, gained airplay in certain markets. Two weeks later, the trade magazines were (rightly) calling "Rock Around The Clock" the A-side. The song started getting played all around the northeast, and the Comets returned to the studio to record their next single, "Shake, Rattle And Roll," a cover of Joe Turner's number one R&B side. "Rock Around The Clock" had been a regional success, but nothing more, before it disappeared temporarily.

In his book *Rock Around The Clock: The Record That Started The Rock Revolution!*, pop culture author Jim Dawson describes how the song became a million seller. One of the buyers of the original Decca single was young Peter Ford, the nine-year¬old son of actor Glenn Ford and an avid listener of popular music. Glenn was the star of a new movie about teen delinquency – *The Blackboard Jungle*. In early 1955, Glenn raided his son's record collection for samples of what kids were listening to. One of Peter's favorite songs was "Rock Around The Clock." At Glenn Ford's suggestion the song was placed into the soundtrack of *The Blackboard Jungle*, which premiered March 19, 1955. Based on the song's appearance in the movie, the record broke onto Billboard's Best Sellers in Stores chart on May 14, 1955. By July 9, it became rock and roll's first number one hit, remaining at the top for eight straight weeks.

The movie itself, though, had little to do with rock and roll. Focusing on the growing problem of violence and rebellion in schools, it proved to be highly controversial. While the March 28, 1955 Life magazine described it as "a brutal and powerful movie on public school juvenile delinquency," Memphis censor Lloyd Binford banned the movie in late March, calling it "the vilest picture I've seen in 26 years as censor." The Atlanta Board of Review responded to the movie shortly thereafter by banning it, even as Memphis reconsidered their ban. An article in the April 28 issue of Jet, then known as "The Weekly Negro News Magazine," suggested that some of the opposition came from people who were "rabidly anti-Negro" because it prominently featured a young Sidney Poitier. Citywide bans prompted court challenges, which usually ended on the side of the movie. Congressional hearings that fall prompted teachers to come forward denying the problem: "there is no blackboard jungle." All of this press helped attract people to the theaters. Whether or not they liked the movie, many of them went out to purchase "Rock Around The Clock." More than two decades later, Glenn Ford was in another film with the song. In 1978's *Superman: The Movie,* Ford appears as Jonathan Kent. "Rock Around The Clock" is played just before his last scene in the film. This may or may not have been a tribute to Glenn Ford's role in making the song a hit. Either way, it's a nice touch.

Bill Haley's rapid rise in popularity led to a slew of "rock and roll movies" starting in 1956. Released that March, *Rock Around The Clock* tells a fictionalized version of the development of rock and roll and the story of Bill Haley. Notable for disc jockey Alan Freed's involvement, the movie features an integrated music venue in which Bill Haley, the Platters, and Puerto Rican star Tony Martinez perform. The film contains 17 rock and roll songs, nine of which are by Haley's Comets. Freddie Bell and the Bellboys, whose rearrangement of "Hound Dog" formed the basis for Elvis Presley's hit that year, also appear in the film. As a soundtrack to the fifties, *Rock Around The Clock* does a good job of demonstrating the direction in which popular music was moving. However, no U.S. label released a soundtrack album even though posters billed the movie as "the screen's first great rock 'n' roll feature." Decca issued Haley's selections as an expanded version of the 1955 LP *Shake, Rattle And Roll*, but without songs by the other artists. The movie leaves much to be desired. It falls short of being a realistic biopic and comes across as an exploitation film.

Elvis Presley's first movie, *Love Me Tender*, was released on November 15. Although the film's poster billed Presley as "MR. ROCK 'N' ROLL!," the movie contains no genuine rock and roll music. Its four songs are country and western tunes suitable for the movie's western plot. *The Girl Can't Help It* hit theaters on December 1. The film is a parody of the music business starring Tom Ewell and Jayne Mansfield, and features Little Richard, Fats Domino, Julie London, the Platters, Eddie Cochran and Gene Vincent. Critics were split, with some regarding the film as nothing more than a musical pin-up magazine, and others finding its romantic and comedy elements charming. The movie's bright colors and expertly-filmed musical performances make it essential viewing. In 1968, the Beatles interrupted their "Birthday" recording session to watch the film on TV. On December 7, *Rock! Rock! Rock!* appeared on the scene as a teen drama. A schoolgirl, played by Tuesday Weld in her first leading role, tries to earn enough money to buy a new dress so she can go to the prom. The plot essentially jumps from song to song, showcasing the talents of Chuck Berry, Frankie Lymon and the Teenagers, LaVern Baker, the Flamingos, the Moonglows, and others. As a substitute for a concert, the movie does well, but fails as a motion picture. Even Billboard's review was negative: "A low-budget film of no great dramatic pretensions. The story is a frail framework which is all but lost in the parade of acts...The music is the thing...." *Don't Knock The Rock*, released on December 14, gave Bill Haley top billing, but revolves around Alan Dale, who plays a rock and roll singer fighting his hometown's ban on the music. It features Little Richard and Alan Freed.

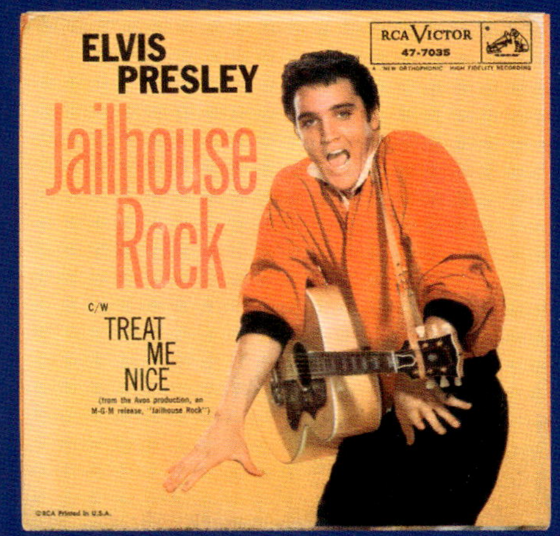

In 1957, Elvis finally got to rock the big screen with his films *Loving You* and *Jailhouse Rock*. In the former, Elvis plays a delivery man who gets discovered and becomes a rock and roll star. The film's title song was written by the legendary production and writing team of Jerry Leiber and Mike Stoller. Better still are "(Let Me Be Your) Teddy Bear" and "Got A Lot O' Livin' To Do." In *Jailhouse Rock*, Elvis' character gets into a bar fight and is convicted of manslaughter. In what would be typical in Presley movies, he's basically a singer who also happens to do something else. His cellmate hears him sing in jail and recognizes his potential. Elvis does a great job with this one, but otherwise, the plot is somewhat empty. The film features six Presley songs, including four written by Leiber-Stoller: the dynamite "Jailhouse Rock," "Treat Me Nice," "(You're So Square) Baby I Don't Care" and "I Want To Be Free." Stoller even appears in the film as Elvis' piano player. The title track becomes a dance production number. Although reviewers largely panned the film, it deserved better. Elvis certainly comes across well, but ultimately the motion picture tells no great story.

King Creole (1958) is more interesting. Once again, the music is quite good, pairing Elvis with jazz musicians on "King Creole" (written by Leiber-Stoller), "Hard Headed Woman" and "Trouble." Making Elvis into a James-Dean-esque figure who deals with organized crime in New Orleans was a good idea. This might be the best early rock and roll film, and for those who must see only one such movie, this one is recommended. Surrounded by film stars like Walter Matthau, Presley's job is very believable, but at times the music seems to interrupt the plot. Of course, being a rock and roll movie, it attracted little attention from the people who gave out awards.

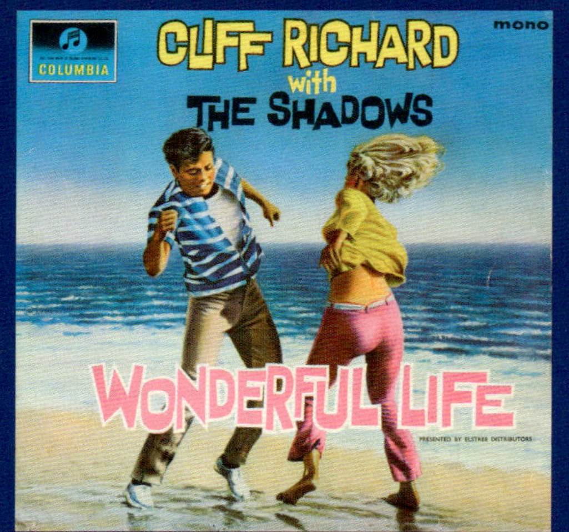

Over the next few years, there were few rock and roll movies that are truly interesting for their storytelling, acting and music. When the acting was good, often the music was substandard. Teen idol Frankie Avalon moved further into acting with roles in *The Alamo* (1960) and *Voyage To The Bottom Of The Sea* (1961). While Avalon fared well as an actor, he would later star in a series of "beach" teen exploitation films whose music was more pop than rock, although a few featured Dick Dale and Little Stevie Wonder. *Twist Around The Clock* is basically a 1961 remake of *Rock Around The Clock* made to capitalize on the popularity of "The Twist." Starring Chubby Checker, the Marcels, and Dion, the focus of the film is getting the music out. This was followed immediately by Joey Dee and the Starlighters' vehicle *Hey, Let's Twist!* And borrowing its title from *Don't Knock The Rock*, Hollywood gave us *Don't Knock The Twist* in 1962.

In England, pop singers were expected to appear in films. Cliff Richard began his movie career in 1959 with a minor role in the melodrama *Serious Charge*, directed by Terence Young, who would recruit Sean Connery to play James Bond and direct the 007 films *Dr. No*, *From Russia With Love* and *Thunderball*. After co-starring in *Expresso Bongo* in 1960, Richard starred in a trio of musicals: *The Young Ones* (*Wonderful To Be Young* in the U.S.), *Summer Holiday* and *Wonderful Life*, which was released the same month as *A Hard Day's Night*. Adam Faith had a prominent role in the 1960 British teen exploitation drama *Beat Girl* (*Wild For Kicks* in the U.S.), which also featured Christopher Lee. Billy Fury starred in the 1962 musical *Play It Cool* with British teen singer Helen Shapiro and American teen idol Bobby Vee. The musical comedy play (and later film) *Half A Sixpence* was written to utilize the talents of Tommy Steele.

The most interesting of the British teen flicks is 1962's *It's Trad, Dad!* The movie stars pop singers Helen Shapiro and Craig Douglas and features Chubby Checker, Del Shannon, Gene Vincent and Gary (U.S.) Bonds, along with several jazz-oriented artists including Mr. Acker Bilk and his Paramount Jazz Band, Chris Barber's Jazz Band with Ottilie Patterson, Terry Lightfoot's New Orleans Jazzmen, and the Dukes of Dixieland. It was the music played by these traditional jazz acts, known as "Trad," that gave the film its name. In America, where the term was not used, the movie was retitled *Ring-A-Ding Rhythm*.

The basic plot is one that is used over and over again. Youngsters are upset when the mayor and town elders shut down juke boxes that are playing jazz records. Two teenagers (Shapiro and Douglas) decide to organize a jazz concert to showcase and legitimize the music. Along the way, assisted by the film's narrator, they visit television studios, a nightclub and a recording studio, recruiting BBC disc jockeys Pete Murray, David Jacobs and Alan Freeman to obtain commitments from performers and set up a live television broadcast of the show. After learning that jazz musicians are involved, the mayor sets up a war room to coordinate police blockades aimed at preventing the musicians' bus from entering the city limits, but this only delays their arrival. To keep the waiting crowd from growing restless, Douglas sings "Rainbows" and Shapiro performs the upbeat "Let's Talk About Love" and the ballad "Sometime Yesterday." The musicians finally arrive and put on a great show highlighted by female blues singer Ottilie Patterson belting out the jazz classics "Down By The Riverside" and "When The Saints Go Marching In." Realizing that the jazz concert is delighting even adults and is being broadcast live by the BBC, the mayor changes his tune and takes credit for the successful show. The film ends with Douglas and Shapiro, backed by Sounds, Inc., singing "Ring-A-Ding."

It's Trad, Dad! showcases 27 songs performed by 20 artists. But what separates the film from other rock and roll movies is Dick Lester directing his first full-length film. Lester uses surreal elements and sight gags to add comedic touches. The musical performances are enhanced with imaginative camera angles, quick cuts and close-ups. These concepts would be put to use by Lester in *A Hard Day's Night*. David Robinson of The Times wrote: "Lester's immoderate interest in technical tricks – speeded up action, multiple exposures, eccentric angles, tricky masking and so on...is all done with such frank enjoyment and at such a determined pace that criticism is disarmed."

While *It's Trad, Dad!* is an effective film that gained praise from The Times (of London), its format of featuring 20 musical acts held together by a flimsy plot was not attractive to the Beatles. A little over a year after the movie's release, John told Melody Maker: "We have been offered scene parts in a package show sort of film where about twenty different pop stars all appear with no story and no meaning. We prefer to wait until we find a film with a good plot that will hold the interest of the teenagers. Otherwise it might do us more harm than good." The Beatles would find that film four to five months later in what would become *A Hard Day's Night* with Dick Lester as director.

At this point, a good question is, "Which rock and roll movies were nominated for Academy Awards?" In 1955, *The Blackboard Jungle,* with its one true rock and roll song, received four Oscar nominations, winning none. Were these for Best Motion Picture or Best Actor? No. They were for Art Direction, Film Editing, Screenplay, and Cinematography. *The Girl Can't Help It* was totally snubbed by the Academy, but Jayne Mansfield did win a Golden Globe for Most Promising Newcomer–Female. The Academy continued to ignore rock and roll movies for nearly a decade, even in the music categories. Finally, the 1963 Elvis Presley parody *Bye Bye, Birdie*, previously a musical comedy hit on Broadway, was nominated for Best Sound and for Best Scoring of Music–Adaption or Treatment. It was also nominated for two Golden Globes, including Best Motion Picture–Musical or Comedy. Ann-Margret received a Best Actress nomination.

It took the Beatles for the Academy to finally take appropriate notice of rock and roll movies. But even *A Hard Day's Night* was not given its proper due at the Academy Awards held on April 5, 1965. Although George Martin received a nomination for Best Scoring of Music–Adaption or Treatment, he did not win. And none of the Beatles songs from the film were even nominated for Best Music (Song). Alun Owen was nominated for Best Writing (Story and Screenplay–Written Directly for the Screen), but did he win? No. The screenplay for *Father Goose* beat *A Hard Day's Night* that year. Anyone remember *Father Goose*? Although not a winner, the appearance of *A Hard Day's Night* put the Academy on notice that rock music was a force to be reckoned with – or at least considered. In the years that followed, other rock songs were nominated in the Music category. *The Graduate* (1967), featuring music by Simon & Garfunkel, was the first movie with rock music to be nominated for the Academy's Best Picture award. It is fitting that the first movie featuring rock music to win the Oscar for Music (Original Song Score) was the Beatles *Let It Be*.

In the film revenue category, only the film adaptation of the play *Bye Bye, Birdie* precedes *A Hard Day's Night* in being a rock and roll movie that appears on the Top Ten list of Top-Grossing Films of its year. These led the way to *The Graduate* being the top-grossing movie of 1967.

A Hard Day's Night was a good movie. The screenplay was excellent, showcasing the individual actors' personalities while providing a realistic parody of the true lives of the Beatles. George Martin's instrumental score was strong, with his single version of "Ringo's Theme (This Boy)" holding its own in the middle of the charts for a few months. The actors, particularly Wilfrid Brambell (Paul's "other" grandfather) and Victor Spinetti (the television director), did a terrific job of bringing the comedy to life, and even the Beatles themselves acted reasonably – with Ringo faring especially well. While we could certainly say that the movie's centerpiece is the music, as we look back at the film itself, we see that the movie actually holds up – not merely as a vehicle for the songs but also as a movie. The surprising thing about it is that you don't need to know who the Beatles were in order to have a good time watching the film. You could show it to your children or your grandchildren today, and they might enjoy it as much as you did. Finally getting the credit that it was due in 2010, Time magazine ranked *A Hard Day's Night* as one of the 100 best movies of all time. Variety placed it on a similar list in 2022. With two dozen reflections from major media outlets, Metacritic also places it among the best movies ever.

During the early years of rock and roll, it was hard to create a movie that was well liked for its acting and plot and which featured chart-worthy rock and roll. *The Girl Can't Help It* was a step in the right direction, giving audiences a romantic comedy with Jayne Mansfield that poked fun at the entertainment business and showed performances of rock and roll artists in glorious color. But in my opinion, *King Creole* was the best rock and roll movie before the Beatles came around, and that's certainly fitting. With *A Hard Day's Night*, rock music had finally reached a point of near acceptance among movie critics. The genre may or may not be here to stay, but thanks in part to the Beatles, to Richard Lester, to Alun Owen, and to the actors and others who put the Beatles first film together, people came to recognize that movies could be "good" and contain rock and roll music at the same time. That alone makes *A Hard Day's Night* one of the most, if not the most, important piece of rock and roll movie history.

Postscript: Rock 'n' Roll Films After *A Hard Day's Night*

You might think that after the box-office success and critical acclaim of *A Hard Day's Night*, producers of rock and roll films thereafter would improve their product to match the Beatles success, but you'd be wrong. While *A Hard Day's Night* prompted more movies to be made, the same quality was never achieved. The industry continued to embrace the old formula of peppering a flimsy plot with rock and roll performances. *Get Yourself A College Girl*, released in December 1964, tells the story of a female college student who runs afoul of her school's board of trustees when her secret career as a successful pop songwriter is exposed. So she and her friends spend Christmas break skiing in Sun Valley. Along the way, the film works in performances by the Dave Clark Five, the Animals, the Standells, and Stan Getz & Astrud Gilberto, who perform "The Girl From Ipanema." In 1965's *Ski Party*, the beach party gang goes skiing and is treated to performances by Leslie Gore, the Hondells, and James Brown & the Famous Flames.

Film producers did take notice that movies could be built around a single rock and roll group; however, they frequently had trouble coming up with a viable concept. For Gerry and the Pacemakers, the creative team went with a theme similar to the Beatles film debut. *Ferry Cross The Mersey* was quickly shot and rushed out in Great Britain in December 1964 and America two months later. The movie opens with the group being greeted by screaming fans upon their return from America. After the band is shown recording "It's Gonna Be Alright," the film flashes back to tell the story of how they made it big. The group performs nine songs. The producers of the Dave Clark 5's *Catch Us If You Can* (titled *Having A Wild Weekend* in the U.S.) took a different approach in the group's 1965 film. The band members are stuntmen who live together in a church building. Dave runs off with an actress known as the Butcher Girl while filming a meat commercial. They go to a swimming pool and then journey towards Burgh Island, meeting beatniks and fleeing from the police along the way. Although the DC5's music is heard throughout the film, the band does not perform. It comes across as a mild weekend. The plot to Herman Hermit's 1966 film *Hold On!* doesn't hold up. NASA faces a PR disaster when the children of astronauts name the next Gemini capsule "Herman's Hermits." Its sole redeeming feature is the group's performance of eight songs. The film's initial title was *A Must To Avoid*. 'Nuff said!

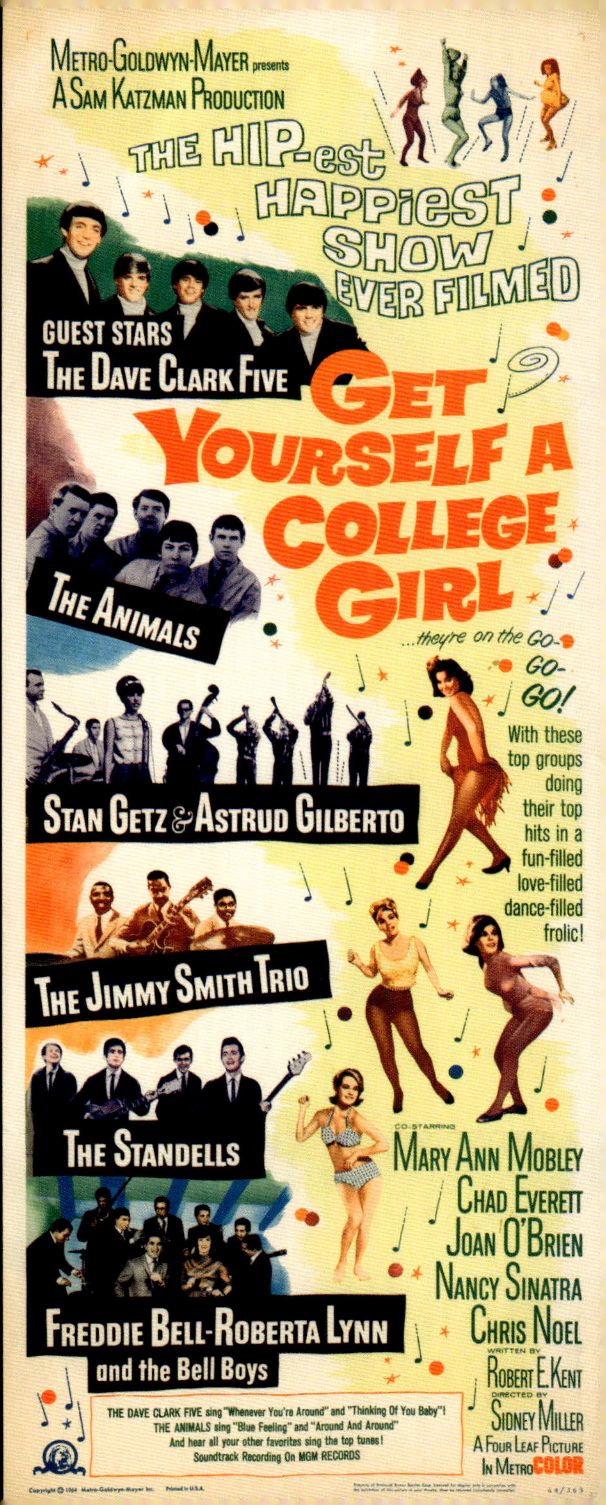

METRO-GOLDWYN-MAYER presents
A SAM KATZMAN PRODUCTION

THE HIP-est HAPPIEST SHOW EVER FILMED

GUEST STARS
THE DAVE CLARK FIVE

GET YOURSELF A COLLEGE GIRL

...they're on the GO-GO-GO!

THE ANIMALS

With these top groups doing their top hits in a fun-filled love-filled dance-filled frolic!

STAN GETZ & ASTRUD GILBERTO

THE JIMMY SMITH TRIO

THE STANDELLS

FREDDIE BELL-ROBERTA LYNN
and the Bell Boys

CO-STARRING
MARY ANN MOBLEY
CHAD EVERETT
JOAN O'BRIEN
NANCY SINATRA
CHRIS NOEL

WRITTEN BY ROBERT E. KENT
DIRECTED BY SIDNEY MILLER
A FOUR LEAF PICTURE
IN METROCOLOR

THE DAVE CLARK FIVE sing "Whenever You're Around" and "Thinking Of You Baby"!
THE ANIMALS sing "Blue Feeling" and "Around And Around"
And hear all your other favorites sing the top tunes!
Soundtrack Recording On MGM RECORDS

Copyright © 1964 Metro-Goldwyn-Mayer Inc. Printed in U.S.A.

The Beatles in Film Before *A Hard Day's Night*

The Beatles Come To Town

Dating back to the days of silent films in the 1910s and continuing into the 1960s, movie theaters frequently showed short newsreels that compiled current news events prior to the start of the feature film. These black and white newsreels were typically four to five minutes long. Pathé News, a well-know producer of cinema newsreels in Great Britain, deemed the Beatles newsworthy as the group's popularity increased after their appearances on Val Parnell's Sunday Night At The London Palladium on October 13, 1963, and at the Royal Variety Performance on November 4. The company obtained permission from Beatles manager Brian Epstein to film two songs performed by the Beatles at their November 20, 1963 concert at the ABC Cinema in Ardwick, Manchester, England. Although newsreels were normally black and white, British Pathé filmed the Beatles in color.

The Beatles Come To Town begins with a shot of the front entrance of the theater, with the newsreel announcer informing viewers: "The fans bought half the tickets by post, and then five thousand queued, some of them for two nights in hope of obtaining the rest. Here are some of the lucky two thousand five hundred who are really going to see the Beatles at the ABC Ardwick, Manchester." After images of fans waiting to get in, the theater's manager is shown getting his staff ready "to cope with the terrific audience response evoked everywhere by the Beatles." This is followed by more screaming fans and Paul being touched by girls as he heads inside the theater. There, the boys show members of the press their latest present, a giant panda bear. Ringo hams it up, and George joins the press in taking pictures of the other Beatles. As fans are let into the cinema, the studio recording of "From Me To You" plays in the background. The Beatles head to their dressing room. Once inside, Paul comically struggles to comb his hair.

After a wide shot of the audience and closeups of screaming fans, the Beatles perform a tight, energetic rendition of "She Loves You." The film cuts back and forth between the Beatles and enthusiastic members of the audience made up almost entirely of young girls. The screaming is so loud that some members of the audience place their fingers in their ears. After the Beatles customary bow at the end of the song, the group performs its shortened concert version of "Twist And Shout." In addition to the up close and personal screaming girl shots, there are images taken from behind the Beatles to show their perspective of the crowd. Richard Lester would film similar viewpoints for the Scala Theatre concert scene at the end of *A Hard Day's Night*. There is also a shot of a British bobby bobbing his head to the music. When the song comes to its climactic end, the Beatles bow and the curtain closes as the Beatles play a brief instrumental passage of "From Me To You." The 6:23 newsreel catches the Beatles at their peak and provides a wonderful glimpse into the excitement generated by the group.

The Beatles Come To Town was shown in British cinemas during the week of December 22, 1963. United Artists obtained the rights to distribute the newsreel in North America. The New York Daily News reported in its April 9, 1964 edition that the United Artists film *Flight From Ashiya*, starring Yul Brynner, Richard Windmark and George Chakiris, would open on April 22 in New York. The movie was an adventure drama involving the U.S. Air Rescue Service. The article noted that a featurette titled *The Beatles Come To Town* would be on the same program. The Daily News panned *Flight From Ashiya* in its April 23 edition. Wanda Hale's review, titled "Mediocre Melodrama Wastes Good Actors," described the film as a "fumbling story...belaboring every incident to the point of boredom." Although Hale did not review the Beatles short film, she called it a "magnet to draw in customers."

While United Artists may have believed that placing the Beatles newsreel on the same program as *Flight From Ashiya* would draw youngsters into theaters to see its sea rescue film, the plan failed. *Flight From Ashiya* had little to attract youngsters, who would have been reluctant to pay for and sit through a one hour, 40 minute adult film to see the Beatles for less than six and a half minutes even if theaters had aggressively marketed the newsreel. By May, *The Beatles Come To Town* began appearing in theaters and drive-ins with more teen-friendly films such as *Muscle Beach Party*, *Wonderful To Be Young* (starring Cliff Richard), *Teenage Millionaire* and *For Those Who Think Young*. The August 3 Daily News reported that United Artists had pulled all prints of *The Beatles Come To Town* so as not to compete with the upcoming release of *A Hard Day's Night*.

What's Happening! The Beatles In The U.S.A.

Two hours prior to the Beatles arrival in New York on February 7, 1964, Britain's Granada TV hired Albert and David Maysles to film the Beatles during their first U.S. visit. Albert filmed the events with his hand-held 16mm camera while David recorded the sound on a Nagra portable tape recorder. The Maysles Brothers style was to film and record what was actually happening without any direction or interference, or as Albert described it, to be "in the thick of it, unobtrusive so as to give the viewer the feeling of actually being there." This "fly on the wall" perspective became known as Direct Cinema.

The Maysles Brothers gathered their equipment and arrived at JFK Airport just as the Beatles plane was landing. They filmed fans rushing to see the group and filmed the Beatles as they exited the Boeing 707 jetliner. They shot footage of fans outside the Plaza Hotel where the group were staying. They filmed the Beatles watching themselves on the CBS Evening News With Walter Cronkite. They filmed WINS disc jockey Murray the K wearing a Beatles wig while playing records. On Saturday, they filmed John, Paul and Ringo in Central Park, where the group posed for the press. When the trio left the Park, they were inside the car recording Paul, Ringo and John reacting to American radio and seeing female fans pressed against the car window as they headed to their Ed Sullivan Show rehearsal.

On Sunday, they filmed Murray interviewing and recording station promos from the Beatles in their Plaza suite. The group was shown listening to the radio and sipping tea. They captured the Beatles leaving their suite on their way to The Ed Sullivan Show. After being told they could not film the Beatles performance, they entered a tenement building and filmed a family watching the Beatles on their television. That evening, they went with the group to the Peppermint Lounge and captured Ringo on the dance floor dancing the night away. On Monday, they filmed Beatles manager Brian Epstein conducting Beatles business on the phone and later in a car.

The Maysles Brothers supervised a quick edit of the show for Granada TV, placing scenes out of chronological order to tell the story and capture the excitement of the Beatles first few days in New York City without the need for voiceovers. The program, titled *Yeah! Yeah! Yeah! The Beatles In New York*, was broadcast in the U.K. on February 12, 1964, at 10:25 PM on ITV. In Canada, a 30-minute edit of the documentary titled *Stalking The Beatles* was shown on February 21 on Telescope Portraits in Television with Fletcher Markle at 9:30 PM.

Although their Granada TV duties were complete, the Maysles kept going. On February 11, they filmed the Beatles arriving by train in Washington, D.C., followed by bits of their concert at the Washington Coliseum. The next day they were on the train taking the Beatles and the press back to New York. They captured George and Ringo shooting pictures of the press. George, dressed as a porter, carried cans of 7-Up on a tray, pulled back his porter's hat and, pretending that no one recognized him, said, "It's me." Ringo interacted with a little girl and took her to meet the others, signing autographs along the way. The group's shenanigans were similar to the fictional train scene filmed three weeks later for *A Hard Day's Night*.

They also filmed the Beatles at the Deauville Hotel in Miami Beach as the group was packing and getting ready to head back to London via New York. George played a blues song on an out-of-tune acoustic guitar. Finally, the group was filmed arriving back in London, where they were greeted by thousands of screaming fans.

The Maysles produced an 81-minute film, *What's Happening! The Beatles In The U.S.A.*, that has had only limited screenings. On November 13, 1964, CBS broadcast an edit of the documentary titled *The Beatles In America* as a special edition of the network's hour-long Friday night variety show, The Entertainers. The program was promoted as: "The astonishing phenomenon called 'The Beatles'–four smiling boys with unschooled Liverpudlian accents, lots of hair, a curious mixture of wild yet controlled abandon, and a battering beat–gets a 'living camera' type treatment here for fans to relish and sociologists to ponder." In 1991, Apple Films prepared a new documentary, *The Beatles: The First U.S. Visit*, that was released by MPI on VHS tape and LaserDisc that November. It mixed portions of the Maysles' film with other footage, including the Beatles New York press conference and performances from the February Ed Sullivan shows. Apple issued a re-edited version of the program on DVD in February 2004, the fortieth anniversary of the Beatles first U.S. visit.

The Washington Coliseum Concert

The Beatles February 11, 1964 concert at the Washington Coliseum was filmed in black and white by CBS. Most of the concert was shown in American and Canadian movie theaters on March 14 and 15, 1964 (two shows a day) by close circuit TV broadcast by National General Corporation. The Beatles set was preceded by unrelated concert footage of the Beach Boys and Leslie Gore. The full Beatles performance has been available as a download on iTunes.

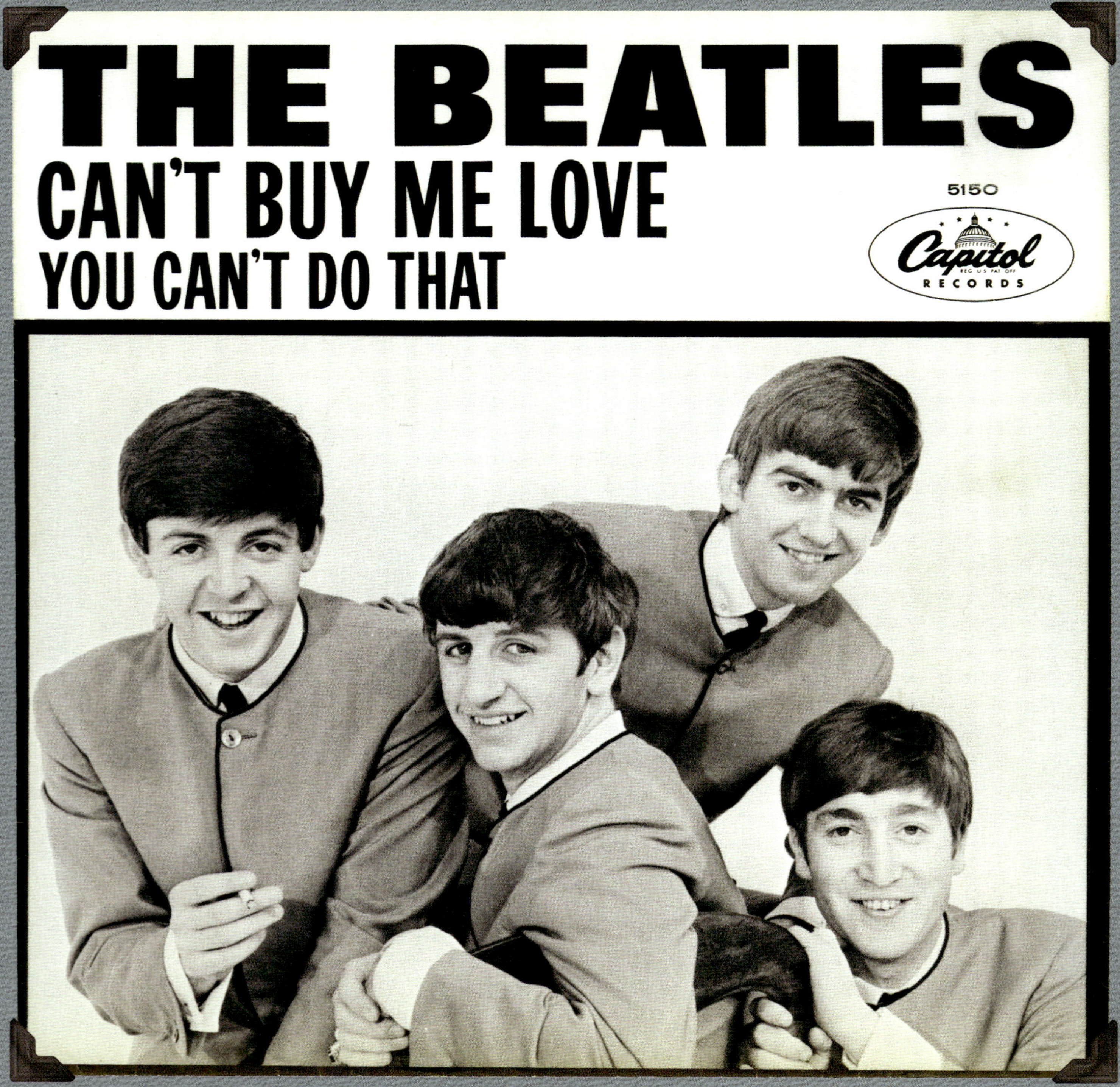
THE BEATLES
CAN'T BUY ME LOVE
YOU CAN'T DO THAT
5150
Capitol
RECORDS

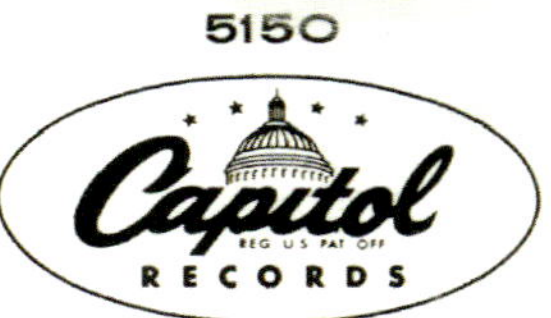

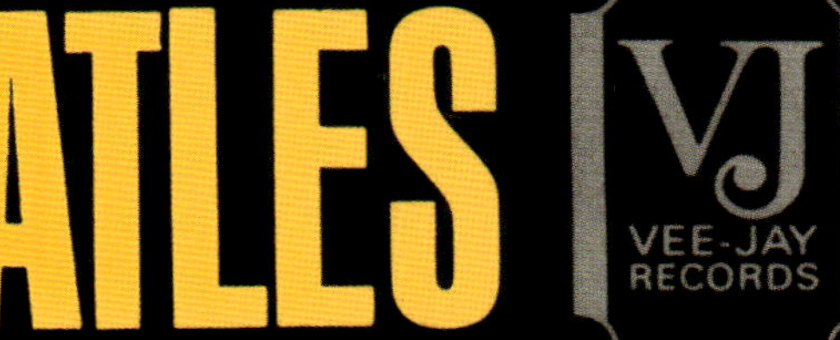
VJ-587
THE BEATLES
VJ
VEE-JAY
RECORDS
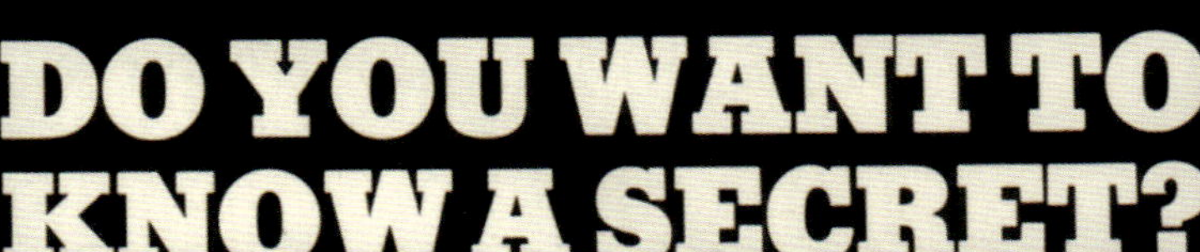
DO YOU WANT TO
KNOW A SECRET?
AND
THANK YOU GIRL
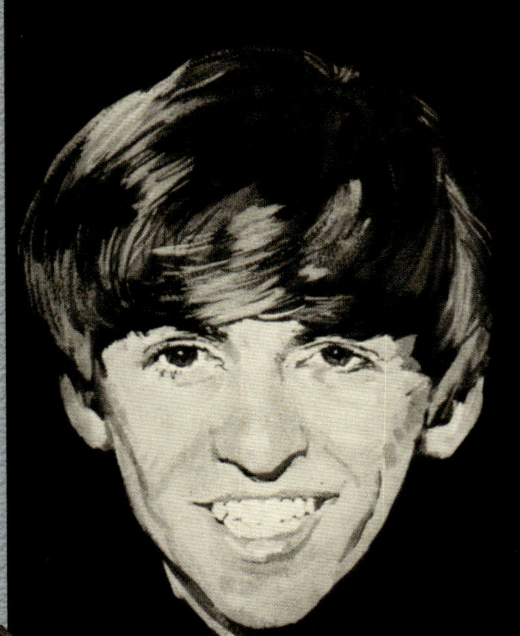

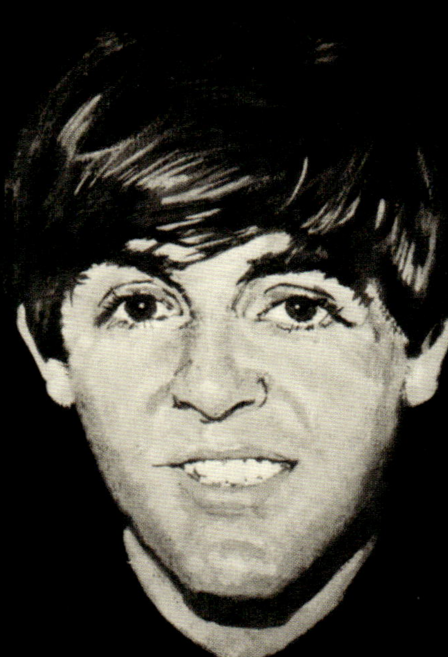

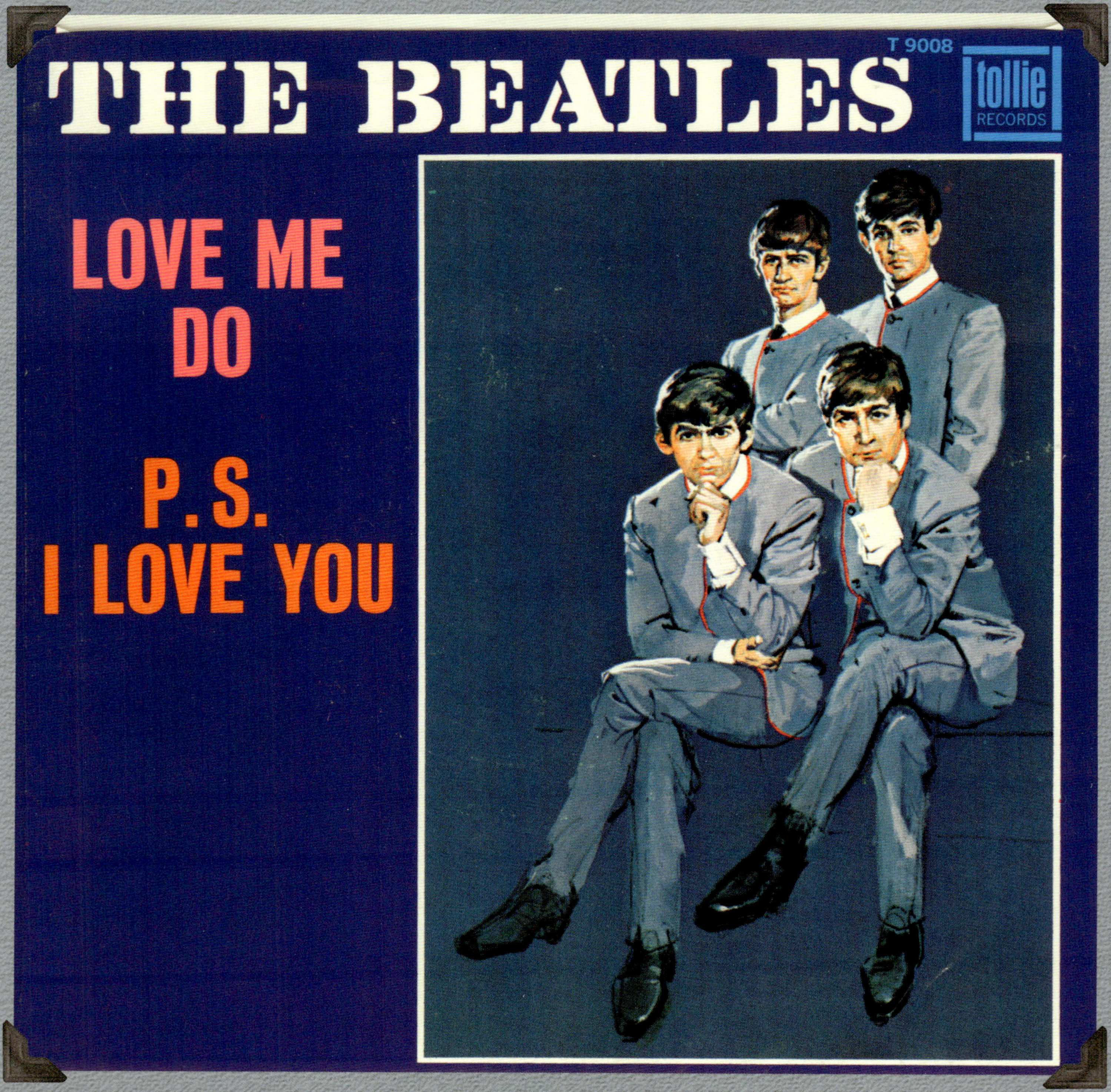
T 9008
THE BEATLES
tollie
RECORDS
LOVE ME
DO
P.S.
I LOVE YOU

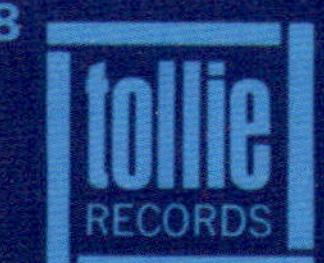

THE BEATLES

A HARD DAY'S NIGHT

I SHOULD HAVE KNOWN BETTER

5222

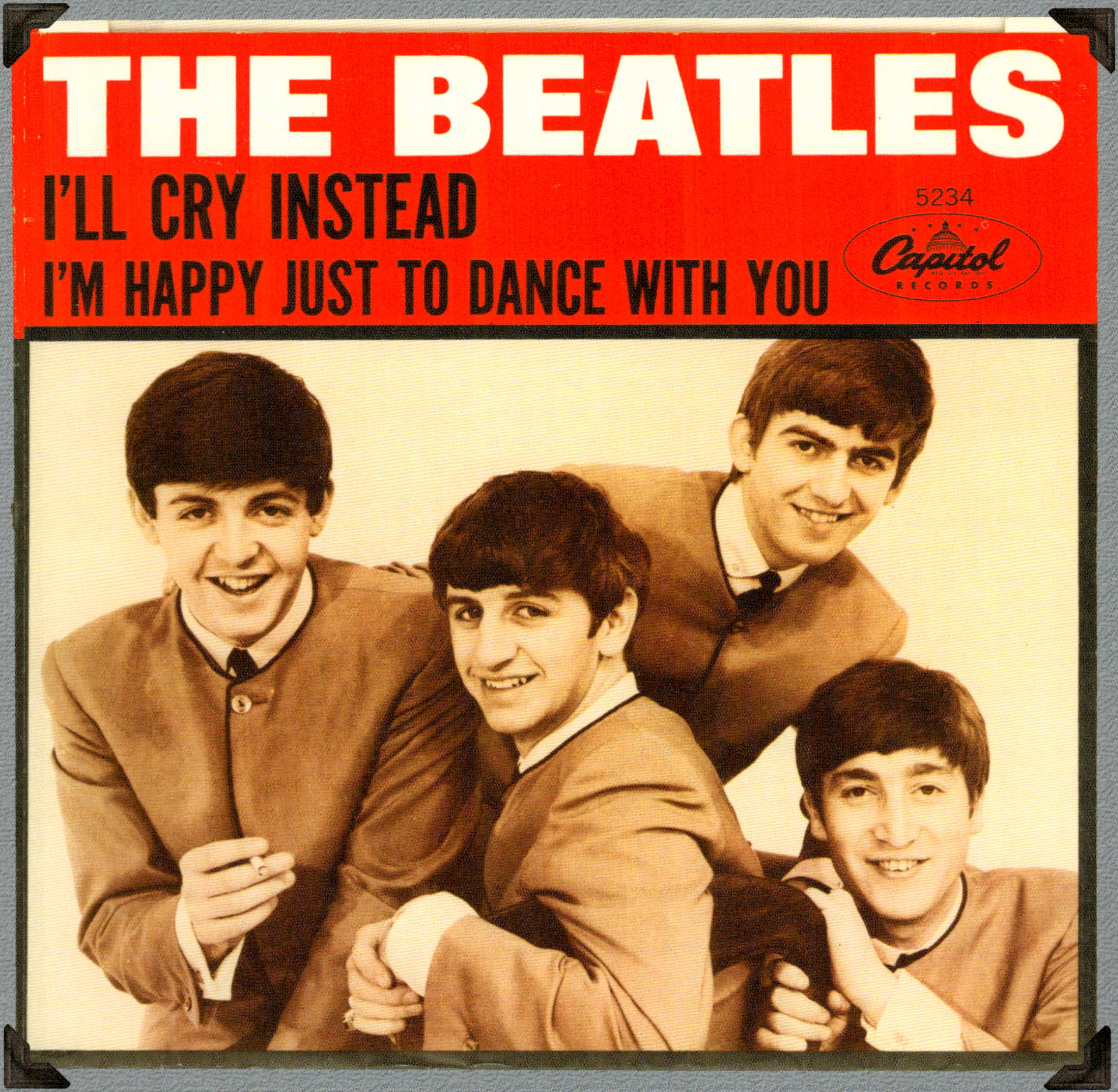
THE BEATLES
I'LL CRY INSTEAD
I'M HAPPY JUST TO DANCE WITH YOU
5234
Capitol
RECORDS

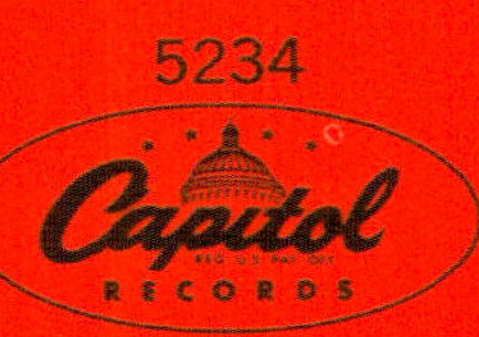

THE BEATLES
AND I LOVE HER
IF I FELL

5235
Capitol
REG. U.S. PAT. OFF.
RECORDS

THE BEATLES
MATCH BOX
SLOW DOWN
5255
Capitol
RECORDS
THE
BEATLES

ask me why
the beatles

an E.P. that is selling like a single
...at single record prices

here is your special D. J. promotion
copy — EPI-903

STILL ONLY
8 IN SALES

FAN RECOLLECTIONS

Meeting George on the Set of *A Hard Day's Night*
by Pattie Boyd

It all started one afternoon in early 1964. I was a fashion model who worked for various magazines. I was having a session with my photographer when my agent phoned him and asked him to tell me to go to a certain address for an interview. I brought my portfolio photographs with me and waited for my turn with the usual amount of girls. When I went in, I recognized one of the guys, Dick Lester. I had done some TV commercials with him for Smith's Crisps [potato chips]. I had to lisp it, and it was funny. It was great fun. I left the interview thinking it's gonna be another Smith's Crisps commercial.

When I got home, my agent called and said I got a part in a Beatles film. This was really confusing. I hadn't been told it was an interview for a Beatles film. I had no idea. I panicked. I never wanted to be an actress. I was a bit too shy. I said, "Oh, no, I don't think I can do that." And she said, "Yes you can." And I thought about it and of course I wanted to do it. So I said, "Yes, I'll do it."

I met the other girls at the train station. We got on the train and off it went. We were dressed in schoolgirl uniforms. But one thing seemed very odd. We hadn't seen the Beatles. Anyway, the train went on for a while and then it stopped at this tiny little station. Then I saw four figures on the platform. It could only be them. It was kinda exciting. Then they all jumped on and they came into the carriage where these other girls and I were. And they were so polite. They shook hands with us and then they disappeared. And we thought, "Woo, what was that? That was exciting!"

GEORGE & PATTIE

As for our first scene, I think an awful lot was ad-libbed, you know, 'cause with the Beatles, you can't really tell them what to do. Dick would tell us roughly what to do and what the story was going to be. It seemed chaotic to me. It was all a muddle. I didn't understand what was going on. I was told to just sit down, and Paul was going to come over to me and say something or other. Anyway, he did, and the whole thing was great fun. I had one line: "Prisoners?"

During our lunch break, I sat next to George [see photo on previous page]. Being close to him was electrifying. I thought all the Beatles were fascinating and very funny. But a lot of their humour went over my head. Liverpudlians have a different way of talking, different ways of expressing themselves. I didn't always understand what they were saying. As the train neared London on our return, George asked me to marry him. It went over my head—I didn't get it! And then he said, "Will you come out to dinner tonight?" I said, "I'm so sorry, I'm going to see my boyfriend." And his face dropped. And I thought: "Oh, poor guy. He's from Liverpool. He probably doesn't know anyone in London." So I said, "Why don't you join us?" He was not amused. "No thank you," he said.

A week or so later, I and the other schoolgirls were at Twickenham Studios where we were filmed watching the Beatles playing a song in the train's luggage car. I didn't spend much time with George, so I didn't know if he would ask me out again. That could have been it. But Dick Lester, I think, was determined for George and I to be together. Because about five days later, during which time I fired the boyfriend, I and the other schoolgirls were called to Twickenham for a press shoot where we had to stand behind a Beatle and pretend to do their hair [shown on page iv]. I stood behind George. I don't think I ever saw the other girls again, but at Beatles conventions, sometimes you see women dressed as the schoolgirls from the film. It's so funny. Well, as for George, he asked how my boyfriend was, and I said, "I don't have a boyfriend." He grinned and asked me to dinner. Less than two years later, we were married. And that is how I got together with George on the set of *A Hard Day's Night*.

Like most teens after seeing the Beatles on The Ed Sullivan Show, we were curious. When *A Hard Day's Night* came to the Vogue Theater in East Chicago, Indiana, I told my family that I was going to the first show. Unfortunately, it was also filled with screaming girls. I had to sit through four screenings (as you could do back then) to finally hear it properly. By that time it was 8 o'clock at night and my family was worried I had been abducted! I got into trouble but it was well worth it. My Beatles love affair was founded on that day.

Arthur Stessl

In the summer of 1964, my father took me to the Kimball theater in Yonkers, New York to see A *Hard Day's Night*. As an eight-year-old boy, still not on the Beatles Band Wagon, I didn't understand what all the girls screaming was about! And each time the screaming started, I put my hands over my ears. In spite of that, I enjoyed the movie and loved the music. If I knew then what I know now, I would have been screaming too!

Ted Amoruso

I was 10½ years old in August 1964. I was with my family at the Sunnycroft Bungalow Colony and Day Camp in Highland Mills, New York, just one hour north of my home in The Bronx. *A Hard Day's Night* opened at the Monroe Theater in Monroe, a ten-minute drive from Sunnycroft. By overwhelming popular demand, parents chauffeured their kids to the theater for a Saturday matinee. The place was packed. As soon as the lights went down and that first shot of John, Ringo and George hit the screen, the screaming didn't stop for the rest of the film! I don't know what the parents thought, but man, it was exhilarating to be there, even if I couldn't hear a thing being said on-screen.

Steven Springer

My father didn't like the Beatles. He thought them trouble. Almost every month, my father, then Assistant Superintendent of Education, Rapides Parish, Louisiana, called me aside to discuss the problem at hand. He did his very best to help me "come to my senses."

"You're in love with this John Lennon!" my father would rail, genuinely disturbed by Beatlemania. "You think he's great, but trust me, I know boys like that! I've been a coach, a principal, a ***career educator***! And I've seen boys like that all my life. They lead gangs. They hate authority. They're hoodlums!"

"No," I began. I never let him have the final word on John Lennon, if the word wasn't a good one. "He's not..."

"He is!" My father grew frustrated. "He is! John Lennon is 100% a hoodlum!"

That's why I found his offer to escort me to see *A Hard Day's Night* so incredible. My hometown, Alexandria, Louisiana, had two main movie theaters: the Paramount and the Don. And *A Hard Day's Night* was coming to the luxurious Don Theater on Bolton Street. For Beatles fans like me, this was THE event of 1964, since I would clearly not be allowed to see the Beatles live in New Orleans at City Park Stadium.

I remember dressing to ride "downtown" for the film. I had on my red and white polka dotted sleeveless shirt with layers and layers of sassy ruffles. I wore white slim slacks and red sandals. That's what you did in 1964. You "dressed up" to go out to dinner, to go shopping in a department store, to attend a movie. You made an effort. I don't remember the theater being air conditioned.

My family had recently purchased a window AC unit for our family room, so we could eat dinner and watch Bonanza or Hazel or Dr. Kildare in comfort. But no other rooms in our house had such luxury, and I don't think the Don did, either. But they had a popcorn machine and ice-cold Coca-Colas, and we had two of each.

I'm sure there were previews; maybe a cartoon. I don't remember them. All I recall are the butterflies in my stomach, the thrill of getting to see the Beatles on the big screen for two whole hours. I couldn't wait to hear the songs and hear the boys talk. It was, as John would say in years to come "a red lettuce day."

A Hard Day's Night did not disappoint. Once the boys began to run from their squealing fans (was that ***really*** John's run?), I forgot about everything else...my Coke and popcorn, the taller girl who had plunked down in front of me, even my father. I was riveted. Strangely, my dad was riveted, too. Once he said something to me about "the Marx Brothers and the Keystone Cops," and I nodded. But that was it. There's wasn't a peep about the boys being hoodlums – not even when they ran alongside the train car heckling that "suit" with cries of, "Can we have our ball back?" Even then, Daddy just chuckled.

When the lights came up as *A Hard Day's Nigh*t played out on the screen, my father didn't rise from his seat. He didn't hurry me along to get back to his preparations for Monday's meetings or the week's teacher evaluations. He just sat there and let me listen to every last word. Then, he said it: "Would you like to stay and see it again?" I was stunned. "We can stay and see it again," he offered, a second time. And, of course, we did.

That unexpected kindness accomplished so much in bridging what a year or so later would be known as "the generation gap." It was a tangible way for me to understand what John meant when years later he told us to "Come Together." My father was giving me the gift of sacrificial love. And 60 years later, it still matters. More than ever.

P.S. I think John Lennon would have loved being referred to as a hoodlum.

Jude Southerland Kessler
Author of The John Lennon Series

In 1964, I was seven years old and completely in love with The Beatles. When I heard *A Hard Day's Night* was coming to the neighborhood theater, that's all I could think or talk about. My grandmother surprised me and took me to a Saturday matinee. I was wearing my Paul McCartney guitar pin, anxiously waiting for the movie to begin. The theater was filled with excited neighborhood kids. Within minutes, the lights went down and there they were in front of me, the Beatles, larger than life. Their looks, their music, their accents. I was in love and in awe (and still am).

The concert at the end of the film captures it all. The screaming fans were not only on the screen but in the theater that afternoon. "She Loves You" was jubilant as everyone joined in with the smiling, singing Beatles! I consider that to be my first concert experience. It ended all too soon as they took their final bows and helicoptered away. It was Beatlemania, it was magic, and I was a part of it!

Many years later I had the good fortune of illustrating Volume 4 of Jude Southerland Kessler's John Lennon Series. That was and is an honor. In my way, that was my contribution. My thank you to the band that changed everything for me.

Susan Derbacher, New Haven, CT

In February 1964, my friend Kathy Talkin and I became Beatles fans for life. Our interest really grew that summer as we discovered teen magazines and purchased the 45 "A Hard Day's Night" and whatever albums came to our small town of Aledo, Illinois. I got *Something New* and Kathy bought the movie soundtrack, so we had it covered. I went with Kathy to see *A Hard Day's Night* on August 15 even though I had a tonsillectomy two days earlier. Despite a very raw throat, I had to join her for the movie, the memories and pizza that wonderful day!

Two years later we formed an all girl rock band called The Mod 4. We had no world tour, movie or record contracts in our future, but did cut two 45 RPM singles of our own and even appeared on Dick Clark's Happening TV show. We, like so many kids back then, were inspired by the Beatles and are totally grateful for the tremendous joy and influence they brought to our lives beginning in that pivotal year of 1964.

Nellie Hastings

I saw an evening showing of *A Hard Day's Night* when it debuted at our local movie theater. The place was packed (with about 98% young girls). They screamed at the screen from the beginning of the film until the end. I could not hear any dialogue. I was able to recognize the songs, but I could hardly hear them. At one point, I actually got up and yelled: "You know, the Beatles can't hear you. They're not actually on the screen! Why are you screaming?" But it was to no avail; they just kept it up.

I went back the next morning for an early matinee and I was the only person in the theater! I was able to figure out what the movie was about, but had difficulty understanding some of the lines due to heavy British accents. I thought it was cool how wonderful the title song sounded over the film's beginning and ending credits. The movie gave me a new appreciation for the song "A Hard Day's Night." Seeing it as part of the film made me realize what a great tune it was!

Bob Pratt, Minneapolis, Minnesota

I was seven years old and a big Beatles fan in 1964. I couldn't wait to see *A Hard Day's Night* at the Stanley Theatre in Vancouver BC. I remember the girls screaming throughout the film as if it was a concert. I experienced Beatlemania at full force. It's still one of my favorite films.

Greg Delaney

South Dakota was usually the last stop for pop cultural movements to take hold. The Beatles changed all that on February 9th, 1964. Our small town of Sisseton, on a Native American Reservation, was now as cool as the rest of the world. It was intoxicating to feel a part of the energy these four lads were spreading.

Ringo launched my drumming career as trash can lids, pots and pans, and garbage baskets became my first drum kit in our basement. Carefully stenciling "The Beatles" with crayons on an upside-down laundry tub, I was instantly transported to a stage somewhere with John, Paul and George; the audience at a fever pitch waiting for the curtain to rise. That's when I would drop the needle on our portable RCA record player, and their new LP, *A Hard Day's Night*, crackled to life. The lone naked light bulb in that dark basement became my spotlight and for one brief and glorious moment, I was a Beatle.

Something New would come out weeks later. Its cover, with those songs, still encapsulates perfectly the excitement I felt back in 1964. Our world had changed forever.

John Erdahl

In 1964 I was a five-year-old Beatlemaniac residing in Brooklyn, New York. My Aunt Fran, who was 15, was the person who introduced me to the Beatles through the *Meet The Beatles!* LP. When the *A Hard Day's Night* film was released, she allowed me to tag along with her and her friends to see the movie. The theater was packed with teenagers and kids of various ages. As the movie started and the Beatles appeared on the screen, there was a chorus of screams of fandom and appreciation. The audience gradually calmed down enough me to hear the movie and follow the story. Similar to the end of the film when the publicity stills were thrown out of the helicopter, the ushers at the theater distributed the same glossy 8" x 10" photos to the fans in the audience. There were two choices of photos. The first was the one which was used for the single "I Want To Hold Your Hand" and the second option was the photo that was used on the back cover of *Meet The Beatles!* I remember not getting the photo I wanted but it was impossible to exchange or trade with anyone in the audience.

After the movie ended, my Aunt Fran took me to the local Woolworth store to buy the single "A Hard Day's Night." When we arrived at the store I found a single with the picture sleeve matching the American album cover. We quickly bought the record and brought it back to my aunt's home to play it on her record player. Once the needle was placed on the record to my surprise it wasn't John Lennon singing, but rather an instrumental version of a Beatles film song performed by the George Martin Orchestra. My disappointment was very noticeable. My aunt returned the record and bought me the Beatles version. Ironically, as an adult Beatles collector I am currently trying to find the George Martin single and sleeve [see page 261] at a reasonable price to add to my collection as a memento of my childhood.

Mark Sippin

I am from Canada. I was 11 years old in April 1966 when I saw the movie *A Hard Day's Night* in French (*Quatre Garçons dans le Vent*) on a Sunday afternoon during Easter time at the parish hall of my local church in Montreal where I used to see *Sinbad The Sailor* and science-fiction movies. (Yes, someone agreed to show this movie of the Beatles despite their rock music.) Everybody there was really in high spirits.

Even if I then listened to less Beatles music in favor of songs in French, I still liked Beatles songs, especially "I Should Have Known Better" and the amazing sound of the harmonica. But after seeing the movie and hearing the instrumental song "This Boy," I was more excited. The Beatles style and look had impressed me to the point that I no longer wanted to have short shaved hair.

Later, when my hair grew long, I went shopping with my mum at Eaton, downtown Montreal, for something that would give me a Beatles look, like a cap that Ringo wore in the movie. And, of course, I got myself some 45 RPM singles to listen on my blue Shine ED100 mono record player, including "Slow Down" b/w "Matchbox." This amazing rock music gave me joy and made me happy!

Norman Trembley

When *The Beatles' Second Album* and the *Long Tall Sally* LP were both available in Canadian record stores at the same time, it created some real mystery to us youngsters. We would stare at the covers and notice subtle colour discrepancies and picture placings, etc., and then try to figure out why two records appeared so similar. I bought *Long Tall Sally* and my friend got the American import album. We would debate which was better. I really liked "Misery," so I preferred *Long Tall Sally*, then and now! Even 60 years later, if I play these LPs I can anticipate the exact running order and sound.

Terry Ott

Being a Canadian Beatles fan, I had the first three albums, *Beatlemania – With The Beatles*, *Twist And Shout* and *Long Tall Sally*, all of which were only issued in mono. My friend and I each ordered a copy of *The Beatles' Second Album* through the Capitol of Canada Record Club. When the albums arrived, we were stunned to hear George's opening guitar riff coming out of the right speaker only. Our copies of the album were in glorious stereo! The whole LP was an amazing listening experience. I'll never forget the thrill of hearing "Roll Over Beethoven" in stereo for the first time!

Richard Zahn

November 23, 1977, the night before Thanksgiving, so for eighth-graders like me, it was a TV night with no homework. The schedule for WGN Channel 9 in Chicago that evening included a screening of *A Hard Day's Night.* I'd recently become interested in the Beatles, but didn't know about the film, so it was thoughtful of my mom to tell me that it would be on. At the appointed time, I scooped out a generous bowl of chocolate marshmallow ice cream and took a seat in the family room in front of the color TV. But although my mom was thoughtful, she had her own shows to watch. She banished me upstairs to my bedroom black and white TV. "But, Mom," I doubtlessly wailed, "the upstairs TV is not in color." "Neither is the movie," she must have said. Well, okay, then.

I closed my door and watched in the dark, and everything changed. My ice cream melted in its bowl, forgotten, as I stared at the screen, sorting out the faces and voices, watching and listening to the music. That was it, the event. My life has not been the same since. The Beatles, 13 years later than the original showing, on a small bedroom TV in rural Hampshire, Illinois, worked a spell on one more person who would owe nearly a lifetime of happiness to them.

Karen Duchaj

I was introduced to the Beatles in 1979 at age 11. Three years later I realized that *A Hard Day's Night* was a movie as well as a song. I'd listened to the song so many times, and in an age where the VHS was just becoming popular, I begged my parents to buy me the VHS tape of the movie. Due to low availability and high cost, it wasn't until June 18, 1985, that I received the tape on my birthday and finally got to watch the film. I will never forget that day. I was so mesmerized that I couldn't remember much about the film. I had to watch it again and just let it play instead of trying to concentrate on specific aspects of it. I was so impressed at how the music portions lined up with much of what was on MTV at the time. I had a big party that weekend where we played the movie. While I expected it to be background noise and entertainment while everyone mingled, I was surprised to see everyone gathered around the TV, just loving the film. One of the greatest birthdays EVER!

Donald Jack

After becoming a Beatles fan in 1977, *A Hard Day's Night* was the one film in their oeuvre that eluded me. Both *Yellow Submarine* and *Help!* appeared regularly on TV. I saw *Magical Mystery Tour* at a library screening and *Let It Be* at a midnight movie. Finally, the tragic circumstances of 1980 led to the re-release of *A Hard Day's Night* in 1982, and I eagerly went to see it. Because I saw it last, I was somewhat disappointed. It didn't help that I didn't get all the jokes, being 14 and not as versed in British culture as I would become. Flash forward 40 years, and *A Hard Day's Night* is a favorite and ironically, easily available on home video and streaming, while the other Beatles films, not so much.

Mark Funideas

In the winter of 1977 I was 12 years old and had only heard a few Beatles songs on WABC radio. With the prodding of my Aunt Barbra, I ventured forth to the Finkelstein library annex in Spring Valley, New York for a showing of the Beatles film *A Hard Day's Night*. This was the day a Beatles fan was born.

I consumed everything Beatles after that night–records, magazines and books, getting my first copy of the soundtrack album at a garage sale. I became a record dealer by the time I was 16 years old. By my twenties, I was a staple at Beatlefest in New Jersey every year.

Paul Garfunkel, Blackbird Records

It was about three months after my third birthday when the Beatles first appeared on The Ed Sullivan Show, so I was probably fast asleep when that monumental event happened. But soon after I was made aware of the Beatles and, in particular, the song "I Want To Hold Your Hand" because children in my apartment building were constantly singing it. However, it was in September 1964 when my mother took me and my older brother to see *A Hard Day's Night* at the Fresh Meadows Theater in Queens, New York that I began my lifelong Beatles fanaticism, which continues to grow as the years progress.

Something New was my first Beatles album (and the first album I personally owned); it was a gift from my aunt for my fourth birthday. Maybe it's because of the impression it made upon me that I have for decades maintained that the U.K. version of *A Hard Day's Night* is group's most perfect LP (with the U.K. *Help!* a close second). Or maybe it's because it is dominated by the writing and singing of John Lennon more than any other Beatles record. And while the film changed my life and made me a hard core Richard Lester devotee, what I most remember about that initial screening was how irate, to the point of tears, my five-year-old brother was for days after we saw the film. He was outraged that the many girls in attendance would not stop screaming and wailing and drowning out the dialogue and song lyrics.

Bruce Bernstein

I was ten years old when I went to see *A Hard Day's Night* with my two best friends. As we were waiting for the movie to start, an instrumental version of "And I Love Her" began to play. My buddies and I began softly singing the song, knowing every word. It's a very sweet memory of three friends enjoying each other's company complements of the greatest band ever!

Tommy Rayburn

I was six years old in 1964, but I remember everything. I had a sister who was ten years older than me, and she kept me up with what was happening. To me, she seemed so wise and so old!

I always liked music, but when I heard "I Want To Hold Your Hand," it seemed so out of the ordinary. Then my sister got *Meet The Beatles!* It was an amazing record. When she went out on a date, I would sneak into her room and play her 45s.

I remember hearing the Beatles on WABC and WMCA, and seeing the group on The Ed Sullivan Show, including the time Ed showed a clip of the group performing "You Can't Do That." When *A Hard Day's Night* came out, my sister took me to the film with her friends. The girls just kept screaming every time a Beatle would appear on the screen, which happened a lot.

My parents didn't discourage my love of music and bought me a drum set. I also got a Beatles wig at Woolworths. I loved banging on the drums, pretending to be Ringo, although sometimes I was Dave Clark. The picture [above] shows me in action in our basement, complete with wig to cover my buzz cut.

Wayne Edward Olsen

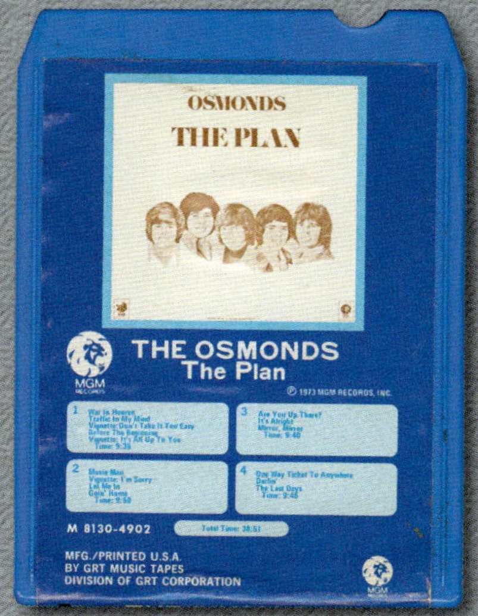

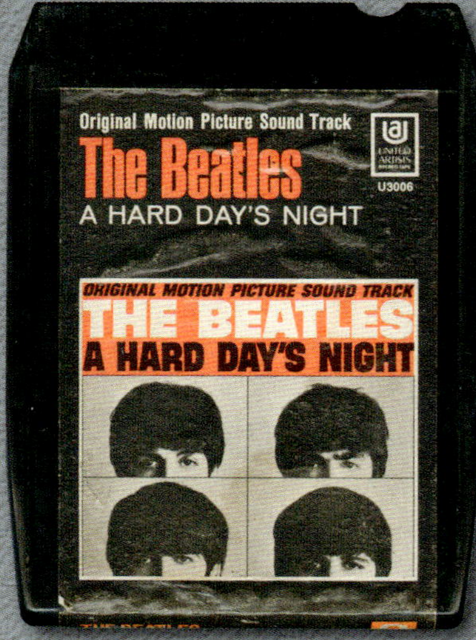

When I was five years old in 1978, I found an old 8-track in the basement that someone in my family had purchased–*The Plan* by the Osmonds. I played that tape a ton and loved it. Then I found another 8-track called *A Hard Day's Night* and played that one like crazy as well. One day, I had the idea to compare them by playing one track at a time and switching the tapes after each song. I did a song by song comparison of the two albums. *A Hard Day's Night* was the clear winner and started my obsession. It will always have a special place in my heart.

Scott Lempa

My obsession over the Beatles recordings began during my first semester of high school in 1977 when a friend gave me a copy of *Something New* on 8-track. Up until then, I was playing *The Red Album* and *The Blue Album* constantly, so most of the titles of this tape were unknown to me. But they had energy and swinging grooves. "I'll Cry Instead," "Slow Down," "Matchbox," "When I Get Home" and "Tell Me Why" got me moving like Beavis and Butthead while I'd listen with my Koss headphones attempting to complete my homework.

The 8-track includes "Thank You Girl" as a bonus, and the album's music has a nice emotional balance. I found myself mooning over my first high school crush listening to "And I Love Her," "Things We Said Today," "If I Fell" and "Anytime At All." The girl wasn't aware, but I got the courage to make a move. For Valentine's Day, I ordered a dozen roses to be delivered to her in school. I told my plan to a friend in confidence, but word spread rapidly among the kids in my class, who were in as much anticipation as I for her reaction, which turned out bad. She was angry and said that she was embarrassed.

I was absolutely mortified and immediately went home to the sanctuary of my headphones. That was my first experience where the Beatles music could provide reassurance and comfort as well as obvious happiness and fun. Over all these years, classic rock has provided a soundtrack to my life, and particularly ALL of the Beatles recordings have been like Linus' security blanket that I can wrap myself in for both good times and bad. I still possess the *Something New* 8-track although I haven't been able to play it for years. I'm so grateful for the Beatles music always being accessible and reassuring.

As for the roses, the other girls at school thought it was a sweet and beautiful gesture, and that I was "such a nice guy." I got plenty of popularity mileage from that!

Art Greinke, Milwaukee, Wisconsin

I was ten years old in the summer of 1964 when I saw *A Hard Day's Night* at a local drive-in theater with my mother and three of my brothers. In the relative safety of our station wagon, I was able to enjoy the film immensely as I heard every word being said and every song being performed. A few weeks later, I saw the film again at a local movie theater where all the girls in town decided to scream their lungs out during most of the movie. That viewing was obviously just about the visuals.

"Can't Buy Me Love" was played twice during the film–a running and jumping scene and a police chase. This inspired me, those same three brothers and a few of our friends to play the "Can't Buy Me Love" 45 at top volume as we leaped and ran around our living room, out the doors that led to a patio, and off the concrete edges of the elevated patio to the ground below. Over and over again. Unfortunately, nothing was captured on film but the memory remains.

Martin E. Horn

In the summer of 1964, my then 31-year-old Mom wanted to see *A Hard Day's Night*. Her mother, my grandmother, who was then just a few years older than I am today, was willing to come along. Mom was okay bringing my older brother, but she was worried about how I would react, being as I had never been in a movie theatre before and was a few months short of being two years old! My grandmother said: "Bring the kid along. If he cries, we'll take him outside!"

As it turned out, my Mom did not have to worry. I was absolutely mesmerized by the movie and did not make one sound throughout the entire show. I think this experience is what turned me into a Beatles fan for life! My Mom, now almost 91, recently verified this story with me.

Paul Friend

My parents' first date was to see *A Hard Day's Night* at the local drive-in. They began going steady, and "If I Fell" became their song. By 1979, at age 12, I was a rabid Beatles fan and loved listening to the song on our family jukebox. That year I saw *A Hard Day's Night* for the first time at the Chicago Beatlefest. Years later, my father, Jim, gave me the movie ticket he purchased to take my mom, Becky, to the Beatles film. I treasured this small ticket all the more after he passed away all too soon. It's amazing to think that the first Beatles movie was instrumental in bringing me into existence and carrying the love of the Beatles through the next generation.

Dr. Jennifer Sandi

A Hard Day's Night is my all time favorite album. Not the British LP, but the American version with all its orchestral fill and amazing energetic songs. That disc had, by far, the most impact on me in terms of the magic of Beatlemania. I was a mere six years old when it came out. My three older brothers, who were more "in tune" with what was "happening" in the music world than I, turned me on to the Beatles. But my initial exposure was limited to the "I Want To Hold Your Hand" single my teen-age aunt owned, along with all the Beatles saturation radio air play we heard in those early days.

That all changed in the Summer of 1964 when the incredible *A Hard Day's Night* LP was released! It changed my life's trajectory forever. I quickly gained a flood of incredible childhood memories of the Beatles. It was the only album my parents bought for us during the the 1960s, so my bond and connection to the LP was and is very profound. That bond remains to this day. At my young age, I thought the Beatles were very special to be able to play and sing all those great rock songs and also play those classical instrumental songs. Back then, the albums didn't tell you who actually "performed" on the album. So, being young and naive, we simply credited the Beatles for all of it and that made them even more bigger than life! We thought: "Man, these guys were amazing singers AND trained classical musicians!"

Now and then, that album, more than any other, captures the pure driving energy and magic of Beatlemania! Those songs were so good, so melodic, so drenching into the ears and down to the soul, that it truly launched the Beatles into stratospheric superstardom. So remarkable that even the great *Sgt. Pepper* album could only tie its Billboard Top LP's chart success of being number one for 14 weeks! So many great albums came before it and so many after, but it truly was that one that reached into the fans' hearts and minds around the world and spoke to every age group about just how appealing and talented these four young men were.

When I played "And I Love Her" for my mom, she said: "It's nice you're listening to some pretty music now!" When I told her it was the Beatles, she was shocked and astounded at how pretty their songs could be! So much so that she really didn't think it was even them at all! She soon became a fan admitting they were really talented.

In 1965, when the Beatles played the Hollywood Bowl, I was in Long Beach, California. My two female cousins (aged 14 and 15) went to the show while I was left behind. When they got back, their hair was messed up and their makeup was still streaming down their faces from seeing the Beatles and screaming and crying their eyes out! That is a fond image forever burned into my memory. We then played the *A Hard Day's Night* all night long, arguing who got to be John or Paul with each song!

That's how it was. There's never been anything since to match it. Years later, when my deep-rooted memories and love for the Beatles followed me into adulthood, I became a collector and dealer of all things Beatles, and put together a string of price guides and contributed to others. It all really stems from my experience and love affair with that one very special soundtrack album, *A Hard Day's Night*. I've also taken a very strong liking to the original U.K. version of the album as it has more Beatles tracks to love. So now I proudly have and play both. And yes, I still like George Martin's instrumentals on the American LP even though I've known for years that the Beatles didn't play on them. I can't wait to read the other fan recollections in Bruce's great new book. I'm sure you all share the same love and magical memories for this incredibly important Beatles album that brought beautiful high energy sound to the world in an explosive meteoric way. Long live *A Hard Day's Night*!

Perry Cox

I was 7 years old in February 1964, living in New York City. I caught the Beatle bug right away. The first time I saw *A Hard Day's Night* was right after it came out in August 1964. The theatre was packed with screaming kids with everyone reacting to the film as if they were seeing the Beatles live! I was just as excited as everyone else. Although I didn't catch much of the dialog the first time I saw the film, I've caught up in the ensuing years. Certainly one of the greatest films of the 20th Century.

Hugh Jones

On a Saturday afternoon in August 1964, my mom drove my friend David and me to the Willow Theatre in North York, Ontario to see *A Hard Day's Night*. Being huge nine-year-old Beatles fans, we were so excited! We sat in the middle of a noisy, sold-out audience of mostly teen girls. However, once the theatre darkened and the movie began, we couldn't hear a thing for most of the film due to the non-stop screaming from the girls. When my mom heard about this and told my dad, he took David and me to see the film at the 400 Drive-In Theatre the next weekend so we could actually hear the film!

Jon Young

I saw *A Hard Day's Night* at my local downtown theater in Dover, New Hampshire when it first came out. I was 11 and had been a Beatle fan since January 1964. I was so excited to see them on the big screen rather than our tiny TV. But my main memory of the showing is that it was almost ruined by other girls screaming in the theater every time they sang. I'm still annoyed to this day!

Susan Gagne

Leave it to my dad to make a last minute offer to take my brother and me to see *A Hard Day's Night* on the night that the TV show Bewitched premiered on September 17, 1964. Of course we opted to see the Beatles, even knowing that we might never see that episode of Bewitched. (This was before VCRs or streaming.) I subsequently recorded the film audio of *A Hard Day's Night* the first time it was on television directly from the TV speaker to my primitive mono reel-to-reel recorder. That broadcast on NBC opened with the statement "The following very, very special program is brought to you in lively black and white." Instead of the colorful NBC peacock, they showed a black and white penguin. What a great alternate opening by the first American network to broadcast in color.

Robert Jakubiec

In mid-1964, my family was living in Providence, Rhode Island. My parents decided to buy their three-year-old son, me, *Meet The Beatles!* and the *A Hard Day's Night* soundtrack LP. This was somewhat strange since by then they were in their early thirties and well beyond experiencing Beatlemania! But they said there was something about this new band from England, and all the hysteria surrounding them, that prompted them to buy a couple of albums to play for me. The story goes that I would bounce up and down and side to side on my spring-loaded pinto pony horse to these two albums! When a record ended, I would whine until they played the Beatles music over and over again. My father says, in particular, I loved the song "A Hard Day's Night." They wore the grooves out playing that one for me!

Matthew Street, Beatles YouTuber

Due to the large number of fan recollections submitted for this book, we were unable to fit them all in! For additional fan recollections and bonus content, go to www.beatle.net/fr/Hardday for a free supplement download of more, along with a place to post your own recollections. (Note: the free supplement is already included in the digital edition.)

A Fan's Notes:
A Hard Day's Night

by Bill King

I wasn't quite 12 years old in the summer of 1964 when the Beatles first movie, *A Hard Day's Night*, and its soundtrack LP came out. Newspaper ads generally had the mono album on sale for around $2.98 (regularly $3.98) and the stereo version for a little less than a dollar more. As I wouldn't start delivering newspapers on my bicycle for another six months, I was at the mercy of my parents when it came to buying new Beatles LPs. But my mother, bless her heart, made the soundtrack LP her July selection from the Columbia Record Club.

Although they'd only been known in the U.S. for six months or so, the Beatles were ubiquitous that summer of '64. They were a frequent topic in the Saturday TV Mailbag of The Atlanta Journal, though mostly journalists still viewed the Beatles with disdain, condescension or indifference.

Still, the Fabs got mentioned in the paper a lot, whether by various stuffed shirts declaring them a sign of the demise of Western civilization or parents of Beatles fans admitting they didn't think the group was that bad.

In its July 7 edition, the Journal ran a picture of the Beatles being greeted by Princess Margaret at the film's London premiere. And the band regularly made the paper's celebrity newsmakers page, as on July 13, when it was reported that George Harrison's sleek new sports car had been involved in a London collision, or the July 15 report on John Lennon buying a $56,000, 20-room hideaway in the country to get away from his fans.

The Beatles even made it into advertisements that had no relation to the band, such as a linens "white sale" being held at Davison's department store that said: "Right now you'll find more excitement at Davison's than a busload of teens off to see the Beatles!"

The day after the release of the *A Hard Day's Night* LP, the afternoon Journal published a story out of London about the girls (as they called them) working as the Beatles fan club secretaries. It called them "the most envied girls in Britain — possibly the world."

I constantly was updating my Beatles scrapbook that I'd begun on the night of the first Ed Sullivan Show appearance in February. And, in fact, those three shows were repeated that summer by CBS on July 12, August 23 and September 20. Meanwhile, I kept clipping articles: Syndicated gossip columnist Dorothy Kilgallen reported in the July 24 Journal that Brian Epstein was "said to be ready to unload" the Beatles for half a million pounds; the fashion editor did a feature on the famous Mary Quant cap worn by Lennon; and there was a report on Pat Boone having snapped up rights to sell some Beatles portraits. "They're the freshest young talent of the day," he said of the band, "with bounce, humor and a brand-new sound."

On the other hand, a singer from the Metropolitan Opera in Atlanta for a performance of "La Traviata" opined that "the reason the Beatles have had such enormous success is because parents have not subjected their children to enough good music."

There also was a report that the U.K. was going to include *A Hard Day's Night* in a cultural exchange with Prague, and that United Artists had ordered between 1,500 and 1,800 prints of the film for distribution, which was a previously unprecedented number.

1964 was an election year, and the political parties held their presidential nominating conventions. I remember watching on TV as the Democrats paid tribute to President John F. Kennedy, who'd been assassinated the previous fall, and nominated President Lyndon B. Johnson for another term. I'd missed the earlier GOP gathering when the Republicans picked Sen. Barry Goldwater. (I was at Boy Scout camp that week.)

On July 10, shortly after the *A Hard Day's Night* album was released, the morning Atlanta Constitution's front page included news of 39 people being killed in a Tennessee plane crash, Teddy Kennedy recovering in the hospital from a broken back suffered in a different plane crash and Pennsylvania Gov. William Scranton demanding that the Republican Platform Committee condemn the John Birch Society.

A month later, when the Beatles movie had opened in theaters, the afternoon Journal's front page reported on an integration battle at an Atlanta restaurant, the U.S. Senate passing LBJ's $947 million anti-poverty bill, China sending MIG fighters to aid the Viet Cong in Vietnam, and Turkey and the Greek Cypriot government accepting a United Nations ceasefire in Cyprus.

Mom's copy of the *A Hard Day's Night* soundtrack LP had arrived from the record club by then, and the film opened in my hometown of Athens, a little over an hour's drive from Atlanta, at the Georgia Theatre (now a venerated music venue). Mom treated my brothers and me to an afternoon screening, complete with a handful of teenage girls screaming from a few rows behind us.

Besides the thrill of getting to see the Beatles perform their music on the big screen, I remember certain lines of dialogue resonating with me, even at that age.

One was when George advises one of the TV crew not to play with Ringo's cymbals because: "he's very fussy about his drums, you know. They loom large in his legend." And, during the press conference segment, when Ringo is asked, "Are you a mod or a rocker?" and replies: "Um, no. I'm a mocker." Also, John being asked how he found America and replying: "Turned left at Greenland."

And, best of all, a line that I'd find myself using in the future when writing about pop culture. It came in the film when the ad man and his secretary, shocked by George putting down their teen spokeswoman, wondered whether he could be "an early clue to the new direction."

When my brothers and I got home, we did our early version of "air guitar" as we played the LP on our suitcase stereo, dressing up semi-Beatles-style in our Sunday school jackets and ties.

In later years, when I was exposed to the original Parlophone *A Hard Day's Night* LP, it took me a while to get used to the different track listing. However, I found the British version to be vastly superior to the American album, which included George Martin instrumentals in some sort of misguided attempt to be more like other movie soundtracks of the time.

As for the film, the morning Constitution's movie editor ran quotes from producer Walter Shenson that were, of course, very positive about the Beatles and their work on the picture. It opened August 5 in metro Atlanta at 15 drive-ins and neighborhood theaters [see pages 86-87] but did not play at any of the more prestigious downtown theaters.

The Journal's amusements editor, who looked to be near retirement age, actually gave the film a very positive review, calling it a "wacky, fast-paced 83 minutes of tomfoolery with music" and saying that "it is frenetic, of course, but, at the same time, gives the viewer a pretty good idea of how the Beatles REALLY live. A capable cast of supporting players contributed considerably to the success of the picture." He concluded that it was "a breezy and funny film."

The Journal's business page reported that the Beatles film grossed $261,671 in its first five days in just 27 U.S. and Canadian theaters.

Opening at the same time was *McHale's Navy*, a film spinoff from the popular Ernest Borgnine TV comedy. Other movies playing that week included Debbie Reynolds in *The Unsinkable Molly Brown*, Jack Lemmon in *Good Neighbor Sam*, Peter Sellers in *The World Of Henry Orient*, Hayley Mills in Walt Disney's *The Moon-Spinners*, John Wayne in *Circus World*, Shirley MacLaine, Paul Newman, Robert Mitchum and Dean Martin in *What A Way To Go!*, Robert Goulet in *Honeymoon Hotel*, Peter Sellers again in *The Pink Panther*, Michael Callan in *The New Interns*, George Kennedy in *Island Of The Blue Dolphins*, and, in an art theater, Ingmar Bergman's *The Silence*.

As I got ready to begin seventh grade (school always opened on the day after Labor Day back then), the papers were running reports from the Beatles North American tour. Also, the August 26 Journal ran a photo of George throwing a drink at a photographer who was pestering the Beatles in a Hollywood jazz club.

And, in a back-to-school ad placed by Rich's, Atlanta's main department store, one of the items touted was a colorful 3-ring binder with the Beatles picture and autographs on the cover for $1.19 and another was a Beatles lunchbox for the same price.

My middle brother, Jonathan, got one of those blue Beatles lunchboxes. A decade later, when I realized those things were collectables, we discovered to our dismay that it had gotten left out on the carport and rusted, and Dad had thrown it away.

Fast-forward 18 years for the first rerelease of *A Hard Day's Night*. This time it was me reviewing the film for The Atlanta Constitution. I noted director that Richard Lester, a veteran of TV commercials, "utilized the jump-cutting and breakneck pacing of that mini-medium, along with some of the New Wave cinema verite techniques, such as handheld camerawork and gritty black-and-white cinematography, to convey the frantic, exuberant, almost surreal atmosphere surrounding The Beatles."

I further wrote: "Coupled with the incisive, working class Liverpudlian wit of Alun Owens' screenplay and the natural, unforced charisma of The Beatles themselves, Lester's approach broke new ground, effectively killing off the old-style jukebox musical typified by Elvis Presley's moronic cinematic endeavors."

That 1982 rerelease gave me the chance to experience *A Hard Day's Night* in a movie theater for the first time since the mid-1960s. Naturally, I also picked up the 1984 VHS release and the first DVD release in 1997. In 2000, I hit one of the local art houses for yet another rerelease of the film, followed by buying various DVD reissues through the years.

But I think my favorite time seeing the Beatles first movie after 1964 was when my wife Leslie and I found ourselves with front-row seats for the world premiere of the 50th anniversary remastered reissue (complete with an onstage Q&A appearance by director Lester) at the British Film Institute in London. The film was as fresh and funny as ever. You could say that *A Hard Day's Night* looms large in the Fab Four's legend.

Bill King's Interview with Walter Shenson

(Originally appeared in Beatlefan #16, June 1981)

How's this for a deal? You're asked to produce a movie, despite the fact you've produced only a couple of low-budget comedies before. You're given almost complete freedom to do the film as you see fit, as long as you bring it in under budget.

You don't have to put up any funds; it's completely financed by the distributors. And because they're primarily interested in the money they can make off the soundtrack album, they go right along with the suggestion that complete rights to the film and its sequel revert to you after 15 years.

And, if that wasn't enough, you're also given the Beatles as stars.

Sound like the offer of a lifetime? That's exactly what it turned out to be for a then 45-year-old Walter Shenson when United Artists came knocking on his door in London in late 1963. UA asked him to make the Beatles, about whom he knew almost nothing, into movie stars.

Considering the worldwide popularity of the group, that assignment was not particularly challenging.

But the fact that Shenson and director Richard Lester exceeded UA's requirements and gave them art with the critically lauded and much imitated *A Hard Day's Night* continues to intrigue film buffs.

When I first spoke with Shenson in early 1981, he was preparing to give new audiences a chance to see the landmark black-and-white film as it should be seen — with new prints and a new Dolby stereo soundtrack — in the first proper rerelease of *A Hard Day's Night*, which took place a year later.

The fact that the 1964 film has been consigned mostly to midnight showings and occasional local TV viewings for the past dozen years or so irritates the normally mild-mannered Shenson, now 61.

"I'm angry with United Artists," he said. "I don't think they ever had the respect for the [Beatles] films that they deserve. They considered them exploitation films and let them go for stupid $100 bookings and TV. They should have held them back."

That didn't happen, he said: "mainly because they were very greedy and because they did not realize the quality of the craftsmanship. [*A Hard Day's Night*] is archival, a landmark. Nobody ever got near it — the cutting, the handheld camera work. I think it is the best example of what I call an 'actuality film.' I use that word instead of 'cinema verité'."

UA's attitude, Shenson said, "resulted from the distributor's viewing The Beatles as 'a fad.'"

A former publicity man for Columbia Pictures, Shenson, a San Francisco native educated at Stanford, was living in London in 1963 and working as an independent film producer. He had done the charming British comedy *The Mouse That Roared* with Peter Sellers in 1959 and its sequel, *The Mouse On The Moon*.

He recalled: "I had a reputation for making low-budget comedies. I was efficient."

"The producers of the James Bond films wanted to make a film with The Beatles, but UA said no because they didn't know how to make a movie at a price. UA was looking to make a low-budget comedy with The Beatles so that their music division could release a soundtrack album. They told me as long as the film came in under budget, it didn't matter if it lost money. They'd make it all back on the record. All they asked for was a Beatles film. But we made the movie we wanted to make."

Combining a witty, intelligent screenplay by Liverpudlian Alun Owen (who was suggested, Shenson thinks, by Paul McCartney, and who spent a weekend on tour with the Beatles), the clever, innovative direction of Lester (a veteran of TV commercials whom Shenson had hired for *The Mouse On The Moon*), and the refreshing, winning personalities of the Beatles themselves, Shenson came up with a pseudo-documentary send-up of the Beatlemania phenomenon.

The critics, expecting the sort of teen idol quickie drive-in picture that Elvis Presley and other pop singers had starred in, were shocked to find instead what The New York Times called "a whale of a comedy" with scenes approaching "audiovisual poetry."

Costing a mere $500,000, *A Hard Day's Night* went on to gross $13.5 million (as did the zany but less critically successful *Help!,* which cost three times more at $1.5 million). But its impact on the Beatles careers far exceeded the healthy profit participation they still retain.

"I wanted to reach out and grab an audience beyond the audience for which the film was intended," Shenson said. "And it did. I converted more adults to The Beatles with 'A Hard Day's Night' than ever would have happened through records. That movie did more to legitimize The Beatles with the older audience than anything else."

UA had qualms about the Beatles as actors before production began but, Shenson said: "they did just fine. The acting we required was very difficult. The most difficult thing is to be yourself. This is what The Beatles did beautifully. It never bothered them to do it again and again."

John Lennon and Ringo Starr drew the most attention from critics, but actually it was George Harrison who impressed Shenson early on. "George came along well with his acting, so I asked the writer for another short scene for him because I liked his 'shirt scene.'"

"He came up with the 'shaving scene.' The art director put a bathtub in, so I said to the director, 'why don't we put John in the bath?' He didn't have any dialogue, but the scene became John's instead of George's."

In later years, Lennon was critical of the stereotypical roles fashioned for the Beatles in their films. "I'm sorry John felt that way," Shenson said, "but I have to take the credit or the blame. I wanted them to have separate identities, so they wouldn't come across as this four-headed monster."

A primary concern in Shenson's mind at the time was: "I had a tremendous obligation never to lose sight of their young audience. I also wanted the critics and my peers to think I'm a fine moviemaker and that the pictures I made were tasteful.

"It would have been easy to defer to The Beatles on matters of taste, but I did put reins on, because I didn't want anything to offend 11- or 12-year-olds. These boys were very progressive, ahead of the average mentality. It would have been very easy to let them make a surrealistic comedy."

In fact, they did just that later when left to their own devices in *Magical Mystery Tour*. What does Shenson think of the Beatles home movie? "That, I think, was The Beatles doing what they wanted to — having fun."

Shenson was also greatly impressed with the songwriting talents of Lennon and McCartney. "The Beatles wrote the songs for the first film before it started shooting and before we had a title (which came from Lennon repeating a saying of Starr's to Shenson). We had just about finished filming when it dawned on me we didn't have a song called *A Hard Day's Night*. One night, after we'd been doing a looping [dubbing] session, I asked John to write one. He asked what we would use it for, and I said to play under the titles. I said we needed something uptempo. That was about 11 at night.

"The next morning on the set at about 8 or 8:30, I was told John wanted to see me in his dressing room. He and Paul were standing there with guitars and he took out — I think it was a matchbook cover or something — with the lyrics on it and they sang and played 'A Hard Day's Night.'" [The lyrics were actually written on the back of a birthday card for John's son, Julian (see pages 234-235).]

The Beatles record producer, George Martin, handled the incidental music for the film. Shenson recalls asking him to write something for Starr's big solo scene (with the truant boy). "He came to my office and played a piece of original background music and I said, 'George, that's very pretty, but it's not for The Beatles.' I asked him to arrange a Beatles song. We selected 'This Boy' because he's with a little boy in the scene.

"When I played the picture for the four Beatles the first time, Dick Lester didn't even show up — he was chicken and didn't know if they would like it. Anyway, when Ringo's theme came on, Paul turned on me with venom and said, 'Who put THAT in there?' It was not in their mode, and they didn't like it. I said, 'George Martin did, and I suggested it.' They really did like George very much and respected his opinions, so Paul said, 'Oh, all right, if George did it.' It's funny, now I can go into the supermarket and hear Muzak playing the goddamn thing all the time."

While Shenson thinks the Beatles second effort for him, *Help!*, was "a more complete film," he said his favorite is the first one. "There's a purity in *A Hard Day's Night* and it's a tribute to Dick Lester that it doesn't look like a film made on a tight budget and schedule [six to seven weeks shooting]."

Also, he said: "I appreciate the brilliance of Alun Owen's screenplay. It was well deserving of its Oscar nomination, and I think Dick should have had one, too, as director."

In terms of gross receipts at the box office, he said both films were big for the period. "They made a lot of money because the actual cost of the negatives was very low and there weren't these crazy marketing expenses you have now. It cost us $4 million [to] $6 million to put them out. We spent $1 million on advertising, press and prints. We had a big margin of net profit, but it was peanuts by today's standard."

Of course, Shenson said, the Beatles were not the film's only attraction. "You've got to remember that this movie's a first-rate comedy."

While Shenson now owns the film, he doesn't claim to have had any greater foresight than anyone else involved with it.

"The clause giving me the film after 15 years was suggested by my English accountant," he admitted. "United Artists agreed, because they were sure The Beatles were a fad that would soon fade away. I didn't even think about it. I was only concerned with making a good movie and not just an exploitation film. At the time, I wasn't that thrilled."

And now? The twinkle in his eye and the smile on his face attest to the fact that Walter Shenson isn't blasé about his little low-budget comedy anymore.

[Walter Shenson died on October 17, 2000, at the age of 81.]

The Beatles Live At The Hollywood Bowl

On August 23, 1964, the Beatles played before more than 17,000 screaming fans at the Hollywood Bowl in Los Angeles, California. All 17,256 available tickets for the event held at the prestigious outdoor concert venue sold out in less than three hours when they had gone on sale four months earlier on April 25.

Capitol recorded the performance with the intent of issuing a live album. The concert recording was produced by Capitol Vice-President Voyle Gilmore, with George Martin's assistance and Hugh Davis serving as engineer. Prior to the show, Billboard reported that Gilmore was hoping the open-air venue would allow the anticipated screaming to dissipate and not overshadow the band's sound. Yeah, right. The concert was recorded on a mobile three-track unit, recording vocals on one track, guitars on the second track and bass and drums on the third. The vocal mikes also picked up the sound of the guitars coming through the amplifiers. The non-stop shrieking by the enthusiastic fans bled over to the Beatles stage microphones.

George Martin was less than enthusiastic about recording a live Beatles album. He knew "the quality of recording could not equal what we could do in the studio." Further complicating the recording of their outdoor performances was what Martin described as "arduous in the extreme" conditions for engineers and the chaos and panic that reigned at Beatles concerts. In addition, "the Beatles had no 'fold back' speakers, so they could not hear what they were singing, and the eternal shriek from 17,000 healthy young lungs made even a jet plane inaudible." EMI was uninterested in releasing a live album as the company believed that sophisticated British consumers would not be interested in purchasing a collection of songs already available in better quality on studio albums and singles.

Capitol didn't share this view, knowing that Americans would eagerly buy a souvenir live album of a Beatles concert. Capitol had done quite well with live albums by the Kingston Trio and was set to release a live Beach Boys album for the 1964 Christmas season. A live Beatles album was a no-brainer as the disc was sure to be a chart-topping million seller.

On August 27, 1964, Gilmore and Davis prepared stereo mixes from the three-track concert tape, which was edited by eliminating the time between the introduction of the band and the first song and by removing some of Paul's introductory comments to Ringo's rendition of "Boys." Side One contained "Twist And Shout," "You Can't Do That," "All My Loving," "She Loves You," "Things We Said Today" and "Roll Over Beethoven." Side Two had "Can't Buy Me Love," "If I Fell," "I Want To Hold Your Hand," "Boys," "A Hard Day's Night" and "Long Tall Sally." A fold-down mono acetate of the proposed album, with a total running time of less than 30 minutes, was cut on September 3, 1964.

Much to Capitol's horror and dismay, George Martin and the Beatles were dissatisfied with the group's performance and the sound quality of the recording. They blocked the release of the live album, disappointing Capitol's sales force and accountants. When the label's *Beach Boys Concert* spent four weeks at number one on the Billboard Top LP's chart in December 1964, Capitol could only dream about what might have been.

The surviving acetate reveals that the Beatles were too hard on themselves. While John and Paul's vocals failed to match the perfection of their studio recordings on songs like "If I Fell" and "A Hard Day's Night," the energy of the performance and the excitement of the screaming crowd outweigh any deficiencies.

Although Capitol's LP of the 1964 concert was never officially released, the label issued an album in 1977 containing performances from both the 1964 and 1965 Hollywood Bowl concerts. *The Beatles At The Hollywood Bowl* contains the following songs from the 1964 show: "Things We Said Today," "Roll Over Beethoven," "Boys," "All My Loving," "She Loves You" and "Long Tall Sally." The album also contains the following performances from 1965: "Twist And Shout," "She's A Woman," "Dizzy Miss Lizzie," "Ticket To Ride," "Can't Buy Me Love," "Help!" and "A Hard Day's Night." Volume 4 of the *Anthology* video contains black and white footage of the group performing "All My Loving." In 2016, Apple released a remixed and expanded version of the 1977 LP titled *Live At The Hollywood Bowl*, which added "You Can't Do That" and "I Want To Hold Your Hand" from the 1964 and "Everybody's Trying To Be My Baby" and "Baby's In Black" from 1965.

Capitol did not prepare a cover for its hoped-for 1964 album. The cover shown on the following page was created by the author and his graphic designer, Diana Thornton, for his book *The Beatles' Story on Capitol Records, Part Two: The Albums.* This cover has been used without permission on several bootleg albums.

File Under: The Beatles • Vocal Group. TAO 2222

THE BEATLES

Capitol RECORDS

HIGH FIDELITY

LIVE AT THE HOLLYWOOD BOWL

INSIDE: CONCERT PROGRAM WITH ON-STAGE PHOTOS AND NOTES ON THE SHOW

featuring the #1 hits

I WANT TO HOLD YOUR HAND
SHE LOVES YOU
CAN'T BUY ME LOVE
A HARD DAY'S NIGHT

...with the great rockers

ROLL OVER BEETHOVEN
LONG TALL SALLY
YOU CAN'T DO THAT
ALL MY LOVING
THINGS WE SAID TODAY
IF I FELL

plus, for the first time on Capitol, the hit single

TWIST AND SHOUT

and Ringo's rendition of

BOYS

A Zany and Animated Cover

After photographing the striking and innovative cover for the album *With The Beatles*, Robert Freeman was once again selected to shoot and design the cover for a Beatles LP. In his book *The Beatles A Private View*, Freeman told of how the producer of *A Hard Day's Night* sought his involvement in the project. "The job came about when Walter Shenson, the film's producer, showed me the designs submitted by United Artists' publicity department for use on the film posters. They were cartoon illustrations of Beatle wigs stuck on top of guitars: quite out of character with the Beatles. Shenson discussed the matter with Brian Epstein and together they were able to influence the choice of design."

While the revised film poster released for the U.S. market (shown on page 89) has cartoonish screaming female fans and a guitar with a knotted neck, the British poster (shown on page 35) is strikingly different than the typical movie posters of the day.

Freeman explained his concept that was used for both the poster and the album cover: "The Hard Day's Night cover used photographs in an animated fashion because that's how the Beatles came across in the feature film–zany and animated. I used a studio for the portraits, shot individually with varying expressions. A white background, a soft sidelight, and the Beatles wearing black. The pictures were edited in a sequence to animate their expressions, one in line for each Beatle, on the same principal as polyphotos, where a person is photographed with different expressions from a fixed camera position. The grid format worked equally well for the album cover and the film poster...I used the same photo-portraits for the title sequence which ran at the end of the film, so everything finally came together nicely."

Both the poster and album cover have a blue background and four rows of photos, with each row featuring a Beatle in the order, from top to bottom, of John, George, Paul and Ringo. The poster has eight columns, while the album cover has five, meaning it has three less photos dedicated to each Beatle. The first photo in each row is the same for the poster and LP cover. Both feature a picture of John pretending to be looking through binoculars and a picture of the back of George's head. The poster has a portrait of Paul's fictional grandfather (Wilfrid Brambell) in Paul's row. Both have "A HARD DAY'S NIGHT" in the same font towards the top.

TRADE MARK
PARLOPHONE

THE BEATLES

mono

A HARD DAY'S NIGHT

The back cover (shown on page 218) has "Songs from the film A HARD DAY'S NIGHT" at the top, with text in four columns. The first column has "THE BEATLES" in large block letters followed by the Side One song titles, "From the soundtrack of the United Artists film 'A HARD DAY'S NIGHT'" and "Words and Music: JOHN LENNON AND PAUL McCARTNEY." Tony Barrow's liner notes about the film and its songs flow through the top of the third column.

After the list of the Side Two songs, Barrow's liner notes continue. He writes of the challenge faced by John and Paul to create and perfect new songs for the film. Faced with a "shooting schedule deadline," they had to write the songs "during a season of concerts in Paris and a now legendary visit to America." Barrow adds that "the two boys had a grand-piano moved into their hotel suite at the George V in Paris."

By the beginning of March, the Beatles had nearly a dozen songs ready for final rehearsal. However, they did not want their first film to "turn into a continuous parade of Beatles performances." Instead, it would "portray as many different facets of the four boys' individual personalities as possible" and "display their on-the-spot sense on humour." The number of new songs in the film would be limited to six. But because "it seemed most unfair to hold back the remainder of the boys' new songs when each one was of such excellent quality," the Beatles recorded all the new songs and included the extra titles on the second side of the album.

Barrow writes: "When you listen to the second side of this record you will agree that it would have been a pity to cast aside such a fabulous set of songs." He concludes by pointing out that this is the group's first album to contain all self-composed songs.

The back cover also features a portrait of each Beatle taken during the shooting of the film.

The United Artists' Original Motion Picture Sound Track album cover (shown right) has a bright red background and features the same Robert Freeman portraits of each Beatle cropped below the eyes above the bottom of the nose that appear on the American poster for the film (shown on page 89). "THE BEATLES" is in large white block letters and the film's title is in black.

The back cover (shown below) also incorporates elements from the U.S. poster, with the group's name and film's title in the same font as on the poster. The top third of the cover also has the film credits from the poster plus additional credits such as "Musical Director George Martin" along with the album's song lineup.

The lower part of the cover features 15 Robert Freeman portraits of John, Paul, George and Ringo in a grid of three rows and five columns. Some of the photos are different than those appearing on the U.K. poster and album cover.

ORIGINAL MOTION PICTURE SOUND TRACK

THE BEATLES

A HARD DAY'S NIGHT

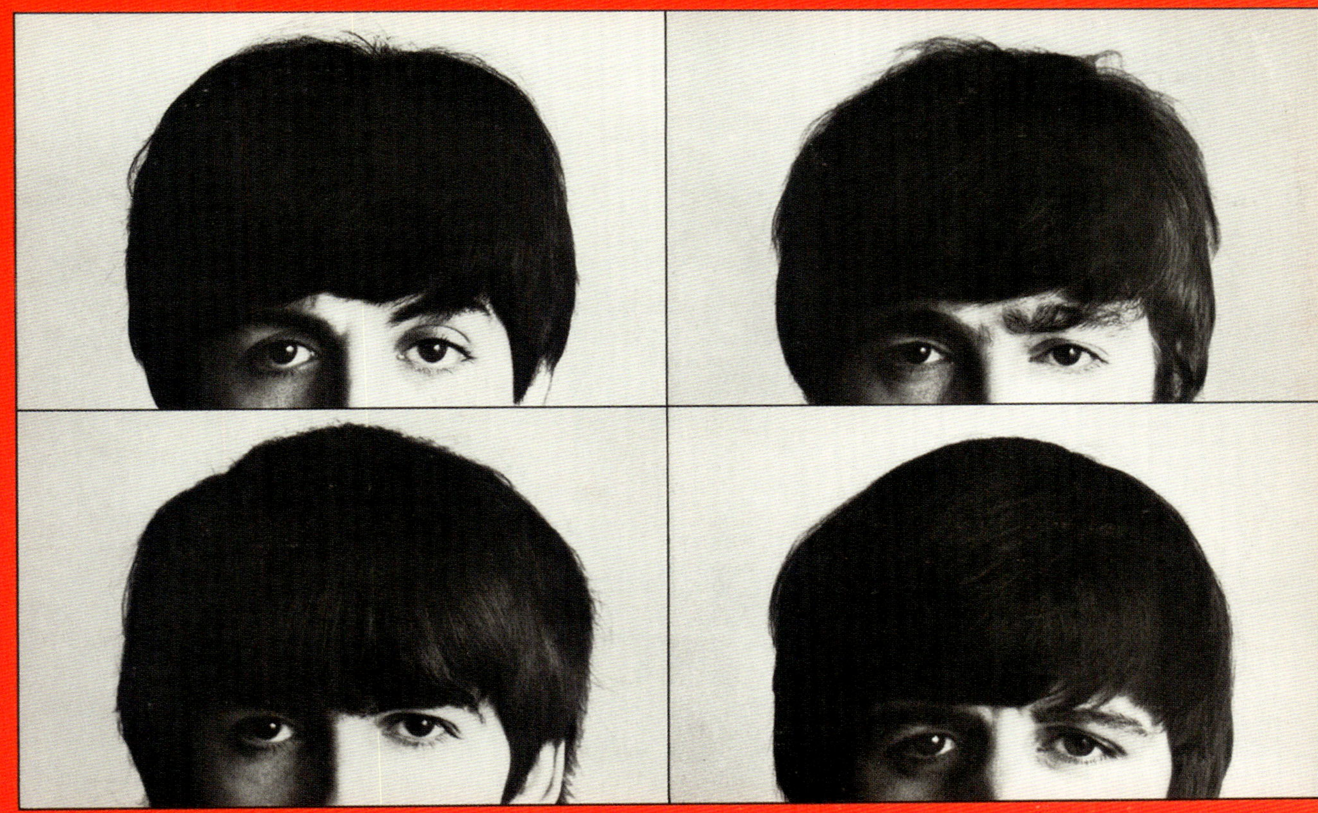

high fidelity THE BEATLES • A HARD DAY'S NIGHT • UNITED ARTISTS UAL 3366

UNITED ARTISTS RECORDS

Capitol's second Beatles album, titled *The Beatles' Second Album*, was the first in a series of Capitol LPs that had either no or only a partial resemblance to one of the group's Parlophone LPs. With the album drawing from a variety of sources (see page 62), Capitol had to create its own cover.

The front cover was designed by George Osaki, head of Capitol's art department. It features a layout of sepia-tinted photographs of the band. There are two group shots: one in front of a curtain at The Ed Sullivan Show and one from the Kennedy airport press conference. Each Beatle's head is featured in a small photo and a larger picture. Of the larger pictures, Ringo is the only one whose face is fully shown. The others are cropped to draw attention to the hair and eyes. There is also a photo of Paul and George sharing a mic (from The Ed Sullivan Show) and of John strumming his guitar.

The album's title is at the top in stylized letters with "The Beatles'" in reddish-brown and "Second Album" in black. This is followed by: "Electrifying Big-Beat Performances by England's Paul McCartney, John Lennon, George Harrison and Ringo Starr." Knowing that hit singles make hit albums, Capitol added "featuring She Loves You and Roll Over Beethoven." The former song had been a number one hit on Swan, while the latter was a Canadian import disc that was nearly issued as Capitol's second Beatles single (see page 51).

The placing of the band member's names on the cover was unique. Prior to the Beatles, bands either had a featured leader or were an anonymous group of musicians and singers whose names were known only by their fans. The Beatles were different. By early 1964, their names were household names. Capitol wanted to capitalize on their individual popularity.

The back cover also features photos of the band. Four feature Ed Sullivan Show performances: Ringo on

drums, Paul at the mic, George and John strumming their guitars and the entire group in the arrow set. There is also a performance shot from the Washington Coliseum concert, a picture of a crowd in front of a banner that says "WWDC Welcomes The Beatles" and the same curtain photo used on the cover. Once again, each Beatle is given a solo head shot, with the picture of George being a full head shot of the cropped picture from the front cover. There is also a picture of John looking over Ringo's shoulder.

The top portion of the back states "Never before has show business seen and heard anything like them... and here they are!...The World's most popular foursome singing and playing their new collection of hits." This is followed by the album's title. The left side of the back cover has the album's track listing, a plug for the group's first LP and the credits "Produced in London by GEORGE MARTIN" and "All Photos/Joe Covello/Black Star."

File Under: The Beatles • Pop Rock, Vocal Group

T 2080

THE BEATLES' SECOND ALBUM

ELECTRIFYING BIG-BEAT PERFORMANCES BY ENGLAND'S Paul McCartney, John Lennon, George Harrison and Ringo Starr

featuring

SHE LOVES YOU

and

ROLL OVER BEETHOVEN

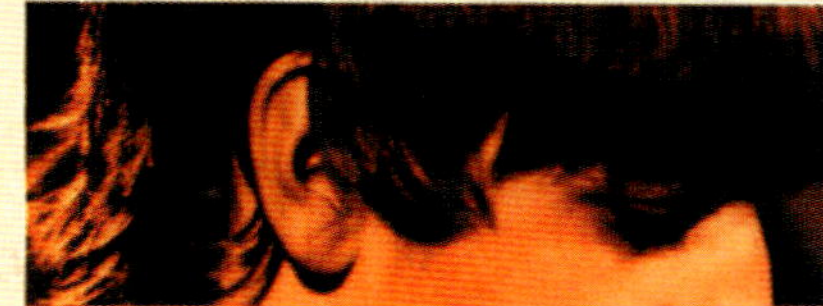

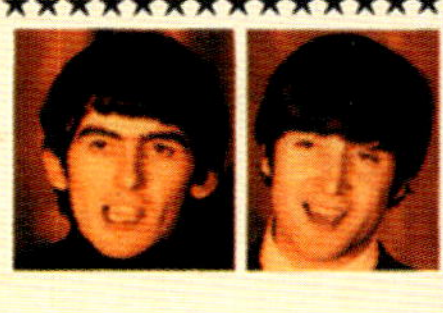

The front cover of the *Something New* album features a color photograph taken by Capitol's Ken Veder at the February 9, 1964 dress rehearsal for the Beatles debut appearance on The Ed Sullivan Show. Paul is shown singing "I Saw Her Standing There," which was the opening number of the group's second set on the show. The 10½" x 7¼" photo is on the left side of the black background front cover.

The album's title logo appears in doubled offset lettering at the top of the right side in white. "THE BEATLES" is under the album title in orange, with the Capitol logo and "HIGH FIDELITY" in white below the group's name. Moving downward, this is followed by the titles to the six non-movie tunes in white, the phrase "...plus the hit vocals from the Motion Picture 'A Hard Day's Night' (A United Artists Release)" in orange and the titles to the album's five film songs in white. The usual filing information, black dot and record number are on the top right of the wrap-over back liner.

The back cover has the title logo centered at the top above "THE BEATLES." The song titles and running times appear below the group's name on the right side. The text on the left states that the album is: "the third great Beatles album for Capitol. And needless to say it's wonderful in the very special and exclusively marvelous Beatles way! Here are the **latest, greatest new Beatles hits** the boys have come up with since their first two phenomenal Capitol albums." This was Capitol's way of telling fans that Capitol Beatles albums were superior to the discs issued by other labels. The notes claim that "One of the most popular is Komm, Gib Mir Deine Hand, the German-language version the boys made of their sensational Capitol hit, I Want To Hold Your Hand." The second paragraph of text plugs the film and tells fans that they "can see John, George, Paul and Ringo giant-size on the screen and play the big hits from the picture on their HiFi and Stereo sets between trips to the movies!"

The liner notes are followed by the first of what would become a series of dubious production credits. This time the credit states "Produced in England by George Martin and in the U.S.A. with the assistance of Dave Dexter, Jr." Dexter's sole contribution to the album was the selection and sequencing of the songs. He was not involved in the production of the songs. And yes, this is the same Dave Dexter who had advised Capitol to turn the Beatles down four times. No wonder George Martin resented Dexter's claim that he had assisted Martin with the production of the album.

The lower portion features images of the covers of the first two Capitol Beatles albums and *The Beatles Song Book by the Hollyridge Strings*. The first three Capitol singles are also plugged. The bottom has the usual factory information and the RIAA logo.

The first order of business at the February 25 session was to complete the sides for the Beatles next single. The "Can't Buy Me Love" tape from the January 29 session at EMI Pathé Marconi Studios in Paris was embellished with Paul's double-tracked vocal and George's rhythm guitar and solo. The group also recorded John's "You Can't Do That," which would serve as the single's B-side. The session ran from 10:00 AM to 1:00 PM.

Both sides of the single, "Can't Buy Me Love" and "You Can't Do That," were mixed during a morning session prior to the Beatles arrival. During the day's 2:30 to 5:30 PM session, the Beatles began work on two other film songs, Paul's "And I Love Her" and John's "I Should Have Known Better." The group returned to and completed the latter song with a remake the next day on February 26 during the 2:30 to 5:30 PM session. They recorded a remake of "And I Love Her" during a 7:00 PM evening session that ended at 10:00 PM without the group having recorded a satisfactory version.

The group was back in EMI's Studio Two the next day on February 27. During the 10:00 AM to 1:00 PM session, the group quickly finished a remake of "And I Love Her" and completed John's "Tell Me Why." The Beatles also recorded John's ballad "If I Fell" during the 2:30 to 5:30 PM afternoon session.

On Friday, February 28, the Beatles took a break from their EMI session to record songs for a BBC special to be broadcast on Easter Monday, March 30. In addition to taping six songs from the *With The Beatles* sessions, the group recorded "Can't Buy Me Love" and "You Can't Do That" to promote their upcoming single.

The Beatles returned to EMI Studios on Sunday, March 1, for a productive 10:00 AM to 1:30 PM session. The group completed George's vocal contribution to the film and album, "I'm Happy Just To Dance With You," which had been written primarily by John, an incredible one-take performance of Little Richard's "Long Tall Sally" sung by Paul, and John's "I Call Your Name," a song which had been previously released as the B-side to Billy J. Kramer's "Bad To Me" (another song penned by John).

The next day the Beatles began filming their first feature-length movie, *A Hard Day's Night*. On March 3, George Martin, assisted by engineer Norman Smith and tape operator A.B. Lincoln, produced mono mixes of the six new songs then intended for the film: "I Should Have Known Better," "If I Fell," "Tell Me Why," "And I Love Her," "I'm Happy Just To Dance With You" and "I Call Your Name." These mixes were sent to United Artists to enable director Dick Lester to incorporate the new songs into the film's soundtrack.

After the film was named *A Hard Day's Night*, producer Walter Shenson asked John and Paul to come up with a title song to run at the start and end of the film. This task was quickly completed, with the Beatles back at EMI Studios on April 16 to record "A Hard Day's Night" in nine takes during a 7:00 to 10:00 PM session.

On April 20, George Martin, assisted by Norman Smith and A.B. Lincoln, made rough mono and stereo mixes of the title song, with the mono mix sent to United Artists. The Beatles finished their work on the film on April 24.

After a well-deserved break for most of the month of May, the Beatles were back at EMI Studios on June 1 to record additional songs that would appear on the second side of the British *A Hard Day's Night* LP and on an extended play (EP) disc. During the 2:30 to 5:30 PM session, the group recorded Carl Perkins' "Matchbox" with Ringo on lead vocal. Perkins, who was in England for a promotional tour, attended the session but did not play on the track. The group then recorded John's "I'll Cry Instead" in two sections that would be edited to form a single track. George Martin expected the song would be included in the film. As then edited, the film featured "Can't Buy Me Love" in two separate places, the romping in the field sequence and the police chase. Martin wanted "I'll Cry Instead" to run behind the latter scene, but was overruled by Dick Lester, who thought the song was relatively weak. The group also knocked out the Larry Williams rocker "Slow Down" with John on lead vocal. Martin overdubbed piano to the track on June 4. During the day's 7:00 to 10:00 PM session, the Beatles recorded John's "I'll Be Back."

On June 2, the group recorded John's "Any Time At All" and Paul's "Things We Said Today" during the 2:30 to 5:30 PM slot. The middle eight to the former track caused difficulties, so it was set aside. After the Beatles knocked out John's "When I Get Home" during the 7:00 to 10:00 PM session, they returned to and completed "Any Time At All."

During a morning photo shoot on June 3, the day before the Beatles were set to depart for a near-month-long tour of Denmark, the Netherlands, Hong Kong (then under British control), Australia and New Zealand, Ringo took sick and was replaced by Jimmy Nicol. The recording session turned into a rehearsal of six songs with the new drummer. After Nicol left, the remaining Beatles recorded demos of George's "You Know What To Do" and John's "No Reply," along with a bit of Cilla Black's current hit, "You're My World." Mixing sessions for the album were held on June 4, 9 and 22, with Martin and Smith assisted by different tape operators on each day.

It's been a hard day's night
And I've been working like a dog
It's been a hard day's night
I should be sleeping like a log
But when I get home to you
all right
You know I work all day
to get you money to buy you things
So why on earth should I moan
'Cause when I get you alone
You know I feel O.K.
When I'm home
When I'm home ...
145 AB 2

A Hard Day's Night

Recorded: April 16, 1964
Mixed: April 23 (mono); June 22 (stereo)

Producer: George Martin
Engineers: Norman Smith; Geoff Emerick

John: Lead vocals; acoustic guitar (Jumbo)
Paul: Lead (on bridge) and backing vocals; bass guitar (Hofner)
George: Lead guitar (12-string Rickenbacker)
Ringo: Drums (Ludwig kit); cowbell (Ludwig Clear Tone)
George Martin: Piano (1905 Steinway Vertigrand)
Norman Smith: Bongos

The origin of the film's title *A Hard Day's Night* has long been attributed to Ringo, although the story varies slightly among people's memories. During the Beatles 1964 tour of America, Ringo told Los Angeles disc jockey Dave Hull: "We went to do a job, and we'd worked all day and we happened to work all night. I came up still thinking it was day I suppose, and I said, 'It's been a hard day ...' and I looked around and saw it was dark so I said, '... night!' So we came to 'A Hard Day's Night.'" Depending on when Ringo made that statement, it was either preceded in usage by John or borrowed by John, who said in 1980 that "it was an off-the-cuff remark by Ringo." The phrase appears in the short story "Sad Michael" in Lennon's book *In His Own Write*, published on March 23, 1964. John writes: "He'd had a hard days night that day, for Michael was a Cocky Watchtower."

Walter Shenson, the movie's producer, recalls having lunch with John on the film set when Lennon mentioned the phrase as an example of Ringo's distinctive use of the English language. Shenson immediately realized this "Ringoism" would be the perfect title for a movie depicting a hectic day and a half in the life of the Beatles. After receiving positive feedback from director Dick Lester and the other Beatles, Shenson phoned the title to United Artists' New York office. Although there was initial resistance, on April 13, 1964, United Artists issued a press release that the movie's title was *A Hard Day's Night*.

Towards the end of filming, Shenson decided the movie should open with a song bearing the film's title. At the end of an evening voice-over session, he asked John to write an up-tempo tune to serve as the title song. The next morning, John and Paul, armed with their guitars and the lyrics John had written on the back of a card for his son Julian's birthday, previewed the song "A Hard Day's Night" for Shenson in their dressing room on the movie set.

On April 16, the Beatles filmed the police chase scenes in London. Journalist Maureen Cleave recalled picking up John in a taxi and taking him to an evening session at EMI to record the title song. "The tune to the song 'A Hard Day's Night' was in his head, the words scrawled on a birthday card from a fan to his little son Julian: 'When I get home to you,' it said, 'I find my tiredness is through ...' 'Rather a feeble line about tiredness,' I said. 'OK,' he said cheerfully and, borrowing my pen, instantly changed it to the slightly suggestive: 'When I get home to you/I find the things that you do/Will make me feel all right.' The other Beatles were there in the studio and, of course, the wonderful George Martin. John sort of hummed the tune to the others – they had no copies of the words or anything else. Three hours later I was none the wiser about how they'd done it but the record was made." The birthday card (shown left) indicates that John had trouble with the bridge beyond "When I'm home."

The productive session ran from 7 to 10 PM. Despite having spent the day being pursued by the police on the set, the session tapes reveal that the group was full of energy and in good spirits. As the song would open both the film and the soundtrack album, a distinctive beginning was essential. The song opens with the jarring strum of a strident-sounding chord played by George on his 12-string Rickenbacker guitar, believed to be an F chord with a G on top (Fadd9) and George wrapping his thumb around the neck of the guitar to cover the G note. He is joined by John playing a Dsus4 chord (not the Fadd9 he played in concert) on George's Gibson Jumbo acoustic electric guitar, Paul playing a D note on his bass and Ringo hitting his snare drum, crash cymbal (and possibly bass drum). During the overdubs, George Martin added the notes D/G/D/G/C on the studio's 1905 Steinway Vertegrand piano.

After an effective pause, John launches into the song with his lead vocal, and the rest of the band falls into place. Paul sings backing vocals on a few of the lines and the solo lead vocal on the bridge because it contained notes beyond John's range.

The song was recorded with George's 12-string Rickenbacker, Paul's Hofner bass and Ringo's drums on track 1, and John and Paul's vocals, along with John on George's Jumbo acoustic-electric guitar, on track 2. Engineer Norman Smith recorded the Jumbo both miked acoustically and through John's Vox amplifier. During the first few takes, the opening guitar chord was treated with heavy echo. This idea was wisely abandoned. George had difficulty with the guitar solo during the first four takes, so he did not play a solo on the remaining takes knowing that he would later overdub a solo.

Take 1, which is on *Anthology 1*, is a rough but fun run through of the song that reveals George's trouble coming up with a suitable solo. Paul sounds tentative during the first bridge and for its second line sings: "When I'm home, feeling you holding me tight all through the night." On the second bridge, he has trouble remembering the words, prompting John to ad-lib: "Ha, ha!" The song's ending is treated with echo.

After false starts on Takes 2 and 3, the group completed Take 4. John and Paul muff a few of the words. On the bridge, Paul replaces "all through the night" with "tight, tight, yeah!" George is still having problems with his guitar solo. The ending has Paul adding a few bass notes, causing John to laugh and ask, "What's that?"

Take 5, misidentified as "Take 4," is also complete. The echo on the opening chord has been dropped, and the band is starting to find its groove. John and Paul's harmony vocals on the fifth and sixth lines of the verses are at last sung with precision. George doesn't attempt a guitar solo, but rather plays his rhythm patterns. By this time the decision had been made for him to overdub his solo. The group has worked out the song's ending with a series of guitar notes. The laughter at the end of the take shows that the group is still enjoying the session.

After the engineer calls out "Take 6," Paul hits a few bass notes and ad-libs "Scooby dooby scooby." John counts in the song and the band hits the opening ensemble chord. The song is taken at a slower tempo and breaks down when John muffs the words at the end of the second verse and says "I heard a funny chord." After Take 7 is announced, John once again explains that he "heard a funny chord." Paul hits some bass notes and practices his vocals on the bridge. After the engineer calls "Take 7" for a second time, the Beatles turn in a complete performance at a faster pace than the previous attempt. The song is clearly coming together, although Paul makes a few vocal errors and John breaks a string on his guitar.

After Take 8 is announced, John admits, "I wish we had the words written out." John quickly counts in the song, but the group doesn't get past the crashing opening chord. Paul gets in a brief practice of the bridge before John shouts out: "Go! One, two, three, four." The band delivers its best performance of the song with Take 9.

The group superimposed additional instruments and vocals onto Take 9 on the two remaining open tracks. The first set included John and Paul double-tracking their vocals, Ringo on cowbell on the song's bridge and Abbey Road engineer Norman Smith on bongos. George Martin then worked out the song's instrumental break. With the tape running at half-speed, Martin played piano in tandem with Harrison on his 12-string, both at an octave lower than desired so that the instruments would be at the correct pitch when the tape was played at the proper speed. Finally, Martin added piano to the opening chord, and Harrison added electric 12-string guitar to the fade out ending. Rough mono and stereo mixes were made on April 20. The final mono mix for the single was made on April 23 with Norman Smith and David Lloyd assisting George Martin as engineers. The stereo mix was made on June 22 with Smith and Geoff Emerick. The finished product successfully fulfilled three purposes: hit single; lead track for the soundtrack album; and the opening and closing song for the film.

The Beatles performed "A Hard Day's Night" twice for the BBC. On July 14, 1964, the group recorded the song at Broadcasting House, London, for airing on the July 16 premiere show of Top Gear. As George Martin was not available to play the piano instrumental break, the BBC edited the instrumental passage from the single into the BBC tape. *Live At The BBC* contains this recording. The group's July 17, 1964 performance for the BBC, which has George playing a guitar solo for the instrumental break, was broadcast on the August 3 From Us To You. The group's live television rendition of the song for the July 19, 1964 Blackpool Night Out is not currently available. "A Hard Day's Night" was part of the Beatles set list for the 1964 North American Tour and remained in their show for most of 1965. The band's August 30, 1965 performance is on the *Hollywood Bowl* LP.

I Should Have Known Better

Recorded: February 25 & 26, 1964
Mixed: March 3 (mono); June 22 (stereo)

Producer: George Martin
Engineers: Norman Smith; Richard Langham

John: Lead vocals; Jumbo acoustic-electric guitar; harmonica
Paul: Bass guitar (Hofner)
George: Lead guitar (12-string Rickenbacker)
Ringo: Drums (Ludwig kit)

"I Should Have Known Better" appears twice in the film. First, the group is shown playing the song during a card game taking place in the baggage car of the train as adoring fans look on. The band later performs the song as part of its TV concert at the Scala Theatre. In both scenes, Paul is shown lip-syncing even though he does not sing on the record.

"I Should Have Known Better" was written by John during the Beatles first U.S. visit in February 1964. Although the song is a fan favorite from the film and soundtrack album, John did not consider it one of his better efforts. In his 1980 interview with David Sheff appearing in Sheff's book *All We Are Saying*, John commented: "Just a song; it doesn't mean a damn thing." This, however, is another example of John being dismissive in assessing his own work.

The recording's most distinctive feature is John's harmonica. Although at least one side of each of the Beatles first four singles featured harmonica, the group started moving away from the instrument, perhaps considering it a gimmick that had outlived its day and was no longer necessary to ensure a hit. None of the songs on the group's previous two singles and only one track on their previous album, "Little Child," had mouth organ. But the group's expansion of its musical palate apparently renewed John's interest in harmonica.

Just prior to the Beatles first U.S. visit, the band was in Paris, France for a series of performances at the Olympia Theatre from January 16-February 4, 1964. The group stayed at the George V Hotel where they spent time writing songs for their upcoming film. The trip also marked the first time the Beatles listened to Bob Dylan. John recalled Paul getting a copy of the folk singer's second album, *The Freewheelin' Bob Dylan*, from a French DJ. "We were doing a radio thing there and the guy had the record in the studio. Paul said, 'Oh, I keep hearing about this guy,' or he'd heard it, I'm not sure—and we took it back to the hotel." John remembered: "And for the rest of our three weeks in Paris, we didn't stop playing it. We all went potty on Dylan." George also has fond memories of his introduction to Dylan's music: "The highlights of the Paris trip were that we discovered Bob Dylan's *Freewheelin'* album and sat around playing it all the time, and that 'I Want To Hold Your Hand' went to No. 1 in the USA."

The Beatles first attempted "I Should Have Known Better" on the afternoon of February 25. The song features John on lead vocal, Gibson Jumbo acoustic-electric guitar and harmonica, George on his 12-string electric guitar, Paul on his Hofner bass and Ringo on drums. Of the three takes recorded that day, only one was complete. At this stage, the song opened with a harmonica solo from John and ended with lead guitar by George. John used a harmonica neck rack to enable him to simultaneously play guitar and mouth organ. By doing so, John was unable to manipulate the slide button on the harmonica with his hand. This resulted in John playing more in the style of Bob Dylan, who frequently alternated between blow (exhaling) and draw (inhaling) notes.

The song was remade and finished the following day. John's vocals on some of the early takes sound raw. After a breakdown, John says: "Can't breathe after I've done that mouth organ bit. Can we skip the mouth organ?" For Take 9, John gets his wish, singing and playing the song without harmonica. George uses his electric 12-string sparingly, single strumming open chords leading into and during the bridge and playing the song's guitar solo. Take 9 serves as the basic track over which two overdubs were added: John's harmonica (which has more of a blues feel than on the earlier takes because John's hand was free to move the slide button) and his double-tracked vocal. The finished master, Take 22, is an energetic rocker worthy of being the album's second track. George Martin, assisted by engineer Norman Smith and tape operator A.B. Lincoln, mixed the song for mono on March 3. In the stereo mix, made on June 22 with Smith and Geoff Emerick assisting Martin, the harmonica drops out briefly during the song's introduction towards the end.

The Beatles recorded the song twice for the BBC. These performances were broadcast on the July 16, 1964 Top Gear and a few weeks later on the August 3 From Us To You.

If I Fell

Recorded: February 27, 1964
Mixed: March 3 (mono); June 22 (stereo)

Producer: George Martin
Engineers: Norman Smith; Richard Langham

John: Lead harmony vocals; acoustic guitar (Jumbo)
Paul: Lead harmony vocals; bass guitar (Hofner)
George: Lead guitar (12-string Rickenbacker)
Ringo: Drums (Ludwig kit)

"If I Fell" also appears twice in the film. After arriving on the theatre stage for a rehearsal of their televised performance, Ringo gets into an argument with a sound man who had messed with his drums. After Paul observes that the drummer is sulking, Lennon remarks "I'll show him" and proceeds to sing the song to Ringo. The tune is also featured in the Scala Theatre concert scene.

John completed the song in early 1964 in Paris. He told David Sheff: "That's my first attempt to write a ballad proper. That was the precursor to 'In My Life.' It has the same chord sequence as 'In My Life'...And it's semi-autobiographical, but not consciously. It shows that I wrote sentimental love ballads, silly love songs, way back when." John wrote the lyrics on the back of a Valentine's Day card.

Ludwig
THE
BEATLES
Ludwig

Although "If I Fell" was primarily written by John, Paul claimed he co-wrote the song with John and was responsible for the song's preamble (introductory section). Paul has described the song as a "nice harmony piece." On John's home demo, his voice is raw and sounds very vulnerable. Towards the end of the demo, he sings words over a melody similar to that of "I Should Have Known Better."

"If I Fell" was the third and final song recorded on February 27, 1964. The song starts with John's solo voice and the strumming of the Gibson Jumbo acoustic guitar behind the introduction, which is followed by the steady taps of Ringo's drums and the rest of the band falling into place, with George on his 12-string Rickenbacker and Paul on bass. The remainder of the ballad features an exquisite vocal harmony between John and Paul. The song, with its wonderfully complex chord changes, shows how far the group had progressed in just a few years. The group took 14 takes to perfect the song using three of the four tracks. John and Paul then double-tracked their vocals, and George added some more 12-string guitar on the remaining track to form Take 15, which was used as the master. The song was mixed for mono on March 3 and for stereo on June 22. For the song's preamble, John's vocal is double-tracked only on the stereo mix.

The Beatles recorded "If I Fell" twice for the BBC, first on July 14, 1964, along with "And I Love Her" and four other tunes, for broadcast two days later on Top Gear, and again on July 17, 1964, for the August 3rd airing of From Us To You. The Top Gear performance is on *On Air - Live At The BBC Volume 2*. "If I Fell" was performed throughout the Beatles 1964 summer tour of North America. Although the song was recorded by Capitol at the Hollywood Bowl concert on August 23, 1964, it was not included on the label's 1977 *Live At The Hollywood Bowl* LP or Apple's 2016 remixed and expanded album, *The Beatles: Live At The Hollywood Bowl*. The group also performed the song live on Blackpool Night Out.

I'm Happy Just To Dance With You

Recorded: March 1, 1964
Mixed: March 3 (mono); June 22 (stereo)

Producer: George Martin
Engineers: Norman Smith; Richard Langham

George: Lead vocals; rhythm guitar (Rickenbacker 12-string)
John: Backing vocal; rhythm guitar (Rickenbacker Capri)
Paul: Backing vocal; bass guitar (Hofner)
Ringo: Drums (Ludwig kit); Arabian bongo drums

"I'm Happy Just To Dance With You" makes its debut in the film as a piano instrumental backing the rehearsal of a choreographed dance routine featuring Lionel Blair and four costumed dancing girls. As the Beatles cross the stage, John and George attempt a few dance steps, while Ringo gets behind his drum kit and plays along. As the tune comes to an end, John, poking fun at typical teen music exploitation movies, shouts: "Hey, kids, I got an idea. Why don't we do the show right here, yeah!" After Paul lets out a laugh, John counts-in the song, and the group performs the rocker with Harrison on lead vocal. At the end of the song, John says: "Very good that, George."

According to John, "I'm Happy Just To Dance With You" was "written *for* George to give him a piece of the action." In this case, a lead vocal in the film and on the album as Harrison had yet to come up with another song on his own after completing "Don't Bother Me" for the group's second album. Paul recalls the track being a "straight co-written song for George" that "pandered to the fans," adding: "It was a bit of a formula song. We knew that in E if you went to an A flat minor, you could always make a song with those chords; that change pretty much always excited you." Although based on simple ideas, Paul correctly summed it up: "The nice thing about it was to actually pull a song off on a slim little premise like that."

The song was recorded on Sunday, March 1, 1964, with George and John on electric guitar, Paul on bass and Ringo on drums. John plays a churning, slashing rhythm guitar part that is somewhere in between a Bo Diddley beat and John's earlier work on "All My Loving." George keeps his guitar simple so that he can concentrate on his singing. Paul provides some nice melodic bass lines to go along with John's rapid guitar patterns. The first three takes were recorded without vocals, with only the first two complete. George, backed by John and Paul, sang live for Take 4. John and Paul's backing vocals are treated with echo. George double-tracked his lead vocal and Ringo superimposed loose-skinned Arabian bongo drums onto Take 4. The latter gives the song a bit of a Latin-flavored mood. The song was mixed for mono on March 3 and for stereo on June 22.

Lyrically, the song's dance theme brings back memories of "I Saw Her Standing There." George sincerely sings the innocent lines "I don't want to kiss or hold your hand" and "I don't need to hug or hold you tight" that contradict the sensuality of earlier songs such as "I Want To Hold Your Hand," "Hold Me Tight" and "Please Please Me." The Beatles recorded "I'm Happy Just To Dance With You" for the BBC at the company's Paris Studios in London on July 17, 1964, for broadcast on the August 3 From Us To You.

And I Love Her

Recorded: February 25, 26 & 27, 1964
Mixed: March 3 and June 22 (mono); June 22 (stereo)

Producer: George Martin
Engineers: Norman Smith; Richard Langham

Paul: Lead vocals; bass guitar (Hofner)
John: Rhythm guitar (Jumbo)
George: Lead guitar (José Ramirez nylon-string classical)
Ringo: Bongos; claves (possibly George Harrison)

The sequence of the Beatles performing "And I Love Her" in *A Hard Day's Night* is one of the highlights of the film. The group is shown rehearsing the song from the perspective of the television control room. In addition to close-ups of band members, there are shots of the four television monitors in the booth and an effective pan shot through the front glass window. At the end of the song, the film's TV director, played by Victor Spinetti, comments from the booth, "Thank you, very nice." Very nice, indeed.

Paul was the primary composer of "And I Love Her," though John claims he helped with the song's middle eight. The song was inspired by Paul wanting to tell his then girlfriend Jane Asher that he loved her. In his 2021 book *The Lyrics,* Paul recalled: "I do think it's a nice melody. It starts with F-sharp minor, not with the root chord of E major, and you gradually work your way back. When I finished it, I felt, almost immediately, proud of it. I thought, 'This is a good 'un.'"

Because the song reached him, Paul thought it might reach other people as well, so he brought it to the recording session and played it for George Martin. According to Paul: "George Martin was inspired to add a chord modulation in the solo of the song, a key change that he knew would be musically very satisfying; we shifted the chord progression [at the beginning of the solo] to start with G minor instead of F-sharp minor–so, up a semitone. I think George Martin's classical training told him that that would be a really interesting change. And it was. And this sort of help is what started to make The Beatles' stuff better than that of other songwriters... And then of course, the song–which is now in F major, or arguably D minor–eventually finishes on that bright D major chord, a lovely, pleasing resolution. So, I was very proud of that."

The Beatles first attempt at "And I Love Her" was on February 25, 1964. The group recorded two takes, but only completed the second. For this early incarnation, Paul was on lead vocal and bass, John on Jumbo acoustic guitar, George on his 12-string Rickenbacker and Ringo on drums. Take 2 of this version, which was later released on *Anthology 1*, has a totally different feel than the finished master. Although some of the same elements are present, such as George picking the chord notes during the verses and the basic melody of his guitar solo, the song has no middle eight, which would soon be composed by John and Paul, most likely in the studio.

The group returned to the song the following evening. Paul recalls Martin saying, "I think it would be good with an introduction." McCartney continues: "And I swear, right there and then, George Harrison went, 'Well how about this?' and he played the opening riff, which is such a hook; the song is nothing without it. We were working very fast and spontaneously coming up with ideas."

For these takes, George abandoned his 12-string electric guitar for a José Ramirez nylon-string classical guitar. Midway through this session, Ringo switched from his drum kit to bongos. During Take 11, Paul flubbed the lyrics by singing; "And if you saw my love, I'd love her" before letting out a "ppffffff" sound. This blooper is part of a studio banter medley in the *Anthology* video. A few takes later, when Norman Smith called out "Take 14," Paul humorously responded: "Ha, Take 50!" Although the group recorded Takes 3 through 19, neither George Martin nor the Beatles were satisfied with any of these performances, so they called it a night.

The next morning everything came together for Take 20. The lineup for this remake of February 27 features Paul on his trusty Hofner bass, John on Gibson Jumbo acoustic guitar, George on the José Ramirez nylon-string classical acoustic guitar and Ringo on bongos. Paul then double-tracked his vocal and Ringo added claves onto Take 20 to form Take 21, which would serve as the master.

The song was mixed for mono on March 3 with Norman Smith and A.B. Lincoln assisting George Martin. Mono Remix 1 only has Paul's voice double-tracked for the bridge and title line. This mix was sent to United Artists for the film and is on the UA soundtrack LP.

On June 22, the song was remixed for mono (MR 2) and mixed for stereo (SR 1) for the British *A Hard Day's Night* LP with Norman Smith and Geoff Emerick serving as engineers. These mixes have Paul's vocal double-tracked throughout except for the first time he sings the lines "Bright are the stars that shine/Dark is the sky" in the third verse. This "unplugged" recording is one of Paul's best loved ballads. In *The Lyrics*, Paul looked back fondly: "It was very satisfying to make that record and to have written that song for Jane."

The Beatles BBC performance of the song broadcast on the July 16, 1964 Top Gear is on *On Air - Live At The BBC Volume 2*.

Property of United Artists Corp. Ltd. Leased for restricted use only. Must be returned to United Artists Corp. Ltd. and must not be sold, leased or given away by any other party.

Tell Me Why

Recorded: February 27, 1964
Mixed: March 3 (mono); June 22 (stereo)

Producer: George Martin
Engineers: Norman Smith; Richard Langham

John: Lead vocals; rhythm guitar (Gibson Jumbo)
Paul: Backing vocal; bass guitar (Hofner)
George: Backing vocal; rhythm guitar (12-string Rickenbacker)
Ringo: Drums (Ludwig kit)
George Martin: Piano (Steinway)

"Tell Me Why" appears once in the film during the Scala Theatre concert scene for which it was apparently written. According to John: "They needed another upbeat song and I just knocked it off. It was like a black-New-York-girl-group song." Although John was later dismissive of the track, back in 1964 he listed it as one of his favorites in the film: "There are four I really go for: 'Can't Buy Me Love,' 'If I Fell,' 'I Should Have Known Better'...and 'Tell Me Why,' a shuffle number that comes at the end of the film." The song's shuffle beat is reminiscent of that of "Chains" by the Cookies, a black New York girl group. (The Beatles recorded "Chains" for their first LP.) "Tell Me Why" may also have been influenced by the upbeat girl group classic "Heat Wave" by Martha & the Vandellas, but it is not known how familiar John was with the song. While "Heat Wave" (Gordy 7022) was a number four hit in the U.S., it failed to chart when issued in the U.K. on Stateside SS 228. "Tell Me Why" was most likely written in February 1964 during the Beatles first U.S. visit.

The song, recorded during the morning session on February 27, 1964, opens with Ringo's thundering drums, and then proceeds directly into the chorus with John on lead vocal backed by Paul and George. John plays George's Gibson Jumbo acoustic-electric guitar, while George strums his 12-string Rickenbacker and Paul plays his Hofner bass. John sings the first and third lines of each verse by himself and is joined in harmony by Paul and George on the second and fourth lines. During the four-line bridge, John sings solo on all but the third line, which he, Paul and George sing "Is there anything I can do?" in falsetto.

The group recorded seven takes of the song before they got it right. Take 4 quickly broke down, with Paul admonishing: "Yeah, you've done it again. You made a mistake, I know you did!" John (and possibly Paul and George) added double-tracked vocals, and George Martin added piano onto the open tracks on what was designated Take 8. The finished product is a high-energy rocker propelled by Ringo's explosive drums, churning rhythm guitars played by John and George, and Paul's walking bass lines.

The spirited instrumental backing overshadows the song's less-than-upbeat lyrics about a troubled relationship. In Barry Miles' *Many Years From Now*, Paul observed: "I think a lot of these songs like 'Tell Me Why' may have been based in real experiences or affairs John was having or arguments with Cynthia or whatever, but it never occurred to us until later to put that slant on it all."

The song was mixed for mono on March 3. George Martin had engineer Norman Smith fade out John's second vocal track on the lines he sings by himself during the verses. This has the effect of making those lines more personal. When the song was mixed for stereo on June 22, Martin and crew did not do this, so John's vocal is double-tracked for the entire song. Either they forgot what they did on the mono mix or, to save time, just didn't bother. Oddly, the shortened version of "Tell Me Why" used for the Scala Theatre sequence in the film appears to have a different John vocal.

Although the Beatles lip-synced "Tell Me Why" in front of hundreds of screaming fans for the film, the group never performed the song in concert. Nor did they record "Tell Me Why" for the BBC.

Can't Buy Me Love

Recorded: January 29, 1964 (Pathé Marconi Studios);
February 25, 1964 (EMI Studios)
Mixed: February 26 (mono); March 10 (stereo)

Producer: George Martin
Engineers: Norman Smith; Jacques Esmenjaud (January 29) & Richard Langham (February 25)

Paul: Lead vocals; bass guitar (Hofner)
John: Rhythm guitar (Jumbo)
George: Lead guitar (Gretsch & Rickenbacker 12-string)
Ringo: Drums (Ludwig kit)

Side One of the British album closes with the hit single "Can't Buy Me Love." Although the Beatles are not shown performing the song in the film, it is twice used as background music. The song is first heard during the scene where the boys break out of the Scala Theatre by heading down the fire escape onto an open field where they randomly run and jump. It is also used for the police chase sequence preceding the group's TV performance. The song's youthful exuberance and energy perfectly fit these zany, manic scenes.

THE
EATLES

"Can't Buy Me Love" was written by Paul during the second half of January 1964 while the Beatles were in Paris for a series of concert appearances at the Olympia Theatre. During their stay at the George V Hotel, the Beatles had a piano brought up to their suite to assist John and Paul in writing songs for the group's upcoming film. Paul composed the song on that piano.

In Miles' *Many Years From Now*, Paul said that "Can't Buy Me Love" was his "attempt to write a bluesy mode." Paul provided additional details in his 2021 book *The Lyrics*: "It's a twelve-bar blues, with a Beatles twist on the chorus, where we bring in a couple of minor chords. Usually, minor chords are used in the verse of a song, and major chords bring a lift and lighten the mood in the chorus. We did it the other way around here." As for its message: "The idea is that all these material possessions are well and good, but money can't buy you what you really need. The irony here is that just before Paris, we'd been in Florida where, if not love, money could certainly buy you a lot of what you wanted. But the premise stands, I think. Money can't buy you a happy family or friends you can trust."

Actually, the Beatles were not in Florida until *after* Paul wrote the song in Paris, but as the man said, "the premise stands." Paul told Miles it was a "very hooky song" and that he was honored when Ella Fitzgerald recorded the song shortly after its release by the Beatles.

During their stay in Paris, the Beatles, under the supervision of George Martin and engineer Norman Smith, reluctantly recorded German lyric versions of "I Want To Hold Your Hand" and "She Loves You" at EMI's Pathé Marconi Studios on January 29, 1964 (see pages 256-257.) After completing this task, the group took advantage of available studio time to record one of their recently written songs, introduced on the two-track tape by Smith as "Money Can't Buy Me Love."

At the suggestion of George Martin, the song was rearranged to begin with its chorus as an attention grabber. Martin explained: "I thought that we really needed a tag for the song's ending, and a tag for the beginning; a kind of intro. So I took the first two lines of the chorus and changed the ending, and said 'Let's just have these lines, and by altering the second phrase we can get back into the verse pretty quickly'. And they said, 'That's not a bad idea, we'll do it that way.'"

The Beatles recorded four takes in Paris before completing the song at EMI Studios in London on February 25, 1964, three days after the band's triumphant return from America. The early takes of the song were performed in the bluesy mode that Paul initially envisioned, with John on George's Gibson Jumbo acoustic-electric guitar, George on his Gretsch Country Gentleman, Paul on his Hofner bass and Ringo on his same Ludwig drum kit used for the band's Paris concert appearances. During the first two takes of these live-in-the-studio performances, Paul's lead vocal was augmented with John and George providing backing vocals on the chorus singing along with "love" and "no, no, no, no, no" and, starting with the second verse, singing responses to Paul's lead with lines such as "ooooh, love me too," "ooooh, give to you," "ooooh, just can't buy" and "ooooh, satisfied." While this approach was dropped after the first two takes, the Beatles would later use call-and-response vocals for the single "Help!" Initially, George played lead guitar lines under the vocals of the song's chorus. This was dropped after the third take.

The first two takes were complete. For Take 1, Paul sang "I'll buy you a diamond ring, my love" and "I'll get you anything, my love" in the first and third lines of the opening verse. Afterwards, Paul replaced "my love" with "my friend." On Take 2, Paul forgets the lyrics during the final verse and improvises a scat vocal that Louie Armstrong would have been proud of. George had trouble coming up with an effective solo. His first attempt opens with some stinging-sounding notes before George plays notes from the song's melody for the last two lines. His solo on the second take has more of a blues feel, but is a bit disorganized. *Anthology 1* contains Take 2 of the song with George's solo from Take 1.

Beginning with Take 3, Paul sings solo. This take breaks down shortly after Paul accidentally re-sings the second line of the first verse at the start of second verse. Take 4 was the best of the Paris session, though George still was having trouble with his solo. On all takes, Paul's vocal was treated with echo.

On February 25, Paul double-tracked his vocal and George superimposed a new guitar solo, though parts of his earlier solo can be heard. Harrison explained that "they'd tried to overdub it, but in those days they only had two tracks, so you can hear the version we put on in London, and in the background you can hear a quieter one [recorded in Paris]." British singer Helen Shapiro was at the session and recalls Ringo adding more cymbals.

Martin, assisted by Norman Smith and Richard Langham, mixed the song for mono on February 26. When the tape was spooled for the stereo mix on March 10, there was a noticeable ripple that caused an intermittent loss of treble on Ringo's hi-hat cymbal. Geoff Emerick took over as balance engineer while Smith headed down to the studio and overdubbed hi-hat to a few bars of the song.

The Beatles performed "Can't Buy Me Love" three times for BBC radio. The first performance was recorded at Piccadilly Theatre, London on February 28, 1964, for broadcast on From Us To You on March 30. This version is included on *Live At The BBC*.

BBC television also provided an opportunity for the band to promote their new record. On March 19, 1964, the group entered the BBC's Television Theatre in Shepherd's Bush, London, to lip-sync both sides of the single for broadcast on the March 25 Top Of The Pops. The group also recorded "Can't Buy Me Love" on April 19, 1964, at IBC Studios, for miming on the television special *Around The Beatles*. This performance appears on the video *Ready Steady Go! Special Edition/The Beatles Live*.

"Can't Buy Me Love" was quickly added to the Beatles live repertoire. The band played the song at the New Musical Express 1963-64 Annual Poll-Winners' All-Star Concert held at Empire Pool, Wembley, on April 26. The Beatles spirited performance was aired on British ABC Television on Big Beat '64 on May 10. A portion of this performance appears on Volume 3 of the *Anthology* video.

The song remained in the Beatles set list throughout 1964 and 1965. Thus, it was played at several famous concerts, including all their Hollywood Bowl appearances and the 1965 Shea Stadium concert. *The Beatles At The Hollywood Bowl* album contains the August 30, 1965 performance of the song. The Beatles are shown performing the song in *The Beatles At Shea Stadium*, which was filmed on August 15, 1965, and broadcast in England in black and white on March 1, 1966, and in the United States in color on ABC TV on January 10, 1967.

Although "Can't Buy Me Love" started out as a blues song with call and response vocals on its first two takes, it evolved into an exciting rocker dominated by Paul's powerful vocal, showing the band's ability to modify musical ideas in the studio.

Any Time At All

Recorded: June 2 & 3, 1964
Mixed: June 4 (mono); June 22 (stereo)

Producer: George Martin
Engineers: Norman Smith; Ken Scott

John: Lead vocals; acoustic guitar (Jumbo); piano (Steinway)
Paul: Backing vocals; bass guitar (Hofner)
George: Lead guitar (12-string Rickenbacker); guitar (Jumbo)
Ringo: Drums (Ludwig kit)

Side Two of the British *A Hard Day's Night* album contains songs that were not featured in the film. It opens with "Any Time At All," which was the first song attempted at the group's June 2, 1964 session. The song was most likely written by John in May when he, his wife Cynthia, George and George's new girlfriend Pattie Boyd were on vacation in Tahiti. In 1980, John described the song to David Sheff as "An effort at writing 'It Won't Be Long' – same ilk: C to A minor, C to A minor – with me shouting." Although both songs open by repeating the song's title three times and have the same major to minor chord progression, neither is in the key of C. "It Won't Be Long" goes from E to C# minor, while "Any Time At All" is D to B minor. John's recollection about shouting the song is indeed correct.

At the time John presented the song to the other members of the band and George Martin in the studio, it did not have a bridge. The group recorded seven takes of the song while trying to come up with a suitable middle eight. By the seventh and best take, the group had an instrumental bridge in place, but the song still felt incomplete. These takes featured John on lead vocal and George's Gibson Jumbo acoustic-electric guitar, George on his Rickenbacker electric 12-string, Paul on backing vocal and his Hofner bass and Ringo on drums.

The tight spacing of words between the third and fourth line of each verse caused problems for John to sing. This was solved by having John skip the first few words of the fourth line knowing he would add them when overdubbing the vocals. For example, in the first verse, John sang "I'll be there to make you feel right," passed over "If your feeling" (saving it for the overdubs) and sang "sorry and sad."

Due to uncertainty over the bridge (perhaps hoping to give it lyrics), the group took a break from the song after Take 7 and moved on to a pair of other new songs, "Things We Said Today" and "When I Get Home." Towards the end of the evening session, they returned to "Any Time At All," recording three takes of superimpositions onto Take 7, with Take 10 being the best. These featured Ringo adding accent snare drum hits at the end of each verse and George contributing additional acoustic guitar on the Jumbo.

The song was completed with final overdubs, which may have been recorded on June 3. Take 11 added more vocals from John and Paul, as well as piano from John on the middle eight. It is not known if John and Paul ever intended to add lyrics to the bridge. The song was mixed for mono on June 4 and stereo on June 22. The tape operators were Richard Langham (June 4) and Geoff Emerick (June 22).

I'll Cry Instead

Recorded: June 1, 1964
Mixed and edited: June 4 (mono); June 22 (stereo)

Producer: George Martin
Engineers: Norman Smith; Ken Scott

John: Lead vocals; rhythm guitar (Gibson Jumbo)
George: Lead guitar (Gretsch Country Gentleman)
Paul: Bass guitar (Hofner)
Ringo: Drums; tambourine

John's "I'll Cry Instead" is a country-influenced rocker that George Martin had the group record specifically for the film. In the June 13, 1964 Disc, Martin said: "Originally 'Can't Buy Me Love' was going to be featured twice during the film, but I thought a new song would be better for the second spot [involving the Beatles being chased by the police], and the boys came up with ['I'll Cry Instead']. It's another good up-tempo number and features George on twelve string guitar." While George Harrison used his 12-string Rickenbacker electric guitar on several of the songs recorded during the sessions for *A Hard Day's Night*, Martin's recollection is incorrect. For this country-flavored tune Harrison played his Gretsch Country Gentleman six-string electric guitar. Others have said that "I'll Cry Instead" was intended for the running and jumping scene following the boys escape from the Scala Theatre, which marks the first soundtrack appearance of "Can't Buy Me Love."

Although Martin was the film's musical director, he was overruled by director Richard Lester, who thought that "I'll Cry Instead" was relatively weak. In addition, the song's lyrical content belied the exuberant nature of the film. This led Lester to wisely stay with his plan to have the upbeat "Can't Buy Me Love" appear twice.

In his 1980 interview with David Sheff appearing in *All We Are Saying*, John commented: "I wrote that ["I'll Cry Instead"] for *A Hard Day's Night*, but Dick Lester didn't even want it. He resurrected 'Can't Buy Me Love' for that sequence instead. I like the middle eight to that song, though – that's about all I can say about it."

Although John had little to say about the song, others have commented on how the lyrics express a range of personal emotions, including sadness, embarrassment, shyness and revenge. McCartney thought the song reflected John's difficulties with his relationship with his first wife, while Cynthia herself thought it was a cry for help: "It reflects the frustration he felt at that time. He was the idol of millions, but the freedom and fun of the early days had gone."

"I'll Cry Instead" was recorded on June 1, 1964, more than three months after the initial recording sessions for the film. The initial recording of the song features John's lead vocal on Track 3, John on George's Gibson Jumbo acoustic-electric guitar on Track 2, and George on his Gretsch Country Gentleman, Paul on bass and Ringo on drums on Track 1.

The song was taped in two sections, most likely to facilitate an edit lengthening the song for the film soundtrack. The Beatles recorded five takes of Section A, consisting of the introduction, first and second verses, bridge and third verse. Take 5 of Section A was edited to form Take 6. The group then recorded a single take of Section B, designated Take 7, which may have been comprised of the first verse, bridge, third verse and the song's ending. This performance was edited to form Take 8. John then double-tracked his vocal onto Track 4 on Sections A and B. At the same time, a tambourine part was added, most likely by Ringo (although some sources attribute the instrument to John).

On June 4, George Martin, assisted by Norman Smith and Richard Langham, mixed both sections of the song for mono. They then made two edits of the song from Sections A and B. The first edit, with a running time of 2:04, utilizes all of both sections. The edited song's structure is verse one/verse two/bridge/verse three (from Section A) followed by verse one/bridge/verse three (from Section B). A second edit, with a running time of 1:43, dropped the repeat of the first verse at the start of Section B.

When tapes of the best mono mixes of the eight songs then slated for the film were made for United Artists and Capitol on June 9, the longer 2:04 edit of "I'll Cry Instead" was included. Thus, the long version of "I'll Cry Instead" appears on the mono United Artists soundtrack album, the stereo UA album which has fake stereo mixes of the Beatles songs created from the mono mixes, the mono version of Capitol's *Something New* LP and the Capitol single of the song.

By the time the stereo version of "I'll Cry Instead" was mixed and edited on June 22, Martin was almost certainly aware that the song would not be included in the film. Thus, the stereo edit made at that time excluded the repeat of the first verse, leading to a running time of 1:44. This edit, made with the assistance of Norman Smith and Geoff Emerick, was used for the stereo version of the Parlophone LP. Capitol also used this mix for its stereo version of *Something New*. The mono version of the British album, which was compiled after the song was dropped from the film, has the shorter edit missing the repeat of the first verse made on June 4.

Things We Said Today

Recorded: June 2 & 3, 1964
Mixed: June 9 (mono); June 22 (stereo)

Producer: George Martin
Engineers: Norman Smith; Ken Scott

Paul: Lead vocals; bass guitar (Hofner); tambourine
John: Backing vocals; rhythm guitar (Gibson Jumbo); piano
George: Lead guitar (Gretsch Country Gentleman); tambourine
Ringo: Drums (Ludwig kit)

"Things We Said Today" was written by Paul while he, then girlfriend Jane Asher, Ringo and Ringo's future wife Maureen were on holiday in the Virgin Islands in May 1964. (Paul mistakenly placed this vacation in the Bahamas in Miles' *Many Years From Now*, but corrects this in his book *The Lyrics*.) It was a well-earned vacation as the group had just finished filming *A Hard Day's Night*, taping the television special *Around The Beatles* and recording eight songs for an installment of their From Us To You BBC radio show.

Paul wrote the song on the yacht Happy Days out of St. Thomas, U.S. Virgin Islands. In *The Lyrics*, Paul talks of how he enjoyed going to his cabin where he "could lock the world out" and "strum away [on his Epiphone Texan acoustic guitar] for a little while and see if anything came." As for "Things We Said Today," he recalled: "That particular day on the boat, I started with an A minor chord. A minor to E minor to A minor, which gave me a sort of folksy, whimsical world. And then in the middle, on 'Me, I'm just the lucky kind,' it goes to the major and gets hopeful. The thing I always loved and still love about writing a song is that, at the end of two or three hours, I have a newborn baby to show everyone. I want to show it to the world, and the world at that moment was the people on the boat."

In *Many Years From Now,* Paul described the song: "It was a slightly nostalgic thing already, a future nostalgia; we'll remember the things we said today, some time in the future, so the song projects itself into the future and then is nostalgic about the moment we're living now, which is quite a good trick. It has interesting chords....It was a sophisticated little tune."

The group started work on Paul's "sophisticated little tune" on June 2. After a false start on Take 1, the Beatles nailed down the basic track on their second try. The up-tempo ballad features Paul on lead vocal and bass, John on George's Jumbo acoustic-electric guitar, George on his Gretsch Country Gentleman electric guitar and Ringo on drums.

The following day, the group, minus Ringo, added overdubs onto Take 2 in what was designated Take 3. Paul double-tracked his vocal and added tambourine, while George played an additional tambourine and John added the quickly strummed acoustic guitar flourishes heard at the start of the song, between the first and second verses, and during the song's fade-out ending. John also superimposed a bit of piano on the Steinway Music Room Model B Grand. His piano is heard only on the twice-played bridge of the song. The tambourines are heard only on the bridge and fade. The song was mixed for mono on June 9 with Smith and Ken Scott as engineers and for stereo on June 22 with Smith and Geoff Emerick.

Paul's vocal effectively varies throughout the track. In the first verse, the first lines are sung solo. Paul then adds a harmony part over "Someday, when I'm lonely/Wishing you weren't so far away" before singing "Then I will remember" solo and double-tracking the line "Things we said today." For the remaining verses, Paul's voice is doubled throughout. On the second verse, he sings harmony on the lines "Someday, when we're dreaming/Deep in love, not a lot to say" and on "Things we said today." Paul's voice is double-tracked for the bridge, but not in harmony. For the third verse, Paul once again sings harmony on the lines "Someday, when we're dreaming/ Deep in love, not a lot to say," but not on "Things we said today." After a repeat of the bridge, Paul sings the third verse again, but breaks his pattern, with the lines "Be the only one" and "We'll go on and on" in harmony. This is especially effective for the latter line.

Because "Things We Said Today" was the B-side to "A Hard Day's Night" in Great Britain, the group promoted the song on TV and radio. On July 7, the Beatles taped a mimed performance of the song for broadcast on July 29 on BBC-1's Top Of The Pops. The group also mimed the song on a Saturday night live broadcast on the July 11 Lucky Stars (Summer Spin), the summer version of ABC Television's Thank Your Lucky Stars, and on the July 19 ABC show Blackpool Night Out. The Beatles recorded the song twice for the BBC. Their July 14 performance aired on the premiere of the show Top Gear, while their July 17 recording was broadcast on the August 3 From Us To You. The former version is on *Live At The BBC*.

The Beatles added "Things We Said Today" to their set list for the 1964 North American tour. For these live performances, the group kicks it up a notch for the bridge. George sings along with Paul during some parts of the song. The band's August 23 performance on the song is on the 1977 album *The Beatles At The Hollywood Bowl* and the 2016 remixed *Live At The Hollywood Bowl* LP.

When I Get Home

Recorded: June 2, 1964
Mixed: June 22 (mono & stereo)

Producer: George Martin
Engineers: Norman Smith; Ken Scott

John: Lead vocals; rhythm guitar (Rickenbacker 325 Capri)
Paul: Backing vocal; bass guitar (Hofner); piano
George: Backing vocal; rhythm guitar (Gretsch Country Gentleman)
Ringo: Drums (Ludwig kit)

"When I Get Home" was written by John, who described the track as "a song with chords all over the place" and "another Wilson Pickett, Motown sound, a four-in-the-bar cowbell song." The recording's rhythm is reminiscent of Motown artist Marvin Gaye's "Hitch Hike," but doesn't have cowbell. John apparently was thinking of the cowbell in other songs recorded during the sessions such as "You Can't Do That," "I Call Your Name" and the title track. Rather than Pickett, John's vocal was influenced by Arthur Alexander. His pronunciation of the word "more" on the line "I'll love her moe" copies the American R&B/soul singer's "But if he loves you moe" in "Anna." The song's catchy "whoah-ho-ho-I, whoah-ho-ho-I" intro to the refrain is an expanded variation of the "Oh, oh, oh, oh, oh, oh" that ends the bridge in "Anna." The lyrics are about John wanting to get back home to his love. Only John could write "no time for trivialities" and "till the cows come home" in a single song and make it work.

The Beatles recorded the energetic bluesy rocker as the last song for the album on June 2. The basic track, completed in ten takes with the last one deemed the best, consists of John on lead vocal backed by his Rickenbacker 325 Capri, Paul on his Hofner bass guitar, George on his Gretsch Country Gentleman and Ringo on drums. For Take 11 (superimposition onto Take 10), John double-tracked his vocal for the refrain, with Paul and George joining him with harmony vocals. The title phrase "when I get home" is sung solo by John and is only doubled during the final refrain and the ending, where Paul and George join in. Paul also overdubs some basic piano.

The song was initially mixed for mono on June 4; however, improved mixes were made on June 22, with Remix Mono 2 (RM2) used on U.K. pressings and RM3 sent to Capitol for its *Something New* LP. The song was also mixed for stereo on June 22. Norman Smith and Geoff Emerick served as engineers with George Martin for the June 22 mixes. Paul's piano is buried in the mixes, although it can be heard on RM3, particularly during the bridge and later verses.

You Can't Do That

Recorded: February 25, 1964
Mixed: February 26 (mono); March 10 (stereo)

Producer: George Martin
Engineers: Norman Smith; Richard Langham

John: Lead vocals; rhythm guitar and solo (Rickenbacker Capri)
Paul: Backing vocals; bass guitar (Hofner); cowbell (Ludwig)
George: Lead guitar (Rickenbacker 12-string)
Ringo: Drums (Ludwig kit); bongos (Premier)

"You Can't Do That" was written by John in mid-February 1964, while the Beatles were in Miami Beach during their first U.S. visit. Lyrically, John shows emotions of jealousy and insecurity, as well as admitting he can't help his feelings and goes out of his mind. He issues a stern warning: If he catches her "talking to that boy again" he will let her down and leave her flat. As was the case with the later-recorded "When I Get Home," John credits Wilson Pickett as an influence: "That's me doing Wilson Pickett. You know, a cowbell going four-in-the-bar, and the chord going chatoong!" While "You Can't Do That" is a blues four-in-the-bar song with cowbell, Pickett was most likely not an influence as the American R&B/soul singer's career did not really take off until 1965 with his hit single "In The Midnight Hour." A more likely influence is Barrett Strong's "Money (That's What I Want)," which was recorded by the Beatles with John on lead vocal for the group's second album, *With The Beatles*. Both songs have a dominant two-measure riff, call-and-response backing vocals and, in the case of the Beatles arrangement, slashing guitars.

"You Can't Do That" was recorded at the same February 25 session during which overdubs were added to "Can't Buy Me Love" (pictures from the session are shown on pages 7 and 9). Prior to the recording of the song, George came up with a catchy two-measure riff that he would play through most of the song. As for where the riff came from, George later told Tom Petty: "I was just standing there (in the studio) and thought, 'I've got to do something.'" George's ability to create an effective riff significantly enhanced the song and would also come in handy for "And I Love Her," where he did the same.

The Beatles ran through eight takes of the song, with only four being complete. These performances feature John's soulful lead vocal. For at least the first six takes, he sings solo as evidenced by Take 6, which is on *Anthology 1*. By Take 8, Paul and George joined him with their backing vocals, although some sources have their backing vocals added as superimpositions onto Take 8.

John plays his newly acquired Rickenbacker 325 Capri that was sent to him at the Deauville Hotel in Miami Beach as a gift from the Rickenbacker company. George is on his Rickenbacker 12-string electric guitar that he received courtesy of Rickenbacker the evening before the group's first appearance on The Ed Sullivan Show. Harrison used this guitar on several of the songs recorded during the sessions. Paul is on his Hofner bass and Ringo plays his new 1964 Ludwig Oyster Black Pearl Downbeat drum set.

The song opens with George's two-measure guitar riff, joined by John. For the repeat of the riff, John switches to strumming chords while Paul and Ringo join in. George continues playing the riff as John sings the first two lines of the verse. Starting with the second verse, Paul and George sing response backing vocals on the verses and together with John on the bridge. John's exciting guitar solo is preceded by a Lennon howl. His solo is a mixture of aggressively played chords, bending strings and riffs reminiscent of Chuck Berry. The song ends with George's guitar riff accompanied by Paul's bass. For the Take 9 superimpositions, Paul added cowbell, Ringo played bongo drums and John double-tracked his vocal on the bridge.

The song was mixed for mono on February 26, with Norman Smith and Richard Langham assisting George Martin as engineers. This mix was used for the B-side of the "Can't Buy Me Love" single, Capitol's *The Beatles' Second Album* and the Parlophone *A Hard Day's Night* LP. The song was first mixed for stereo on March 10, but this mix was not used. On May 22, while the Beatles were enjoying a well-deserved vacation, George Martin superimposed his piano onto the song as Take 10. This version of the song has yet to be released. The stereo mix on the Parlophone LP was made on June 22, with Norman Smith and Geoff Emerick as engineers.

The group recorded "You Can't Do That" four times for BBC radio. The Beatles July 14, 1964 performance (broadcast July 16 on Top Gear) is on *On Air - Live At The BBC Volume 2*.

"You Can't Do That" was added to the group's set list in April 1964 and performed at the New Musical Express Poll-Winners' Concert on April 26. During the 1964 North American tour, the song immediately followed "Twist And Shout" at the start of the set. Although the song was recorded by Capitol at the August 23, 1964 Hollywood Bowl concert, it was not included on Capitol's 1977 album *The Beatles At The Hollywood Bowl*. It is, however, a bonus track on the 2016 remixed and expanded edition of the album titled *The Beatles Live At The Hollywood Bowl*. The song was dropped from the group's set list after the 1964 North American tour.

Early press releases regarding the movie *A Hard Day's Night* announced that "You Can't Do That" would be included in the film. Although the Beatles lip-synced the song before 350 screaming fans at the Scala Theatre in London on March 31, 1964, during the filming of the television performance sequence at the end of the movie, the song did not make the final cut. Prior to that decision being made, the Scala performance was broadcast on The Ed Sullivan Show on May 24, 1964. It is featured in the 1994 video *The Making Of A Hard Day's Night*, which is hosted by Phil Collins, who, at age 13, was one of the lucky fans participating in the mayhem. On June 17, 1964, the band's concert at the Festival Hall in Melbourne was taped for Australian broadcast on a July 1st TV special titled *The Beatles Sing For Shell*. The group's performance of "You Can't Do That" from the show is included in Volume 3 of the *Anthology* video.

I'll Be Back

Recorded: June 1, 1964
Mixed: June 10 (mono); June 22 (stereo)

Producer: George Martin
Engineers: Norman Smith; Ken Scott

John: Lead vocals; rhythm guitar (Gibson Jumbo)
Paul: Backing vocals; bass guitar (Hofner)
George: Lead guitar (José Ramirez classical nylon-string)
Ringo: Drums (Ludwig kit)

The album's closing selection, "I'll Be Back," is a beautiful acoustic ballad. John remembered the song being entirely his, while Paul considered it "co-written but it was largely John's idea." Paul explained to Miles: "When we knew we were writing for something like an album he would write a few in his spare moments, like this batch here. He'd bring them in, we'd check 'em. I'd write a couple and we'd throw 'em at each other, and then there would be a couple that were more co-written. But you just had a certain amount of time. You knew when the recording date was and so a week or two before then we'd get into it." In this case, John would have found some spare time during his May 1964 vacation in Tahiti to write this and other songs for the album's final sessions.

Lyrically, the song is quite different from the bravado of "I'll Cry Instead" (where, in an act of revenge, he's gonna break the hearts of girls all round the world) and the stern warning of "You Can't Do That." Here, John shows vulnerability, confessing that if she breaks his heart he'll go, but he'll be back again.

As for the music, John called it a "variation of the chords in a Del Shannon song ["Runaway"]," which topped the American and British charts in 1961. The structure of "I'll Be Back" is a bit unconventional. It has two two-line verses leading into the first bridge followed by two more two-line verses before a second different bridge. The song then repeats the third and forth verses and the first bridge, but with different lyrics, before returning to the first verse and a fade-out ending. The verses are six measures long, while the first bridge has six and a half measures and the second bridge has nine and a half. There is no chorus or instrumental solo.

The Beatles recorded "I'll Be Back" during the evening session held on June 1, 1964. It was first attempted as a waltz in 6/8 time with John on his Rickenbacker 325 Capri, George on his Rickenbacker 12-string, Paul on his Hofner bass and Ringo on drums. John and Paul sang the verses in harmony, while John soloed on the bridges except for the ending "oh, oh, oh, oh/oh, oh, oh, oh" where Paul joined in. As John did not feel comfortable singing the song in a waltz tempo, it was most likely someone else's idea that the song be performed that way. This was probably George Martin's idea, although it could have been suggested by Paul. *Anthology 1* contains Take 2 of the song, which breaks down during the second bridge with John struggling through his vocal, confessing it's "too hard to sing."

Prior to Take 3, it is decided that the song should be played in 4/4 time. When John presumably discusses the difficulty duetting on the part at the end of the bridge where he "starts going 'oh, oh' about eight times," Paul says "I just won't sing that bit." Take 3 is complete, with John and George remaining on their electric guitars. At this stage, John does not repeat the first verse after singing the first bridge for a second time. Instead, the song ends with him repeating the "oh, oh, oh, oh/oh, oh, oh, oh"s during the fade.

As the Beatles continued working on the song, other changes were made. The band opted for a gentler sound, with the guitarists abandoning their electric instruments. John switches to George's acoustic-electric Jumbo, while George changes to his José Ramirez nylon-string classical acoustic guitar. Harrison also comes up with the simple but effective riff heard at the beginning and other places in the song. By Take 9, the instrumental backing is fixed.

Take 12 quickly came to halt, with John announcing: "Paul forgot to sing." As engineer Norman Smith calls out "Thirteen" from the control room, John starts to mention something George didn't do, and Paul apologizes: "God I'm so sorry...I just wasn't doin' it and I thought it must be alright." Take 14 is also a false start.

It all comes together for Take 16, which is then augmented by Paul singing a high harmony part over his and John's vocals on the verses, and George adding depth with additional nylon-string guitar.

Although a mono mix was made on June 10, it was not used. On June 22, George Martin, assisted by Norman Smith and Geoff Emerick, created mono RM2 for the U.K. and RM3 for the U.S., and stereo mix RS1.

The finished master blends three acoustic guitars and a three-part harmony. Ending the record with the fade of the song's gentle acoustic guitars was a drastic departure from the frenzied rockers that closed the group's first two albums. Oddly, Capitol chose not to include the song on its semi-soundtrack album *Something New*. "I'll Be Back" was not issued in America until mid-December 1964 when it appeared on *Beatles '65*.

Banding and Mastering–Parlophone LP

EMI initially planned on issuing an LP that featured the eight songs recorded for the movie along with soundtrack music. The May 9, 1964 Record Mirror reported that the new Beatles LP would have six Beatles songs, with the rest of the record filled with incidental music from the film and informal conversation between the group and their producer, George Martin. There was also a rumor that the album would be a mixture of film songs and humorous dialog from the movie. Another idea was an LP containing the six Beatles songs making their debut in the film plus the five former hits featured in the movie: "I Wanna Be Your Man," "Don't Bother Me," "All My Loving," "Can't Buy Me Love" and "She Loves You."

All of the above ideas were scrapped, with EMI determining that the best approach was to release an album containing the songs appearing in the film on Side One with a batch of freshly recorded Beatles songs on Side Two. John and Paul were up to the task, with the group recording five original compositions on June 1 and 2, 1964, before heading off on their world tour. The released album contains seven film songs on the first side backed by six other Beatles songs on the non-film side. All of the tracks were written by John and Paul, making the *A Hard Day's Night* LP the only Beatles album consisting exclusively of Lennon-McCartney compositions. The only previously released songs on the album were "Can't Buy Me Love" and "You Can't Do That." Two other songs, "A Hard Day's Night" and "Things We Said Today," were issued on a single at the same time the LP appeared in stores.

While the Beatles first two Parlophone albums each had 14 tracks, *A Hard Day's Night* only had 13 songs. In all likelihood, George Martin planned on recording an additional track for the album, but fate intervened.

The June 3, 1964 Session

June 3 was scheduled to be the last day of recording for the new album; however, plans for the afternoon and evening sessions had to be revised when Ringo took ill during the morning's photo shoot and was rushed to the hospital. When it was learned that he had severe tonsillitis and would remain hospitalized for a week or more, Brian Epstein and George Martin quickly lined up Jimmy Nichol to serve as replacement drummer for at least the first segment of the group's upcoming world tour, set to start the following evening in Copenhagen, Denmark. The planned afternoon recording session was canceled and replaced with a 3:00 to 4:00 PM rehearsal of six songs at EMI Studios with Jimmy Nicol and the remaining Beatles.

John, Paul and George returned to the studio for a 5:30 PM session. The trio recorded a demo of an original Harrison song, "You Know What To Do." After a 30-second run through of Cilla Black's current number one hit "You're My World," John and Paul recorded a single take of a new Lennon song, "No Reply." John sang lead and played guitar, while Paul provided backing vocal and bass. They were accompanied by a drummer whose identity remains unknown. This recording, which was later issued on *Anthology 1*, has John and Paul laughing along with their vocal gaffes. The song was later recorded for *Beatles For Sale*. At the end of the session, the group added overdubs to "Any Time At All" and "Things We Said Today."

Had Ringo not become ill, the group could have properly recorded either of these new originals. Although Paul had written "One And One Is Two" in Paris, the song was not up to the group's standards. A demo of the song with Paul's solo vocal backed by piano and acoustic guitar was recorded for music publisher Dick James, most likely in Paris. The tune was offered to Billy J. Kramer, who declined, and recorded but not released by the Fourmost with Paul on bass. The song was issued as a single on Philips BF 1335 by the Strangers with Mike Shannon on May 8, 1964. It did not chart.

You Know What To Do

Recorded: June 3, 1964
Mixed: For *Anthology 1* in 1995

Producer: George Martin
Engineers: Norman Smith; Ken Scott

George: Lead vocal; rhythm guitar (Jumbo)
Paul: Bass guitar (Hofner)
John: Tambourine

After having "Don't Bother Me" on *With The Beatles*, George took another stab at composing. The June 1964 edition of The Beatles Book reported that a new George song would probably be on the album but not in the film (see page 26). For this demo recording, George sang lead backed by his Gibson Jumbo acoustic-electric guitar, Paul on bass and John on tambourine. Although "You Know What To Do" is a charming little tune, George Martin, John and Paul were not impressed. The Beatles never returned to the song, leaving Harrison with no composition on *A Hard Day's Night* or *Beatles For Sale*. The song was issued on *Anthology 1* in 1995.

The Long Tall Sally EP

Although *Long Tall Sally* was the fifth Beatles extended-play disc, it was their first EP to feature recordings not previously issued in the U.K. (see pages 18-20). The songs on Side 1, "Long Tall Sally" and "I Call Your Name," had been previously issued in America on Capitol's *The Beatles' Second Album*, released on April 10, 1964. The songs on Side 2, "Slow Down" and "Matchbox," were recorded specifically for the EP. With the Beatles policy of placing only original compositions on their singles, and the decision having been made that their third album would not have any cover versions, the EP was the perfect format for the British release of "Long Tall Sally."

Long Tall Sally

Recorded: March 1, 1964
Mixed: March 10 (mono & stereo U.S.); June 4 (mono U.K.)

Producer: George Martin
Engineers: Norman Smith; Richard Langham

Paul: Lead vocal; bass guitar (Hofner)
John: Rhythm guitar (Rickenbacker 325 Capri)
George: Lead guitar (Gretsch Country Gentleman)
Ringo: Drums (Ludwig kit)
George Martin: Piano (Steinway Music Room Model B Grand)

The EP gets off to a rousing start with a high-energy cover of "Long Tall Sally," which was originally recorded by American singer/pianist Little Richard. The song, written by Enotris Johnson, Robert "Bumps" Blackwell and Little Richard, was recorded on February 7, 1956, at J&M Recording Studios in New Orleans. When issued on Specialty 572 on March 12, 1956, "Long Tall Sally" became Little Richard's biggest hit and a million seller in the U.S. The song spent 16 weeks on the Billboard Rhythm & Blues Records charts, including eight weeks at number one on the separate Best Sellers, Juke Box and Jockey charts. The rocker remained in the Billboard Hot 100 for 19 weeks, peaking at number six, and was charted at number seven by Cash Box. The single was released in the U.K. on London 45-HL-O 8366. It charted for 16 weeks, peaking at number three.

The Beatles recorded "Long Tall Sally" in one incredible take on March 1, 1964. Paul gives one of his greatest vocal performances in front of a flawless instrumental backing of Paul on bass, John on his Rickenbacker Capri, George on his Gretsch Country Gentleman, Ringo on drums and George Martin on piano. Highlights include George's guitar riffs and solo, Martin's rollicking piano and Ringo's pounding drums, particularly at the end of the song. There was no need for additional takes on this instant rock 'n' roll classic.

Martin and Norman Smith created mono and stereo mixes of the song for Capitol Records on March 10. The pair, assisted by Richard Langham, remixed the song for the mono EP on June 4.

"Long Tall Sally" had long been a part of the Beatles stage show through much of their performing career. The earliest known Beatles recording of the song is on *Live At The Star Club,* which was recorded during the 1962 Christmas season. Prior to their EMI session, the group performed the song four times for the BBC. The July 16, 1963 recording of the song at BBC Paris Theatre in London aired on the August 13 Pop Goes The Beatles and is on *Live At The BBC*.

The Beatles performed the song before an excited audience for the Swedish television program Drop In on October 30, 1963. This performance was broadcast in Sweden on November 3 and is on Volume 2 of the *Anthology* video.

Even though the Beatles had yet to record "Long Tall Sally" for EMI at the time of their first U.S. visit, the group closed their all-important first American concert on February 11, 1964, with the rocker. The wildly enthusiastic response of the audience at the Washington Coliseum hearing the Beatles version of the song for the first time may have contributed to the group recording "Long Tall Sally" at EMI Studios shortly after their return from America.

On April 19, the Beatles recorded the song at IBC Studios in London as part of their performance for the Jack Good—produced television special *Around The Beatles*. Nine days later the group was filmed miming the song to the pre-recorded IBC tape before a live audience. The program was broadcast in the U.K. on May 6. The back cover liner notes to the *Long Tall Sally* EP describe the group's performance of the song as "the hit of the show."

During 1964, "Long Tall Sally" was often used as the closing number for the group's concerts. The band's August 23, 1964 performance of the song closes out *The Beatles At The Hollywood Bowl* LP. The song remained the concert finale until the group's 1965 North American tour, when it was replaced by the Little Richard-influenced "I'm Down." The Beatles went back to "Long Tall Sally" as the closing number for their 1966 North American tour. Thus, "Long Tall Sally" was the last song the Beatles performed at their last regularly scheduled concert, held at San Francisco's Candlestick Park on August 29, 1966. Unfortunately, the cassette tape used by Tony Barrow to record the show ran out prior to the end of the song.

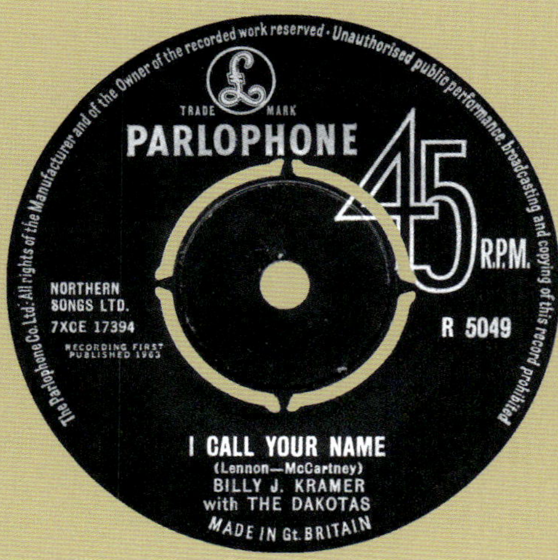

I Call Your Name

Recorded: March 1, 1964
Mixed: March 3 (mono U.S.) & 10 (stereo U.S.); June 4 (mono U.K.)

Producer: George Martin
Engineers: Norman Smith; Richard Langham

John: Lead vocals; rhythm guitar (Rickenbacker 325 Capri)
George: Lead guitar (Rickenbacker 12-string)
Paul: Bass guitar (Hofner)
Ringo: Drums (Ludwig kit); cowbell (Ludwig Clear Tone)

According to John, "I Call Your Name" was one of his first attempts at a song. Paul recalls working on the song with John at John's Aunt Mimi's house on Menlove Avenue, Liverpool. "I Call Your Name" was first recorded by Billy J. Kramer with the Dakotas on June 27, 1963, at EMI Studios. It was issued as the flip side to another Lennon-McCartney tune, the chart-topping "Bad To Me."

The Beatles recorded "I Call Your Name" on March 1, 1964. Its arrangement is similar to that of the Kramer single, but has a different rhythm for the solo section. The recording features John on lead vocals and his Rickenbacker Capri, George on his Rickenbacker 12-string, Paul on his Hofner bass and Ringo on drums. The song's straight-forward beat is replaced by a ska rhythm behind George's guitar solo. The Beatles needed seven takes to complete the song. John then double-tracked his vocal while Ringo added steady four-on-the-bar cowbell onto Take 7. Because George's solo was better on Take 5, the finished master edits the solo section from Take 5 into Take 7. Thus, there is no cowbell during the solo. Details regarding the song's various mixes are in the section for *The Beatles' Second Album* on page 259. The mono mix for the EP was made on June 4.

Slow Down

Recorded: June 1 & 4, 1964
Mixed: June 4, 1964 (mono); June 22, 1964 (stereo)

Producer: George Martin
Engineers: Norman Smith; Ken Scott

John: Lead vocals; rhythm guitar (Rickenbacker 325 Capri)
Paul: Bass guitar (Hofner)
George: Lead guitar (Gretsch Country Gentlemen)
Ringo: Drums (Ludwig kit)
George Martin: Piano (Steinway Music Room Model B Grand)

"Slow Down" was written and recorded by singer/pianist Larry Williams, who was born in New Orleans. It was released in the U.S. on Specialty 626 in spring 1958, and on London 45-HL-U 8604 in the U.K. Although "Slow Down" did not chart, its flip side, "Dizzy Miss Lizzy," reached number 69 on the Billboard Hot 100. Both sides of this single, along with another Larry Williams' song, "Bad Boy," were recorded by the Beatles. John had been singing lead on the Larry Williams songs in the Beatles stage show for years. The group's first recording of "Slow Down" was for the BBC on July 16, 1963. It aired on Pop Goes The Beatles on August 20 and is on *Live At The BBC*.

"Slow Down" was recorded at EMI Studios on June 1, 1964. The group took three takes with John on his Rickenbacker Capri, George on his Gretsch Country Gentleman, Paul on his Hofner bass and Ringo on drums to get an acceptable backing track. Three overdub takes added lead guitar and a wonderfully raunchy double-tracked John Lennon vocal. On June 4, George Martin superimposed piano onto Take 6 and produced mono and stereo mixes of the song. Norman Smith and Richard Langham served as engineers.

Matchbox

Recorded: June 1, 1964
Mixed: June 4, 1964 (mono); June 22, 1964 (stereo)

Producer: George Martin
Engineers: Norman Smith; Ken Scott

Ringo: Lead vocals; Drums (Ludwig kit)
John: Rhythm guitar (Rickenbacker 325 Capri)
Paul: Bass guitar (Hofner)
George: Lead guitar (Gretsch Country Gentleman)
George Martin: Piano (Steinway Music Room Model B Grand)

"Matchbox" is a traditional blues song which was recorded as "Match Box Blues" by blues singers Blind Lemon Jefferson in 1927 and Leadbelly in 1934, and country artist the Shelton Brothers in 1949. Carl Perkins, at the suggestion of his father, recorded the song on December 4, 1956. As his father could only remember some of the words, Perkins had to improvise his singing with typical blues lines. Perkins' rocking guitar and Jerry Lee Lewis' boogie-woogie piano turned the song into a rockabilly classic. Perkins' "Matchbox" was released on Sun 261 in the U.S. and on London 45-HL.S 8408 in the U.K. in 1957. John, who had purchased the singer's "Blue Suede Shoes" the year before, bought a copy of the London single. Although the song did not chart, its flip side, "Your True Love," was a number 13 country hit that reached number 67 on the Billboard Hot 100.

"Matchbox" was a staple of Beatles stage shows during the early years. It is believed that John, George and Ringo each took their turns on lead vocal. John is the lead vocalist on the version of the song appearing on *The Beatles Live At The Star Club*. Prior to recording the song for EMI, the Beatles performed the song twice for the BBC with Ringo on lead vocals. The first, recorded on July 10, 1963, for the July 30 Pop Goes The Beatles, is on *Live At The BBC*.

The Beatles recorded "Matchbox" at EMI Studios on June 1, 1964. The song was quickly completed in five takes, with Ringo simultaneously singing and playing drums backed by John on his Rickenbacker 325 Capri, George on his Gretsch Country Gentleman, Paul on his Hofner bass and George Martin on the studio's Steinway Music Room Model B Grand Piano. Ringo double-tracked his vocal and George Harrison added a second solo over his first. Although Carl Perkins attended the session, he did not participate.

The June 4 mono mix contains Harrison's full double-tracked solo, whereas the June 22 stereo mix starts with both solos, but quickly fades one of the two.

The German Language Recordings

On January 29, 1964, the Beatles recorded German-lyric versions of "I Want To Hold Your Hand" and "She Loves You" at EMI Pathé Marconi Studios in Paris, France. The recordings were made at the request of Gunter Ilgner, production manager for EMI's West German branch, Electrola, for release on its Odeon label. The songs were released as a single on March 5, 1964 (see page 70). George Martin gave the following explanation for the single. "Odeon was adamant. They couldn't sell large quantities of records unless they were sung in German. I thought that if they were right then we should do it." The German lyrics were written by Camillo Jean Nicolas Felgen, who wrote under the names Jean Nicolas, Heinz Hellmer and Lee Montague. Felgen, a Luxembourg-born singer, lyricist and TV and radio presenter, attended the session to coach the boys.

Martin booked studio time in Paris during the three weeks the Beatles were there for a series of concerts at the Olympia Theatre. He and engineer Norman Smith flew to Paris to record the Beatles performing German-lyric versions of their two most recent hits. After waiting an hour past the late-morning scheduled session time with no sign of the Beatles, Martin phoned the group's suite at the George V Hotel and was told by road manager Neil Aspinall that the boys were in bed and had decided not to go to the studio. An angry Martin took a taxi to the hotel. He described the scene as follows:

"I barged into their suite, to be met by this incredible sight, right out of the Mad Hatter's tea party. Jane Asher–Paul's girlfriend–with her long red hair, was pouring tea from a china pot, and the others were sitting around there like March Hares. They took one look at me and exploded, like in a school room when the headmaster enters. Some dived onto the sofa and hid behind the cushions, others dashed behind curtains. 'You are bastards!,' I screamed, to which they responded with impish grins and roguish apologies. Within minutes, we were on our way to the studio."

Although the Beatles did not want to record the German versions of the songs, once at the studio they dutifully performed their duties. When Beatlemania quickly spread to non-English countries throughout Europe and the Far East, EMI's foreign branches realized that the group's records would sell in those markets despite any language barrier. This success spared them from ever being asked to record in a foreign language again. George Martin admitted, "They were right, actually. It wasn't necessary for them to record in German, but they weren't graceless, they did a good job."

Komm, Gib Mir Deine Hand

Recorded: October 17, 1963 & January 29, 1964
Mixed: March 10, 1964 (mono); March 12, 1964 (stereo)

Producer: George Martin
Engineers: Norman Smith; Jacques Esmenjaud (1964 only)

John: Lead vocal; rhythm guitar (Rickenbacker Capri); handclaps
Paul: Lead vocal; bass guitar (Hofner); handclaps
George: Backing vocal; lead guitar (Gretsch Country); handclaps
Ringo: Drums (Ludwig kit); handclaps

The German-lyric version of "I Want To Hold Your Hand" was the first song the Beatles recorded at the Paris session. The instrumental backing from the original four-track master tape was played and copied to one track of a two-track tape machine while the Beatles superimposed their vocals onto the other track. Although they knew a little German from their Hamburg days, the group had difficulty with the words, necessitating the recording of 11 takes. After Takes 5 and 7 were edited together, the edited take was bounced down to another two-track tape for the overdubbing of handclaps.

"Komm, Gib Mir Deine Hand," credited to Lennon-McCartney-Nicolas-Hellmer, is not a direct translation of the Beatles song, but rather German words that fit the music which express similar sentiments. Translating the German words back into English shows how different the lyrics are. "I want to hold your hand" becomes "Come, give me your hand." The first verse opens with "Oh come, come to me, you drive me out of my mind." The second verse opens with "Oh you are so pretty, as pretty as a diamond." The middle eight becomes "In your arms I'm happy and glad/It was never that way with anyone else/Never that way, never that way."

Sie Liebt Dich

Recorded: January 29, 1964
Mixed: March 10, 1964 (mono); March 12, 1964 (stereo)

Producer: George Martin
Engineers: Norman Smith; Jacques Esmenjaud

John: Lead vocal; rhythm guitar (Rickenbacker 325 Capri)
Paul: Lead vocal; bass guitar (Hofner)
George: Lead vocal; lead guitar (Gretsch Country Gentleman)
Ringo: Drums (Ludwig kit)

It is believed that the two-track master for "She Loves You" had either been lost or recorded over, requiring the Beatles to re-record an instrumental backing of the song. This was accomplished in 13 takes. The Beatles played the same instruments as they played on the original July 1, 1963 session, except that John played his Rickenbacker Capri electric guitar rather than his Jumbo acoustic-electric. The instrumental track was then bounced down to another two-track tape for the group to superimpose their vocals. Although Mark Lewisohn states in his book *The Beatles Recording Sessions* that this was done in one take, the master recording appears to consist of edits of different vocal takes.

"Sie Liebt Dich" is credited to Lennon-McCartney-Nicolas-Montague. Unlike "Komm, Gib Mir Deine Hand," the German-lyric version of "She Loves You" matches the Beatles song title and, for the most part, follows the story line. The opening verse is "You think she loves only me, yesterday I saw her/She only thinks of you, and you should go to her." The chorus translates as "She loves you, yeah, yeah, yeah, She loves you, yeah, yeah, yeah/For with you alone, can she only be happy."

The American Albums

While British LPs typically had 14 songs, American albums normally had 12. This was due to the different way publishing royalties were calculated in the two countries. In the U.K., the royalty amount owed by a record company for an album was a fixed amount regardless of the number of songs on the LP. Each publisher received a pro-rata share of the royalties based on the number of songs it had on the disc. However, in the U.S., a mechanical license fee was paid for each song. In the sixties, this fee was normally two cents per song. Record companies could save four cents per album by having 12 rather than 14 songs.

Capitol determined that it could save even more money by limiting a Beatles album to 11 tracks. The company reasoned that fans would buy a Beatles album whether it had 11 or 12 songs, so it might as well save an additional two cents per LP. If an album sold two million copies, Capitol would save $40,000 by having one less song on the record. As the value of money has increased nearly ten times from 1964 to 2024, this would be a savings of $400,000 in 2024 dollars.

Capitol's reconfiguration of Beatles albums was affected by more than royalty considerations. The company believed that hit singles made hit albums. Thus, Capitol wanted to include singles on its albums even though Brian Epstein and George Martin often decided against doing so under their belief that it was wrong to make fans pay for the same songs twice if they had already purchased the songs on a single prior to buying the album.

Although Capitol's reconfiguration of the Beatles carefully crafted albums may seem callus today, back in the 1960s, it was standard practice. We were not living in a global community. Each country was viewed as a separate market. Foreign countries such as Canada, Japan, France, Mexico and others had their own unique Beatles albums tailored for their own markets. Similarly, U.S. albums by groups such as the Rolling Stones, Dave Clark Five and the Hollies were different from the albums issued in the U.K.

Some songs on the U.S. Beatles albums sound different than those on the Parlophone LPs. Sometimes Capitol added echo to the songs or created a fake stereo mix from a mono tape or folded down a stereo mix for its mono version of the song. Occasionally, Capitol would receive an earlier mix of a song or even one prepared especially for the U.S. market by George Martin. Nonetheless, the American albums are an important part of the Beatles history.

The Beatles' Second Album

Put simply, *The Beatles' Second Album* is a great rock 'n' roll LP. Its admirers include those who are otherwise critical of how Capitol handled the Beatles catalog. Capitol had five cover versions from the U.K. album *With The Beatles* that were not included on its *Meet The Beatles!* LP. The radio air play and sales of the imported Canadian single of "Roll Over Beethoven" made it clear that U.S. Beatles fans were receptive to Beatles renditions of songs originally recorded by American artists. These five songs would form the core of the album, with "Roll Over Beethoven" marketed on the cover as if it were a hit single (see pages 222-223).

Because Swan's licensing agreement for its sole Beatles single was limited to the singles format, Capitol was able to place the number one hit "She Loves You" and its excellent flip side "I'll Get You" on the album. That brought Capitol up to seven tracks for its second Beatles album. After the addition of the B-side of Capitol's second Beatles single, "You Can't Do That," the company was only three short of its goal of 11 Beatles songs for its next LP.

In discussions of its planned album with EMI, Capitol was most likely told of an unreleased stereo mix of the B-side to the Beatles third British single, "Thank You Girl," made on March 13, 1963. Capitol negotiated with the American music publisher for the song, Conrad Music, for a reduced royalty rate of 75% of the standard rate. Capitol almost certainly was not aware that Conrad Music was owned by Vee-Jay Records or that Vee-Jay had released "Thank You Girl" as the B-side to its "From Me To You" single one year earlier. Capitol scored a real coup by obtaining from EMI two recently recorded Beatles songs, "Long Tall Sally" and "I Call Your Name," that would not appear in the upcoming Beatles film. This gave Capitol the worldwide debut of two Beatles songs.

The tape box for *The Beatles' Second Album* indicates that the stereo master lacquers were cut by Capitol engineer Maurice Long on March 17, 1964. The tape box further reveals that the songs were dubbed with E/Q and limiter plus echo. This added echo is quite noticeable on the five cover songs, particularly "Roll Over Beethoven" and "Please Mister Postman." These five songs use the same stereo mixes found on the U.K. album. Capitol obtained a tape of the unissued stereo mix of "Thank You Girl" and the stereo mixes of "Long Tall Sally" and "I Call Your Name" specifically made for Capitol on March 10, 1964. Capitol created fake stereo "duophonic" mixes for "You Can't Do That," "She Loves You" and "I'll Get You."

For its stereo albums, Capitol created duophonic mixes from mono tapes when stereo mixes of a song were not available. The engineers transferred the mono master to a two-track tape and then boosted the low bass frequencies in one track and tweaked the high treble frequencies in the other. Capitol's engineers enhanced the stereo illusion by running the two tracks slightly out-of-sync.

The mono version of *The Beatles' Second Album* was mastered by Don Henderson, also on March 17, 1964. As it had done on *Meet The Beatles!*, Capitol created its own mono mixes from existing stereo masters on some of the songs by combining the left and right channels of the stereo master into a single-track mono mix. Internal Capitol documents and acetates identify these stereo-to-mono mixdowns as "mono Type B." It is not known why Capitol created its own mono mixes from the Beatles stereo masters. Perhaps Capitol's engineers thought they could achieve a fuller sound this way.

The five rock 'n' roll cover songs from *With The Beatles*, as well as "Thank You Girl," are mono Type B mixes. These mixes are not enhanced with echo as on the stereo LP. Because no stereo mix of "You Can't Do That" was available when the album was assembled, "You Can't Do That" is the single's mono mix. "I'll Get You" and "She Loves You" are the same mono mixes as on the British single.

For "Long Tall Sally" and "I Call Your Name," Capitol used mono mixes specifically prepared by George Martin for the American LP. Unlike the stereo version of "Long Tall Sally," the mono mix of the song was not treated with echo during the mastering of the album by Capitol. When "Long Tall Sally" was remixed for mono on June 4 for the British EP, the song was given a touch of echo. The song was also remixed for stereo during the marathon mixing session of June 22. This mix was not issued in 1964.

"I Call Your Name," which may have briefly been considered for the film, was first mixed for mono on May 3, with George Martin assisted by Norman Smith and A.B. Lincoln. The guitar solo from Take 5 was edited into Take 7 just after John sings "I call your name" before the start of the solo. Thus, cowbell is not present during the solo. For the March 10 stereo mix, Take 5 of the song's introduction was edited into the beginning of Take 7. The edit for the solo from Take 5 comes in slightly earlier, just before John sings "I call your name" leading into the solo. Thus, there is no cowbell during that vocal line and the solo, as well as the song's introduction. The vocals and cowbell are in the right channel. The June 4 mono remix for the EP has a similar edit. The song was also remixed for stereo on June 22. This stereo mix was used on the 1976 album *Rock 'N' Roll Music*.

The United Artists Soundtrack Album

Under its movie deal with the Beatles, United Artists was given the American and Canadian rights to a soundtrack album of the group's first film, *A Hard Day's Night*. Capitol Records could also release the Beatles songs from the film, but could not issue a soundtrack album. On June 9, 1964, George Martin, assisted by balance engineer Norman Smith and tape operator Ken Scott, prepared separate (but apparently identical) tapes for United Artists and Capitol containing the best (as of that date) mono mixes of the eight songs then intended for the film: "I Should Have Known Better;" "If I Fell;" "Tell Me Why;" "And I Love Her;" "I'm Happy Just To Dance With You;" "I'll Cry Instead;" "Can't Buy Me Love;" and "A Hard Day's Night."

The tape's mono mix of "I'll Cry Instead" is the longer 2:04 edit of the song from June 4 which contains a repeat of the first verse placed between the third verse and the repeat of the bridge (see page 248). This edit was used for the United Artists soundtrack LP, Capitol's single release of the song and the mono version of Capitol's *Something New* album. Both the mono and stereo versions of Parlophone's *A Hard Day's Night* LP and the stereo version of Capitol's *Something New* album have the shorter 1:43 edit of the song.

Although "I'll Cry Instead" was later dropped from the film, apparently UA and Capitol were not informed of this development until after preparing their releases. The song was mistitled "I Cry Instead" on the first run pressings of UA soundtrack album, as well as the first print run of the back liners to the album's cover. Due to the large amount of albums initially prepared by United Artists, the majority of the records sold in 1964 have this error.

The tape's mono mix of "And I Love Her" is RM1 from March 3, which has Paul's voice double-tracked only when he sings "and I love her" at the end of the verses (he actually sings "I love her" at the end of the first verse) and during the bridge. This mix was also used for Capitol's single release of the song and on the mono version of its *Something New* LP.

"And I Love Her" was remixed for mono on June 22, 1964. This mix, known as RM2, has Paul's voice double-tracked throughout the song except for the first time he sings the lines "Bright are the stars that shine/Dark is the sky" in the third verse. The stereo mix, RS1, also has the same double-tracked vocals. These mixes were used on the mono and stereo versions of Parlophone's *A Hard Day's Night* LP.

United Artists most likely received its tape of the Beatles eight film recordings on June 10, 1964. These songs were not enough for an album, so the company had to turn to another source for the remaining tracks–the film's musical director, George Martin.

In addition to producing the Beatles recordings for the movie, Martin had arranged and recorded a jazzy rendition of the title track for use as incidental music during the scene where Paul's grandfather, played by Wilfrid Brambell, is trying to break into the theater to inform the group that Ringo is being held by the police. Martin also recorded an arrangement of "This Boy," which served as the musical background to Ringo's "parading" scene in which he roams the streets after deserting the band.

As UA needed four more tracks to get to the U.S. standard of 12, Martin re-recorded "This Boy" and "A Hard Day's Night" and arranged and recorded two additional film songs, "And I Love Her" and "I Should Have Known Better." Although an instrumental passage of "I'm Happy Just To Dance With You" precedes the group's rehearsal of the song in the film, he did not record the song for this LP.

George Martin's arrangement of "I Should Have Known Better" is dominated by horns, piano, electric guitar and drums. The horn section mimics John's harmonica riffs from the Beatles recording, and electric guitar replaces the lead vocals for the first two verses and the following bridge. The next verse has a saxophone lead, which is followed by a verse in which the horn section takes its turn up front. The electric guitar retakes the lead for the remainder of the track, with a saxophone supplying counterpoint riffs. The arrangement has that "swinging London sound" which would come into prominence months later on Petula Clark hit singles such as "Downtown" and "I Know A Place."

Martin's arrangement of "And I Love Her" opens with the same nylon-string guitar riff as the Beatles version. The melody of Paul's lead vocal is replaced on the verses by a string orchestra backed by horns, piano and percussion, including claves. During the first bridge, the horn section handles the lead. George Harrison's guitar solo is duplicated note for note, but is performed blandly compared to Harrison's rendition. The strings then return to carry the next verse. The second bridge features a flute solo. For the final verse, the strings are augmented at the end of each melody line by trumpet flourishes. The song ends with four repeats of the opening riff, each time followed by piano triads. This instrumental track is played at a noticeably slower tempo than the Beatles recording, leading to a running time of 3:42.

Martin's re-recorded album version of "This Boy" is a lush instrumental. The track opens with rhythm guitar and drums, with the lead vocal melody line played on guitar. At first, the strings, horns and harp are in the background, but by the time the song reaches the first bridge the strings become more prominent. When the song gets to the next verse, the horns and strings take over and carry the melody for the remainder of the song.

This recording differs significantly from the stripped-down instrumental version of the song used in the movie during Ringo's "parading" scene. The film version of the song has the same basic arrangement, but lacks the strings, horns and harp present on the album track. Instead, the instrumental features rhythm and lead guitar, bass guitar, drums, piano, saxophone and flute. It is unfortunate the soundtrack album has George Martin's heavily orchestrated version of "This Boy" instead of his superior film version. Because of the song's association with Ringo in the film, United Artists titled this George Martin recording as "Ringo's Theme (This Boy)."

Martin's jazz arrangement of "A Hard Day's Night" features a lead saxophone backed by drums, Dave Brubeck-style piano, a punchy horn section and, on the first bridge, swinging strings. The track ends with a flourish of saxophone notes and drums.

United Artists differentiated the four George Martin tracks from the Beatles recordings by adding "(Instrumental)" after the song's title on the label and back cover of its soundtrack album. The Beatles performances have "(Vocal)" following the song title. These recordings led United Artists Records to sign George Martin to a recording contract. The company would release four albums credited to George Martin and His Orchestra.

Although UA was prohibited from issuing Beatles singles, the company released the four George Martin songs on two singles. The first disc, UA 745, was released in early July and featured "And I Love Her" and "Ringo's Theme (This Boy)." In a full-page ad in the July 11 Billboard, United Artists touted the disc as: "A blockbuster single by The Beatles' brilliant musical director, George Martin and his orchestra." The ad stated that the record was issued "in a special sleeve illustrated with thirteen pictures of The Beatles!"

The second single, UA 750, was issued in either late September or early October 1964. The record paired "A Hard Day's Night" with "I Should Have Known Better." Some of the singles were issued in an attractive sleeve featuring a picture of the Beatles below a blue rectangle containing text. The back side of the sleeve has a Robert Freeman photograph of the Beatles and George Martin.

AND I LOVE HER/RINGO'S THEME (THIS BOY)

GEORGE MARTIN AND HIS ORCHESTRA

UNITED ARTISTS

FROM THE ORIGINAL MOTION PICTURE SOUND TRACK

The BEATLES A Hard Day's Night

UA 745

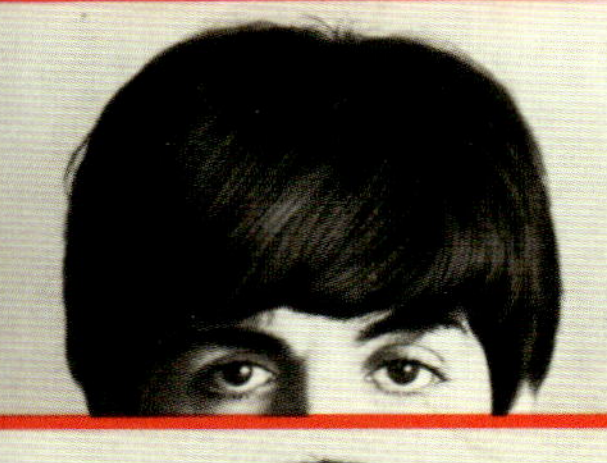
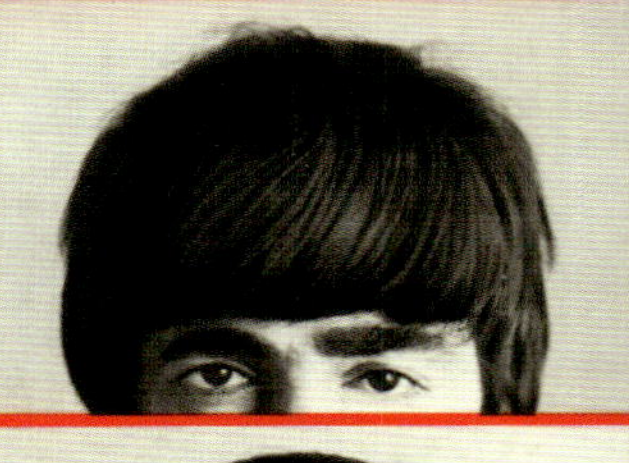
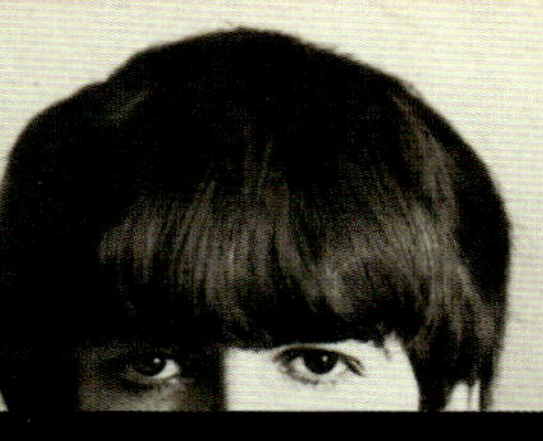
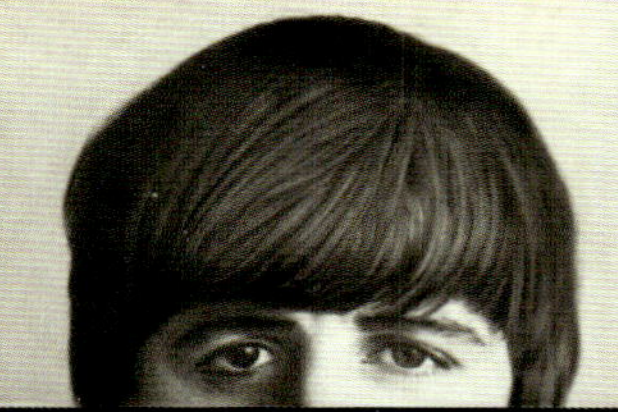

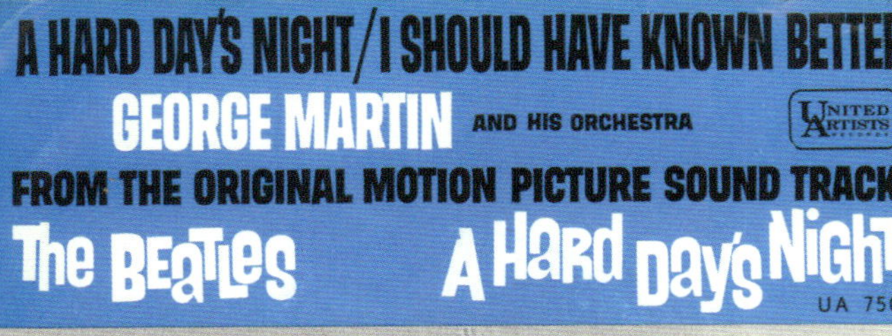

The first UA George Martin single was reviewed in the July 18 issues of the trade magazines. Although Billboard failed to review the soundtrack LP and brushed off the film's title tune with a sarcastic one-liner (see page 74), it reviewed the disc with "Ringo's Theme (This Boy)" listed as the A-side. "Music by and about the Beatles for those who can't stand them. Lush instrumental with plenty of strings." Cash Box featured the record on its Pick of the Week page, describing "And I Love Her" as a "haunting melody in the 'More' tradition played by George Martin and his ork and penned by Beatles John Lennon and Paul McCartney for their debut film." The magazine added: "Inventively arranged and orchestrated, this one could be the first big instrumental theme for the rock-oriented group. The pattern continues on the undercut with an easy-listening version of a previously released vocal tabbed, 'This Boy.' Loads of loot to be made here."

Record World, which showed the single on its cover as its Number One Pick of the week, observed: "And it's still The Beatles on the disk score. 'Ringo's Theme (This Boy)'...looks like the runway single this week. The instrumental is arranged for easy listening and has a nice tang to it." "And I Love Her" was also described as "top drawer material."

Cash Box's Radio Active chart indicated that as of July 15, both sides of the George Martin single were getting airplay, with 13% of its reporting stations adding "Ringo's Theme" and 23% adding "And I Love Her." One week later, "And I Love Her" was added by only 10% of the stations, bringing its total to 33%. The song's airplay dried up when Capitol issued a single featuring the Beatles recording of the song. However, "Ringo's Theme" faced no competition from a competing Beatles single and was added by 41% of the stations, increasing its airplay up to 54%. As of July 29, the song picked up another 12%, bringing its total to 66% of the reporting stations.

Billboard charted "Ringo's Theme (This Boy)" for eight weeks with a peak at 53, Cash Box for eight weeks with a peak at 57, and Record World for ten weeks with a peak at 54. Although Cash Box charted "And I Love Her" for three weeks with a peak at 71, the song could not break into the Top 100 of the other trades, stalling at 103 in Record World and 105 in Billboard. The single sold 200,000 copies.

The second Martin single pulled from the soundtrack album was reviewed in the September 26 issues of the trades. Cash Box wrote that Beatles musical director George Martin should get "more well-deserved recognition" with these "programming musts." The topside was a "cool, swingin' jazz-waltz rendition" of "A Hard Day's Night," while the flip-side was a "driving, rock-a-twist reading" of "I Should Have Known Better." Billboard predicted that the disc's two songs would be as popular as the previous two-sided chartmaker. Neither side made the Top 100 in any of the trades, although "A Hard Day's Night" charted at 122 in Billboard, and "I Should Have Known Better" stalled at 111 in Billboard and 122 in Cash Box.

Because United Artists adopted the strategy of releasing its soundtrack LP as soon as possible, it decided not to wait for stereo mixes of the songs. (The stereo mixes would not be made until June 22, 1964, four days prior to the record's release.) Thus, the Beatles songs appearing on the United Artists stereo album are fake stereo.

These fake stereo mixes were created by transferring the mono master of each song to a two-track tape and then slightly boosting the low bass frequencies in the left channel and tweaking the high treble frequencies in the right channel. This was similar to the process used by Capitol for its duophonic mixes.

In addition, most of the songs also have a panning effect. This was achieved by increasing the volume in one channel and lowering the volume in the other channel during certain vocal or instrumental passages. For example, during the title song "A Hard Day's Night," the volume is increased in the left channel and lowered in the right during the bridge, thus giving prominence to Paul's vocal on the left side. Conversely, the volume is decreased in the left channel and raised in the right during the instrumental break, thus shifting the focus to George Harrison's guitar and George Martin's piano on the right side. The guitar fade out at the end of the song is also panned to the right.

While much of the panning is subtle, the vocals in "Tell Me Why" appear to jump from speaker to speaker in a call and response pattern. The vocals on the chorus are centered; however, during the verses the lead vocals are panned to the left, while the response vocals are panned to the right. The song also pans to the right during its ending.

The panning on the album's next few Beatles songs is not as drastic. Some of the guitar fills on "I'll Cry Instead" sound like they are slightly panned left. There is no noticeable panning on "I'm Happy Just To Dance With You." The harmonica riffs and guitar solo on "I Should Have Known Better" appears to have been slightly panned to the right. The first verse of "If I Fell" is given slight prominence in the left channel and the song's volume increases in the right channel during its ending. George's guitar solo in "And I Love Her" sounds like it has been slightly panned to the right.

The album's final Beatles song, "Can't Buy Me Love," has panning during the lines "I don't care too much for money/Money can't buy me love." The vocals start in the center, but pan right for "much for money" and left for "Money can't buy me love" before shifting back to the center. While the panning of the vocals on "Tell Me Why" creates a call and response effect, here it is just plain weird.

Although the Beatles songs on the album are fake stereo, the four George Martin instrumentals are presented in full glorious stereo. On most of these tracks, the strings are in the left channel, while guitars and other solo instruments are normally heard in the right channel.

Something New

Although Capitol was prohibited from marketing a soundtrack album for *A Hard Day's Night*, it was allowed to issue the songs from the film on singles and albums. The company originally planned on releasing an album similar to the Parlophone album, most likely with the six new film songs on Side One and the second side opening with "Can't Buy Me Love" followed by the five new songs on Side Two of the 13-track British album. The only track missing on the 12-track Capitol album would have been "You Can't Do That," which Capitol had already issued on *The Beatles' Second Album*. The disc was set for release in early August to coincide with the U.S. release of the film. But when United Artists rushed out its soundtrack LP in late June, Capitol pushed up its release date and altered the content.

The new Capitol disc would have six new songs not available on the UA soundtrack album plus five songs from the film (including "I'll Cry Instead," which, unbeknownst to Capitol, had been dropped from the movie). The new songs would include three tracks from the non-movie side of the Parlophone LP, namely "Things We Said Today," "Any Time At All" and "When I Get Home," two songs from the *Long Tall Sally* EP that were not on *The Beatles' Second Album*, namely "Slow Down" and "Matchbox," and the German language version of Capitol's first Beatles hit, "Komm, Gib Mir Deine Hand." To save money on licensing fees, Capitol went with an 11-track album, holding "I'll Be Back" for future release. It would be issued five months later on Capitol's next Beatles album, *Beatles '65*.

The mono *Something New* album was mastered by Billy Smith on June 29, 1964. Its film songs, including "I'll Cry Instead," were pulled from the tape sent to Capitol by EMI on June 9, which had the same mixes as those sent to United Artists on the same day. Thus, "And I Love Her" is RM1 from March 3, which has Paul's voice double-tracked only on the last line of each verse ("I love her" for the first, "and I love her" for all others) and during the bridge. "I'll Cry Instead," which opens the LP, is the longer version of the song with the repeat of the first verse. At the start of the track, there is a split-second extraneous sound unique to the mono *Something New* album. It is either a guitar sound that was not edited off the beginning of the song or an error made when the master tape for the album was compiled by Capitol.

The mono mixes for "Any Time At All" and "When I Get Home" were made during the album's June 22 marathon mixing session. Separate mixes of these songs were made for the American and British markets. Capitol was sent Remix 3 of both songs, while Remix 2 of the songs was used in England. The American version of "Any Time At All" has the piano and crashing drum beat preceding the chorus mixed more in the background than on the British mono and stereo versions. On the American mono mix of "When I Get Home," the piano is more up front and the cymbals are not as loud as on the British mix. George Martin also made different British (RM2) and American (RM3) mono mixes for "I'll Be Back." Capitol used RM3 of the song on its *Beatles '65* album.

George Martin did not make different mono mixes for the June recordings that were mixed prior to June 22. These included the B-side of "A Hard Day's Night," "Things We Said Today" (June 9) and the two new EP tracks, "Slow Down" and "Matchbox" (June 4). "Komm, Gib Mir Deine Hand" is the same March 10 mono mix made for the German single.

The stereo album was mastered by Maurice Long on July 1, 1964. For the eight songs that were on the British *A Hard Day's Night* album, "I'll Cry Instead," "Things We Said Today," "Any Time At All," "When I Get Home," "Tell Me Why," "And I Love Her," "I'm Happy Just To Dance With You" and "If I Fell," Capitol used the same June 22, 1964 stereo mixes as the British album. Thus, "I'll Cry Instead" is the shorter 1:49 edit without the repeat of the first verse (although the record label and back cover list the running time as 2:04, the time of the extended mono mix).

Although "Slow Down" and "Matchbox" were only issued in the U.K. on a mono EP, Martin made stereo mixes of these songs for Capitol on June 22. Capitol also used Martin's March 12 stereo mix for "Komm, Gib Mir Deine Hand." *Something New* was the first stereo Beatles album issued by Capitol to contain true stereo mixes for all the songs.

VISIT

www.beatle.net

for more books by Bruce Spizer

SUBSCRIBE TO BRUCE'S EMAIL LIST
FOR EXCLUSIVE BEATLES ARTICLES AND CONTENT

THE BEATLES
ALBUM SERIES

AVAILABLE IN
DIGITAL,
HARD COVER AND
SPECIAL COLLECTOR'S EDITIONS

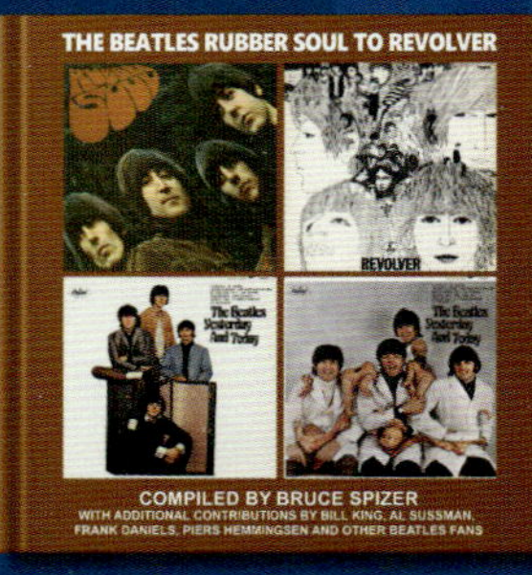

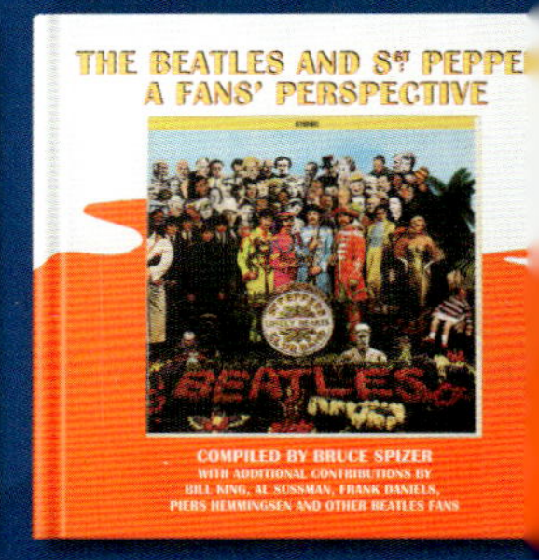

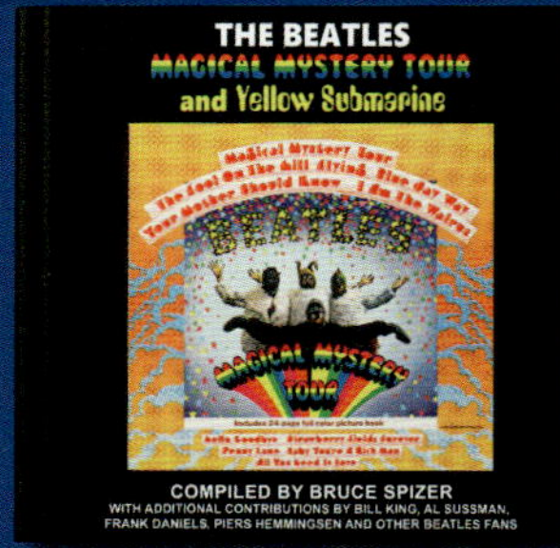

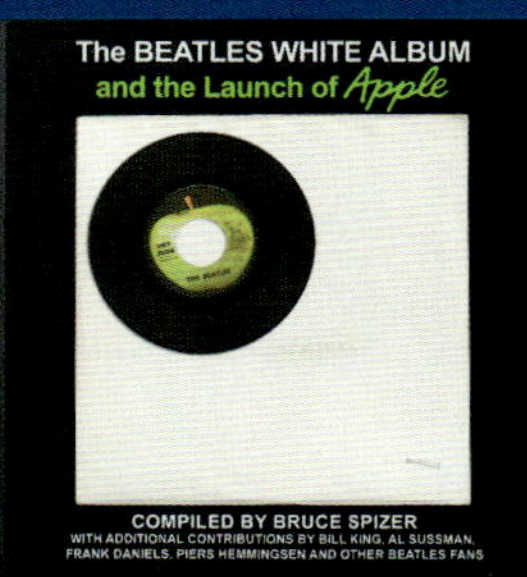

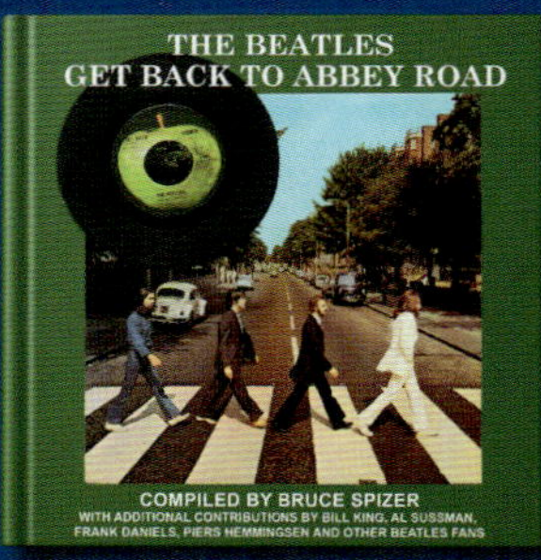

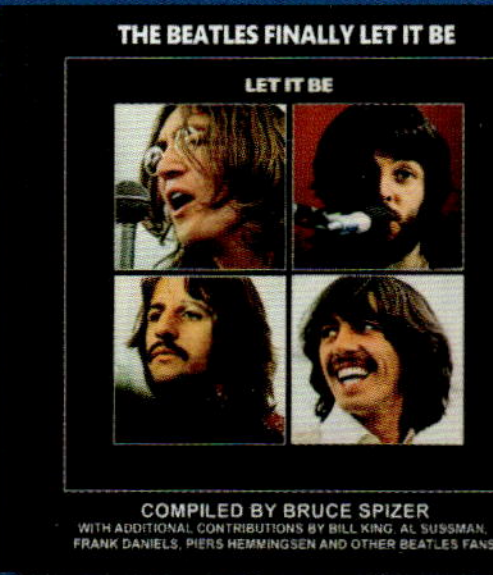

ORIGINAL SERIES: DIGITAL EDITIONS, FIRST EDITION HARDCOVER AND SPECIAL COLLECTOR'S EDITIO

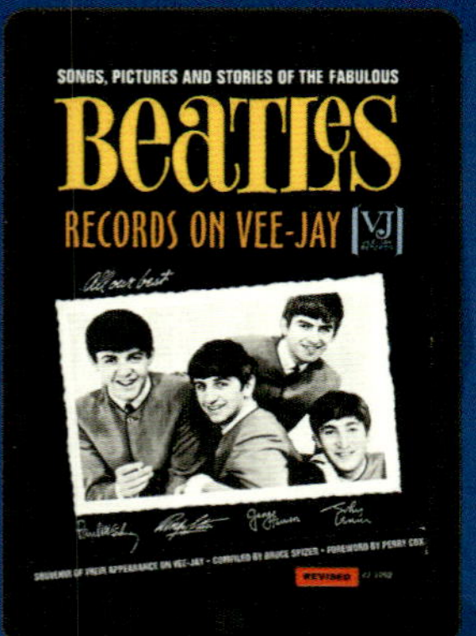

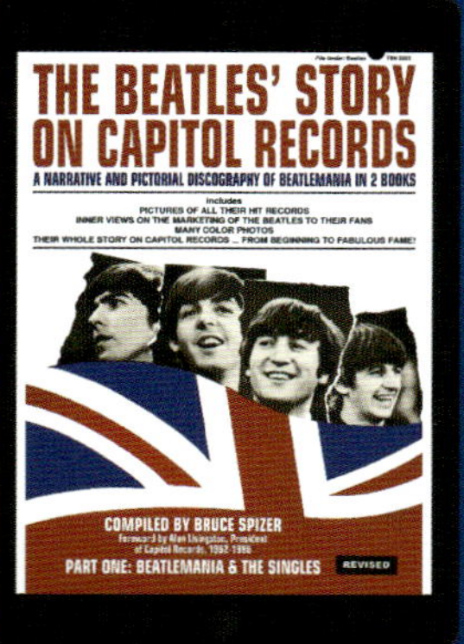

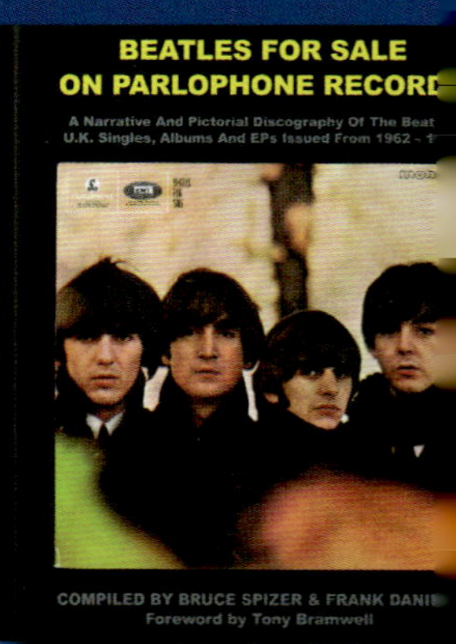

BEATLES
MOVIE
"A HARD DAY'S NIGHT"
A United Artists' Release
BUBBLE
GUM
5¢